James Gylby Lonsdale

The Works of Virgil

Rendered into English prose with introductions, running analysis and an index

James Gylby Lonsdale

The Works of Virgil
Rendered into English prose with introductions, running analysis and an index

ISBN/EAN: 9783337373542

Printed in Europe, USA, Canada, Australia, Japan

Cover: Foto ©Thomas Meinert / pixelio.de

More available books at **www.hansebooks.com**

The Globe Edition.

THE

WORKS OF VIRG

RENDERED INTO

ENGLISH PROSE

*WITH INTRODUCTIONS RUNNING ANALYSIS
AND AN INDEX*

BY

JAMES LONSDALE M.A.

LATE FELLOW AND TUTOR OF BALLIOL COLLEGE OXFORD
AND CLASSICAL PROFESSOR IN KING'S COLLEGE LONDON

AND

SAMUEL LEE M.A.

LATIN LECTURER AT UNIVERSITY COLLEGE LONDON
AND LATE SCHOLAR OF CHRIST'S COLLEGE CAMBRIDGE

London:
MACMILLAN AND CO.
1871.

PREFACE.

THIS translation of Virgil is intended partly for the use of Students; and the original has therefore been faithfully rendered, and paraphrase altogether avoided. At the same time, the translators have endeavoured to adapt the book to the use of the English reader. Some amount of rhythm in the structure of the sentence has been generally maintained; and, where in the Latin the sound of the words is an echo to the sense, (as so frequently happens in Virgil,) an attempt has been made to produce the same result in English.

It is indeed no easy task, especially in translating so consummate a master of language as Virgil, to present a version at once literal, and also in any measure a reflection of the style of the original. The translators cannot hope that they have attained a high degree of success in a work of so much difficulty; but they trust that they have not altogether failed to convey, though in a literal translation, some faint idea of the many beauties of the language and style of Virgil.

CONTENTS.

	PAGE
General Introduction . .	1
Introduction to the Eclogues	9
The Eclogues . . .	12
Introduction to the Georgics	30
The Georgics . . .	32
Introduction to the Æneid	78
The Æneid . .	82

GENERAL INTRODUCTION.

No authentic life of Virgil has come down to us; and Virgil, unlike his friend Horace, is not his own biographer. But what we are told about Virgil's loss of his property near Mantua in the life written by the so-called Donatus is confirmed by the first and ninth Eclogues, from which it appears that the poet was twice in danger of losing his paternal farm. In the same Eclogues we have descriptions of scenery, which, unlike those in the other Eclogues, appear to be real. Lycidas in the ninth Eclogue says :

> *Your country friends are told another tale,*
> *That from the sloping mountain to the vale,*
> *And doddered oak, and all the banks along,*
> *Menalcas saved his fortune with a song—*

which passage describes scenery that Keightley, (quoted by Conington), professes to recognise not far from Mantua. Again, the so-called Donatus tells us that Virgil learnt from Syro the Epicurean tenets, but that he afterwards preferred the opinions of the Academicians, and esteemed Plato above all other philosophers. Now in the first and second books of the Georgics Virgil seems to propound the Epicurean tenets; in the fourth book of the Georgics and in the sixth book of the Æneid he seems to adopt the Pythagorean doctrines, which in many points were the same as those of Plato and his followers. It is said that Virgil at first intended to have published only nine Eclogues, for "unequal numbers please the god," and the nine Eclogues would have answered to the nine Muses, but he added a tenth Eclogue in honour of his dear friend the poet Gallus; the fourth book of the Georgics also ended with the praises of the same Gallus; but Gallus falling under the displeasure of Augustus was compelled to put himself to death; and Virgil substituted for the praises of Gallus the unoffending tale of Aristæus. The story of the shepherd who lost his bees is very beautiful; but perhaps the tribute to a friend and brother poet might have been more touching. In the concluding lines of the last book of the Georgics, the genuineness of which there seems no sufficient reason to doubt, Virgil speaks of his own life during the time that Augustus was in the east after the battle of Actium, as thus spent: '

> *While I at Naples pass my peaceful days,*
> *Affecting studies of less noisy praise.*

This also agrees with the old life of the poet, in which we read that he directed that his bones should be taken to Naples, where he had lived so long and so happily. The same life gives a very pleasing account of the poet, mentioning his modest and retiring disposition, his singular freedom from vanity and jealousy, his patient and affectionate temper, his generous liberality, his temperate and frugal habits, his attachment to his friends, his dutiful conduct towards his parents, his learning, his care and fastidiousness in the composition of his verses, his taciturnity, his love of philosophical studies, his intimacy with Augustus and Mæcenas; much of which may be illustrated from his poems, indirectly it is true, and yet in such a way as to make it probable that the ancient biographer has given in the main a true account of the poet's life and character. In agreement with this are the notices of Virgil by his friend Horace. We cannot help wishing Horace had told us more. Horace was five years younger than Virgil, and outlived him eleven years. An ode by Horace on the death of Virgil might have ranked among the most charming tributes to friendship and genius. Horace has mentioned Virgil nine times; in six of these places the names of Varius and Virgil are united. There seems to be no certain reason to lead us to conclude that the Virgil in the Odes is a different person from the poet. In one ode Horace prays the gods to bring Virgil safe to the Attic shores, "faithfully guarding the half of my soul." Another ode contains an invitation to Virgil to dinner. The allusions in it to his friend's love of gain are probably only playful. The meeting of Virgil and Varius with Horace at Sinuessa gives occasion to a burst of enthusiasm in praise of friendship: "there is nothing," says Horace, "comparable to a pleasant friend; and never were there souls purer and more free from stain than the souls of my friends." From a passage in the same satire we learn that Virgil suffered from indigestion; this also is mentioned in the ancient life. It was the good Virgil and Varius that first told Mæcenas what the character of Horace was; thus to Virgil and Varius Horace owed the prosperity and happiness of his easy and joyous life. While to Varius Horace ascribes the vigorous and manly epic style, probably in allusion to the lost poem on Death, Virgil he speaks of as dear to the Muses of the country for his elegant and refined poetry, Virgil having at that time not yet written the Æneid, perhaps only the Eclogues. Virgil and Varius the poets are spoken of as dear to Augustus; they may have been then dead. In Horace's *Art of Poetry* the brother poets are mentioned as the highest authority of the age in which they lived, as Cæcilius and Plautus were of a former age.

The modest Virgil felt the hopes that genius inspires, when he says:

New ways I must attempt my grovelling name
To raise aloft, and wing my flight to fame.

He promises that the affection of Nisus and Euryalus shall not be forgotten so long as the Capitol shall remain unmoved and the Roman empire endure. But he could not have divined what undying fame was to attend his name through all generations, outliving the empire of Rome by many centuries. Propertius and Ovid speak of Virgil with the partial enthusiasm of national pride. We are told that Cæcilius the grammarian lectured on Virgil in the poet's lifetime, as professors in Universities do at the present time; that when he entered the theatre, the spectators rose to him as to Cæsar; that though his modesty shrank from observation, the people, as he passed through the streets, spoke of him as the darling of Rome. Juvenal mentions the Æneid as recited with the Iliad, the glory of which it rivalled; the learned ladies wearied their husbands and friends with discussions on Virgil; Horace and Virgil were even then used as school books. Among the many points of Roman life on which the writings of Martial throw light, none is clearer than that in those days Virgil was familiar to all literary men; his birthday, the 15th of October, was kept as a holyday; Virgil is ranked with Diana and Mercury. Pliny says that the poet Silius kept the birthday of Virgil more religiously than he did his own, and that he used to visit his sepulchre near Naples, as he would have visited the shrine of a god; as Niebuhr so many hundred years after, though a very unfavourable critic of Virgil, yet says that he went to his tomb as a pilgrim, and that the laurel branches plucked at the poet's grave were dear to him as relics. The later poets of Rome laboured, though in vain, to equal the matchless rhythm of the Virgilian hexameter. Tacitus was evidently a most diligent student of Virgil; the brevity of the style of the poet, his careful selection of epithets, his inverted constructions, his variety of expression, his fondness for the dative case, his frequent use of what is called Zeugma, of the plural number, of the infinitive mood, his power of painting a scene with few touches, many of his favourite words and expressions, are imitated with great effect by the historian; poet and historian alike dwell on the power of fate; they both at times are exaggerated in their expressions; they both fully understood the majesty of the Roman tongue and the greatness of the Roman empire; there is in both of them a sad solemnity, and a melancholy feeling of the misfortunes of man's uncertain life. At times Tacitus himself becomes a poet almost; like Virgil, he uses adjectives for adverbs; he speaks of inanimate objects as having life. Quinctilian repeats what he was taught by Afer Domitius, that if Homer was first, Virgil was second, and nearer to the first than to the third. The same critic calls Virgil a lover of antiquity. Aulus Gellius is full of quotations from Virgil, on some of which he comments at great length after his gossiping manner. The desire to destroy Virgil's poems was regarded as one of the wildest extravagances of the madness of the emperor Caligula. Macrobius in his *Saturnalia* quotes many passages of the early Roman poets, which were borrowed by Virgil; he is fond of drawing comparisons between the two great epic poets of antiquity, with as strong a preference for the earlier as, many ages after, Scaliger shewed for the later poet. Macrobius speaks of Virgil as introducing philosophy into many parts of his poems. It is probable that the life of Virgil ascribed to Donatus was written about this time. Servius too, about the same time, wrote a commentary on Virgil, deficient in judgment, but full of curious antiquarian lore, especially interesting in the elucidation of a poet, who displays, as Niebuhr says, a learning from which the historian can never glean too much. This Servius says that Virgil was skilled in medicine and in philosophy. As the Sibylline books were consulted for the indications of the divine will, so the poems of Virgil even in early times were opened at random to obtain directions from them. It is said that the emperor Alexander Severus was encouraged by lighting upon the passage in the sixth book of the Æneid which bids the Roman "rule mankind and make the world obey." Dryden says these "Sortes Virgilianæ were condemned by St Austin and other casuists." Perhaps the most famous instance is that of the passage in the fourth book of the Æneid; which it is said King Charles I. opened, and which runs as follows:

> *And when at length the cruel war shall cease,*
> *On hard conditions may he buy the peace;*
> *Nor let him then enjoy supreme command,*
> *But fall untimely by some hostile hand.*

St Jerome and St Augustine speak of Virgil as a philosopher. Some of the fathers regarded the fourth Eclogue as a prophecy of the Messiah taken from the ancient writings of the Cumean Sibyl; and it was said that St Paul coming to Naples wept over the ashes of the heathen poet, grieving that he came too late to convert him to the faith of Christ.

Gradually the poet of the days of Augustus was changed into a magician, sometimes capricious, but usually benevolent. As we have seen, some of the ancients regarded him as a famous mathematician and physician; his grandfather is called magus; he is said to have studied astronomy and astrology. The word "vates" in Latin is ambiguous. The emperor Alexander Severus had his image in the shrine of his house, together with the statues of his household gods; the women of Mantua worshipped at a tree sacred to their beloved poet, as at an altar, and in later days his name was joined in their praises with that of St Paul. In the middle ages[1] all that was extraordinary was regarded as strictly supernatural; and the imagination of the writers of these days added strange tales, which popular belief readily accepted. Virgil was born not at the close of the republic, but in the days of Remus, the son of Remus, the brother of Romulus; enraged at a slight he received from a certain lady of Rome he put out all the fires in the houses of the city, which could not be kindled again, till the great magician had received an apology; he built a wonderful palace, so constructed that all that was whispered at Rome was heard there; in it was a miraculous image of bronze, and a light that continued to burn long after the Roman empire had passed away; he made an orchard which rivalled Paradise, which no man could enter, wherein were all kinds of fruits; he married the daughter of the Soldan of Babylon, who visited her husband, and was visited by him, travelling along a bridge of air; when he was taken once at Babylon by the enraged father, and condemned to be burnt together with his wife who refused to abandon him, he made all the barons of Babylon swim like frogs in the market-place of the city, which appeared to their imagination to be filled with the river, while he and his beautiful wife escaped to the land of the Franks along the bridge of air. Afterwards he founded the city of Naples on an egg, miraculously defeated the assaults of the emperor of Rome, made a wondrous serpent of bronze, which by instantaneous punishment convicted the perjurer of his guilt; at last, like Romulus, he disappeared amidst a tempest of wind, leaving behind him treasures protected by guards of bronze. These and other similar tales are told of Virgil with sundry variations. We find him in what we should now call strange company, for he is joined with Aristotle, Euclid, Hippocrates, Samson, David, Solomon, King Arthur. Apart from his fame as a magician, he had a place in the schools of the middle ages. St Augustine had recommended his works, and styled him the first and noblest of poets; St Jerome, on the other hand, condemned the admi-

---

[1] Quæ vices, quæque mutationes et Virgilium ipsum et ejus carmina per mediam ætatem exceperunt explanare tentavit Franciscus Michel. Lutetiæ Parisiorum ex typis Maulde et Renon, 1846.

ration of Terence and Virgil. In agreement with this it appears that throughout the middle ages many of the abbots and teachers condemn him, while others quote him with praise. Copies of his works were kept in the monasteries; the Benedictine monks of Casino studied them; in the abbey of St Augustine at Canterbury were MSS. of his poems: yet, on the other hand, the study of the heathen poet is represented as antagonistic to that of the Psalms, and as even encouraged by the evil spirits of darkness. Considering the place Virgil held in the schools of the middle ages (for the favourable view of the poet was the predominant one) and the popular belief in his supernatural powers, it is not to be wondered at that Dante should have chosen him as his guide into the other world. In the days of Dante Greek was almost entirely unknown, and if it had been better known, and Dante had read Homer, yet the description of the dead in the Odyssey is vague and indefinite: and properly speaking there is no descent into the lower world at all. But Virgil, assisted by later and fuller legends and by the writings of the philosophers, far surpasses his master in this subject; his description of the regions of the dead is full of details; in places it has the grotesque character, the exact measurements, and precise delineations, though in a much less degree, of the poem of the middle ages. The sixth book of the Æneid probably in part suggested the idea of the descent to Dante, which was afterwards filled out from other sources, and from the imaginations of a genius essentially different from that of his adopted guide. Again, Virgil was a familiar name. He was the predecessor of Dante in Italian poetry. He was his dear master, from whom he had taken that fine style which gave him his name. Both poets came from the northern part of Italy. The Ghibelline Dante might regard the Imperialist Virgil as so far connected with him. Still more would Dante be glad to place himself under the guidance of the poet, as that "famous sage," reckoned, as we have seen, with Aristotle and Plato, and as one who by his knowledge of magic and necromancy was acquainted with the secrets of the spiritual world.

Gradually and slowly did the opinion of Virgil, as a magician, give way: it is even said that the expedition of the French to Naples so late as the year 1494 spread the fame of Virgil as a great magician. But the first person who appears to have questioned the accuracy of the popular belief had been Petrarch : who said that the only fascination exercised by Virgil was that of his poetry. Long after, about the year 1630, Gabriel Naude wrote "an apology for the great men who have been accused of magic," and amongst them for Virgil. After this time the opinion seems to have died out. Other strange opinions were held. Tasso, who had imbibed a love of allegory from the study of Plato, regarded the Æneid as a continued allegory, as he did his own poem. The hero Æneas represented sometimes the active, sometimes the contemplative life. Hardouin, a learned French Jesuit, maintained that almost all the writings that bear the names of Greek and Latin authors are spurious productions, written chiefly in the thirteenth century, excepting only some inscriptions. And yet he did admit the Eclogues and Georgics as genuine; but he considered the Æneid to have been written by mediæval monks.

To the editions of Virgil we may apply his own words,

> *Which who would learn as soon might tell the sands*
> *Driv'n by the western winds on Libyan lands.*

Heyne has given an account of these editions. Since the first edition at Rome in the year 1469 there has not, Heyne says, been a year in which there has not been at least one edition of Virgil. Servius' commentary was first edited in 1471. N. Heinsius' edition of the poet appeared in 1676, "a noble edition," says Heyne, "from which at last a brighter light shone on Maro." The Delphin edition, by Charles de la Rue the Jesuit (Ruæus), did perhaps more than any other single edition has done to advance the study of Virgil. Other names are well known in connection with Virgil, as those of Burmann, Martin, Maittaire, Baskerville, Heyne, Wagner, Forbiger, Keightley, Conington, and Gossrau, whose Latin commentary on the Æneid is remarkable for accurate, clear, and sensible criticism.

The influence of Virgil on modern poets has perhaps been greater than that of any other single poet of antiquity. We may mention a few instances out of very many. Garcilaso de la Vega imitated the Eclogues. The *Aminta* of Tasso owes much to the same source. The *Bees* of Rucellai follows the fourth book of the Georgics. Thomson, in his *Seasons*, has put into an English dress many of the passages of the Georgics. Many stanzas of Tasso's chief poem are little else than elegant, but often rather feeble translations of the Æneid. It is probable that Racine owed the exquisite grace of his style to the study of the Latin poet. Milton, though his genius was far more nearly related to the stern sublimity of the Hebrew prophets than to the refinement of the Roman bard, yet has not disdained to draw many beauties from particular passages of Virgil. The *Lusiad* of Camoens is much indebted to Virgil. The *Henriade* is not without imitations from the poet, whose writings, together with the sermons of Massillon, are said to have been Voltaire's favourite companions.

If the influence of Virgil on other poets has been great, his influence

on education has been far greater. There seems never to have been any
time since his poems were written, in which they have not been so used.
In ancient Rome, in the middle ages, in the schools of the Jesuits, in
those of Europe in the present day, nowhere more than among us
Britons,

A race of men from all the world disjoined,

the study of Virgil has held and holds a prominent place. The union of
Horace and Virgil, begun in their youth, has extended beyond the few
years of their lives through many generations. A few scholars have no
doubt preferred Catullus to Horace, and Lucretius to Virgil, esteeming
the earlier poets as writers of a more free and original genius; but the
great majority of readers regard Virgil as the prince of Latin poets,
while for Horace they have almost a personal affection. If the writings
of these two friends had been lost, it is probable that Latin had never
been made the basis of education in the schools of Europe. Virgil's exquisite taste, his brevity of diction, the matchless rhythm of his verse, his
power of putting the right word in the right place, his very difficulties
and obscurities, all unite in making his writings an excellent school book.
What has been well said by Lord Lytton of Horace may be said almost,
perhaps not quite so truly, of Virgil: " It is an era in the life of a school-
boy, when he first becomes acquainted with Horace." When the days of
school are past men return with fondness to their favourite passages of
Virgil. The cadence of his verse still haunts the ear. It has been said
that men like Virgil better as they grow older. Few authors are more
often alluded to. A happy quotation from and adaptation of Virgil have
weight even in serious questions and in august assemblies. Criticism can
point out innumerable faults in Virgil, but criticism is as powerless
against the poet as the sword of the mortal hero against the immortal
temper of the Vulcanian shield: and what Macrobius said so many years
ago is still true: " Such is the glory of Maro, that no man's praise can
increase it, no man's censure can diminish it."

INTRODUCTION TO THE ECLOGUES.

VIRGIL is the founder of the artificial school of pastoral poetry. And so, though he has taken very much from Theocritus, though he not only borrows from him the design of several of the Eclogues, but even translates many of his phrases literally, yet there is this one great difference between the two poets. Theocritus is a genuine writer of pastoral poetry; his whole object is to describe poetically the characteristics of a shepherd's life, its simple joys and griefs, its coarseness, and humour, and childishness, and superstition. But of Virgil's Eclogues only a very few can be called pastoral in this literal sense; and even these contain frequent allusions to the persons and events of Virgil's own age. Indeed, the dress of pastoral poetry is often used by Virgil, as it has been by so many imitators in later times, only to disguise his own personality, and to clothe in poetic allegory incidents in his own life, or circumstances of his own day.

If we examine the Eclogues one by one, we find that the first tells the story of an event in the life of Virgil. The triumvirs had made an assignment of lands in the north of Italy to their veterans, and the poet's farm near Mantua had been seized by one of the soldiers as his allotment. Virgil recovered his land by the influence of Octavianus (afterwards the emperor Augustus), and this Eclogue is mainly a tribute of gratitude to his patron. It has many points highly characteristic of the artificial style of the Eclogues, and of Virgil's disregard for consistency in the accessories of his pieces. Tityrus (Virgil) at one time looks to Octavianus as a divine guardian, to protect him in the possession of his land, at another as a master, from whom he begs for freedom from slavery. The scenery too, in this Eclogue as in several others, entirely wants uniformity; at one time it is Mantuan, at another Sicilian. In fact, the whole outline of the Eclogues is painted in a manner that is more or less conventional, and not drawn directly from nature.

The second and third Eclogues are closely imitated from Theocritus, and yet distinctly marked by the peculiar style of Virgil.

The subject of the fourth Eclogue has made it better known than all the rest, though it hardly stands first in intrinsic merit. It was written, as we learn from the poem itself, in the consulship of Pollio, B.C. 40, and about the time of the peace of Brundisium. The poet imagines that the cycle of the "great year" of the world is beginning anew, and the golden age returning. But the principal event celebrated in the poem is the birth of a wondrous child, who is to be king of the world in this age of peace. The language employed is very vague and indefinite, but it seems more probable that the child is to be the son of Octavianus (who had lately been married to Scribonia), rather than of Pollio, whose chief glory would appear to consist in the fact that the child is to be born in his consulship. But the Eclogue is best known on account of the resemblance of its language in some passages to descriptions in the Hebrew prophets, especially Isaiah ; and from the idea that the Sibylline books contained predictions of a coming Messiah, also derived originally from the prophecies of the Old Testament. But the vague looking forward to a golden age in the future has been hardly less universal than the dream of it in the past ; and though the language used in describing the birth and career of the child, who is to be the universal king, is certainly sometimes striking, and though it is remarkable that the poem was written at a time so near the birth of Christ, yet there seems no sufficient reason to connect the legends employed by Virgil with the prophecies of the Old Testament. For the idea of the advent of a great and beneficent ruler of the world has been hardly less wide-spread than that of the coming of an age of peace ; so that, on the whole, it is perhaps going too far to attach much weight to the points of resemblance which have been mentioned.

The fifth Eclogue, which probably surpasses all the others in excellence, is modelled in its plan on Theocritus, but much of its finest poetry may fairly claim to be original. There can be little doubt of the correctness of the old notion, which supposes the death and apotheosis of Daphnis, the ideal shepherd, to represent allegorically the assassination of Julius Cæsar, and the honours paid to him after death. Several passages in this poem are imitated in Milton's *Lycidas*, in Spenser's *Lament for Dido*, and by other modern writers.

The immediate source whence Virgil derived the subject of the sixth Eclogue is doubtful ; but the introduction to the song of Silenus bears a general likeness to the story of the binding of Proteus by Menelaus, in the fourth book of the *Odyssey*, which Virgil has himself imitated in the fourth Georgic. The Epicurean account of the creation of the world is evidently modelled on that given by Lucretius.

The plan of the seventh Eclogue is similar to that of the third.

The incidents of the eighth are mainly adapted from Theocritus, but the arrangement is different, and much of the poetry is apparently original. It is entitled "The Enchantress" (*Pharmaceutria*), from the subject of the second of the two songs.

The ninth tells of the difficulty experienced by Virgil (Menalcas) in regaining possession of his farm, and how his life was threatened by the soldier who had seized upon the land. Virgil, it seems, has gone to Rome a second time, to seek the protection of Augustus; and his successful return is hoped for in the last line of the poem.

Virgil wrote his last Eclogue in honour of his friend Cornelius Gallus, whose love-complaint forms the subject and greater part of the poem. Nothing is known with any certainty as to the occasion on which this Eclogue was written. Its framework is borrowed from the first Idyll of Theocritus.

Though it is impossible to look upon Virgil as a writer of genuine pastoral poetry, yet the Eclogues abound in excellence, and in beauties of description and style. Virgil was in truth naturally unfitted to be a pastoral poet ; the flow of his hexameter in the Eclogues is hardly less heroic than in the Æneid; and he everywhere treats his subject with a certain dignity and grandeur, which is quite at variance with rustic simplicity and rudeness. He now and then, by the introduction of a coarse or antiquated expression, makes some attempt to give a rural colouring to his descriptions; but this only serves to mark more strongly the general refinement of his tone. But he excels in pathos and tenderness, as in the first Eclogue; in splendour of language and elevation of style, as in the fourth and fifth ; in touches of natural description, and in dramatic power, as in the first, eighth, and tenth ; and everywhere in the beauty of his rhythm, and marvellous power over words.

In originality of style, in artistic subtleness of phrase, in skilfully varied music of verse, and in highly wrought and complex beauty of workmanship, he has probably never yet been matched; and though there is some ground for the charge of plagiarism, which again and again has been brought against Virgil, yet it must surely be allowed that he almost always makes what he borrows fairly his own, by his peculiar style, by additional touches, by giving phrases and metaphors a new setting, as it were, which imparts fresh brightness to their former beauty.

The Eclogues have been imitated more or less by a multitude of poets of various times and nations. In Virgil's own country, by the later pastoral poets of Rome, Nemesianus, Calpurnius, and others, none of whom reached to excellence, except in a few passages of their works ; and in the *Aminta* of Tasso, and the *Pastor Fido* of Guarini. In Spain, Garcilaso de la Vega is the most meritorious of those who have imitated the Eclogues at second-hand, as followers of the Italian school of pastoral. In France, Florian has modelled his Pastorals on the pattern of Virgil. Among English poets, Spenser, Milton, Drayton, Drummond, Pope, Shenstone, Phillips and Gay have in different degrees taken Virgil for their master in pastoral poetry. Most of these may be with good reason accused of that unreality which has so persistently been imputed to Virgil ; and very few of them at all approach the excellence of their original; though one or two passages in Milton's *Lycidas* perhaps surpass in beauty the lines of Virgil on which they are based; and the poems of Guarini, Tasso, Spenser, and a few others, have peculiar merits and beauties of their own. The *Gentle Shepherd* of Allan Ramsay, though it sometimes contains ideas which seem borrowed from Virgil, certainly owes him but little, and may undoubtedly claim to belong to the genuine school of natural pastoral poetry.

It must be allowed that the branch of the pastoral of which Virgil was the founder has fairly been charged with the fault of unreality. And much of the modern pastoral has other and worse blemishes than this : false sentiment, useless ornament, coldness, dulness, and prolixity. But it would be indeed unreasonable to accuse Virgil of any one of these latter defects. The Eclogues will always be read with delight and admiration, for their own peculiar charm and sweetness ; and if the first place as the bard of the country must be yielded to Theocritus, yet, in that region of rural poetry which he has chosen for himself, Virgil is still without an equal.

ECLOGUE I.

1—18. *Melibœus, forced to leave his farm, wonders to see Tityrus in ease and safety. Tityrus tells him that one whom he shall always regard as a god has been his benefactor. Melibœus asks him who this benefactor is.*

M. TITYRUS, you, reclining beneath the canopy of your spreading beech, on slender pipe practise your woodland lay; we leave our country's bounds and pleasant fields; we flee our native country; you, Tityrus, at ease within the shade, teach the woods to echo back the name of your fair Amaryllis.

T. O Melibœus, 'twas a god that wrought for us this repose. For he shall ever be to me a god; his altar a tender lamb from our folds shall often stain with blood. He it was who made my oxen free to range, as you behold, and myself to play the sportive songs I chose upon my rustic flute.

M. In sooth I feel not envy, but rather surprise: on all sides over all the fields the confusion is so complete. See, I myself wearily drive my she-goats on their way; and this one, Tityrus, I scarce can lead along. For here among the tangled hazel bushes she just now left with the pangs of labour her twin offspring, the hope of the flock, alas! on the bare flint-stones. Ofttimes, if my sense had not been blinded, I remember that oaks blasted from heaven foretold me this distress. But yet let me know, Tityrus, who is that god you speak of.

19—45. *In answer to Melibœus, Tityrus tells the cause of his visit to Rome, and how he received his freedom from Octavianus.*

T. The city which they call Rome, Melibœus, I in my folly had thought like this town of ours, whither we shepherds are often wont to drive in the tender young of our sheep. So I knew that dogs resembled puppies, and kids their dams, so I used to compare great things with small. But this city exalts her head among all other towns, as high as cypresses are wont to tower among the bending osiers.

M. And what was the pressing cause that took you to see Rome?

T. Freedom; who, though late, yet smiled upon my slothful self, when my beard had begun to fall in whitening locks beneath the barber's hand; yet she smiled upon me, and came after a long time, since Amaryllis has been my mistress, and Galatea forsaken me. For I must in truth confess that so long as Galatea was my charmer, I had no hope of freedom, and no care to hoard my savings; though many and many a victim went forth from the fences of my fold, and rich the cheese that was pressed for the thankless town, not once did my hand come back home heavy with its load of coin.

M. I used to marvel why your Amaryllis would mournfully invoke the gods, and for whom she suffered the fruit to hang upon its tree: Tityrus was far away. Even the pine-trees, Tityrus, even the fountains, even these vineyards used to call you home.

T. What was I to do? It was not in my power either to escape from servitude, or elsewhere to discover gods so strong to help me. 'Twas here

I saw that youth, Melibœus, for whom twelve days a year our altars
smoke; 'twas here he first bestowed an answer to my prayer: "Ye swains,
feed as of yore the oxen; rear the bulls."

46—63. Melibœus congratulates Tityrus on the happiness of his lot.
Tityrus declares his deep thankfulness to his benefactor.

M.   O blest old man, your fields will then be still your own, and large
enough for you, albeit all the farm bare stone o'erspreads, and marshy
ground with muddy sedge chokes up your pasture-land.   Strange herbage
will not vex your teeming flocks, nor the baneful infection of a neighbouring
herd do them harm.   O blest old man, here among familiar streams and
hallowed springs you will court the coolness of the shade!   From yonder
neighbour-bound the hedge, whose willow bloom is quaffed by Hybla's
bees, will ofttimes, as it has done ever, with gentle hum invite the approach
of sleep; yonder, beneath the lofty rock, the pruner will raise his song to
heaven: nor yet meanwhile will cease the hoarse note of the wood-
pigeons you love, nor from the towering elm the turtle-dove's complaint.

T.   So first in air the nimble stags shall feed, and the seas leave the
fish uncovered on the beach, first the Parthian and the German shall both
o'erpass their bounds, and drink in exile the Arar and the Tigris, ere from
my heart his look shall pass away.

64—83. Melibœus deplores his banishment, and the ruin of his farm.
Tityrus invites him to stay for this night at least.

M.   But we shall go away, some to thirsty Africa, some to Scythia,
and the rushing stream of Cretan Oaxes, and to the Britons sundered
quite from all the world.   Ah! shall I e'er, in time far off, viewing my
native fields, and humble cabin's turf-built roof, my own domain, hereafter
see it with amazement nought but some few ears of corn?   Shall a
sacrilegious soldier hold this soil that I have tilled so well? a barbarian
these cornfields?   See to what a depth of woe discord has drawn down
our hapless citizens!   'Twas for these we sowed our fields!   Now,
Melibœus, graft the pears, plant the vines in rows.   Go then, go my
she-goats, that were a fortunate herd.   Never again shall I, stretched
within a green grot, see you afar hanging from a bushy crag: no more
songs shall I sing; no more tended by me, my goats, will you browse on
flowery lucerne and bitter willow plants.

T.   Yet here this night with me you might repose on fresh leaves; we have
mellow apples, soft chesnuts, and a wealth of curded milk: and now yon
cottage-roofs begin to smoke, and from the hill-tops larger shadows fall.

ECLOGUE II.

1—18. Corydon's hopeless love.   He complains that he is distracted while
all the world is at rest; and warns Alexis not to presume too much
on his beauty.

CORYDON the shepherd deeply loved the fair Alexis, his master's choice,
and found no place for hope: nought could he do but again and again
come to wander among the clumps of beech with shadowy tops; there
with bootless passion he used to pour to hills and woods this artless
moan: " Cruel Alexis, care you nothing for my lays?   Have you no pity
at all for me?   You will force me at last to die.   Now even the cattle woo

the coolness of the shade; now even the green lizards are hidden close
in thorny brakes; and Thestylis is bruising for the reapers o'erspent by
the scorching heat garlic and wild thyme, savoury herbs. But to keep
me company, while I trace your footsteps, beneath the burning sun the
copses are loud with the creaking cicalas. Was it not easier to endure
the dread wrath of Amaryllis, and her proud disdain? Was it not easier
to endure the scorn of Menalcas, albeit he was dark, and you are fair?
O beauteous boy, trust not too far your bloom! White privet flowers are
left to fall, dusk hyacinths are plucked."

19—55. *Corydon boasts of his wealth, accomplishments, and comeliness.
He talks of the presents he designs for Alexis, and says the nymphs
are making nosegays for him.*

I am your scorn, Alexis, and you ask not who I am, how rich in kine,
how wealthy in snow-white milk: a thousand lambs of mine wander on
the hills of Sicily; new milk fails me not in summer heat or winter cold.
I sing the songs which, whenever he called home his herds, Amphion of
Dirce used to sing on Attic Aracynth. I am not so passing uncomely;
lately I saw myself on the beach, whilst the winds allowed the sea to
rest in calm; I would not fear Daphnis, in your judgment, if the reflected
image ne'er deceives. O that you would but please with me to live in
homely fields and lowly cots, and pierce the stags, and drive the herd of
kids to the green hibiscus! Along with me you will in the woods rival
Pan in song. 'Twas Pan that first devised the art to join with wax many
a reed; Pan guards the flocks and the masters of the flocks as well. And
let it not displease you with the pipe to gall your lip; to know this same
accomplishment what would not Amyntas have done? A flute is mine,
neatly fashioned with seven unequal hemlock stalks, which Damœtas
once gave me as a present, and dying said, "That flute has now for its
master you, second to me alone." So spoke Damœtas: envious was the
foolish Amyntas. Besides, two young roes, that I found in a dell by no
means safe to reach, whose coats are still spotted with white, drain the
udders of a ewe twice every day; these I am keeping for you. Long has
Thestylis been striving by intreaties to draw them from me; and so she
shall, since in your eyes my gifts are vile. Hither come, fair youth; lo
for you the nymphs bring baskets filled with lilies; for you the beauteous
Naiad, plucking pale violets and poppy-heads, blends the narcissus and
the flower of fragrant dill; next, with yellow marigold she sets off the
pliant hyacinth, twining it with casia and other scented herbs. I myself
will cull the quinces with hoary delicate bloom, and the chestnuts that my
Amaryllis used to love; I will add plums of waxen hue; this fruit too
shall have its honour; and you, O laurels, I will gather, and myrtle, you,
the laurel's mate; for thus arranged you mix your odours sweet.

56—73. *Corydon feels his gifts must be unavailing; yet, to conciliate
Alexis, he extols the country. He deplores his endless passion. At
last he sees his madness, and resolves to go back to his neglected work,
trusting to find another love.*

You are but a clown, Corydon; and Alexis cares not for gifts; nor
would Iollas yield to you, should you in gifts attempt to match him.
Alas! alas! what have I meant to do to my hapless self? Lost as I am,

I have let in the south wind on my flowers, and wild boars to my crystal springs. Whom flee you, O blinded one? The gods too have dwelt in the woods, and Dardan Paris. Let Pallas by herself haunt the citadels she has built; above aught else, let woods be dear to me. The grim lioness pursues the wolf; the wolf in his turn the goat; the wanton goat pursues the flowery lucerne; you, Alexis, Corydon pursues; each one is attracted by his own delight. See, the bullocks bring home the plough that hangs from the yoke, and the parting sun doubles the growing shades; yet me love burns; for what bound is set to love? Ah, Corydon, Corydon, what frenzy has seized you? Your vine, half-pruned, hangs on its leafy elm. Rather, do at least set yourself to weave of osiers and pliant rushes some one of the things of which you have actual need. If this one scorns you, you will find another Alexis.

ECLOGUE III.

1—31. *The Eclogue opens with the quarrelsome conversation of two shepherds, Menalcas and Damœtas. At last, in reply to a taunt from Menalcas, Damœtas challenges him to a singing-match.*

M. TELL me, Damœtas, whose flock is that? Does it belong to Melibœus?

D. No, but to Ægon; Ægon of late entrusted it to me.

M. O ye sheep, a flock ill-fated ever! While the master pays his court to Neæra, and fears she may prefer me to himself, this hireling keeper milks the ewes twice in the hour; and fatness is filched from the sheep, and milk from the lambs.

D. Yet be careful to fling those taunts more sparingly at men. We know your story too, when the he-goats looked askance, and in what chapel it was; but the easy-tempered nymphs laughed.

M. It was then, I suppose, when they saw me with malicious knife lop Mico's vineyard-trees and tender vines.

D. Or when here beside the old beeches you broke the bow and arrows of Daphnis; for you not only felt pain at the sight, when you saw them given to the boy, you spiteful Menalcas, but also you would have died, had you not done him some harm.

M. What would the masters do, when their knaves are so audacious? Did I not see you, worst of men, catch by craft Damon's goat, while all the time his mongrel barked? And when I cried, "What is that rogue pouncing at now? Tityrus, drive the flock together;" you lay hid behind the sedge.

D. Ought he not, as he was vanquished in singing, to have given up to me the goat, which the melodies of my pipe had won? If you know it not, that goat was mine; and Damon himself confessed it to me; but said he could not give it me.

M. You in song beat him? Why, did you ever own a pipe cemented with wax? Used you not in the streets, you dunce, on a creaking reed to murder your sorry lay?

D. Will you then that one against the other we prove in turn what each can do? I, (lest perchance you try to retreat) lay this heifer; twice she comes to the milking pail, two calves her udder feeds : say you, with what stake you will make a match with me.

32—59. After a dispute about the stake each is to lay, the shepherds agree to make Palaemon, a passer by, the judge of their singing. He bids them compete.in alternate couplets.

M. I would not venture to lay with you any stake taken from the flock; for I have at home a father; I have an unkind stepmother; and twice a day both count the flock, and one of them the kids as well. But since it is your pleasure to play the madman, I will lay a pawn which you will yourself allow to be far greater than your own,—beechen cups, the carved work of divine Alcimedon ; where a streaming vine, engraved thereon by the cunning knife of the carver, mantles the straggling clusters of the pale-green ivy. In the midst are two figures, Conon, and —— who was the other, that with his wand marked out for the nations all the sphere of heaven, what seasons the reaper, what the bending plough-man was to own? And not yet have I applied them to my lips, but keep them treasured up.

D. For me too that same Alcimedon wrought two cups, and clasped the handles round with twining acanthus, and in the midst set Orpheus and his train of woods. And not yet have I applied them to my lips, but keep them treasured up. If you look at the heifer, you have no ground for praising the cups.

M. You shall never escape to-day; I will come whithersoever you call me. Only let this match be heard by ——, or by him who is approaching; see, Palæmon. I will cause you never hereafter to challenge any man in song.

D. Well, come, if aught you can; no delay shall be owing to me, and I shrink not from any judge; only, neighbour Palæmon, store up these verses in your inmost soul, for the business is not slight.

P. Sing ye, since we are seated on the velvet grass. And now each field, now every tree buds forth; now the woods break into leaf, now fairest is the year. Begin Damœtas; then follow you, Menalcas. You shall sing in turn; to sing in turn the Muses love.

60—111. The shepherds repeat alternate couplets, the second always being on a subject similar to that of the first, or forming an antithesis to it. Palaemon praises both the singers, and confesses that he cannot decide between them.

D. From Jove is my beginning, ye Muses; all things are full of Jove; 'tis he who makes fruitful the earth, 'tis he who is the patron of my lays.

M. And me Phœbus loves; ever with me are the offerings proper to Phœbus, bays and sweetly-blushing hyacinth.

D. Galatea pelts me with an apple, the playful girl, and runs away to the willow-copse, and desires to be seen first.

M. But Amyntas, the object of my love, uncalled presents himself to me; so that now not even Delia is better known to my dogs.

D. I have found out presents for my fair one; for I have marked the spot, where the wood-pigeons high in air have built their nest.

M. I have sent to the youth ('twas all I could do) ten golden apples picked from a forest tree ; to-morrow I will send as many more.

D. Oh, how many and how sweet are the words Galatea has spoken to me! Some part of them, ye winds, waft to the ears of the gods!

M. What boots it, Amyntas, that in your own heart you scorn me not, if, while you hunt the boars, I watch the nets?

D. Send Phyllis to me; it is my birthday, Iollas: when I sacrifice a heifer on behalf of my crops, come yourself.

M. Phyllis I love beyond all other maids; for she wept that I parted from her, and still she said "Adieu, adieu, my fair Iollas."

D. Dreadful is the wolf to the stalls, showers to the ripened crops, winds to the trees, the wrath of Amaryllis to me.

M. Sweet is rain to the new-sown corn, the arbutus to weaned kids, the bending willow to the teeming herd, Amyntas alone to me.

D. Pollio loves my verse, all rustic though it be; a heifer, my Muses, for your reader feed.

M. Pollio himself too makes new lays: feed for him a bull that is beginning to butt with his horn, and spurn with his feet the sand.

D. Let him who loves you, Pollio, attain the bliss he joys to see in you; for him let streams of honey flow, and the rough bramble bear the fragrant spice.

M. Let him that hates not Bavius, love your verses, Mævius; and let him yoke foxes too, and milk he-goats.

D. Ye that pluck flowers and strawberries that grow on the ground, flee hence, ye swains! a clammy snake is lurking in the grass.

M. Beware, my sheep, to go too far; 'tis ill to trust the bank; even now the ram himself is drying his fleece.

D. Tityrus, drive off the browsing she-goats from the stream; I myself, when the season comes, will wash them all in the brook.

M. Drive together the ewes into the shade, ye swains; if the parching heat first check the milk, as of late it did, in vain shall we squeeze their udders with our hands.

D. Alas, alas, how lean is my bull amid the fattening vetch! Love is the bane of the herd, and the master of the herd as well.

M. Not even love is the cause of ill to these of mine in sooth; their skin scarce clings to the bones. Some evil eye bewitches my tender lambs.

D. Say in what land (and my great Apollo you shall be) the space of heaven is but three ells in width.

M. Say in what land flowers spring inscribed with monarchs' names; and possess Phyllis for yourself alone.

P. It is not given to me to decide so high a contest between you. Both you deserve the heifer, and also he; and whoever else shall fear the sweets or prove the bitters of love. Ye swains, close up the sluices now; the meadows have drunk enough.

ECLOGUE IV.

1—17. Let my pastoral song rise higher, and be worthy of Pollio. In his consulship the golden age shall come round again, and a godlike child be born, who shall rule a world of universal peace and innocence.

MUSES of Sicily, let us raise a somewhat loftier strain. Not all the copses please, and tamarisks low: if we sing of the woods, let the woods be worthy of a consul.

Now has come the latest age of the Cumæan hymn; the mighty line of cycles begins its round anew. Now too the maiden Astræa returns, the reign of Saturn returns; now a new generation of men is sent down from the height of heaven. Only be thou gracious to the birth of the child, beneath whom the iron brood shall first begin to fail, and the golden race to arise in all the world, O chaste Lucina! Thine own Apollo now is king. And it shall be in your consulship, in yours, Pollio, that this age of glory shall commence, and the mighty months begin to run their course; under your auspices, whatever traces of our nation's guilt remain shall be effaced, and release the earth from everlasting dread. He shall receive the life of the gods, and see heroes mingled with gods, and shall himself be seen by them, and with his father's virtues shall rule a reconciled world.

18—47. Nature will do homage to the infant child, and serpents and poisonous herbs will disappear. In his youth corn, grapes, and honey will everywhere be found; but there will still be adventurous voyages, and wars. When he is grown to manhood, even commerce will cease, and nature will everywhere produce her fairest gifts; so the Fates ordain.

Then for you, O child, the earth shall begin to pour forth far and wide without aught of tillage its simple gifts, straggling ivy twined with foxglove, and the Egyptian lily blended with smiling acanthus. Of themselves the she-goats shall bring back home their udders swollen full with milk, and the herds shall fear not mighty lions: of itself the ground that is your cradle shall pour forth flowers to please you. The serpent too shall perish, and the treacherous poison-plant shall perish: Assyrian spice shall spring up everywhere. But so soon as you shall begin to be able to read of the glorious exploits of heroes, and the deeds of your sire, and to learn what virtue is, slowly the plain shall grow yellow with gently waving corn, and on wild brambles shall hang the ruddy grape, and hard oak-trunks exude the honey-dew. Yet a few traces of ancient guile shall still be left behind, to prompt men to provoke the main with barks, to circle towns with walls, to cleave the earth with furrows. Then shall be a second Tiphys, and a second Argo to carry the flower of the heroes, and a great Achilles shall again be sent to Troy. Next, when your age, grown to its strength, has now made you a man, even the merchant shall quit the sea, and the pine-built ship shall not exchange its wares; every land shall every product bear. The soil shall not feel the hoe, nor the vineyard the pruninghook; also the stout ploughman shall now unloose his oxen from the yoke; and wool shall not learn to counterfeit various hues; but of himself the ram in the meadows shall now begin to change the whiteness of his fleece for sweetly-blushing crimson, and for saffron dye; scarlet of its own accord shall dress the browsing lambs. "Ye ages, be such your career," the Destinies to their spindles said, agreeing in the stedfast will of fate.

48—63. *Come quickly to receive your power, for all the world awaits you. O that I may live to see so noble a subject for my verse! Hasten to smile upon your mother; else you cannot expect the favour of Heaven.*

Begin to assume, I pray, your sovereign honours, (the time will soon arrive,) dear offspring of the gods, majestic child of Jove! See the world nodding with its ponderous vault, and lands, and plains of sea, and deep of heaven! See how all things exult in the age that is to come! O may there be left me the latest portion of a life so long, and breath so much, as shall suffice to sing your deeds! Truly neither Thracian Orpheus shall surpass me in song, nor Linus, albeit his mother aid the one, and his father the other, Orpheus Calliopea, and Linus the fair Apollo. If even Pan, with Arcadia for judge, were to compete with me, even Pan, with Arcadia for judge, would pronounce himself vanquished. Begin, little child, to recognise your mother by a smile: ten months have brought your mother lingering sickness; begin, little child; him, on whom his parents have not smiled, no god has deemed worthy of his table, and no goddess of her couch.

ECLOGUE V.

1—19. *Two shepherds agree to sing and play in turn, in a cave shaded with the wild vine. Menalcas asks Mopsus, the younger of the two, to begin.*

Me. MOPSUS, since we two have met together, both good men, you to inspire the light reed, I to sing verses, why do we not sit down here among the elms and blended hazel-trees?

Mo. You are the elder; it is fair I yield to you, Menalcas, whether we go beneath the restless shades the Zephyrs ever stir, or choose to descend into the cave. See, how the woodland vine with scattered clusters has o'errun the cave.

Me. On our hills Amyntas only strives with you in song.

Mo. Why, 'tis he who would strive to vanquish Phœbus in singing.

Me. Begin first Mopsus; if you have either any love-songs to Phyllis, or praises of Alcon, or satires on Codrus. Begin; Tityrus will tend the browsing kids.

Mo. Nay, I will try these verses, which lately I carved on the green bark of a beech-tree, and set the tune, and marked the time in turns: then do you bid Amyntas rival them.

Me. As far as the bending willow yields to the pale-green olive; as far as the lowly Celtic reed yields to the bright-red rosebeds, so far, in my judgment, Amyntas yields to you.

Mo. Well, say no more, O youth; we have come within the cave.

20—44. *An elegy on the death of Daphnis, who is represented as the ideal shepherd. Now that he is gone, the gods have left the fields, and a curse has come on the land. Let us make his tomb, and write his epitaph.*

The Nymphs for Daphnis wept destroyed by a cruel doom; ye hazel-trees and brooks attest the Nymphs' lament; while his mother, clasping her loved son's piteous corpse, exclaims against the cruel gods and stars. No herdsmen on those days, Daphnis, drove their oxen from pasture to the cool streams; no cattle either tasted the river, or touched a blade of grass. Daphnis, both savage hills and woods proclaim that even Cartha-ginian lions deplored your death with groans. 'Twas Daphnis who first made it a custom to yoke Armenian tigers to the car, 'twas Daphnis who introduced the wild dances of Bacchus, and taught us with curling leaves to wreathe the pliant shafts. As the vine is the glory of trees, grapes of vines, bulls of herds, harvests of wealthy fields, in you was every glory of your friends: since fate has carried you away, even Pales, and even Apollo, have left the fields. Oft in the furrows to which we have com-mitted great grains of barley, unfruitful darnel and barren wild oats spring; instead of the gentle violet, instead of the bright narcissus, the thistle rises up, and the thorn with prickly spikes. Strew the ground with leaves, ye shepherds, curtain the fountains with shade; such are the honours that Daphnis desires you to pay him; and build a mound, and place above the mound this epitaph: " I Daphnis rest in the woods, famed even from earth to heaven, a fair herd's guardian, fairer still myself."

45—55. Menalcas praises the verses and skill of Mopsus, and undertakes to reply with a song on the ascent of Daphnis to the sky.

Me. Such is your song to me, O heavenly bard, as slumber on the grass to weary men, as 'tis to quench our thirst amid the heat with the sweet water of a dancing brook. You match your master not on the pipe alone, but in voice as well. Blest youth, you now will be next after him. Yet I will sing somehow to you this lay of mine in turn, and will exalt your Daphnis to the stars; Daphnis I will waft to the stars; me also Daphnis loved.

Mo. Can any favour be to me greater than such a gift? Not only the boy was himself worthy to be sung of, but long has Stimicon praised your songs to me.

56—80. The apotheosis of Daphnis. He showers blessings on the fields, as the patron god of shepherds and husbandmen.

Daphnis in beauty wonders as he views the portal of the sky unseen before, and underneath his feet beholds the clouds and stars. So sprightly pleasure charms the woods and all the fields beside, and Pan and shepherd swains and Dryad girls. The wolf against the herd no ambush plots, and nets no treachery against the stags; kind Daphnis loves repose. Even unshorn hills fling in delight their voices to the stars; even rocks, even copses, now cry aloud, "A god, Menalcas, a god is there!" Be kind, I pray, and gracious to thine own! Behold four altars; see two for thyself, O Daphnis, two for sacrifice to Phœbus. Each year two goblets foaming with new milk, and two bowls of rich olive oil I will dedicate to thee, and specially making the banquet merry with flowing wine, before the hearth if it be cold, if harvest-time within the shade, I will pour out from flagons the new-made nectar of Arvisian wine. Damœtas and Lyctian Ægon shall sing to me ; Alphesibœus shall imitate the dances of the Satyrs. Ever to thee these honours shall be given, both when we pay the Nymphs our annual vows, and when with offerings we go round the fields. While the boar shall love the mountain-heights, while the fish shall love the sea, while bees shall feed on thyme, while grasshoppers on dew, thy honour, name, and praises ever shall remain. As to Bacchus and to Ceres, so to thee the husbandmen shall make their vows each year ; thou also shalt bind suppliants to their vows.·

81—90. *Mopsus extols the song of Menalcas. The two shepherds exchange gifts.*

Mo. What gifts are there that I can give you in return for such a lay? For neither the whistling of the south wind as it comes, nor billow-beaten shores delight me so, nor streams that hurry down 'twixt pebbly vales.

Me. I first will present you with this fragile hemlock-pipe : this taught me, "Corydon deeply loved the fair Alexis ;" this taught me too, "Whose flock is that? To Melibœus does it belong?"

Mo. Take you next a crook, Menalcas, which, though he asked me oft, Antigenes won not from me (and he was then worthy of love) ; a crook with well-matched knots and brazen rings adorned.

ECLOGUE VI.

1—12. *Virgil, in the character of Tityrus, excuses himself from writing an heroic poem in praise of Varus, but hopes a pastoral song may spread his fame.*

'Twas my Thalia first who stooped to sport in Syracusan verse, and blushed not to haunt the woods. When I would sing of kings and battles, Phœbus plucked me by the ear, and warned me thus : "'Tis a shepherd's business, Tityrus, to feed fat sheep, to sing a thin-drawn lay." I now (for bards more than enough you will have, O Varus, who will be eager to hymn your praises, and record your grisly wars,) on slender reed will practise my rustic lay. Forbidden themes I sing not. Yet if these lines also anyone, anyone inspired with fondness for the song shall read, of thee our tamarisks, Varus, of thee each grove shall sing ; and no page is dearer to Phœbus, than that which on its front has inscribed the name of Varus.

13—30. *Two shepherds once found Silenus asleep, bound him, and claimed a song he had promised them. Silenus begins his song, which fills all nature with delight.*

Proceed, ye Muses. Young Chromis and Mnasylos saw Silenus lying in a cave asleep, his veins swollen, as they ever are, with the wine of yesterday ; the wreaths had slipped from his head, and lay but a short space from him, and in his grasp his heavy tankard hung by its well-worn handle. They assailed him, (for oft with the promise of a song the old god had cheated them both,) and cast upon him fetters twined of his own garlands. Ægle makes herself their comrade, and comes to join the timorous swains, Ægle fairest of the Naiads ; and when his eyes are opened, she paints with blood-red mulberries his face and brows. He, laughing at the trick, says "Wherefore twine ye fetters?

Loose me, boys; it is enough that you have seemed to have this power. Listen to the song ye wish to hear; you for your prize shall have the song, she another reward." He spoke, and at once begins. Then it was that you might see fawns and wild beasts bounding to the measure, then might you see stiff oak-trees nod their tops; neither does the cliff of Parnassus so much rejoice at Phœbus' voice, nor do Rhodope and Ismarus so much admire their Orpheus.

31—86. *The song of Silenus. He describes the creation of the world from the four elements, and the early history of man, and tells some legends of old mythology. His song lasts till evening calls the shepherds home.*

For he sang how massed throughout the mighty void were the seeds of earth and air and sea and unmixed fire withal; how from these principles all early forms, and the sphere of the universe itself, still soft, grew into substance; how next the ground begins to harden, and shut out Nereus within the sea, and by degrees assume the forms of things; and how the earth is soon amazed at the rising and growing light of the new-made sun, and showers fall from the uplifted clouds; when first the woods begin to rise, and here and there the creatures roam o'er hills that know them not. Then he tells of the stones that Pyrrha cast, of the reign of Saturn, of the birds of Caucasus, and the theft of Prometheus. Besides these tales, he sings how the mariners had called aloud on Hylas, left behind at the fountain, how with "Hylas! Hylas!" all the shore was loud. And he tells of her, blest if herds had never been, Pasiphae, solaced with her love for a snow-white steer. Ah, hapless damsel, what frenzy has seized you? The daughters of Prœtus with counterfeited lowings filled the fields; and not one of them was led away by so disgraceful a passion for the herd, albeit she feared lest her neck might feel the yoke of the plough, and on her smooth brow often sought for horns. Ah, hapless damsel, you now are roaming on the hills; while he, on soft hyacinth flowers resting his snowy side, under the dusky ilex chews the pale-green grass, or follows some heifer in the mighty herd. "Close, Nymphs, Dictæan Nymphs, now close the forest glades, if anywhere perchance the steer's vagrant steps may lead him to meet my gaze; perhaps, while he is intent on the green pasture, or as he follows the herds, some cows may draw him on to the Gortynian stalls." Then of the girl he sings, whose eyes were charmed by the apples of the Hesperides; then he tells how Phaeton's sisters were circled with the bitter mossy bark, and upward rose, high-towering alder-trees. Then he sings how one of the sisterhood guided Gallus to the Aonian hills, as he wandered beside the streams of Permessus, and how all the choir of Phœbus rose up to greet their guest; how Linus, shepherd with a gift of song divine, his locks with flowers and bitter parsley decked, spoke to him thus; "To you the Muses give these reeds (receive them now), which erst they gave the old Ascræan bard, by which in song he used to charm stiff ash-trees from the hills. On these be hymned by you the birth of the Grynean grove, so that there be no other wood, of which Apollo may make higher boast. What shall I next relate? How he sang the story of Scylla, child of Nisus, of whom the legendary tradition tells that she, with barking monsters girt below her beauteous waist, troubled the barks of Ithaca, and in deep flood, alas! mangled with her sea-hounds the affrighted mariners; or how he told of the transformed limbs of Tereus, what feast, what gifts Philomela for him prepared, in what form of flight she sped to the wilderness, and what were the wings on which the hapless one hovered, before she fled away, above her own abode? All that once, as Phœbus played and sung, blessed Eurotas heard, and bid his bay-trees in their memory keep, he sings of; the echo-beaten. vales repeat the sound to heaven; till the Evening-star warned them to drive in their sheep to the fold, and tell their tale, and floated forth in the unwilling sky.

ECLOGUE VII.

1—20. *Melibœus tells how, as he was looking for a goat that had strayed, he heard of a match between two rival singers, Corydon and Thyrsis. He puts off his work to listen to the contest.*

IT chanced beneath a shrill-voiced ilex-tree Daphnis had made his seat, and there Corydon and Thyrsis had gathered their flocks together, Thyrsis the sheep, Corydon the she-goats swollen with milk; both in the bloom of youth, Arcadians both, ready to sing on equal terms, and to reply in verse. Hitherward, while I fenced my tender myrtles from the cold, my he-goat himself, the lord of the herd, had strayed away; and so I caught sight of Daphnis. He, when he saw me coming towards him, said, " Make haste and come hither, Melibœus! Your he-goat and kids are safe; and if you can be idle for a time, repose beneath the shade. Of themselves your steers will come through the meadows hither to drink; here with waving rushes Mincius fringes his verdant banks, and from the sacred oak the swarming bees resound." What could I do? I had neither Alcippe nor Phyllis to shut up close at home my weaned lambs; and great was the contest, Corydon matched with Thyrsis. Yet to my business I preferred their sport. So in alternate verse they both began to strive; alternate verse the Muses bade them shape in mind. These Corydon rehearsed, and Thyrsis these in turn.

21—70. *The shepherds sing four verses each alternately, the second stanza always having in some way reference to the first, as in the match in the third Eclogue. The contest ends in the victory of Corydon.*

C. Nymphs that I love, nymphs of Libethra, either bestow on me the gift of song, such as you grant my Codrus; for he makes verses next to Phœbus' lays; or if we have not all that power, here on this sacred pine my shrill-voiced pipe shall hang.

T. Arcadian swains, with ivy deck your rising bard, so that with envy Codrus' heart may burst; or if he praise me even beyond my due, with foxglove wreathe my brow, that the tongue of malice may not harm the poet that is to be.

C. Delia, young Micon offers to thee this bristly wild-boar's head, and the branching antlers of a long-lived stag; if still his prayers shall be fulfilled by thee, wrought all of polished marble thou shalt stand, thy ankles with the purple buskin bound.

T. A bowl of milk, Priapus, and these cakes, 'tis enough for thee to claim from me each year; poor is the garden which thou dost protect.

Now we have wrought thee in marble for a time; but if the new-born lambs make full the flock, then be thou all of gold.

C.   Galatea, child of Nereus, sweeter to me than Hybla's thyme, fairer than swans, lovelier than light-hued ivy, so soon as to their stalls my steers return from pasture, if for your Corydon any care you feel, come hither.

T.   Nay, may I seem to you more bitter than Sardinian plants, more rough than butcher's-broom, more vile than seaweed cast upon the shore, if this day be not now longer than all the year to me.   If ye have any sense of shame at all, go home from pasturage, my oxen, go.

· *C.*   Ye mossy springs, and grass more soft than sleep, and verdant arbutus, that screens you with its scanty shade, from the midsummer heat protect my herd; now the parching summer comes; now in their fruitful sprout the vinebuds swell.

T.   Here is a hearth, and oily brands of pine; here an abundant fire ever, and door-posts blackened with perpetual soot; here of the north-wind's cold we reck as much as the wolf of the number of the flock, or rushing rivers of their banks.

C.   Fair stand the junipers and shaggy chestnut-trees; beneath each tree its fruit lies strewn around; now all things smile; but if these hills beauteous Alexis quit, even the rivers you would see dried up.

T.   The field is scorched; the grass is parched and dies beneath the tainted air; from the hills the envy of Liber withholds the vine-leaves' shade: at the coming of my Phyllis every grove shall be green, and Jove in a gladdening shower shall plenteously descend.

C.   Most dear to Alcides is the poplar, to Bacchus the vine, to beau-teous Venus the myrtle, to Phœbus his chosen bay-tree; Phyllis the hazels loves; so long as Phyllis shall love them, neither the myrtle, nor the bay of Phœbus shall surpass the hazel-trees.

T.   Fairest is the ash in woods, the pine in gardens, the poplar among streams, the fir on mountain-heights; but if you, beauteous Lycidas, would often come to visit me, the woodland ash, the garden pine, should yield to you.

M.   These verses I remember, and how the vanquished Thyrsis vainly strove.   From that day it has been with us Corydon, none but Corydon.

ECLOGUE VIII.

1—16.   *The songs of Damon and Alphesibœus are to form the subject of this Eclogue.   The dedication to Pollio.   It was just daybreak when Damon began his song.*

· THE shepherd's lay, the lay of Damon and Alphesibœus, on whom, as they vied in song, the heifer heedless of her pasture gazed, by whose melody lynxes were entranced, and streams were changed, and stayed their wonted pace, we will repeat the lay of Damon and Alphesibœus.

Whether you now, my friend, are passing by the rocks of great Timavus, or sailing by the coast of the Illyrian main, say, will that day ever come, when it will be granted me to utter your feats?   Say, will it come to pass that I may spread through all the world your verse, the only verse that deserves the buskin of Sophocles?   From you was my beginning; my ending shall be to you.   Accept the song essayed at your command; and round your temples let this ivy creep among the conqueror's bays.

Scarcely had night's cold shadow passed away from heaven, at the hour when on the tender grass the dew is most welcome to the cattle, when, leaning on a staff of polished olive, Damon thus begins :

17—62. Damon bewails the broken faith of Nisa, his betrothed, and depreciates Mopsus, his successful rival. He complains of the ancient cruelty of Love.

D. Spring to life, O Morning-star, and speed the kindly day, its harbinger, while I, cheated in my love, ill-bestowed on Nisa my betrothed, make my complaint, and, though their testimony availed me nought, yet, as I die, address the gods in this my latest hour. Begin with me, my flute, the strains of Mænalus. Mænalus a shrill-voiced grove and vocal pines possesses ever ; he ever hears the loves of shepherds, and Pan, the first who suffered not the reeds to rest untrained to art. Begin with me, my flute, the strains of Mænalus. Nisa is given to Mopsus ; what may we not hope in love? Presently griffins will with horses mate ; and in the following age with hounds the timorous hinds will come to drink. Begin with me, my flute, the strains of Mænalus. Cut new torch-brands, Mopsus ; the bride is being led home to you ; bridegroom, scatter the nuts ; for you the Evening-star leaves Œta's height. Begin with me, my flute, the strains of Mænalus. O mated with a worthy lord, while you contemn us all, and while my pipe, and while my goats, and shaggy eye-brows, and my length of beard, are hateful in your eyes, and you fancy not one god cares for the deeds of men. Begin with me, my flute, the strains of Mænalus. Within our fence I saw you when a child, gathering with my mother apples wet with dew : I was your guide. Then my twelfth year of life had just begun : from the ground I just could reach the brittle boughs. The moment that I saw, how was I lost ! How a pernicious blindness forced me on ! Begin with me, my flute, the strains of Mænalus. Now know I what Love is ; on flinty crags Tmaros, or Rhodope, or the far remote Garamantes, are they that gave him birth, the boy that comes not of our race or blood. Begin with me, my flute, the strains of Mænalus. 'Twas ruthless Love that taught the mother to pollute her hands in her children's blood ; cruel too were you, O mother ; was the mother more cruel, or that wicked boy? More cruel, that wicked boy ; you, mother, were cruel too. Begin with me, my flute, the strains of Mænalus. Now let the wolf e'en flee before the sheep, let rugged oak-trees golden apples bear, let the narcissus on the alder bloom, let tamarisks from their bark exude rich ambergris. Let screech-owls also vie with swans, let Tityrus be Orpheus,—an Orpheus in the woods, among the dolphins an Arion, (begin with me, my flute, the strains of Mænalus,) yea, even let all the world be made deep sea. Ye woods, farewell ! Headlong from a high-towering mountain's peak I will plunge into the waves ; take this last present of your dying swain. Cease you, now cease, my flute, the strains of Mænalus.

63—110. Alphesibœus, in the character of an enchantress, sings of the various charms by which she endeavours to bring back her lover.

So Damon sung ; ye Muses, rehearse the answer of Alphesibœus ; we all have not power to perform all tasks.

A. Bring water forth, and with a pliant garland wreathe these shrines

and unctuous sacred plants, and choicest incense burn; that I may essay
by magic rites to turn away the sound senses of my betrothed; nothing is
wanting here, except the song. Draw Daphnis from the city home, draw
Daphnis home, my song. Song has even power to draw the moon from
heaven; Circe by song transformed Ulysses' crew; by song the clammy
snake is burst asunder in the meadows. Draw Daphnis from the city
home, draw Daphnis home, my song. First these three threads of three hues
each distinct around you I entwine, and thrice around these altars draw your
image; in an uneven number heaven delights. Draw Daphnis from the
city home, draw Daphnis home, my song. Amaryllis, in three knots three
colours weave; weave them, Amaryllis, pray, and say these words; "Venus'
bands I weave." Draw Daphnis from the city home, draw Daphnis home,
my song. As this clay hardens, and as this wax melts in one and the
self-same fire, even so let Daphnis melt with love for me, to others' love be
hard. Scatter the sacred meal, with brimstone fire the crackling boughs
of bay. Me unkind Daphnis burns; I, to kindle Daphnis, burn this bay.
Draw Daphnis from the city home, draw Daphnis home, my song. May
Daphnis feel love such as the heifer feels, when she, tired out with seeking for the steer through groves and lofty woods, in green sedge by a
water-brook sinks down, all lost, and minds not to retreat as night
grows late; and may I care not to heal his pain! Draw Daphnis from
the city home, draw Daphnis home, my song. These dresses once that
traitor left with me, dear pledges of himself; which I now in the threshold
of the door commit, O Earth, to thee; Daphnis these pledges make my
due. Draw Daphnis from the city home, draw Daphnis home, my song.
These herbs and these drugs at Pontus gathered were given me by
Mœris himself; at Pontus plenteously they spring. By the power of these
I have seen Mœris oft become a wolf and hide within the woods; oft have
I seen him call up spirits from the deep of the grave, and draw sown corn
away to other fields. Draw Daphnis from the city home, draw Daphnis
home, my song. Amaryllis, bear ashes forth, and cast them o'er your
head into the running brook; and look not behind you. With these
charms I will assail Daphnis; nought recks he of the gods, and nought
of magic songs. Draw Daphnis from the city home, draw Daphnis home,
my song. See, while I delay to bear them forth, the ashes of themselves,
of their own accord, have fired the altars up with flickering flames! May
the sign be good! Something it surely means, and Hylax is barking at
the door. Am I to believe? Or do they that love mould in their own
thoughts visions for themselves? Stop you, now stop, my song, from the
city Daphnis comes.

ECLOGUE IX.

1—16. *Lycidas, who has heard that Menalcas has saved his farm by his
poetry, wonders to hear from Mœris that a stranger has seized the
land. Mœris tells him that poetry was no protection against intrud-
ing soldiers.*

L. WHITHER away, Mœris? Go you, as the path leads, to the city?
M. O Lycidas, we have reached this point alive, a woe we never
dreamt of, that a stranger should seize our farm, and say, "These lands

are mine, ye ancient occupiers yield possession." Now vanquished, sad, since Fortune sways the world, we send to him these kids, and may the gift prove no blessing.

L. I surely had heard, that where the hills begin to swell from the plain, and downward drop their ridge with gentle slope, as far as the fountain and the beech-trees, whose tops are shattered now, your master Menalcas by his lays had saved all the land.

M. So you had heard, and so the story went ; but, Lycidas, our lays have as much power among the arms of Mars, as they say the doves of Chaonia have, when the eagle comes against them. Indeed, had not a crow on my left hand warned me from a hollow ilex-tree by some means to break off the new-begun dispute, neither I, your Mœris, nor Menalcas himself would be living.

17—36. *The two shepherds extol the songs of Menalcas, and Lycidas begs Mœris to recite some of them.*

L. Alas, can any man think of crime so foul? Alas, were your delightful lays, and yourself as well, almost snatched from us, Menalcas? Who then would sing of the Nymphs? Who would bestrew the ground with flowering plants, or curtain the fountains with green shade? Or who would sing the verses I silently caught from you of late, when you were journeying to Amaryllis, our darling? "Tityrus, while I am away (the distance is but short) feed my she-goats ; and drive them, Tityrus, when fed, to drink ; and as you drive them on, beware of coming in the he-goat's way, for he strikes with his horn."

M. Nay, rather these, which though not yet finished he used to sing to Varus : "Varus, your name (let Mantua but be spared us, Mantua, alas too near to hapless Cremona) swans in their song shall waft aloft to heaven."

L. So may your swarms shun yews of Corsica, so may your cows on lucerne fed their udders swell,—begin, if aught you can. Me too the Muses have made a poet; I too have lays ; me also the shepherds call a bard ; but I believe them not. For as yet I ween I utter not things meet for the ear of Varus or Cinna, but cackle like a goose among the tuneful swans.

37—55. *Mœris complies with the wish of Lycidas, and repeats some verses of Menalcas. He complains of his failing memory and voice; and tells Lycidas he may hear the songs of Menalcas from his own lips.*

M. So indeed I am doing, Lycidas, and silently pondering in my mind, if I can recollect them ; and it is no common lay : "Come hither, Galatea ; for why care you to play in the waves? Here is the rosy spring, here about the streams earth sheds many-coloured flowers, here the white poplar overhangs the cave, and creeping vines their shadowy arbours weave ; come hither ; let the billows madly beat the shore."

L. How deem you of the verses I heard you singing by yourself beneath the cloudless night? I remember the measure, could I command the words.

M. "Daphnis, why mark you the risings of the ancient constellations? Lo, the star of Cæsar, child of Venus, has come forth, the star beneath whose sway the fields are spread with joyful crops, and the grape deepens its colour upon the sunny hills. Daphnis, graft the pears ; your children's children shall pluck your fruit." Age carries all away, memory too ; I recollect that when a boy I often whiled away long days in song : now all those ditties are by me forgot ; now Mœris also voice itself forsakes ; wolves have looked on Mœris first. But yet Menalcas will oft enough repeat for you those songs.

56—67. Lycidas still presses Mœris to sing. Mœris excuses himself till Menalcas returns.

L. With reasoning you long linger my desire. And now, look all the deep in peace is laid, and lo, all the gales of the whispering wind have dropped. From hence but half our way is left ; for the tomb of Bianor begins to be seen : here, where the farmers strip the abundant leaves, here, Mœris, let us sing ; here set down your kids ; we shall still reach the city. But if we fear lest night first gather a cloud of rain, we may go right onward as we sing,—so, less irksome is the way ; that we may sing as we go, I will relieve you of this burden.

M. Cease, boy, to urge me more, and let us set about our instant business : we will sing songs better then, when the master himself is come.

ECLOGUE X.

1—30. This last pastoral song is in honour of Gallus, and tells of his love for Lycoris, who has forsaken him. The woods and hills of Arcadia mourn for him, and gods and men visit him, to console his despair.

ARETHUSA, suffer me to accomplish this my final task : for my Gallus I must sing a lay, of verses few, but such as Lycoris herself may read ; who would refuse a lay to Gallus? So, when you glide beneath the Sicilian waves, may briny Doris mingle not her flood with thine. Begin : let us discourse of Gallus' torturing love, while my flat-nosed she-goats browse on the tender twigs. Not to the deaf we sing ; the forests every note repeat. What were the groves, or what the glades, that held ye, Naiad maids, when Gallus languished with love ill-bestowed? For surely not the ridges of Parnassus, surely not any height of Pindus, nor Aonian Aganippe, caused you to keep away. For him even bay-trees, even tamarisks wept ; for him as he lay beneath a desolate rock, even piny Mænalus wept, and the crags of cold Lycæus. His sheep too stand around ; they scorn not us, and scorn not you the flock, O god-like bard ; beauteous Adonis too fed his sheep beside the streams : the shepherd came too, slowly the swineherds came; Menalcas came, all wet from steeping winter-mast. "Whence springs that love of yours?" they all inquire. Apollo came : "O Gallus, why so mad?" he says ; "Lycoris, for whom you pine, has followed another through the snow, and through the savage camp." Silvanus also came, his head decked with a rustic crown, wagging his fennel flowers and lilies large. Pan came, Arcadia's god, whom we ourselves have seen, with blood-red elderberries and vermilion stained. "Will there be any bound to your tears?" he says ; "Love regards not such ; insatiate of tears is cruel Love, and grass of running brooks, and bees of lucerne-bloom, and goats of leaves."

31—69. Gallus replies. He wishes he could live the life of an Arcadian shepherd, but mad love of war has made him a soldier. For a moment he resolves to lead a pastoral life, and strive to forget his love; but soon bethinks himself that no change of scene can alter Love, who conquers all things everywhere alike.

But sadly in reply he says: "Still sing, Arcadians, on your hills my woes: Arcadians alone are skilled in song. Oh! then how softly would my bones repose, if e'er your pipe should of my love discourse. And would I had been one of you, and either keeper of your flock, or dresser of your ripened grapes! Surely at least the one I loved, whether it were Phyllis, or Amyntas, or whoever it were, (what then would it matter that Amyntas was dark of hue? Both violets and hyacinths too are dusk:) among the willows would lie with me beneath the creeping vine; Phyllis would gather garlands, Amyntas sing for me. Here are cool springs, Lycoris, here velvet meadows, here a grove; here with you I might slowly waste away only by lapse of time. Now frenzied love for ruthless Mars keeps me ever in arms in the very midst of weapons, and face to face with the enemy: you far from your native land (let me only not believe it!) alone, away from me, hard-hearted one! view Alpine snows and the Rhine's frozen streams. Ah, may the frosts harm you not! Ah, may the jagged ice wound not your tender feet! I will go: and the lays that in Chalcidian verse I have composed will attune upon the pipe of the Sicilian swain. I am resolved rather in forests, among caves that wild beasts haunt, to endure, and carve on tender trees my love; they will grow, and with them you will grow, my love. Meanwhile, amid the throng of Nymphs, I will roam o'er Mænalus, or hunt the fierce boar; and not the keenest cold shall forbid me to encompass with hounds the thickets of Parthenius; even now methinks I speed o'er rocks and through echoing woods; 'tis my delight from the Parthian bow to shoot Cydonian shafts; —as if this could be my frenzy's antidote, or that god could learn to soften at the woes of men! Now a second time neither Dryads nor even songs have charms for me! Even ye woods, a second time adieu! Our toils on him can never work a change, not though in the midst of the time of frosts we should drink the Hebrus and endure the snows of the rainy Thracian winter; nor if, when the inmost bark is parched and dying upon the lofty elm, beneath the star of Cancer we should tend the Æthiopians' wandering flocks. Love conquers all the world; let us too yield to Love."

70—77. The Conclusion of the Eclogues.

'Twill be enough that your bard has sung as much as this, Pierian Ladies, while he sits idle, and twines a basket of slender hibiscus; ye will make these songs of highest worth to Gallus, Gallus, for whom my love each hour grows as much as in the early spring shoots up the vigorous alder. Let us rise: the shade is oft unwholesome to those that sing beneath it; unwholesome is the shade of the juniper; shade hurts the crops as well. Go ye home, go, my goats, for you have browsed your fill; and the Evening-star is rising.

INTRODUCTION TO THE GEORGICS.

IF the Eclogues must on the whole yield to the Idylls of Theocritus, if the Æneid may not claim to be the chief of Epics, yet, as the author of the Georgics, Virgil will generally be allowed to be the prince of didactic poets. It is true that here, as in the Eclogues, he professes to follow a Greek original. He avowedly imitates Hesiod; and speaks of himself as one who "old Ascræan verse in Roman cities sings." But the influence of Hesiod in the Georgics is not like the influence of Theocritus in the Eclogues. Indeed, Virgil owes but little to the *Works and Days* of the Bœotian poet. Except in the general character of the subject, in the constant praise of unwearied industry, and in some few points of detail, there is but little similarity between the two works. For Hesiod is a practical writer; perhaps he only used poetry at all because it was the one form of composition in his time; his digressions are few, and his verse is seldom imaginative. But the practical value of the Georgics is certainly intended to be subordinate to their claims as a poem; their greatest beauties are contained in digressions from the subject; and the verse throughout is elaborately adorned with musical flow and poetic colouring.

It may be mentioned that in the first book of the Georgics Virgil has borrowed part of his matter from the *Diosemeia* (Prognostics) of another Greek poet, Aratus; and that Quinctilian speaks of Virgil as a follower of Nicander, also a Greek poet, who wrote on the art of keeping bees. Still there is no doubt that the poetry of the Georgics owes very little to either of these writers. Virgil has taken from Aratus hardly anything but mere materials for his work; and he everywhere improves what he appropriates, by his own characteristic arrangement and poetical form. Nicander's work on bees is lost; but, judging from his extant writings, we may safely assume that he has not lent much to the charm of the fourth book of the Georgics.

But no small portion of the spirit and poetry of the Georgics Virgil owes to a work of his own nation, the poem of Lucretius *On the Nature of Things*. It is true that at first sight the two writers may seem to possess little in common. Lucretius has an absorbing enthusiasm for his subject; he is filled with a passionate desire to explain and enforce the system of philosophy he treats of; for he firmly believes that, if it be rightly understood, it will relieve the mind of all unhappiness and weakness; that it will drive away the phantoms of superstition, and all the terrors of death. And so, through his very earnestness, his continual pressing of the details of his subject, he naturally grows wearisome to the reader; he wants the lighter touch and greater variety of Virgil. His digressions too, though very beautiful, are but rare, and are not always skilfully introduced; and again, his verse is monotonous, and his diction is often heavy and inelegant. In fact, as an artist he is far inferior to Virgil.

Yet the Georgics owe him much. To him, even more perhaps than to

Hesiod, is due the spirit of earnestness in his subject which Virgil has so well succeeded in imparting to the Georgics; not indeed the overwhelming devotion of Lucretius himself, but a continual conviction of the necessity of severe toil, of grappling with difficulties, of firm resolution. This feeling is strongly brought out in many passages of the first three books; and the same spirit is equally clear in the fourth, which takes for its subject the bee, the emblem of toil and thrift. Like Lucretius too, Virgil expresses his consciousness of the difficulty of giving interest to the details of his subject. The Georgics also contain many actual imitations from Lucretius; the account of the pestilence, at the end of the third book, is modelled on the description of the plague at Athens, which concludes the poem of Lucretius. Virgil has also appropriated many of the phrases and formulas of the older poet.

To the same source are due those indications of love and admiration for natural philosophy which appear here and there in the Georgics. There is an evident reference to Lucretius himself in the famous passage towards the end of the second book, where Virgil extols the blessedness of him "who has had the power to learn the causes of things, and has cast beneath his feet all fears, and inexorable fate, and the roar of greedy Acheron." But the mind of Virgil himself was perhaps hardly suited for philosophy; he seems to regard science rather with admiration than sympathy; his own views "on the nature of things" were certainly not decided and made up; and he had probably little aptitude or enthusiasm for dealing with abstract subjects.

Many writers of later times have been more or less indebted to the Georgics; but, as compared with the Eclogues, the former have had few direct imitators: the didactic poetry of modern Europe has on the whole taken Horace for its model rather than Virgil. Agriculture is a subject difficult indeed to treat poetically; and no great poet since Virgil has ventured to write an elaborate work on husbandry. But several English poets have taken the Georgics for their pattern to a greater or less extent; of these Thomson is the most eminent; but *The Seasons* is more descriptive than didactic, and resembles Virgil in its serious and heroic style, and in particular passages, rather than in general design and arrangement. Phillips' *Cyder* and Dyer's *Fleece* are perhaps best known among the more professed imitations of the Georgics.

The Georgics were probably begun about B.C. 37, and occupied, the so-called Donatus says, seven years of Virgil's life. We learn, from the conclusion of the work, that it was finished during the campaigns of Octavianus in the East, soon after the battle of Actium, which took place B.C. 31. It was written, Virgil himself tells us, at the suggestion of Mæcenas. But there is little ground for the idea that it was part of the design of the poem to encourage the revival of agriculture in Italy, depressed as it was after the long continuance of civil war, and a period of insecurity and violence. For the Georgics certainly cannot be called a practical work; and the tone of the poem on this subject is not hopeful, but melancholy; the poet looks back with mournful regret on the old times when due honour was paid to the plough; when the Romans were simple, honest, frugal, industrious, and at peace among themselves: but

he does not venture to look forward to the return of ancient simplicity
and virtue.

The Georgics have often been praised as the most highly finished of
Virgil's poems. They have all the merits that have been noticed in the
Eclogues, and even more; and they have far fewer defects. They are
also more original; for the Romans, though never a pastoral, had always
been an agricultural people; and dwelt with fondness on the stories of
Curius, Cincinnatus, and others of their old heroes, who had followed the
trade of husbandry; so that Virgil was now treating of one of the principal characteristics of his own nation. And so, though the charge of
unreality may in some degree be brought against the Georgics, as well as
against the Eclogues, as must always be the case in a didactic work
where practical usefulness is made subordinate to poetical treatment, yet
here the defect is far less apparent. And we see in the Georgics a decided
growth in Virgil's genius, a finer sympathy with nature, and a more
splendid and vigorous power of description; more delicate touches of
feeling and observation, greater artistic skill in arrangement, stronger
grasp of the subject, and a command of verse still more varied and
majestic. The praise which Johnson gives to the author of *The
Seasons* may surely with still greater justice and accuracy be assigned
to the poet of the Georgics: "His numbers, his pauses, his diction, are
of his own growth, without transcription, without imitation. He looks
round on Nature and on Life with the eye which Nature bestows only on
a poet; the eye that distinguishes, in everything presented to its view,
whatever there is on which imagination can delight to be detained. He
imparts to us so much of his own enthusiasm, that our thoughts expand
with his imagery, and kindle with his sentiments."

BOOK I.

*1—42. The subjects of the four Georgics. The invocation of the heavenly
powers, especially of Augustus, soon about to rise to heaven.*

WHAT makes the crops rejoice, under what star 'tis meet, Mæcenas,
to plough the land, and wed the vines to elms, how oxen we should
tend, what care in breeding cattle use, what experience we need, if
we would keep thrifty bees, now I begin to sing. And oh, ye brightest
luminaries of the world, guides of the gliding year along the sky,
Liber and Ceres, who sustainest life, if by your bounty the earth
received the rich ear for the acorn of Dodona, and mixed the draughts
of the water of Achelous with the juice of the newly discovered grape;
and ye, oh Fawns, deities ready to aid the husbandmen, yes hither
come, ye Fawns with tripping foot, and ye Dryad maidens; for of
your bounty now I sing. Thou too, for thou art he, at whose command the earth by thy trident struck straight did produce the neighing
steed, oh Neptune; and thou of groves the dresser, for whom three
hundred milk-white steers crop the fruitful bushes of Cæa; and do
thou, great god, leaving thy native grove and lawns of Lycæus, Pan,
thou guardian of the sheep, as thou lovest thine own Mænalus, come
to my help, gracious lord of Tegea; and thou, Minerva, inventress

of the olive, and thou, O youth, from whom we learnt to make the crooked plough, thou too, Silvanus, with tender cypress plucked from its roots in thy hand ; and gods and goddesses all, whose joy it is to protect our fields, who cherish the new fruits of the earth, that spring without a seed, or on sown crops send down from heaven many a plenteous shower ; but chiefly thou, O Cæsar, though we know not yet, what company in heaven thou dost mean to choose, whether to watch o'er our towns, and to protect our lands, so that the mighty world may welcome thee as giver of the fruits of the earth, and lord of seasons, and with thy mother's myrtle crown thy brows ; or whether thou wilt come as the god of the boundless sea, that thy divinity alone the mariners may worship, thee furthest Thule may obey, and Tethys buy thee for a son-in-law with the dowry of all her waves : or wilt thou add thyself as a new star to speed the laggard months, where room for thee appears between Virgo and the grasping claws of the scorpion ; e'en now that burning star of himself for thee contracts his arms, and leaves thee more than thy fair share of heaven : whatever power thou wilt be, for Tartarus hopes not for thee as king, nor would a passion for sovereignty so fell enter thy heart, however Greece may praise Elysian fields, and Proserpine though claimed care not to follow her mother : do thou vouchsafe an easy course, and favour my bold attempts, and with me show pity on the husbandmen, who know not the right path, and enter on thy divine powers, and even now learn how to listen to the vows of men.

43—70. Plough in early spring. A fourfold ploughing will find its reward. Yet understand the soil. Fight not against Nature. Follow her guidance in ploughing.

In early spring, as soon as the dissolving snow melts on the white mountains, and the earth crumbles unbound by zephyrs, e'en then let my plough be pressed deep down, and my bullock begin to groan, and the share be well worn and bright from the furrow. That land alone fulfils the prayers of the covetous farmer, which twice has felt the heat and twice the cold : abundant crops that goodman's granaries burst. Yet ere our iron cuts an unknown plain, first let us learn with care the winds and changing habits of the sky, the natural culture and disposition of the ground, and what each land will produce, or will refuse to bear. Here corn grows happiest, there the vines : there flourish fruit-trees best, and herbs unbidden spring. Seest thou not how Tmolus sends us scented saffron, India ivory, the soft Sabæans their own frankincense, the naked Chalybes iron, Pontus the strong-smelling castor, Epirus mares which win the prize in the Olympic games. From the very first these laws and eternal covenants were laid by nature on certain places, ever since the time Deucalion threw stones into the untenanted world ; whence men are sprung, a hardy race. Come then, let the rich soil be turned up by sturdy bullocks straightway in the first months of the year, let the clods lie exposed, and dusty summer bake them with its mellow suns ; but should the soil be poor, then it will be sufficient to leave it lightly raised with shallow furrow, just before Arcturus rises : so will you prevent in the rich

soil weeds from hurting the joyous corn ; in poor land the scanty moisture will not fail the barren sand.

71—93. *Let your land lie fallow every other season; change your crops;
idle lands are not ungrateful; it is well to burn stubble.*

Further, suffer your land after harvest to lie fallow in idleness every
other season, and let your field grow hard in indolent repose : or 'neath
another star sow yellow corn, whence, before, you have carried the pulse
rejoicing in its quivering pod, or the slight seeds of vetch, or brittle
stalks and thick rattling growth of bitter lupine. A field is burnt by crop
of flax or oats, 'tis burnt by poppies steeped in Lethe's sleep. But to
plough every other season will lighten toil ; only be not ashamed to soak
the arid soil with rich dung, or freely to cast dirty ashes o'er the exhausted fields. Thus too with change of grain the land finds rest ;
meanwhile not thankless is the untilled earth. 'Tis often good to set fire
to the barren fields, and to burn light stubble with crackling flames ;
whether thence the lands conceive some hidden power and rich nourishment ; or whether by the fire all the vice of the ground is baked out, and
redundant moisture thence transpires ; or else that heat opens more
passages, and relaxes the hidden pores, whence juice may reach the
young herbs ; or else it binds and hardens the gaping veins, and prevents
the soaking rain from sinking in, and the fierce power of the devouring
sun, and penetrating cold of Boreas from scorching the land.

94—117. *Harrowing is good, and cross ploughing. Pray for dry
winters, wet summers. Let water in or drain it off as need requires. Let cattle eat down luxuriant corn.*

Very greatly too does he help the fields, who with harrows breaks the
sluggish clods, and drags o'er them osier hurdles ; nor on him does
yellow Ceres look down with idle gaze from high Olympus ; nor on him
who turns his plough, and in new direction breaks thoroughly the ridges
obliquely, which he had stirred when first he cut the surface ; with
frequent exercise he subdues the earth and tames the fields. Ye farmers,
pray for summers wet, and winters fair ; 'tis winter's dust that makes the
corn so glad, that bids the field rejoice : then most does Mysia glory in
her tilling, then even Gargarus marvels at her crops. Or need I tell of
him, who having cast his seed, like soldier in close fight, falls on the
fields, levelling the ridges of the sorry sand? then on the crops brings
rills and flowing streams, and when the parched land is hot, and the
blade is dying, look, from the brow of the sloping path he entices the
water : the falling flood wakes o'er the smooth stones a hoarse murmur,
and with its bubblings cools the thirsty fields. Or what of him, who lest
with heavy ears the stem should forward fall, sends in his flocks to eat
down the luxuriant corn in the tender blade, ere the grain o'ertops the
furrow? or of him, who draws off the collected moisture of marshy ground
by mixing thirsty sand? chiefly, when in the months we cannot trust the
full river o'erflows, and covers all around with layer of mud, whence
hollow ditches steam with moisture warm.

118—146. *But many are the enemies of the farmer. Jove has so ordained
it. The golden age encouraged idleness. Necessity is the mother of
invention.*

And yet, though industrious men and labouring oxen experience all these toils in tilling the ground, this is not all, for greedy goose, and Strymonian crones, and succory with bitter roots, and shade of trees are not harmless, or innoxious. The great Sire himself would not have the path of tillage to be a smooth one, and first disturbed the fields by the husbandman's art, and whetted human wit by many a care, nor suffered heavy sloth to rust his realm. Before the rule of Jove no tillers used to subdue the fields; it was impious then e'en to mark the field or distinguish it by bounds. Men's gains were for the common stock; of her own free will more readily the earth did all things bear, when none solicited her gifts. Jove to black serpents added deadly slime, he bid the wolves to prowl, the sea to swell, he shook from off the leaves honey, and hid fire out of sight, and checked the streams of wine that once ran in every brook, that experience by practice might strike out various arts little by little, seeking for the blade of corn in furrows, striking forth the fire hidden in veins of flint. Then first the rivers felt the hollowed alder; then sailors numbered stars, and called them by their names, the Pleiades, the Hyades, and the bright bear of Lycaon. Then was the taking of wild animals in toils and the snaring of birds with bird-lime discovered, and how to gird great glades of forests with hounds. And now one lashes a broad river with a casting net, throwing it deep, and another draws a dripping dragnet in the high seas. Then was stiff iron, and the blade of the grating saw first used; for the men of the golden age clave the splitting wood with wedges. So various arts succeeded. Labour o'ercame all difficulties, labour that cannot tire, and the pressure of need amidst the pinches of life.

147—159. *Ceres taught men how to till the land. Yet many are the farmer's difficulties. Without industry he would return to acorns once more.*

Ceres was the first to teach mortals how to turn the land with iron share, when the acorns and arbutes began to fail in the holy wood, and Dodona denied men food. But presently to the corn too were added its own troubles, and it was ordained that noxious mildew should eat the stems, and that the lazy thistle should bristle in the fields: see how die the crops, in their stead arises a prickly wood, cleavers and caltrops, and amidst the neat cornfields the unfruitful darnel and barren wild-oats lord it in the land. Now unless too you give the land no rest with diligent harrows, and make a noise to scare the birds, and with your bill restrain the boughs of the dark o'ershadowing country, and with vows invoke the rainy god, alas, you will idly gaze on your neighbour's great heap, and find no comfort for your hunger, but once more to shake the oak in the wild woods.

160—175. *I must not forget the farmer's implements. The plough in particular is curiously wrought.*

I must tell too of the implements of the hardy rustics, without which the corn cannot be sown, or grow to the harvest. There is first the share, and the heavy strong timber of the crooked plough, and the slowly rolling wagons of the Eleusinian mother, the threshing sledges and drags, and harrows of unwieldy weight; further too the common wicker furniture of Celeus, arbute hurdles, and the mystic winnowing fan of Iacchus ; all which remember well to provide and store up long before, if the well-earned honours of the divine country are to be yours. The elm while yet quite young in the woods is bent by strong force, and trained to grow into the shape of a plough-beam, and receives the form of a crooked plough. To the end of this a pole as much as eight feet long, two earth-boards, and share-beams with double back are fitted. Also a light lime-tree is cut down betimes for the yoke, and a tall beech will make a handle, to turn the bottom of the plough from behind ; the wood hung up in the chimney is seasoned by smoke.

176—186. *Let the threshing-floor be level and hard, lest weeds get in, or animals creep through.*

Many are the precepts of the men of old I could repeat to you, did you not start off, as one loth to learn such trifling tedious points. Above all level your threshing-floor with a huge roller, and work it with the hand, and make it solid with binding potter's clay, to hinder weeds from growing through, or lest it give way and chap through dust, lest, too, various plagues mock your hopes ; often does the little mouse build his home under the ground and there make his granaries ; or moles bereft of eyes their chambers dig ; in holes the toad is found, and all the many other vermin that the ground produces ; a mighty heap of corn the weevil wastes, or the ant that dreads an old age of penury.

187—203. *The fruit of the walnut-tree and the corn-harvest correspond. Be careful to pick out the best seeds. All things in nature degenerate to the careless.*

Likewise observe and see how, when the walnut in the woods is clothed with fullest blossom, and seems to bend its scented boughs ; if the fruit abounds, there will be corn in like measure, and a great threshing come with a great heat ; but if the shade of the tree is fuller with luxuriant leaves, your floor shall idly thresh your stalks rich in nought but chaff. Some men I have seen medicate the seeds they sow, and steep them in alkali and black lees of oil, to give a fuller fruit to the deceitful pods, that with any fire however low soon may they be sodden. I have seen these, though picked long before and tested with much care, yet for all that degenerate, if human toil does not pick with the hand the largest, one by one each year. Thus all in nature is fated to speed from worse to worse, and slipping back to run in downward course ; just as when a man with oars painfully rows a boat up against the torrent, if perchance he slacks his arms, lo headlong down the descending stream the current sweeps him on.

204—230. *Farmer and sailor alike must watch the stars. Each seed has its own star, under which to be sown.*

Further, as carefully must the star of Arcturus, and the days of the Kids, and the bright Dragon be observed by us on land, as by those, who, homewards bound across the stormy seas, venture to the Euxine and straits of oyster-breeding Abydos. When the balance has equalized hours of day and sleep, and halves the world exactly 'twixt light and shade, then work, my men, your steers, sow barley in the land, even to the last showers of impracticable winter. Further, now it is time to cover in the ground flax that is to be your crop, and poppy dear to Ceres, and at once to bend to your ploughs, whilst you still have dry ground, and the clouds fall not in rain. In spring sow beans ; then you too, lucerne, the crumbling furrows receive, and millet asks an annual care : when the bright Bull ushers in the year with his gilded horns, and the Dog retiring sets, facing the threatening Bull. But if it be for a harvest of wheat, and for spelt, a hardy crop, you work your ground, and labour earnestly for bearded ears alone, let the seven daughters of Atlas hide themselves from your eyes with the dawn, and let the Cretan star of the blazing Crown retire, ere you commit the expected seeds to the furrows, or hastily trust a whole year's hope to the unwilling earth. Many have begun before Maia sets ; but the desired crop has baffled them with empty ears. But if your mind is to sow vetch or common kidney-beans, and you scorn not the culture of Egyptian lentil, setting Bootes will give no doubtful sign : begin, and extend your sowing even to the midst of the frosts.

231—251. *The Sun's path in the zodiac rules the seasons. There are five zones.*

For this end the golden Sun guides the year's circle, portioned out in regular parts through the twelve constellations of the world. Five zones possess the sky ; whereof there's one, which is ever red with the flashing Sun, and ever torrid with fire. Round this two at the end extend to right and left, with blue ice stiff and gloomy showers of rain. 'Twixt these and the middle zone, two by heaven's grace are granted to suffering mortals ; a path is cut 'twixt both, along which the order of the signs might obliquely turn. As steep to Scythia and the Riphæan crags arises our world, so it is depressed downward to the south of Libya. One pole high towers above our heads; dark Styx and the ghosts in the abyss behold the other beneath their feet. Here forth doth twine with winding coil the Dragon great, after the manner of a stream, around and through the two Bears, the Bears that dread a bath in Ocean's waves. There, as they tell, is either the silence of the dead of night for ever, and darkness thickens 'neath the pall of night ; or else from them to us Aurora comes, bringing back the day ; and when on us the rising Sun first breathes with panting steeds, there blushing Vesper lights his latest fires.

252—258. *The sailor and the farmer can trust nature.*

Hence we can learn coming changes of weather in the dubious sky, hence the days of harvest and the season of sowing, and when 'tis meet with oars to cut the faithless sea, when to launch our rigged fleets, and when at the proper time to fell the pine-tree in the woods : nor will you be disappointed, if you watch the setting and rising of the heavenly signs, and observe the year fairly divided by four distinct seasons.

259—286. *Even wet weather and holydays have their proper work; yet all days are not equally lucky.*

If ever a cold rain confines the farmer at home, 'tis granted to him then to do much at leisure, which otherwise in fine weather he would presently have to hurry over : then does the ploughman sharpen the hard tooth of the blunted share ; then does he scoop troughs out of trees, and marks his cattle, or numbers his sacks of corn. Others sharpen stakes and two-

horned forks, and prepare Sabine willow twigs to bind the creeping vine.
Now let the pliant basket be woven of twigs of briar ; ' now roast your
corn with fire, now grind with stone. Why, even on holydays there is
certain work that gods and men allow ; to make a channel for a stream
no religious scruple ever forbad, or to defend the corn with a hedge, to
set snares for birds, to fire brambles, and bleating flocks to dip in health-
ful stream. Oft too the driver of the slow-paced ass loads his ribs with
oil or common fruit, and on his return brings back from the town an
indented millstone and mass of black pitch. Nay, the Moon of herself
has appointed some days in one degree, some in another, as lucky for
work. The fifth day eschew : it is the birth-day of ghastly Orcus and of
the Furies : then with monstrous labour did the Earth bring forth Cœus
and Iapetus and fierce Typhœus, and the brethren who conspired to tear
down the ramparts of heaven. Thrice did they strive to pile Ossa on
Pelion, yea and on Ossa to roll Olympus with all its woods ; thrice did
the great father hurl asunder the heap of mountains. But the seven-
teenth day is lucky either to plant the vine, or to take and tame oxen,
and to add new threads to the web ; the ninth is good for the runaway,
adverse to the thief.

287—310. *Even in night and early morning and in long winter even-*
ings we need not be idle. Summer is the time for industry; in winter
enjoy yourself, and yet even then work.

Very many are the tasks that you will best set yourself in the cool
night, or when at sun-rising the morn sprinkles the earth with dew.
By night 'tis best to cut the light stubble, by night to mow the dry
meadows ; in night the clammy dew will never fail. One, too, sitting by
the late fire of a wintery night, watches the hours through, pointing
torches with a sharp knife ; meanwhile the goodman's wife with song
beguiles her labour long, and runs through the web with shrill-sounding
comb, or over Vulcan's fire boils down the sweet must, and scums with
leaves the water of the bubbling boiling kettle. But the golden corn of
Ceres is cut down in the heat of mid-summer, in burning mid-summer
the floor threshes the roasted grain. Plough stripped, stripped sow :
winter is a time of idleness for the husbandman. In cold weather farmers
mostly enjoy what they have gained ; and joyously one with another
interchange their feasts ; thereto invites winter, a genial time, dissolving
care ; as when heavy laden ships have just reached the haven, and the
joyous mariners have crowned their sterns. But yet, for all that, even
then is the season to strip the oaks of the acorns, and gather the berries
of the bay, and the blood-berries of the myrtle ; then is the time too to
set snares for cranes, and nets for stags, and to hunt the long-eared
hares ; also to shoot does, as you whirl the hempen thong of the Balea-
ric sling, in the days when snow lies deep, when the streams drive down
lumps of ice.

311—334. *Autumn and spring are stormy. Terrible is the tempest : in*
a moment it sweeps away the work of months.

Need I tell of the changeful weather and stars of autumn ? and
why the husbandmen must watch, when shorter grow the days, less
fierce the heat ? or when in showers downwards falls the spring, just

as the bearded harvest bristles in the fields, just as the milky corn swells on the green stem? Often have I, as the farmer was bringing the reaper into the golden fields, and just gathering the barley with its brittle stalks, seen all the winds engage in battle-shock, and tear up all the full corn far and wide from the very roots, and toss it whisked on high ; so fiercely does the storm with whirlwind dark sweep away the light stalks and stubble flying far. Often too from heaven comes a mighty column of waters, and clouds gathering from the deep mass together the weather hideous with grim storms of rain ; down tumbles the sky impetuous from above, and with a mighty rain washes away the joyous crops, and all the labours of the oxen ; fast fill the dykes, and hollow rivers roaring swell, and the surging sea boils with its straits that breathe with rage. The great father himself in the midnight of the storm-clouds hurls his thunder-bolt with flashing right hand ; trembling thereat quakes the mighty earth ; in an instant flee the beasts of the field ; the hearts of men throughout the world sink prostrate in lowly fear ; the god with his blazing bolt casts down either Athos or Rhodope, or high Ceraunia : then redouble the winds, then thickens the shower ; now woods, now shores moan with the mighty blast.

335—350. *Observe the stars, and neglect not religion. Ceres is the goddess of farmers; honour her in all your actions.*

In dread of this, observe the months and stars of heaven ; noting, whither the cold planet of Saturn retires ; into what circles of heaven the fiery Mercury wanders. Above all, worship the gods, and duly pay your annual offerings to great Ceres, sacrificing amidst the joyous blades of corn, just at the very close of winter, just when fair spring-weather begins. Then lambs are fat, and wines are mellow then ; then sleep is sweet beneath the thick shade on the hills. With one consent let all thy rural labourers adore Ceres ; for her dilute honeycombs with milk and soft wine ; and thrice let the auspicious victim be led round the young corn : then should follow the whole choir of the rejoicing companions, and shouting let them invite Ceres under their roof : nor let a man of them dare to put the sickle to the ripe corn, till in honour of Ceres he has bound his head with oaken wreaths, and danced in uncouth measure, chanting hymns.

351—392. *Many are the signs of coming wind and rain. Nature is a prophet: all things have a voice for the prudent.*

Now that we may know this by infallible signs, both heat and rain, and winds that bring up cold ; the great father himself hath ordained the monthly warnings of the moon ; what foretells the fall of winds ; what farmers seeing oft, should keep their herds nearer to their stalls. Straightway, when winds arise, either the straits of the sea begin to swell with agitation, and a dry crash is heard on the high hills, or far in the distance the shores are filled with confused echoes, and the murmur of the woods thickens on the ear. The wave can but ill forbear to do a mischief to the crooked keels, even then when gulls fly swiftly back from the high sea, sending their screams before them to the shore, and when the sea-coots sport on dry land, and the heron forsaking her familiar fen flies aloft above the high clouds. Oft too, when wind impends, you will see

stars shoot headlong from the sky, and through the shade of night long
trails of flames whiten behind their fall.   Oft will you see light chaff and
falling leaves fly about, or floating feathers dance on the water's top.
But when it lightens from the quarter of grim Boreas, and when the
home of Eurus and Zephyrus thunders, then are the dykes filled and all
the country is flooded, and every mariner out at sea furls his dripping
sails.   Never unwarned are men, when rain does them a mischief; as it
rises from the low valleys, the cranes sailing on high fly swift before it,
or the heifer looking up to heaven snuffs the breeze with open nostrils,
or swallow twittering skims around the meres, or frogs in mud croak out
their ancient grumble.   Often too the ant brings forth her eggs from her
inmost chambers as she tracks a narrow path; and a great rainbow drinks
up moisture: and an army of rooks departing home in a long line from
their feeding make a loud clapping with a mass of thick wings.   Again,
you may see various sea-fowl, and those which round the Asian meadows
in the fresh-water pools of the Cayster grub for their food, as in rivalry
with each other they pour abundant showers of spray o'er their bodies,
then dash their heads beneath the waves, then run into the billows, and
wantonly disport themselves in the joy of their bath.   Then the crow
with clamorous cry importunately summons the rain, and solitary stalks
on the shore's sand.   Not e'en the maids that card the nightly wool are
unwarned of the coming storm, as oft as they see the oil sputter in the
burning lamp, and a rotten growth that forms about the wick.

393—423. *As sure are the signs of the happy return of fine weather. It
   almost seems as if there were inspired prophets in the brute creation;
   but 'tis perhaps only natural changes that makes them so feel.*

Nor less after rain are bright suns and dry open weather to be foreseen
and learnt by sure signs.   For then the stars twinkle with undimmed
light, and the moon is seen to rise, as though not beholden to her brother's beams, nor are thin fleecy clouds, as of wool, borne through the
sky; nor do the halcyons dear to Thetis spread out their wings to catch
the warm sun; nor do the dirty swine remember to toss with their snouts
the bundles of straw into loose pieces.   Then mists come lower down,
and lie along the plain, and the owl watching the setting sun from the
top of a roof keeps up her aimless nightly screech.   On high is seen
Nisus in the clear sky, and Scylla pays the penalty of her sin for the
bright coloured lock; where'er she flying cleaves the light air with her
wings, lo, her fierce foe Nisus follows close with a great whizzing through
the breeze; where Nisus soars upwards, she flying with many a sudden
snatch cleaves the light air.   Then do the ravens in stifled tone three or
four times repeat a clearer note; and often in their high roosts, with more
than wonted pleasure strangely glad, together rustle midst the leaves;
'tis their delight now that the rain is over to revisit their little progeny,
and beloved nestlings; not that I can believe that they have from heaven
any inspiration, or from fate a further foresight of things to come; but
when the weather and changeful moisture of the sky alter the course of
nature, and the god of the air with the damp winds condenses what just
now was rare, and anon rarefies what was dense, the images of their
minds are turned, and their breasts conceive impulses other than what

they felt, while the wind chased the clouds; hence we have the pleasant chorus of birds in the fields, and the joys of the cattle, and the exulting croak of ravens.

424—437. *The moon also gives signs ; a hazy moon portends rain, a red moon wind, a clear moon fine weather.*

But if you pay regard to the scorching sun, and the moons that succeed in order, never will to-morrow's hours cheat you, nor will you be entrapped by the snares of a calm night. If when the moon first gathers up her returning rays, she encloses the dark air within her dim crescent, for husbandmen and mariners a heavy rain is in store; but if she shows her face suffused with maiden blush, then there will be wind; when wind is coming golden Phœbe ever reddens. But if at her fourth rising, for that is a warning that never fails, she rides through the heavens clear with crescent undimmed, the whole next day, and all the days that follow even to the end of the month, will be free from rain and wind, and sailors home returning safe shall pay their vows on the shore to Glaucus and Panopea, and Melicerta Ino's son.

438—460. *The sun is as true a monitor as his sister the moon; his appearances vary to warn us of the weather that is coming.*

The sun also, both when rising and when he hides himself beneath the waves, will give you signs; infallible signs attend the sun, both those which he brings when he returns in the morning, and those he shows when the stars arise. When he at his birth and rising is marked with spots, withdrawn into a cloud, and retires with half his disc, then may you suspect showers, for from the deep comes rising swift the south wind boding ill to plants and corn and cattle. Or when at dawn of day amidst the thick clouds the rays burst forth in different directions, or when with colour pale Aurora rises, as she leaves Tithonus' saffron bed; ah then ill will the leaf defend the ripening grapes, so thick upon the roofs bounds hail that rattles sharp. Remember this e'en more, just as the sun goes down, when through Olympus he has run his course, so will it do thee good; for oft we see o'er the god's face the shifting colours pass: a blue colour announces rain, or fiery winds; but if the spots begin to be mixed with glowing red, then you will see all nature rage with wind and stormy rain together. On such a night let no one advise me to venture on the deep, or pluck my cable from its mooring on the shore. But if both when the sun brings back the day and when he puts to rest the light he brought back, his disc is bright and shining, then stormy rains are but an idle fear, for with a cloudless north wind you will see the forests wave.

461—497. *But the sun foretells greater things than weather. He warns us of hidden changes and revolutions, as by an eclipse he told of Caesar's death: though then all nature combined in the prognostication of ill.*

In a word, whatever the fall of even brings, whence it is that the wind drives before it rainless clouds, what the wet south wind is devising,. of all the sun to you will warnings give. Who dares name the sun a liar? He too often admonishes of the dark approach of alarms in our land, of the swellings of treachery and concealed wars. The sun it was that showed his pity for Rome, when the light of Cæsar's life was extinguished, by covering his bright orb with dusky murky darkness, when an age of impiety feared eternal night. And yet at that time the earth likewise and the expanse of the deep sea, and ominous dogs, and birds foreboding ill gave many a sign. How often did we behold Ætna glow forth with a burning deluge from her vast furnaces into the lands of the Cyclops, and roll balls of flame, and rocks of molten fire. Germany heard a clashing of arms in the whole heaven : with unwonted heavings quaked the Alps. Oft too a voice was distinctly heard through the silent groves, a voice of mighty tones, and phantoms ghastly in marvellous mode appeared in the dusk of twilight; and cattle spoke, (a monstrous portent,) rivers stay their course, the earth opens its mouth, ivory weeps as in sorrow within the shrines, statues of bronze sweat. Eridanus, monarch of waters, whirling forests in his mad eddy, poured forth his flood, and over all the plains bore herds and stalls alike. Nor at the same time did fibres of threatening import ever cease to appear in the entrails that boded ill, or jets of blood to flow from wells, and high cities to resound the night long with the howling of wolves. At no other time did more lightnings shoot through a cloudless sky; nor ever so oft did ill-boding comets blaze. Therefore it came to pass that a second time Philippi saw Roman lines engage in civil fight; and the heavenly powers thought it not unmeet that twice with Roman blood Emathia and the broad plains of Hæmus should be fattened. Yes, and the time will come, when in those lands the husbandman, as he labours, tilling the earth with crooked plough, shall find Roman javelins eaten up with mouldering rust, or with heavy hoes strike empty casques, and as he digs up the earth their grave will marvel at the giant bones of a past age.

498—514. *But, ye gods, spare us at least our Caesar: heaven should not envy earth; we need him sorely in this age of wickedness and war.*

Ye gods of our country, ye heroes sprung from our soil, Romulus, and Vesta our mother, who preservest the Tuscan Tiber and the Palatine hill of Rome, at least hinder not this our youth from coming to the succour of a ruined age. Long ago have we fully expiated by our blood the perjuries of Troy the city of faithless Laomedon ; for some time past the palace of heaven envies us thee, O Cæsar, and complains that mortal triumphs can interest thee ; and no wonder ; for on earth good is put for evil and evil for good ; so many are the wars in the world, so many the forms of guilt; the plough has not its meed of honour; the fields lie rough, the tillers are taken off to war, the crooked pruning hooks are forged into stiff swords : on this side the Euphrates, on that side Germany stirs up war; neighbouring towns break their leagues and bear arms: the impious Mars of civil strife rages in the whole world : thus, when from the barriers started the four-horsed chariots pour forth, with ever quickening pace they speed along the course, in vain does the charioteer tug at the reins, he is borne along by the·steeds, and the chariot heeds not the curb.

BOOK II.

1—8. *The introductory invocation of Bacchus.*

THUS far have I sung the tillage of corn-fields, and the stars of heaven; now thee, O Bacchus, will I sing, and with thee of woodland copses, and the offspring of the olive that slowly grows. Hither come, I pray, O Father of the wine-press; here all things are full of thy blessings; for thee the field blossoms and teems with the vine-leaves of autumn, for thee the vintage foams in brimming vats. Hither come, I pray, O Father of the wine-press; with speed strip off thy buskins, and with me plunge thy naked legs in new-made must.

9—34. *The various modes of rearing trees.*

In the first place, nature has various forms for the production of trees. For some, constrained by no man, of themselves, of their own accord, come up, and far and wide possess the plains and winding streams; as the tender osier, and the pliant broom, the poplar, and the willow-copse with its grey and hoary leaf: again, a class springs from seed that has dropped on the ground; as tall chestnuts, and the giant of the woods, the mast-tree, that bears foliage sacred to Jove, and oaks, revered as oracles by Greece. Others have a crowded growth, sprouting in off-shoots from the parent root, as cherries and elms; the bay-tree of Parnassus too springs up, a tiny plant, beneath its mother's mighty shadow. These methods nature first ordained; by them blooms every kind of forest-trees, and shrubs, and hallowed groves. Other plans there are, which experience by course of practice discovers for herself. One sends away suckers from the tender body of their mother, and sets them in furrows; another buries stems in the soil, and stakes cloven cross-wise, and saplings with sharpened ends; other forest-trees await the time when the layer is bent into an arch, and set in the ground, and the young plants live in a soil that is their own. Others need not aught of root; and the pruner fears not to give back and entrust to earth the topmost spray of the tree. Nay more, when the stock has been cleft in pieces (a wondrous thing to tell), an olive root sprouts from the sapless wood. And oft we see the branches of one tree pass unharmed into those of another, and the pear-tree suffer a change, and bear engrafted apples, and upon plum-trees stony cornels redden.

35—46. *The address to husbandmen. The dedication to Maecenas.*

Wherefore come, I pray you, learn by their kinds the proper modes of culture, ye husbandmen, and tame by training the wildness of your fruit, and let not the soil lie idle. It is sweet to plant Ismarus over with the vine, and dress with the olive great Taburnus. And do you draw near, and with me pursue the toilsome voyage I have begun, you that are my glory, you that are by right the largest part of my renown, Mæcenas, and spread your flying sails far out to sea. Yet I aspire not to embrace all points within my verse; not if a hundred tongues were mine, a hundred mouths, a voice of steel; draw near, and skirt the beach's inmost line; land is within our grasp; I will not now weary you with an unreal song, and lead you through winding ways and tedious prefaces.

47—82. *Trees may be improved by various artificial methods, according to their kind : the distinction between grafting and budding.*

The trees that by their own power lift themselves into the world of light, spring up unfruitful indeed, but vigorous and strong ; for here is native power within the soil. Yet these too, if a man graft upon them, or transplant and commit them to pits of well broken soil, will be found to put off their wild spirit, and by frequent culture will readily pursue any ways of art to which you call them. Likewise the barren tree, which grows up from the root, will do this, if it be planted out over open land ; at present the mother's lofty foliage and branches overshadow it, and spoil it of fruitfulness while it grows, and exhaust it for a bearing tree. Again, the tree that rears itself from scattered seeds comes up slowly, destined to make a shade for late posterity, and its fruit degenerates, and forgets its old flavour, and the vine bears sorry clusters, a plunder for the birds. Be sure that on all trees labour must be spent, and all must be marshalled into ranks, and disciplined at the cost of heavy toil. But olives repay you best when reared by truncheons, vines by layers, Paphian myrtles when raised from the entire trunk ; from suckers hard hazels spring, and the mighty ash, and the umbrageous tree that forms the wreath of Hercules, and the acorns of the Chaonian sire ; so also springs the towering palm, and the fir that is to behold the perils of the sea. On the other hand, the rough arbutus is grafted with the offspring of the walnut, and barren planes oft bear the goodly apple-tree ; the beech is whitened with the chestnut's pale blossom, and the mountain-ash with the pear's, and swine crush acorns underneath the elm. Nor is the process of grafting and budding with eyes one and the same. For where the buds sprout from the midst of the rind, and burst their delicate coats, just in the knot a narrow slit is made ; at this point they insert an eye taken from a different tree, and teach it to grow into the juicy bark. Or, again, boles free from knots are cut open, and with wedges a path is cleft deep into the heart of the trunk ; then fruitful slips are introduced ; and with-out long delay, lo, towards heaven shoots a mighty tree with happy boughs, and views with wonder strange foliage, and fruit that is not its own.

83—108. *Each sort of tree has its varieties.*

Besides the kind is not single only, either in the case of vigorous elms, or the willow, and the lotus, or the cypresses of Ida ; nor do fat olives spring destined to a uniform shape, the oval Orchades, the long Radii, and the Pausian with bitter berry ; and so apples, and the groves of Alcinous ; and cuttings of Crustumian and Syrian pears, and the heavy Volemum, are not the same. The same vintage hangs not on our trees, as Lesbos gathers from Methymna's bough ; there are Thasian vines, there are also the white Mareotic, the former adapted to rich land, the latter to lighter soil ; and the Psithian, more suitable for raisin wine, and the dry Lagean, that will some day try the feet and bind the tongue ; the purple and the precian ; and with what verse shall I extol you, Rhætic vine ? Yet do not therefore compete with the wine-bins of Falerii. There are too Aminæan vines, a wine right sound to keep, to which the Tmo-lian bows down, and sovereign Phanæ itself ; and the lesser Argitis, with

which no other will be found to vie, either in yielding such a stream of
juice, or lasting so many years. I would not pass you by, vine of Rhodes,
welcome to the gods and to the second course, and you, Bumastus, with
your swelling clusters. But we cannot number either how many kinds,
or how many names there be ; and indeed it avails not to reduce them to
a number ; which he who should wish to know, would also wish to learn
how many grains of sand on the Libyan plain are stirred by the west
wind; or to know how many Ionian billows travel to the shore, when the
east wind in his fury lights upon the ships.

109—135. *Different trees are produced on different soils.*

And yet all soils cannot produce all trees. In rivers the willow, in
muddy marshes the alder springs, on rocky hills the barren mountain-ash ;
the shore is fondest of the myrtle grove; lastly, Bacchus loves open
slopes, the yew the north wind and its cold. Observe too the region of
the world tamed by tillers most remote from us, the eastern homes of the
Arabians, and the painted Geloni : separate fatherlands are assigned to
trees. India alone bears black ebony, with the Sabæans alone is the
frankincense bough. Why should I tell you of the balm that exudes from
the fragrant stem, and the berries of the evergreen acanthus? Why of
the woods of Æthiopia, white over with downy wool, and how the Seres
comb off from the leaves the delicate fleeces? Or of the forests that
India, still nearer to the ocean, rears, that nook at the limit of the world,
where no arrow, shot from the bow, can pass above the treetop through
the air? And yet that people is not slow in handling the quiver.
Media bears the generous citron, with acid juice and lingering flavour,
which, whenever fell step-mothers poison the cup, and mix herbs therewith and pernicious words, comes a succour surer than aught else, and
drives the black venom from the limbs. The tree itself is large, and in
look much like the bay ; and a bay it were, did it not fling abroad
another scent ; its foliage falls not off in any wind ; its blossom is right
surely fixed ; with it the Medes wash carefully the noisome breath and
mouth, and use it as a medicine for asthmatic age.

136—176. *The praises of Italy.*

But neither the groves of Media, that land of wealth, nor fair Ganges,
and Hermus turbid with its slime of gold, can vie with the glories of
Italy ; not Bactra, nor the Indians, and all Panchaia rich in sands that
bear the frankincense. This region no bulls breathing fire from their
nostrils have ever ploughed for the sowing of the teeth of a grisly hydra,
nor has the cornfield bristled with crowded casques and spears of men :
but teeming crops o'erspread it, and the juice of the Massic vine ; olive-
trees possess it, and goodly herds ; hence comes the warrior horse, that
proudly bounds into the field ; hence thy snowy flocks, Clitumnus, and
the bull, the chiefest victim, which, often bathed in thy hallowed stream,
lead to the shrines of the gods the triumphs of Rome. Here is ceaseless
spring, and summer in months where summer is strange ; twice the cattle
yield their increase, the tree is able twice to minister its fruit. But ravening tigers are far away, and the lion's savage brood, and the aconite cheats
not hapless gatherers ; and the scaly snake speeds not his monstrous
rings along the ground, nor winds himself up into a coil with that huge

trailing length. Think too of so many glorious cities and laboured works, so many towns piled by the hand of men on steepy crags, and the streams that flow beneath those ancient walls! Shall I tell of the two seas, one that washes it above, and one below? Shall I sing of those mighty lakes? Of thee, great Larius, and of thee, Benacus, swelling with billows and boisterous turmoil like a sea? Shall I tell of havens, and the barrier set against the Lucrine lake, and how the ocean chafes with mighty roar, where the wave of the Julian harbour resounds with the sea rolled backward, and the Tyrrhene surge streams into the channels of Avernus? This land too shows within her veins rivulets of silver and the ore of brass, and flows with a plenteous stream of gold. This land has reared a valiant race of men, the Marsians, and the Sabine manhood, and the Ligurian inured to hardship, and the Volscians that bear the pike; this land has bred the Decii, the Marii, and the great Camilli, the Scipios stout in war, and you, most mighty Cæsar, who now, already conqueror in the distant confines of Asia, drive far from the towers of Rome the unwarlike Indian. Hail, realm of Saturn, mighty mother of fruits, mighty mother of men! For thee I venture to discourse of themes of ancient glory, and works of ancient art, I dare to unlock those sacred springs, and sing through Roman towns the Acræan lay.

177—225. The genius of different soils. Description of the land best suited for the olive, for the vine, for grazing, and for corn-crops.

This is the place to discuss the genius of different soils; what is the vigour of each, what the colour, and what its natural power for bearing plants. First, ground hard to work, and unkindly mountain-land, where meagre clay is found, and pebbles in the thorny fields, delight in the grove that Pallas loves, the long-lived olive-tree. The wild olive springing up abundantly in the same plot, and its wild berries overspreading the fields, afford a sign. But the soil which is rich, and luxuriant with fresh rushes, and the plain which is rank with herbage and prolific in its fruitfulness, (such as often we are wont to look down upon in a mountain's hollow dell; hitherward the torrents pour down from rocky heights, and bring a train of fertilising mud,) and which rises to the southern breeze, and nurtures fern, hateful to the crooked plough; this in time will supply you with vines extremely hardy, and streaming with a wealth of winejuice; this ground is fruitful in the grape, and in that draught, such as we shed for libations from golden bowls, when the well-fed Tuscan blows his ivory horn beside the altars, and in deep chargers we present the smoking entrails. But if your bent is rather to tend herds and calves, or the young of sheep, or she-goats that exhaust the crops, haste to the woodland lawns and distant meadows of well-watered Tarentum, and such a plain as hapless Mantua lost, that feeds in grassy stream the snow-white swans: neither crystal springs nor herbage will fail your flocks, and all that your herds crop in the long days, the cold dew will quite replace in one short night. Ground that is dark in colour, and rich beneath the print of the ploughshare, and the surface of which is friable, (for this quality we imitate by ploughing,) is commonly best for corn-crops; from no plot of land will you see more waggons departing homeward with slowly-pacing oxen; or again, land from whence the surly farmer carries away the trees, and overthrows the groves that have stood idle for many a year, and tears up by the very roots the birds' ancient homes ; they then quit their nests and speed aloft ; but the field, a novice to the plough, shines beneath the pressure of the share. For as for the hungry gravel of a hilly country, it scarce serves the bees with humble casia-flowers and rosemary ; and scurfy tuff-stone, and chalk scooped out by darkhued water-snakes, denote that no other fields afford like. them sweet food for serpents, and provide their winding haunts. Soil which exhales light mist and fleeting vapour, and drinks in the moisture, and, when it pleases, readily discharges it from itself, and which is ever dressed in the greenery of its own grass, and never harms the steel with scurf and salt rust, that soil will wreathe your elms with laughing vines, that soil is fruitful in the olive, that you will prove as you till it, to be both goodnatured to the cattle and able to endure the crooked ploughshare. Such land rich Capua ploughs, and the region near the heights of Vesuvius, and the stream of Clanius, unkind to desolate Acerræ.

226—258. *Various methods of ascertaining the nature of the soil.*

Now I will tell by what means you can learn the nature of each soil. You will need to know whether it be light or more than common close. Because the one is adapted for corn, the other for the tree of Bacchus, (the closer soil for Ceres, all particularly light soils for Lyæus) ; you must first with the eye fix upon a spot, and bid that a pit be driven deep down in solid earth, and put all the soil back into its place, and by treading it in with the feet make level the surface of the ground. If it proves not enough to fill the hollow, it will be a light soil, fittest as productive land for grazing and the generous vine ; but if it shows plainly that it cannot be put within its old space, and there is a superfluity of earth when the trench is filled, that field is stiff soil ; look forward to reluctant clods and tough ridges of land, and with strong teams of oxen cleave the ground. But as for salty soil and that which is called bitter, (it is unfavourable for the fruits of the earth, and never grows tame beneath the plough, and preserves not the vine its lineage, nor the apple its title), it will present the following mark : take you down with speed from the smoky roof baskets of close-woven osier, and strainers of the wine-press ; hither let the soil of that bad field, and sweet water from the spring, be brought, and squeezed in up to the brim ; all the water will slowly ooze out, you will see, and big drops will pass through the wicker-work ; then the taste will unmistakeably give its evidence, and will distort with bitter savour the wry mouths of those that try it. Likewise what ground is rich, we learn, to be brief, in this way ; when shaken about in the hands, it never crumbles, but like pitch cleaves to the fingers as it is handled. The moist rears taller grass than other soils, and is in itself more prolific than is good. Ah, may it be not too productive in my field, nor show itself over-vigorous at the sprouting of the ear ! Soil that is heavy silently betrays its character by its very weight, and so too that which is light. 'Tis the work of a moment to recognise beforehand a black earth, and what is the colour of what particular soil. But mischievous coldness it is hard to find out ; only sometimes pitch-pines and baleful yews, or gloomy ivy, disclose its track.

259—287. Instructions how to prepare the soil for a vineyard, and in what order to plant the vines on plains and slopes.

When you have observed these points, remember first to thoroughly season the land, and with trenches to break up great knolls of earth, first to expose to the north wind the upturned clods, before you plant in the pleasant race of the vine. Plots of friable soil are best; the winds make that their business, and so do chill hoar-frosts, and the stout ditcher, who loosens and stirs the acres. But if there be any men whom no precaution escapes, they search out a tract alike in both its divisions; one where the stock of vines may be first prepared for its trees, and another, to which it may afterwards be removed and planted out, lest the infants disown a mother to whom they are suddenly exchanged. Moreover, they print upon the bark the aspect of the tree, so as to restore each to the position in which it has stood, according to the side on which it had faced the southern heats, and as it has presented its back to the northern pole. To form habits in early life has a force so very strong.

First inquire whether it be best to plant your vines on hills or level ground. If it be the tract of a fertile plain that you measure out for the vineyard, set close the vines; in close array the wine-god is not less vigorous and prolific; but if you choose a plot with sloping knolls and gently-slanting hills, give free room to the ranks, and as before let every avenue, as you plant the trees, with its straight-drawn line be exactly even with the rest. As oft in mighty war, when the long-extended legion has deployed its cohorts, and the line stands firm on the open plain, and the battle-array is set, and all the land far and wide ripples with the flash of·brass, and they do not yet mingle in the grisly turmoil of the fight, but the god of battles undecided roams between the armies; so let all the lines of avenue be marked out in uniform numbers; not only that the view may satisfy the idle mind, but because in no other way the land will bestow on all an equality of vigour, nor the boughs be able to reach forth into free air.

288—314. The trenches for the vine and its supporter. Some practices that should be avoided in planting a vineyard.

Perhaps you may also ask, what should be the depth of the trenches' slope. I would venture to entrust a vine even to a shallow furrow. Deeper, and thoroughly in earth, the tree is fixed,—the mast-tree foremost of all, which extends its root to Tartarus, as far as it points its crown up to the air of heaven. Therefore no winter's rage, no blasts nor storms, can tear up it; unmoved it abides, and in endurance conquers, as it rolls its onward course, many generations of posterity, many cycles of men. Then too, stretching far and wide its brawny boughs and arms on this side and on that, itself the centre, it supports a mighty breadth of shade. Neither let your vineyard slope towards the setting sun; nor plant the hazel-tree among your vines; nor lop their topmost sprays, nor tear off cuttings from the top of the tree; so deep is the love they bear the earth; nor with a blunt knife hurt the tender plants; nor set in the vineyard wild-olive stems. For often on the unwary swains a sudden fire breaks out; which, lurking concealed at first beneath the fruitful bark, gathers strength, and, gliding in a moment to the leafy height, gives forth into heaven a mighty

roar; then, running on, reigns a conqueror along the boughs, along the
loftiest tops, and envelopes all the grove in flames, and, crammed with
pitchy darkness, rolls to the sky a black tumbling cloud; especially if a
tempest from the peak of heaven chance to lower upon the woods, and
a strong-blowing wind drives on the thickening fire. When this disaster
comes, the vines have no life left in their stock, and cannot revive again
by cutting, and, from the earth at their very roots, begin to bloom again
as they were before; the barren wild-olive with its bitter leaves alone
remains alive.

315—345. *Plant your vines in the spring, the season when nature is
prolific; the season when the world itself must have been created.*

And let no counsellor, however shrewd, persuade you to stir the stubborn earth when Boreas blows. Then winter locks the fields with frost,
and suffers not the plant, when the young shoot is set, to foster its root
firmly and make it coalesce with the ground. 'Tis the best season for
planting a vineyard, when in the crimson springtime the white bird has
come, the trailing serpents' hated foe, or just before the autumn's earliest
chills, when the coursing sun reaches not yet the winter in his car, when
summer is passing away. The spring it is that ministers to the leafage
of the groves, and to the forests themselves as well; in spring the land
heaves with fruitfulness, and requires the procreative seed. Then
Heaven, the Almighty Father, comes down in fertilising showers into the
lap of his joyous bride, and in his might, mingling with her mighty frame,
nourishes every product. Then ring the thickets wild with tuneful birds,
and on their days the herds devote themselves to love; the bounteous
field gives birth to life, and beneath the west-wind's breezes warm the
meadows unloose their folds; and all with delicate moisture overflow;
and the herbage safely dares to trust itself to meet the new-born suns;
and the tendrils of the vine fear not the rising of the South wind, or a
storm of rain driven from heaven by the North wind's might; but put
forth buds, and unfold all their leaves. I would believe that even such
were the days that dawned at the first opening of the new-created world,
and such the course they kept; 'twas spring-time then, the mighty globe
was passing a season of spring, and the Eastern gales restrained their
wintry blasts; when the first cattle drank the daylight, and an iron brood
of men reared its head from the hard-bound fields; and wild beasts were
admitted to the woods, and stars to the sky. And in truth the plants
would not be able to surmount their hardships here, did not such a time
of rest elapse between the cold and heat, and the gracious kindness of the
sky welcome the world to itself.

346—370. *Instructions how to plant the young sets, to prepare supports
for the vines, and to restrain the luxuriance of the leaves.*

For the rest, whatever trees you plant throughout the fields, strew them
with rich manure, and remember to cover them in with a mass of earth,
or bury porous stones or rough shells; for the water will glide through
between them, and the delicate vapour will rise up, and the plants you
have set will revive their spirits; and erewhile husbandmen have been
found, who overlaid them from above with a large stone, and a jar of
ponderous weight; this would be a shield against pelting showers, and

when the sultry dog-star cleaves the fields that gape with drought. When the cuttings have been set, it remains to break up the soil repeatedly at the roots, and still strike in the stubborn hoe, or to work the ground beneath the print of the ploughshare, and drive the straining bullocks up and down through the vineyard itself ; next, to fit the vines with smooth wands, and lances of peeled rods, and ashen stakes, and stout forked poles, that, relying on the strength of these, the plants may inure themselves to struggle hard, and scorn the winds, and form tier after tier throughout the height of the elms. And when the early age of the young leaves is growing to youth, the tender foliage must be spared, and while the shoot is joyously speeding towards the sky, set free with loosened reins through clear space, you must not venture yet to make the tree itself feel the edge of the pruning-knife, but with your crooked hands must pluck the leaves, and pick them here and there. After that, when in time the tree has shot aloft, and clasps the elm with vigorous stem, then strip the foliage, then crop the spreading boughs ; before that, they shrink from the steel ; then at last practise a stern command, and curb the streaming branches.

371—397. *Cattle and other animals must be kept away from the young vines. The injury it does to the vine is the reason why the goat has always been sacrificed to Bacchus.*

Moreover, you must twine fences of osier, and shut out all cattle, especially while the tendril is delicate, and knows not the trials that await it ; for, besides unfeeling winters and the overpowering sun, buffaloes of the forest and persecuting roes ceaselessly insult it, and sheep make it their food, and greedy heifers too. And indeed neither winter-cold with its congealed hoar-frost, nor oppressive summer heat, that broods over the parching rocks, do harm so great as those herds, and the poison of their hard tooth, and the scar marked deep on the rind mangled with their bite. For this very offence the goat is slaughtered to Bacchus at all the altars, and the ancient games come upon the stage, and the sons of Theseus set up the prize for genius about their villages and the corners of their streets, and, amid the merriment of their cups, danced in the velvet meadows on oiled goat-skins. Likewise the farmers of Ausonia, a race sent forth from Troy, in uncouth verse and unchecked laughter play, and put on hideous vizards wrought of hollowed bark, and sing thee, O Bacchus, with joyful hymns, and in thy honour hang from the tall pine tiny waving masks of them. By the virtue of this every vineyard blooms with large increase, deep vales and hollow dells are covered o'er, and all lands, whithersoe'er the god bears round his comely face. Therefore in our national hymns we will duly ascribe to Bacchus his proper praise, and will offer to him chargers and cakes ; and the doomed he-goat, led by the horn, shall stand beside the altar, and the fat entrails we will roast on spits of hazel-wood.

397—419. *The labour of dressing the vine is great; and even when that is over you will still have to fear the injury that storms may do.*

There is also the other toil of dressing the vines, whereon you cannot spend enough of pains; for thrice or four times every year you must cleave open all the ground, and endlessly break the clods with the back of the hoe; you must lighten the grove of every leaf. The labour of the husbandman, prolonged into a round, comes back to him, even as the year, passing over its own footprints, rolls back upon itself. And even at the time when the vineyard has cast its latest leaves, and the North-wind has swept away the glory from the woods, even then the diligent rustic extends his care into the coming year, and plying Saturn's crooked knife, with ceaseless cropping persecutes anew the vine he has left, and by pruning moulds it to his pleasure. Be the first to dig the ground, the first to carry home and burn the vine-boughs you have lopped away, and the first to convey the poles within the shelter of the roof: be the latest to reap the produce. Twice thickens the shade of vines; wild plants with thronging briars twice obstruct the crop: to deal with each of these is heavy toil. Praise great estates; cultivate a small one. Moreover, rough twines of butchers' broom amid the wood, and river-reeds on the bank, have to be cut, and the tending of the wild willow forces you to toil. Now the vines are bound, now the vineyard allows the pruning-knife to rest, now the last dresser sings of the completed files: still must you vex the soil, and stir the dust, and fear lest the storms of Jove light on your grapes when fully ripe.

420—425. *The rearing of olives is on the contrary an easy task.*

On the other hand, no tending is needed for olive-trees; and they look not for the crooked pruning-knife and the mattock that grapples with the ground, when once they have fastened on the field, and learnt to bear the gales; the earth of itself, if it be laid open with the curved tooth of the share, gives moisture enough to the plants when set, and teeming crops with the help of the plough alone. Thus nurse the olive, plump, and pleasing to Peace.

426—457. *Fruit-trees are also hardy. Description of various forest-trees. They are in some points even worthier than the vine.*

Fruit-trees too, so soon as they feel that their boles are strong, and when they have gained their proper vigour, with bounds aspire to heaven by force innate, and need no help from us. And not the less, meanwhile, every wood grows heavy with its weight of produce, and the wild haunts of the birds are crimsoned with blood-red berries. The lucerne is cropped by the steer, the lofty forest presents its pine-brands, and so fires by night are fed, and shed forth their light. And are men then slow to plant, and lavish care? Why should I search for greater themes? The willow and the humble broom,—why, they either supply leaves to the herd, or shade to the shepherd, and a fence for the sown crops, and food for the making of honey. And pleasant it is to view Cytorus with its waving box-groves, and Narycium's woods of pitch-pine; pleasant it is to look on fields that owe nought to the mattock, nought to the care of man. Even the un-fruitful forests on the crown of Caucasus, which passionate Eastern blasts constantly break and wreck, give their produce, each according to its kind, give serviceable timber, for ships the pine, for houses the cedar and the cypress; from them husbandmen turn spokes for their wheels, and rollers for their waggons, and fit the vessel with its curving keel; in its osier is the virtue of the willow, that of the elm in its leaves; but the myrtle excels in its strong spear-like wands, and so does the cornel good for war; the yew is bent into the Ituræan bow; likewise, smooth linden-trees, or the box oft shaven with the lathe, adapt themselves to a new shape, and are hollowed with the sharp steel; likewise the light alder swims upon the pouring flood, sped down the Po; likewise bees house their swarms in the bark of hollow trees, and the cavity of a decayed ilex-tree. What so notable as this have the gifts of Bacchus produced? Bacchus too has given causes for offence; 'twas he who tamed with death the infuriate Centaurs, Rhœtus, and Pholus, and Hylæus, that with a ponderous wine-bowl menaced the Lapithæ.

458—474. *The happiness of a husbandman's life.*

O husbandmen, too dear to Fortune, if they know their own blessed-ness! For them of herself, far from the clash of arms, all-righteous Earth pours from her soil an easy sustenance. If no high mansion with proud portals discharge from all the palace its huge tide of early visitants, if they never stare at door-posts variously inlaid with beauteous tortoise-shell, and dresses tricked with gold, and statues of Corinthian brass, and if white wool is not stained with the Assyrian drug, nor the usefulness of the olive's fair oil adulterated with casia; yet, repose without a care, and a life that knows not what disappointment is, a life enriched with manifold treasures; yet ease with wide domains, caverns, and living lakes, and Tempe's cool vale, and the lowing of oxen, and soft slumber beneath the trees, are theirs; with them are woodland glades and the wild-beasts' haunt, and a band of youths inured to toil, and accustomed to little; the sacred rites of Heaven, and reverend sires: Justice, as she departed from earth, planted among them her latest footsteps.

475—542. *The praise of science. If I may not be the philosopher of nature, let me lead a secluded country life, far from the crimes and miseries of the world. Such was the life of the old Romans in hap-pier times of peace and simplicity. The conclusion.*

For myself, may the lovely Muses first above all else, they whose mys-teries I bear, smitten with o'erwhelming passion, take me to themselves, and show me the paths of heaven, and its stars, the various eclipses of the sun and labours of the moon, from whence the earthquake springs, by what force it is that deep seas learn to swell and burst their barriers, and again of themselves sink back into their place; why winter suns make so much haste to dip in Ocean, or what obstacle it is that clogs the course of the lingering nights. But if, to prevent me from having the power to approach these regions of nature, chill blood around my heart shall prove a barrier, may the fields of the country delight me, and the streams that water the valleys; rivers and forests may I love, all inglorious though I be. Oh, where are those plains, and the stream of Spercheus, and Taygetus haunted by the revels of Spartan maids! Oh, who will set me down in the cool dells of Hæmus, and shield me with the branches' boundless shade! Happy is he who has been able to learn the causes of things, and has cast beneath his feet all fears, and inexorable Fate, and the roar of greedy Acheron! Blest too is he who knows the rural gods, Pan, and Silvanus old, and sister-nymphs! Not him the fasces of the Roman People, nor the monarch's purple can sway, and the discord that drives brethren to mutual treachery, or the Dacian sweeping down from his confederated Danube, nor the Roman state, and the kingdoms doomed to fall; and never is he pained through pity for him that is destitute, or envies him that has great possessions. Those fruits that the boughs afford, the fruits that of itself, of its own free will, the country bears, he gathers; and has never seen laws carved on steel, and the maddening forum, or the archives of the Roman People. Other men vex with oars the perilous seas, and rush to take the sword; they press their way into courts and through kingly portals: one assails with ruin a city and its hapless household gods, that he may drink from a jewelled cup, and sleep on Tyrian purple; another hoards up wealth, and broods over the gold he has buried in the earth; one is amazed and dazzled at the eloquence of the Rostra; one the applause of commons and patricians, redoubled as it is along the rows of the theatre, sets agape with the shock of joy; some delight to steep themselves in brothers' blood, and exchange for a place of exile their homes and pleasant thresholds, and seek a father-land that lies beneath another sun. The husbandman with his crooked plough furrows the soil; from this comes the work for the year; by this he maintains his country and little grandsons, by this his herds of oxen, and his bullocks that have served him well. And there is never a time of rest; for either in fruits the season richly abounds, or in the offspring of cattle, or in the sheaf of Ceres' stalk, and loads the furrows with increase, and overflows the barns. Then winter comes; in the olive-mill is bruised the berry of Sicyon, the swine come home, well satisfied with mast, the forest gives the fruit of the arbutus, and Autumn drops his various produce, and on the sunny cliffs the mellowing vintage basks.

Meanwhile his dear children hang about his lips, his stainless house preserves its purity; his cows hang down their udders fraught with milk, and fat kids on the smiling lawn with levelled horns against each other strive. The sire himself keeps holy-day, and stretched along the grass, where is a kindled altar in the midst, and his companions wreathe the wine-bowl, with a libation invokes thee, O Father of the wine-press, and for the masters of his cattle sets upon an elm the target, for a match at the flying dart; and their wondrous hardy limbs they strip for the rustic wrestling bout. This life of yore the antique Sabines lived, and Remus too, and his brother; so, I ween, brave Etruria grew, and Rome became the beauty of the world; and, one within herself, encompassed with her bulwarks seven heights. Likewise, before the Cretan king held sceptred sway, and before an impious age banquetted on slaughtered bullocks, this was the life that Saturn passed on earth, the monarch of the golden age; nor yet too had they heard the clarion blare, nor sword-blades ring, when placed on anvils hard.

But we in our career have traversed o'er a vast expanse of plain, and now 'tis time to loosen from the yoke our horses' smoking necks.

BOOK III.

1—48. Cattle is the subject of the third Georgic. The fabulous subject of the Greeks are trite. The Roman poet will bring the Muses from Helicon, and some day sing of the glories of Caesar Augustus.

THEE too, great Pales, and thee Shepherd from the river Amphrysus, worthy of all remembrance, will we praise in verse; ye too woods and rivers of Lycæus. Other subjects, which might have charmed the idle fancy with song, are trite and common now. Who knows not of Eurystheus, master hard, and the altars of infamous Busiris? By whom has not the boy Hylas been sung, and Delos, Latona's isle, and Hippodame, and Pelops distinguished by his ivory shoulder, the driver of the fiery steeds? I too must essay a way by which I may raise myself from the lowly ground, and fly triumphant through the mouths of men. I first of all as one returning to my country, if life be spared, will bring again the Muses from the Roman peak; first of all I will bear back with me the goodly palms of Edom to thee, O Mantua, and on the green grassy plain will build a marble temple near the water's edge, where mighty Mincius wanders on with slowly winding curves, fringing the bank with waving reed. In the centre I will have Cæsar's image stand, the god who guards my shrine; in his honour I as conqueror conspicuous in Tyrian purple will drive a hundred four-horse chariots by the water's side; with one consent will all Greece for my sake leave the Alpheus, and the groves of Molorchus, and contend in the race and with cestus of raw hide. I myself, my head decked with leafy crown of trimmed olive, will offer gifts to heaven. E'en now I joy to lead the solemn procession to the shrine and to behold the sacrifice of steers; or to see how the scene shifts with changing face, and how the Britons woven in the tapestry raise the purple curtain. On the doors will I represent in gold and solid ivory the battle of the Gangaridæ, and the arms of our victorious Quirinus; and here shall appear the Nile, whose billows threaten war, whose stream flows proudly, and the columns rising with naval brass. Then I will add Asia's vanquished towns, and Niphates defeated in war, and the Parthian, whose trust is in his flight, and arrows backward shot, and two trophies taken by a strong hand from foes in opposite quarters of the world, nations twain each triumphed over on either shore. There shall stand too statues of Parian marble, as though with life and breath, the race of Assaracus, and the honoured names of the stock descended from Jove, Tros our parent, and he of Cynthus founder of Troy. Ill-omened Envy shall dread the Furies, and stern river of Cocytus, and the twisted snakes of Ixion, and the monstrous wheel, and the stone that cannot be pushed over the ridge. Meanwhile let us now pursue the theme of the Dryads' groves and glades, regions of song as yet untouched, no easy tasks, but thy behest, Mecænas. Without thee my heart inaugurates nought that is lofty; come then awake, away with sloth and delay; with clamours loud

Cithæron invites us, and hounds of Taygetus call, and Epidaurus tamer of horses; and the call repeated by the assenting groves re-echoes the cry. And yet hereafter will I gird myself to sing the fiery fights of Cæsar, and to bear the great name of Cæsar through as many years as he is distant in descent from his first origin from Tithonus.

49—71. *Carefully should we choose our cattle for breeding, as to form and age. It is the law of the world that the best comes first, the worst last.*

Whether one admires the prizes of the Olympian palm, and breeds horses, or whether rather bullocks able to draw the plough, with special care must one choose the bodies of the mothers. That cow has the best form, whose look is lowering, head ugly, neck thick, whose dewlaps hanging from the chin reach to the very knees. Then her side should be long past the usual measure, every point large, large foot, large hairy ears under the crumpled horns. Nor do I dislike one marked with spots of white, or one that tosses off the yoke and at times is awkward with her horn, whose face is not so unlike a bull's, whose form is all tall, and who, as she steps, sweeps her tracks with the end of her tail. The right age for Lucina and regular marriage begins after four, to end before ten years; the rest of the life of cattle is neither fit for breeding nor strong to draw the plough. Meantime, ere joyous youth is past to the herds, loose the bulls, be first to send your cattle to breed, and supply a succession of the stock by generation. Each goodliest day of life to suffering mortals flies first, diseases soon steal on, and sad old age, and decay, and cruel inexorable death sweeps life away. There will always be some, whose breed you may wish to change, so always repair your loss; and lest you miss them when too late, anticipate the time, and choose a new stock for the herd year by year.

72—102. *Be careful too about the choice of horses. You must observe shape, colour, age; so will you have horses like the famous ones of olden time.*

Likewise in breeding horses the same careful choice is needed. So do you even from their tender years give special attention to those whom you settle to use in the hope of the increase of your stock. From his earliest years the colt of a noble breed steps higher o'er the fields, and with alternate tread moves on elastic feet; he dares the first to lead the way, he tempts threatening rivers, he trusts himself on an unknown bridge, he starts not at idle noises. Lofty is his shoulder, pointed his head, short belly, broad back; his chest, as though full of spirit, rises luxuriant with knots of muscle: of a good breed are bay and grey: the worst colour is white and dun. Then if any arms clash afar, he cannot stand still, he pricks his ears, his limbs quiver, he rolls in his nostrils the close collected flame: thick is his mane; if tossed, it will lie on his right shoulder: a double spine runs straight along his loins, his hoof hollows the ground, and gives a deep sound with the solid horn. Such was Cyllarus, whom Laconian Pollux tamed with reins, and the steeds of whom Grecian poets tell, the pair of the chariot of Mars and of great Achilles. Such too did

Saturn himself seem, when at the coming of his spouse, as a nimble
steed, he threw a mane from his neck, and flying filled the height of
Pelion with his shrill neighings.   Yet even such a horse as this, when
wasted with disease, or sluggish through age he fails, put aside at
home, nor spare his ignoble old age.   The old horse is frigid, in vain
he strives at a thankless toil, and if ever he comes to the battle, his
rage is fruitless, as when a fire burns in stubble, and its force is spent.
Therefore above all note their spirit and years ; next observe their other
qualities, the race of their sires, and how each chafes at defeat, or glóries
in the prize.

103—122. *Great is the excitement, the glory, the antiquity of the chariot-
race.   The art of riding too traces back to heroes of old.   But any how
youth is necessary in horses.*

See you not, when in headlong contests chariots course o'er the cham-
paign, and pouring from the barriers onwards rapid rush, when the
youthful charioteers are on the tip-toe of expectation, and thrilling excitement draws the blood of their beating hearts ; they ply the twisted lash,
bending forward they slacken their reins ; with force flies the glowing
axle ; now low depressed,· then reared aloft, they seem to be borne
through the open air, and to rise to the sky ; no rest, no respite, whilst
a storm of yellow sand is raised ; they are wet with the foam and breath
of the horses that follow.   So deep is their passion for renown, so dear is
triumph to their hearts.   First of all men Ericthonius dared to yoke four
steeds to the chariot, and victorious to take his stand above the whirling
wheels.   The Thessalian Lapithæ mounted on the horse's back invented
the bit and how to turn in circles, teaching the armed rider how to
manage his horse bounding in the plain and proudly prancing in many a
mazy tread.   Equal was either labour ; equally do the trainers seek out a
young horse, high in spirit, keen to run, and that too although a horse
has often driven before him the foe in flight, and counts back in descent
from Epirus and valiant Mycenæ, nay may trace his origin back to Neptune himself the founder of his race.

123—156. *Horses should be well fattened, mares kept thin, but afterwards they should be kept quiet, and protected from the gad-fly.*

This being well observed, men are careful as the time draws near, and
give all heed to fill out with firm fat him whom they have chosen as leader
and husband of the herd : and cut flowering grasses, and supply running
water, and corn, lest he should fail in the pleasant toil, and lest the weakness of the foals repeat the ill condition of their sires.   But the mares on
the other hand they purposely make spare and lean, and when the time
for breeding is drawing nigh, then they stint their leafy fodder, and keep
them from the springs, often too harass them with galloping, and fatigue
them in the hot sun, during the hours that the floor gives the heavy sound
of the threshing of corn, and to rising Zephyrs the empty chaff is tossed.
Presently on the contrary the care of the sires relaxes, and that of the
dams succeeds.   When their months are fulfilled and they wander
during their pregnancy, let no one suffer them to bear the yokes of heavy
wagons, or to bound across the road, or to scour the fields in swift course,
or to stem strong torrents.   Let them feed at large in glades, by the

margin of full streams, where grows the moss, and the bark is green with
turf; where grottos may give them shelter, and rocks cast forward their
shade. About the groves of Silarus and Alburnus, where holm-oaks
flourish, an insect flies often, we Romans call it asilus, the Greeks gave
it another name, œstros; a stinging fly, whizzing with sharp sound,
thereat terrified all the herds scatter in flight through the woods; shaken
and stirred to madness is the sky by the bellowings, the forests and
banks of dry Tanager resound. This is the monster which Juno once
sent to glut her dreadful wrath, devising a plague for the Inachian
heifer. This insect, for in the mid-day heat its attacks are fiercest, keep
from your pregnant cattle, and feed your herds when the sun is fresh
risen, or the stars usher in the night.

157—178. *After calving, care for your calves chiefly. You cannot begin
too gently: youth requires gentle treatment.*

After the birth to the calves must pass all your care: and from the
first the herdsmen brand them with marks and the name of the stock,
that they may know which they mean to keep for breeding, which for
victims at the altars, with which to cut the land, and break the clods and
turn up the rough plain. The other cattle graze in the green grass;
those whom you would fashion to rural use and end, train whilst still
calves, and enter on the way of taming them; the spirits of the young
are pliant, their age still docile. And first about their necks fasten loose
circles of slender osier; presently, when they have accustomed the
freedom of their necks to bondage, unite the bullocks just by their
collars, and yoke them fairly matched, and force them to step in time.
Next let them often draw o'er the ground the wheels of an empty cart,
and lightly touch with the marks of their footsteps the surface of the dust.
Afterwards let the beechen axle labouring under the ponderous weight
creak, and a brazen pole drag the wheels of the wagon. Meanwhile give
the untamed bullocks not grass merely, or the leaves of willows, sorry
food, or the sedge of the fen, but spare not to pluck for them the corn;
nor, as in the days of your fathers, let your cows after calving fill your
pails with milk as white as snow, but let them consume all that their
udders give on their beloved young.

179—208. *By gentle and spare treatment you may rear a colt to be as
swift as the north wind, a good racer, a good draught-horse.*

But if your taste be war and martial troops, or your passion is to fly
swift on whirling wheels beside Alpheus Pisa's stream, and in Jove's holy
wood to drive the speeding car, remember that what the horse must first
be taught with difficulty is to face steadily the arms of bold warriors, and
to bear the trumpet's voice, and fearless to pull the car rattling as it is
drawn, and to hear the noise of the bit in the stable: then more and
more to rejoice in the flattery and praises of his trainer, and to love the
noise of the patting of his neck. Let him hear these noises as soon as
ever he is weaned from his dam, and in time let him accustom his
mouth to soft bits, whilst still unsteady, still trembling, still untrained and
young. But when three summers are past and the fourth is just come,
let him learn to run in the circle, and to prance with regular steps in
measure, and let him curvet with his legs moving in time, as one that

seems to have a work to do ; so let him challenge the gales in race, and skimming over the open plain, as though free from reins, scarcely let him set the marks of his feet on the surface of the sand. As when a steady north-wind comes down from Hyperborean coasts, scattering the storms of Scythia and the dry clouds ; the tall corn and waving fields are ruffled with the gentle blasts, and the tops of the trees of the forest roar, and long waves press onwards to the shore ; the wind flies sweeping in its course over fields and seas alike. Such a horse as this will sweat at the goal and long courses of the stadium of Elis, and will champ the bloody foam ; or else will better bear the yoke of the Belgic chariot on his obedient neck. Then and not till then, when they are fully tamed, allow their bodies to become plump on thickly mixed food ; for till they are tamed, they will raise their spirits high, and when caught will disdain to endure the tough lash, and to obey the hard bits.

209—265. *Keep your horses and bulls from love. Fierce are the battles of bulls. All animals are maddened by love; even man himself.*

But there is no industry and care that so confirms their strength, as to keep away from them love and the excitement of a blind passion ; whether the practice of rearing horses, or steers, is preferred. Therefore the bulls are banished to a distance into lonely pastures behind intervening hills, and across broad rivers, or shut up in stables at full mangers. For the sight of the female little by little steals away the bull's strength, and consumes him with passion, nor allows him to remember the groves and the grass. Her power lies in her sweet blandishments, often does she force her proud lovers to decide their claims by the battle of their horns. In great Sila feeds a fair heifer ; the bulls in contest engage with mighty force, dealing each other many a wound ; they are bathed in black blood ; as they strive with mighty bellowings their horns are driven against each other, the woods and great Olympus echo back the roar. Nor will the warriors make their lair together ; but the conquered combatant withdraws, and at a distance passes an exile's life in unknown lands, much does he lament his disgrace, and the blows of the haughty victor, and his lost love, and his unavenged defeat, and with his gaze fixed on the stalls departs from his ancestral realms. Therefore diligently does he train his powers, and makes his bed on hard stones, and lies there all the night long, his food rough leaves and sharp-pointed sedge ; then he makes trial of his strength, and learns how to throw his wrath into his horns, pushing at the trunk of a tree, and with blows defies the winds, and spurns the sand, the prelude of the fray. Presently his strength is collected, and his powers recruited, then for the fight he starts, and headlong rushes on the unguarded foe : just as when a wave first whitens out in the open sea, far away from the shore, and even from the deep onwards draws its heaving curve ; then rolling to the land over the rocks roars dreadful, and breaks in tumbling mass not less than a mighty mountain ; the water surges up from beneath in eddies, and casts on high the dark sand. So true is it that every kind of living creatures in the earth, men and beasts alike, and the race that dwell in the sea, cattle and birds with painted plumage, are hurried into the frenzy and flames of passion ; all feel love alike. Then and

at no other time does the lioness forget her cubs, and in fiercest mood
prowl o'er the plain; nor do misshapen bears at other seasons make
so much havoc and destruction in the forests; then is the wild boar
savage, then is the tiger man's worst foe: alas, and then 'tis ill to
wander in the deserts of Libya. See you not how a trembling thrills the
bodies of horses all over, if their snuffing does but bring the familiar
scent? And then no longer do bits stop their course, or the violent
lashes of their drivers, or cliffs or hollow rocks, or the barrier of rivers
whirling crags hurried down their torrent. On rushes the great Sabine
boar whetting his tusks, with his foot he roots up the ground before him,
he rubs his sides hither and thither against a tree, he hardens his shoulders to endure wounds. Need I mention the youth in whose heart cruel
love stirs up a mighty fire of passion? See how, late in a dark night, he
swims the strait troubled by bursting storms; above him thunders the
great portal of heaven, and the cry of the waters dashing against the
cliffs warns him back; nor can his wretched parents recall him home, or
the maiden who will not bear to outlive his cruel death. Need I tell of
the spotted ounces, the team of Bacchus, or the fierce race of wolves and
dogs, or of the battles fought by unwarlike stags?

266—283. *No animals, however, so furious as mares; it is as if Venus
herself possessed them. They say the Zephyrs impregnate them. Wondrous is the magic power of the hippomanes.*

But doubtless the rage of mares is above that of all other creatures;
Venus herself inspires their passion, from the day that the four Potnian
steeds devoured the limbs of their charioteer Glaucus with their jaws.
Love leads mares beyond Gargarus, and across the roaring Ascanius;
they pass the ridges of mountains, they swim across streams. And as
soon as ever their kindled hearts have caught the flame, in spring chiefly,
for in spring warmth returns to the limbs, they all stand on high rocks
with their faces turned to catch the Zephyr, and snuff the light breezes,
and often without wedlock are impregnated by the wind, (marvellous to
tell), then o'er rocks, o'er cliffs, along lowly dales, they fly hither and
thither; but not towards thee, Eurus, nor towards the rising of the
Sun; but towards Boreas and Caurus, or towards the quarter whence
blows dusky Auster, saddening the heavens with chilly rain. Hence at
last a slimy substance distils from their sides, which the shepherds call
by a true name Hippomanes, gathered often by malicious step-mothers,
who mix with it herbs and baneful charms.

284—294. *Let this suffice for herds; now we will sing of sheep and
goats. 'Tis an humble subject, but original, and I am smitten with
the love of it.*

Meanwhile time flies, yes, flies with irreparable speed, whilst we linger
on each detail, charmed with the love of song. Let this suffice for herds;
the second part of my task remains, to teach men how to tend fleecy
flocks and shaggy goats. This too is laborious; hence also hope for
honour, sturdy husbandmen. Nor do I feel any doubt that it is arduous
to overcome this difficulty by my style, and to add dignity to such a
lowly theme. But the sweet love of song hurries me o'er the lonely
steeps of Parnassus. I rejoice to pass the ridges, where no beaten road

of former bards turns aside to Castalia by an easy descent. Now, honoured Pales, now must I sing in lofty speech.

295—337. We must care for sheep in winter, for goats too, a flock not less valuable, independent, and hardy. When spring comes let them feed in early morn, have water and shelter in midday, feed again in cool evening.

With authority I decree first that the sheep should feed on herbage in their soft pens, while in its turn comes leafy summer back: beneath make a bed on the hard ground of thick stubble and handfuls of fern, lest the chilling frost hurt the tender flock, bringing scab and unsightly gout. Next in order I direct that the goats be bountifully supplied with leafy arbutus, and fresh water from the streams; and I wish the pens to be turned from the wind to face the wintry mid-day sun, when the time comes that chilly Aquarius is just setting, sprinkling from his watering-pot the close of the year. With no less care should our goats be tended, nor less their use; however great the price Milesian fleeces fetch, when steeped in Tyrian dye. Goats are more prolific; milk they give in plenteous abundance; the more the milk-pail froths from their emptied udders, so more freely flow the joyous streams of milk from their pressed dugs. Meanwhile no less the goatherd shears the grey beard from the chin of the Libyan he-goat, and clips his thick shaggy hair, for the use of camps, and for the coats of needy mariners. Then they are content to feed in woods and on the very peaks of Lycæus, and browse on prickly briars and on bushes that love steep heights; and unbidden remember to return home, guides to their young, with udders so full that they can hardly step o'er the threshold. Therefore as less they need the care of man, do you with all diligence keep from them frost and snowy winds, glad to bring them provender and twigs to feed on, and have your hay-lofts open all the winter long. But then, as soon as summer rejoicing in the Zephyrs' call, sends either flock unto the lawns and pastures, then let us at the earliest rising of the day-star take our pleasure in the cool country, whilst the dawn is fresh, whilst the grass is white with hoar-frost, whilst the dew on the tender herb is most grateful to the cattle. Presently, when the fourth hour of the day has collected the thirsty heat of the sky, and the plaintive grasshoppers seem to burst the trees of the vineyard with their chirping song, do you bid your flocks at the wells or deep ponds drink the water running in oaken troughs: but in the heat of noon see that they carefully seek a shady dell, where a mighty oak, Jove's tree, stretches its huge branches from an ancient trunk, or where a dark grove of thickly planted holm-oaks casts forward its holy shade. Then once more give them liquid running water, and again let them feed even to the setting sun; when the hour comes that the cool evening freshens the air, and the dewy moon gives the lawns new life, when the shores echo to the voice of the halcyon, and the bushes are alive with the song of the goldfinch.

338—383. Very different are the scenes in Africa and in Scythia; in the one region the cattle feed for months in the boundless plains; in the other they are kept in stalls, for winter and ice are all around, and men live in holes of the earth.

Why need I pursue the theme of Libya's shepherds and pastures, and villages of huts with thinly scattered roofs? Often day and night, yea, a whole month long, day after day the flocks feed, and the cattle go on into the far extending wilderness, where there is no host to entertain ; so far the vast plain stretches. The African herdsman takes all his property with him, his home, his gods, his stuff, his Spartan dog, his Cretan quiver. Just as the Roman soldier under the arms of his country's service marches onwards beneath a cumbrous load, and before the foe expects him, e'en as he marches on, his camp is pitched, and fixed for fight. Far other is the scene, where are the tribes of Scythia, and the lake Mæotis, where turbid Ister rolls his yellow sands, where Rhodope bends and stretches under the middle of the pole. There close they keep their herds in stalls ; no grass is seen on the plain, no leaves on trees ; but the earth lies shapeless under drifts of snow, a wide deep frozen mass, rising seven ells in height. Eternal winter reigns, and north-west winds ever coldly blow. Never does the sun dispel the dull pale mists, neither when riding in his car he mounts the lofty sky, nor when he bathes his fast-descending chariot in the red surface of the ocean. Suddenly crusts of ice form on the running stream, and now the water bears iron-bound wheels on its expanse, once the home of ships, now of broad wagons. Brass splits everywhere, clothes stiffen on men's backs, with hatchets they cleave liquid wine, whole tanks turn into solid ice, the pointed icicle hardens on uncombed beards. Meanwhile the snow-flakes never cease to fall in the whole sky ; the cattle perish, the mighty forms of oxen are seen standing encased in frozen snow, and crowded herds of stags grow numb under the strange mass, above it hardly rise the tips of their horns. Men hunt them not with hounds slipped from the leash, nor entrap them with nets, nor frighten them with the terrors of the crimson feather ; but as the creatures vainly with their breasts push against the bulwark of the snow, the hunters standing close stab them, and slay them braying with deep cries, then joyously carry them home with loud shouts. There do the people dwell in deep-dug holes low down in the earth, at ease and free from care, they heap up logs of heart of oak, and roll whole elms to the hearth and give them to the flames. Here they pass the night in games, and for cups of wine make shift with beer and the cider of sour service-berries. Such are those who live under Charles' wain, a race of wild savage men, buffeted by the Riphæan east wind, clothed in the shaggy tawny skins of cattle.

384—403. *If wool is your object, (and wool tempted a goddess), keep your flock from certain food, and have no rams but white ones : if you set your heart on milk, give salt food, and you will have cheese, when you want it, for sale, or to be kept.*

If wool be your care, first see that your land is free of burrs and caltrops ; eschew rich pastures, and from the very first pick out for your flocks those that are white with soft wool. A ram, who is to be master of your flock, though he be of the brightest white, yet if his tongue only be black under his moist palate, reject him, lest he darken the fleeces of the lambs at their birth with black spots, and do you look round the well-stocked field to find another. Thus with snow-white wool, if to believe the tale insults not the gods, Pan, Arcadia's god, beguiled thee, O Moon, charmed with the gift, inviting thee to the deep groves, nor didst thou scorn the invitation. But he who loves milk should with his own hand bring lucerne and lotus in abundance, and salt herbs to their cribs. Hence they love the rivers more, and more distend their udders, and one can trace a slight taste of salt in the milk. Many keep the kids from their dams as soon as they are born, and put muzzles with iron spokes on their mouths. What at sun-rise or in the hours of the day they milk, that at night they press ; again what they milk at night or as the sun goes down, at day-break the shepherd carries in baskets to the town, or they sprinkle it slightly with salt and store it up for winter.

404—413. *Dogs are useful both to guard your house and to hunt in the fields.*

Nor should the care of dogs be last ; but together feed on rich whey the swift hounds of Sparta and the fierce Molossian ; with these for guards you need never dread for your fold the thief at night, or the attack of wolves, or restless robber coming on you from behind. Often too coursing you will pursue the timorous wild asses, with dogs too hunt the hares, with dogs the does ; often with the baying hounds you will raise the wild boars forth from their woody beds wherein they wallow, and over the high hills with huntsman's cry drive a huge stag into the nets.

414—439. *By fumigation drive away the snakes. They lurk, if you are careless. In Calabria is one which in wet weather lives in pools, in dry weather is dangerous to sleepers in the open air.*

Learn too to light in your stalls the fragrant cedar, and with smell of gum to keep off venomous snakes. Oft beneath uncleansed cribs either a viper deadly to touch is lurking, and frightened has fled from the daylight, or a snake, that grievous plague of oxen, used to steal under a roof or beneath the shade, and shower its venom on the cattle, squats close on the ground : take stones in your hand, take oaken clubs, shepherd, and as he rises menacing, as he swells his hissing neck, down with him to the ground ; see he flies, see quickly he hides his timorous head in a deep hole, his central coils and the extreme lines of his tail are unloosed, and the utmost fold slowly drags its coil. There is too that dreaded snake in the glades of Calabria, a fell beast, which lifts its breast and rolls its scaly back, long is its belly, speckled with large spots ; so long as any streams gush from their sources, so long as the earth is moist with damp spring weather, and with rainy south winds, it haunts the ponds, and dwelling on the banks fills its black greedy maw with fish and croaking frogs : but when the marsh is burnt up, and the ground gapes with the burning heat, forth it springs upon the dry land, and glares with flaming eyes, and rages in the fields, savage through thirst, dazed by the drought. May not the fancy then take me to cull the blessing of soft sleep beneath the sky or to throw myself on a woody slope along the grass, when the snake having cast his

slough, fresh in youthful gloss, rolls along, leaving in his hole his young
or his eggs, with high head erect towards the sun, and three-forked
tongue that quivers in his mouth.

440—477. *The diseases of sheep with their remedies. No time is in*
this case to be lost, as contagion advances quickly spreading desola-
tion far and wide.

I will also teach you the causes and symptoms of diseases. Ugly
scab attacks sheep, when chilly rain and winter stiff with hoary frost
penetrates deeply even to the quick; or when, after shearing, the sweat
not washed off clings to their bodies, or prickly brambles tear their
skin. Therefore in fresh running water the shepherds wash all their
flock, and the ram is plunged in the pool with his dripping fleece,
and is let loose to float down the stream. Or else after shearing
they smear their bodies with bitter lees of oil, making a compound of
litharge and native sulphur, and pitch from mount Ida, and wax
greased with ointment, and squill, and strong smelling hellebore, and
black bitumen. But fortune is never so ready to aid the distressed
by any other method, as if we dare with the knife to lay the head of
the sore open: to cover the distemper gives it life and nourishment;
so long as the shepherd shrinks from applying his healing hands, or
idly sits importuning heaven for happier omens. Moreover, when the
pain rages piercing deep to the very bones of the bleating sheep, and
parching fever preys upon their limbs, then is it good to turn the
course of the kindled heat, and just under the foot to open a vein
and let out the spouting blood; such is the practice of the Bisaltæ
and the active Gelonian, when he flies to Rhodope, and the deserts
of the Getæ, whose drink is a mixture of milk and horse's blood.
But should you see a poor animal often retire to a distance beneath
the soft shade, or listlessly crop the top of the herbage, or lag behind
his companions, or as it feeds lie down in the midst of the plain,
and not give place to night till lonely and late, at once cut off with
the knife the diseased member, before the dire contagion stealthily
spreads through the unwary flock. Nor so thickly does the whirlwind
drive before it a storm, and rush upon the main, as plagues come
crowding upon cattle; nor do the diseases seize single bodies, but lay
waste the whole summer quarters at once, the flock and the hope of
the flock together, and all the nation from its earliest source. This
may any one know, if even after so long a time he should visit the
Alps towering in the sky, and the castles of Noricum on the hills,
or the fields where Timavus of Iapia flows, and sees the desolation of
the pastoral realms, and the glades far and wide without inhabitant.

478—566. *Description of a plague in imitation of Lucretius. It causes*
universal destruction with many varieties of misery. It pollutes
sacred rites. It destroys the noblest hopes. Remedies are even mis-
chievous. The innocent creatures perish. Man has to do the work
of brute beasts. The air itself and the sea are polluted. The fury
is let loose. The contagion spreads even to the hides and wool, which
are now useless.

In this country once upon a time through the corruption of the air suddenly began a woeful time, which glowed like a furnace with the white heat of autumn, and delivered over to destruction all the race of cattle, all the wild beasts of the field, and poisoned the pools, and tainted the pastures as with venom. Nor did they travel a simple path of death; but when the fiery drought coursing through all their veins had contracted their wretched limbs, a change passed over the disease, and the watery dropsy flowed profusely, and spread through all the bones, one by one drawing them into corruption. Oft in the midst of the sacrifice to the gods, as the victim was standing at the altar, while it was being decked with woollen fillet with snow-white ribbons, the creature fell in the agonies of death almost in the hands of the loitering ministers: or if the priest was in time to slay a victim with his knife, yet, when its entrails were placed on the altar, the flame would not kindle, and the consulted seer had no response to give, and the knives beneath the throat were scarcely stained with blood, and the surface of the sand hardly coloured with the thin corrupted gore. Hence the calves are continually dying in the luxuriant herbage, or give up their dear life at well filled mangers. Hence gentle dogs turn raging mad, and a panting asthma shakes the wheezing swine, and throttles them in their swollen throats. Unhappy in all his noble aims, forgetful of his pasture sinks the horse, conqueror in the race; he loathes the fountains, ever and anon he stamps on the ground; his ears droop, on them breaks forth a fitful sweating, and that too, as death draws near, becomes cold; dry is the skin, and resists, all hard, the touch of the hand. Such are the symptoms of the fatal disease during the first days; but as in its advance it waxes fiercer and fiercer, then the eyes burn with heat, the breath is drawn deep, between times it comes laden with a groan, with sobs and sighs the whole length of the sides is racked; black blood flows from the nostrils, the rough tongue cleaves to the obstructed jaws. For a time it does good to pour from a horn the Lenæan juice of wine down their throats; that seemed the only hope of deliverance from death : presently the very remedy was deadly, with rage recruited they burnt with fresh fever, and as their sickness drew on to death (ye gods, give better hearts to the pious, and such an infatuation to our enemies!) they tore and mangled their own limbs with their naked teeth. But behold the bull smoking with the weight of the hard plough suddenly falls, he vomits from his mouth gore mixed with foam, and draws the last groans; sadly goes the ploughman and unyokes the bullock sorrowing at his brother's death, the plough is left fixed in the ground, the work is unfinished. No shades of deep groves, no velvet meadows can gladden his spirit, no stream that rolls o'er the rocks, clearer than amber, in its course to the plain; flabby is the length of his flanks, torpor loads his stupid eyes, his neck droops to earth borne down with heavy weight. Alas, what boots his toil or kind services to man? what avails his having turned up the stubborn earth with the share? And yet the Massic wine, the gift of Bacchus, was not his bane, nor the dainties of loaded tables; his simple food was leaves and grass; his cups were crystal springs and rivers racing in their rapid course; no cares disturb his healthy rest. At such and no other time men say that in these regions kine were sought in vain for Juno's sacrifices, and that ill-matched buffaloes drew the chariots to the lofty shrines. Therefore do men with harrows painfully grub up the earth, and with their own nails plant the corn, and over the high hills straining their necks drag the creaking carts.   No more does the wolf try his wily tricks around the folds, nor nightly prowl about the flocks ; a sharper trouble tames his spirit now ; timorous roes and flying stags now roam close to the kennels of the hounds and the houses of men.   Now the wave washes up on the beach of the shore the progeny of the boundless sea, and all the race that swims in the water, as though they were the bodies of shipwrecked mariners ; sea-calves take refuge in the rivers—an unfamiliar dwelling.   The viper too perishes, her winding hole is a vain defence ; the water-snakes are scared with scales erect.   To the very birds the air is an unkindly home ; headlong they fall, and leave their life within a lofty cloud.   Moreover so sore is the distress that the change of pasture is useless ; the invented methods of medicine are only baneful, beaten are the masters of the craft, Chiron the son cf Philyra, Melampus the son of Amythaon.   Ghastly Tisiphone rages, let loose into the light of day from the Stygian darkness, she drives before her disease and terror, day by day she ever raises higher her greedy head.   With the bleating of sheep and constant lowings of oxen resound the rivers and parched banks and sloping hills.   And now the Fury destroys them heap upon heap, and piles in the very stalls the carcases that stream with foul corrupted gore ; until perforce they learn to cover them in the earth, and put them out of sight in pits.   For even the hides were good for nought ; and no one could cleanse the infection of the entrails by water, or overcome the contagion by fire ; they could not so much as shear the fleeces wasted by the filthy disease, nor even touch the wool that should have been woven, so rotten was it ; but if any one ventured to put on the loathsome clothing, burning pustules and a noisome sweat soon ran o'er his fetid frame, nor was it long before he found that the fiery curse was consuming his infected limbs.

BOOK IV.

1—7. *The introduction.*

I WILL go on to discourse of next the heavenly gifts of honey born in air. Regard, Mæcenas, also this division of my work. Marvellous shows, though made by trifling things, and high-souled captains I will tell you of, and recount in order all the nation's character, and tastes, and tribes, and wars. Slight is the subject of my toil, but not slight the glory, if adverse powers perchance allow me, and Apollo hear my call.

8—32. *Directions as to the situation of the hive, and the plants that should grow about it.*

In the first place, a fixed site must be sought out for the dwelling of the bees, to which the winds may never find a path (for the winds prevent them from carrying home their food), and where no sheep and butting kids may trample on the flowers, or the heifer, as she wanders o'er the plain, sweep away the dew and crush the springing plants. Let the painted lizard's scaly back be also far away from the wealthy home-

stead, and bee-eaters, and other birds, and Procne, her breast marked
with her bloody hands ; for everything far and wide they devastate, and
catch on the wing the bees themselves, and in their beaks bear them
away, a sweet morsel for their cruel nestlings. But close at hand be
crystal springs and pools all green with moss, and a tiny rivulet stealing
through the grass, and let a palm or great wild olive canopy the porch, so
that, when in the spring they love, the new-made kings shall lead forth
their earliest swarms, and the young bees play unprisoned from the
comb, a neighbouring bank may invite them to withdraw from the heat,
and a tree full in their view may charm them to stay within its hospitable
bower. Into the midst of the water, whether it stand idle or gush forth,
cast willow boughs across, and massy stones; that they may have a succession of bridges whereon to settle, and spread their wings out to the
summer sun, if it chance the south-wind has sprinkled them with a
shower of rain as they linger abroad, or with headlong swoop has plunged
them in the deep. About this place let green casia, and wild thyme that
flings its fragrance round, and a wealth of strong-scented savory blossom,
and beds of violets quaff the irrigating spring.

33—50. *The construction of the hive, and precautions to be used to
exclude heat and cold. Nothing that may hurt or offend the bees
should be near the hive.*

Next, let the hive itself, whether you have it sewn together of pieces of
hollow bark, or woven of pliant osier, have its entrances narrow ; for
winter contracts the honey with cold, and summer heat melts it again in
turn. Your bees should be guarded equally against the fierceness of both
extremes ; and it is with good reason that they in their dwellings are all
eagerness to daub with wax the tiny crevices, and with the pollen of
flowers stop up the chinks, and store up gum, which they have gathered
for this special purpose, more binding than birdlime, and the pitch of
Phrygian Ida. Often too, if the story be true, they dig out a hiding-
place, and make their settled home beneath the earth, and have been
found deep within scooped-out pumice rocks, and the cavern of a hollow
tree. Still do you with fostering care anoint all round their chambers
full of cracks with smooth mud, and scatter leaves above it here and
there : and suffer not a yew-tree too near to their home, nor roast in the
fire red crabs ; and mistrust a deep marsh, or a spot where the smell of a
morass is oppressive, or where arched rocks ring with the stroke of sound,
and from the shock rebounds the echoed voice.

51—66. *The activity of bees at the return of spring. Their swarming;
and how to induce them to go back to the hive.*

For the rest, when the golden Sun has banished winter, and driven him
beneath the earth, and with the summer light unlocked the sky, they
straightway range throughout the glades and groves, and crop bright
flowers, and lightly sip the surface of the streams. Hence is it that,
pleased with some vague delight, they cherish their young ones in the
nest; hence is it that they skilfully fashion the fresh wax, and mould the
honey-glues. Therefore, whenever you observe the train, just unprisoned
from its hollow cages, to soar towards the stars of heaven, floating through
the cloudless summer air, and view the dark cloud trailing in the wind,

mark them ; sweet springs and leafy bowers they ever seek.   Hitherward
scatter at once the savoury herbs prescribed, bruised leaves of balm, and
the wax-flower's humble blade, and all about raise tinkling sounds, and
rattle the cymbals of the mother of the gods : of themselves they will
settle down on the spot you have thus prepared, of themselves they will,
according to their habit, hide deep within their chambers' inmost cells.

67—102. *Description of the battle, when there are two rival kings in the*
hive.   When the fight has been stopped, the worst of the two should be
killed.   The common bees are of two sorts, each class being like
its king.

But if perchance for fight they quit the hive, for discord oft with passion
deep two kings inspires, and from the first you may from far divine the
feelings of the crowd and their hearts that throb with the spirit of war ;
for the well-known battle-note of the hoarse clarion startles the loiterers,
and a sound is heard that mimics the trumpet's fitful blasts ; then all
excited they close in combat, and flash their wings, and whet the points
of their beaks, and make ready their arms to fight, and around their king
and close to his pavilion they swarm in throngs, and with loud shouts
defy the enemy.   So when they have found a clear spring day and open
plains, they sally forth from the gates ; high in the air they meet in the
shock of fight ; a din is heard ; mingled they roll into a mighty globe,
and headlong fall ; not thicker pours the hail from heaven, nor such a
rain of acorns from the shaken oak.   The chiefs themselves with conspicuous wings throughout the midst of the array have mighty souls at
work within a narrow breast, utterly resolved not to give way, till the
overpowering conqueror has forced one army or the other to turn and
shew their backs in flight.   These passions of soul, and these conflicts,
fierce though they be, are quelled and laid at rest by the casting of a
little dust.   But when you have recalled both captains from the field,
him that is worst to view consign to doom, that he be not a wasteful
burden ; allow the better one to reign in the palace his rival has left
empty.   The one will be ablaze with spots of golden mail ; for there are
two sorts ; first the better, distinguished in form, and bright with flashing
scales ;   the other of the two squalid through sloth, and trailing in-
gloriously a breadth of belly.   As the shapes of the monarchs are twofold, so are the bodies of their subjects ;   for some are unsightly and
squalid, as when from a depth of dust the traveller comes, and from his
parching mouth spits out the earth ; others brightly gleam and glitter and
sparkle, their bodies ablaze and uniformly marked with golden drops.
This is the nobler stock ; from this at the certain season of the year you
will press sweet honey ; and yet not so sweet, as crystal-clear, and able
to subdue the harsh flavour of wine.

103—115. *How to prevent the bees from straying.   There should be a*
flower-garden near.

But when the swarms fly aimlessly about, and play in the air, and
scorn their combs, and leave their dwellings cold, you should restrain
their wanton minds from idle play.   And the trouble of restraining them
is not great ; do but pluck away the monarch's wings : not one will dare,
while they remain at home, to set out on his airy march, or pull up the

standards from the camp. Let gardens that breathe the odour of saffron
flowers invite them, and the watcher against thieves and birds with his
willow pruning-hook, Priapus, lord of the Hellespont, guard and protect
them. Let him to whom this charge belongs himself bear thyme and pine-
trees from the mountain heights, and plant them everywhere around
their homes ; let him wear with hard toil his own hand, with his own
hand let him set in earth the fruitful herbs, and let loose the welcome
irrigating showers.

116—148. *An apology for not treating of gardens more at length. Description of a garden and orchard near Tarentum.*

And I myself, were I not now, as I draw close to my labours' utmost
bound, furling my sails, and hastening to turn my prow to land, perhaps
would sing what cultivating care makes fertile gardens gay, and tell of the
twice-flowering rosebeds of Pæstum, and how the endive rejoices in the
streams it drinks, and green river-banks in parsley, and how the cucum-
ber coiling through the grass grows and swells in girth ; and I would
not have passed in silence by the late-blowing narcissus, and the pliant
stalk of the twining acanthus, and ivy pale, and the myrtle that loves the
shore. For I remember that beneath Œbalia's stately towers, where
black Galæsus soaks the golden fields, I saw an old Corycian swain, who
possessed a few acres of abandoned land, and it a soil not rich enough
for the ox to plough, nor fit for the herd to graze upon, nor kindly for the
growth of the vine. Yet he, as he planted vegetables here and there on
the thorny ground, and about them white lilies, and the poppy with its
tiny seeds, matched in his heart's content the wealth of kings, and home
returning late at night, with unbought dainties used to pile his board.
The first was he to gather the rose in spring, the fruit in autumn ; and
when stern winter was still bursting the rocks with cold, and bridling the
rivers' speed, he was then beginning to pluck the tender hyacinth bloom,
chiding the lazy summer and lingering western gales. So he too was
first to abound in teeming bees and many a swarm, and from the pressed
honeycomb to collect the frothing honey ; his lime-trees and his pines
were most luxuriant ; and for every promise wherewith his bounteous
tree had dressed itself in early bloom, it bore fruit in its autumn ripeness.
He also latest planted out his elms, and his pear-tree when grown quite
hard, and the sloe when it had begun to bear its plums, and the plane
when spreading enough to minister a shade to the revellers. But I
myself, shut out by want of space, pass by this theme, and leave it for
others after me to treat.

149—196. *The nature and habits of bees. Their commonwealth, division of labour, energy in work, and regularity of system. Their
occupation on stormy days.*

Now come, I will discuss the natural qualities which Jove himself has
bestowed upon bees, I will tell for what wages they, following the Curetes'
ringing noise and rattling brass, fed the king of heaven within a Cretan
cave. They alone have a community of children, and jointly own the
houses of their city, and pass their life beneath majestic laws. They
alone acknowledge a fatherland and settled home, and mindful in summer
of the winter that must come, practise hard toil, and for the common use

store up their gains. For some look to the supply of provisions, and by settled covenant labour in the fields ; part within the confines of their homes lay the tear of the narcissus, and the gluey gum from the bark of trees, to be the first foundations of the hive, next hang aloft the binding wax ; others guide forth the grown offspring, the nation's hope; others pack close a wealth of purest honey, and with clear nectar swell out wide the cells. Some there are to whose lot it has fallen to stand sentinels at the gates, and by turns they watch the watery clouds of heaven, or receive the loads of those that come to the hive, or in close array drive from the homestead the drones, a lazy herd. Hotly the work proceeds, and the stores of odorous honey are sweet with the smell of thyme. Even as when the Cyclops haste to fashion thunderbolts out of malleable masses of ore, some with bellows of ox-hide draw and blow forth the blasts, some dip in the pool the hissing brass ; beneath the anvils piled upon her Ætna groans ; they, one after another, with mighty force raise their arms in time, and turn the iron lump with biting tongs ; so, if small things may be compared with great, an inborn love of gain goads on the Attic bees, each according to his station. 'Tis the charge of the aged to guard the towns, and build the combs, and mould the curious houses ; but deep in the night the younger come back weary home, their legs smeared thick with thyme ; far and wide they feed on arbute trees, and pale-green willows, and casia, and the crocus with its ruddy gleam, and the rich gum of the lime, and dusky hyacinth flowers. All have one season to rest from toil, all one time for work ; at daybreak they throng out from the gates ; nowhere is there aught of sloth ; when at length the Evening-star reminds them to withdraw from their pasture in the fields, and return home, then they speed to their dwellings, then they recruit their bodies ; a noise begins, and they buzz around the entrances and doors. Afterwards, when at last they have settled down in their chambers, there is silence for the night, and the sleep they need possesses their weary limbs. And yet they go not very far away from their stalls, when rain is threatening, or trust the sky when east winds are coming on; but safe around their homes make watering excursions near the shelter of their city-walls, and attempt short expeditions, and often carry up pebbles in their flight, as rocking boats take in ballast, when tossed by the surge ; on these they poise themselves, as they fly through the empty clouds.

197—209. *Bees do not propagate their race, but find their young on flowers and herbs. The shortness of their life.*

You will wonder that such a custom as this is established among bees, that they never yield themselves to sexual love, nor unnerve their bodies to the languor of passion, or bring forth their offspring by the pangs of birth ; but by themselves with their mouths they gather their children from leaves and sweet plants; by themselves they provide a king, and the tiny freemen of their Rome, and fashion anew their palaces and waxen realms. Often too as they wander they bruise their wings on hard stones, nay even yield their lives beneath the load ; so passionate is their love for flowers, and their glory in engendering honey. Therefore, albeit·the limit of a narrow life await the bees themselves, (for indeed it is never prolonged beyond the seventh summer,) still the race remains immortal,

and for many a year stands firm the fortune of the house, and grandsires'
grandsires swell the pedigree.

210—218. *The reverence of bees for their king.*

Besides, neither Egypt, nor mighty Lydia, nor the Parthian tribes, nor
Median Hydaspes, so deeply reverence their king. All are of one mind,
so long as the king is safe ; when he is lost, they are sure to break their
allegiance, and themselves pull down the stores of honey they have
built, and break in pieces their latticed combs. He is the overseer of
their works, to him they look up, and all around him stand in shouting
crowds, and closely thronging form a guard about him, and oft uplift him
on their shoulders, and for him are eager to expose their bodies to the
fight, and seek to gain 'mid wounds a glorious death.

219—227. *The belief that bees are inspired with a portion of the soul of*
the universe.

Judging by these signs and guided by these instances, some have said
that bees possess a share of the divine mind, and draw the breath of
heaven ; for they think that the deity moves through all lands, and
spaces of the sea, and deep of heaven ; that hence flocks, herds, men,
every kind of wild beasts, each one at birth derive the delicate spirit of
life ; and so in course all things are restored to this fountain, and thither
return again by dissolution ; and there is no room for death, but each
flies up into the place of a star, and climbs the height of heaven.

228—250. *Directions how and when to take the honey. If the bees are to*
be saved, the empty combs must be taken out, and the hive fumigated.

Whenever you mean to unseal the narrow dwelling, and the stores of
honey hoarded in the treasure houses, first with a draught of water carefully sprinkle and wash your mouth, and hold forth a stream of piercing
smoke. Men twice collect the teeming growth of honey, there are two
seasons of harvest; so soon as the Pleiad Taygete has shewn to earth her
brilliant face, and spurned and dashed beneath her foot the Ocean river ;
or when the same star, as she flies from the constellation of the rainy Fish,
more sorrowfully descends from heaven into the winter-waves. Beyond
measure is their anger, and when hurt they breathe poison into their
bite, and fixing on the veins leave their stings hidden within, and lay
their lives down in the wound they give. But if perchance you fear the
cruel winter, and mean to spare them for longer life, and pity their
crushed spirits and broken fortunes, still who would hesitate to fumi-
gate with thyme and cut away the empty house of wax ? For oft the newt
undetected eats away the comb, and the chambers are crammed with
beetles that shun the light, and the drone that takes no part in the
work sits beside another's food ; or the savage hornet closes in fight
with arms that are not his match ; or the spider, hateful to Minerva,
hangs in the doorway her drooping toils. The more grievously wasted
they may be, the more earnestly they all will set themselves to repair the
ruins of their fallen race, and will fill up the tiers of cells, and wreathe
their granaries with the pollen of flowers.

251—280. *The symptoms of the breaking out of sickness among bees, and*
the remedies that should be used.

But if (since to bees also life has brought the calamities of us men)

their bodies chance to languish with fell disease, as you will presently be
able to ascertain by no doubtful symptoms:—from the first the sick
change their colour ; a squalid leanness gives them an unsightly look;
soon they bear forth from their dwellings the corpses of the lifeless, and
form the mournful funeral train; or the bees clinging foot to foot hang in
a cluster at their gate, or within their home stay idly in the close-shut
mansion, all listless with hunger, and torpid with numbing cold.   Then is
heard a deep-toned sound, and they buzz with long-drawn murmur, as in
the forests oft the chilling south-wind moans ; as roars with backward
waves the troubled sea ; as when shut in furnaces rages the devouring
fire.   I will advise you then to kindle at once a fire of fragrant gum, and
convey honey through channels of reed, encouraging them besides, and
inviting the sickly bees to their familiar food.   It will be beneficial also to
bruise and mix with the honey the strong-flavoured gall-nut, and dried
roses, or wine-juice made rich with repeated fires, or parched bunches of
the Psithian vine, and Attic thyme and strongly-scented centaury.   Besides, there is a flower in the meadows, for which farmers have made the
name of amellus, a plant easily found by those that seek it ; for from one
sod the root shoots up a spreading growth of leaves ; golden is the eye of
the flower, but among the petals, which are scattered plenteously around
it, a bright gleam peeps beneath a dusky violet hue : often with garlands
twined of it the altars of the gods are decked ; its taste is sharp in the
mouth ; in the close-cropped valley pastures, and near the winding
streams of Mella, it is gathered by the shepherds.   The roots of this
plant boil in fragrant wine, and in full baskets in the doorway serve
it to be their food.

281—314. *If the stock of bees has altogether failed, it may be renewed by
a method much relied upon among eastern nations. Description of
this process.*

But if a bee-master has lost all at once his whole breed, and has no
source whence he may derive the stock of a new generation, it is the time
to reveal also the famed discovery of the Arcadian master, and to tell by
what method the corrupted gore of slaughtered oxen has oft ere now
produced a stock of bees.   From its spring I will unfold the whole story,
and retrace it from its first beginning.   For where the happy people of
Pellæan Canopus dwell beside the lake made by the overflowing Nile,
and are carried round their fields in painted barges, and where the border
of Persia, land of the quiver, joins them close, and the river, that runs in
unbroken stream down from the swarthy Indians, in its rushing course
divides into seven separate mouths, and with black slime makes Egypt
green and rich, all the country round rests on this contrivance its hope of
relief.   First a place is chosen, naturally confined, and straitened for the
special purpose ; this they hem round with a narrowed roof of tiles, and
close walls, and towards the four winds introduce four windows with
slanting lights.   Then a bullock is looked for, on whose brow are beginning to curl the horns of its second year; both its nostrils and the breath
of its mouth are stopped up, in spite of all its struggles ; and then it is
slain with blows, and all its body inwardly crushed and mashed beneath
the still unbroken skin.   In this condition they leave it lying in the

closed room, and strew beneath the sides broken boughs, thyme, and fresh-plucked casia flowers. This is done when the zephyrs are beginning to sweep the waves along, before the meadows are crimsoned with new-born hues, before the twittering swallow hangs his nest in the caves. Meanwhile the moisture, growing warm in the softened bones, begins to ferment, and forms of life of wondrous kind to view, at first short of feet, next with buzzing wings as well, swarm together, and thicker and thicker stem the fleeting air ; until, as a shower shed from summer clouds, they all at once burst forth, or as arrows sped from the string, whene'er the nimble Parthians commence the prelude of the fray.

315—332. *This remedy was first given to Aristaeus, when he had lost his bees, and appealed in despair to his mother, the river-nymph Cyrene.*

What god was it, ye Muses, who worked out for us this device? Whence did this new discovery of man derive its source? Shepherd Aristæus, quitting Peneus and Tempe, when he had lost his bees, as tradition tells, by disease and famine, in sorrow stood beside the sacred fount at the farthest limit of the stream, ever complaining, and with these words addressed his parent: "Mother, mother Cyrene, thou that dost haunt the depths of this flood, why didst thou give birth to me of the illustrious line of gods, (if really, as thou allegest, Thymbræan Apollo is my sire,) to me, a being hateful to destiny? or whither is banished thy love for me? Why wert thou wont to bid me hope for heaven? Lo, even this very ornament of my mortal life, which the sedulous tending of crops and cattle has scarce worked out for me after all experiments, I abandon, while thou art my mother. Nay come, and with thine own hand tear up my wealthy groves, bear hostile fire against my stalls, and destroy my harvests, burn the plants I have sown, and wield against my vines the violent axe, if thou art seized with such deep loathing for my honour."

333—386. *His complaint reaches his mother, as she sits with the Nymphs around her in her palace beneath the river. She bids him enter the cavern, where he sees the sources of all the great rivers of the earth. Cyrene makes a banquet for her son, pours a libation to Ocean, and begins her counsel.*

Then his mother heard the sound within the chamber of the river-depth. Around her the Nymphs were plying fleeces of wool, dyed with the full deep hue of glass; Drymo, and Xantho, and Ligea, and Phyllo-doce, with long bright hair streaming down their snowy necks; Nesæe, and Spio, and Thalia, and Cymodoce, and Cydippe and yellow-haired Lycorias, the one a maiden, the other had then for the first time proved the travail of birth ; and Clio, and Beroe, both daughters of Ocean, both girt with belts of gold, both dressed in painted skins ; and Ephyre, and Opis, and Asian Deiopeia, and fleet Arethusa, her arrows laid aside at last. Among these Clymene was telling the tale of Vulcan's baffled watchfulness, and the stratagems and sweet thefts of Mars, and recounted from the age of Chaos the thousand loves of the gods. Charmed with this song, while with the spindle they roll down the soft material of their tasks, a second time the wail of Aristæus smote his mother's ear, and all were startled on their glassy seats ; but before the rest of her sisters

Arethusa looked forth, and raised her golden head above the surface of
the wave, and from a distance cries : "O thou, struck with no causeless
alarm by a lament so loud, Cyrene my sister, Aristæus himself appealing
to thee, he the chiefest object of thy care, sadly weeping stands beside
the wave of father Peneus, and calls thee cruel one by name." To her the
mother, her mind deep stricken with unwonted dread, "Come, guide him,
guide him to us," exclaims ; "'tis meet for him to tread the threshold of
gods." Withal she bids the deep stream retire far away, to make a
path, by which the footsteps of the youth might enter in : so him the
flood encompassed, rounded into the form of a mountain, and admitted
him within its huge fold, and let him pass beneath the river. And now
he went along, wondering at his mother's home and watery realms, and
the pools enclosed in caves, and the echoing woods ; and amazed at the
mighty tide of waters, he beheld in their several places all the rivers
that glide beneath the whole earth, Phasis, and Lycus, and the fountain-
head whence deep Enipeus first bursts forth, the fount whence father
Tiber springs, and whence the streams of Anio, and stony-sounding
Hypanis, and Mysian Caicus, and he, with both horns gilded on his bull-
like face, Eridanus ; no other river flows through fruitful fields to pour
forth with greater violence into the dark-blue sea. When he reached the
chamber with its hanging roof of pumice-stone, and Cyrene had learnt the
cause of the idle tears of her son, the sisters in due order present for the
hands the water of a crystal spring, and bring towels with nap smooth-
shorn ; part load the tables with the feast, and still replenish the wine-
cup ; the altars are kindled with burnt-offerings of Panchæan spice ;
and the mother says, "Take beakers of Mæonian wine, let us pour a
libation to Ocean ;" withal, she herself makes her prayer to Ocean the
father of the world, and to the sisterhood of the Nymphs, who guard
a hundred woods, a hundred streams. Thrice she bedewed with crystal
nectar the glowing fire on the shrine, thrice the flame that lurked beneath
flashed up to the highest point of the roof. Assuring his spirits with this
omen, she thus herself begins.

387—414. *Cyrene bids Aristaeus go to Pallene to consult Proteus, the
old prophet of the sea; and instructs him how to compel Proteus to
give the counsel he needs.*

In Neptune's Carpathian flood there lives a seer, azure Proteus, who
traverses the mighty main in a car drawn by fishes, and a team of two-
footed steeds. He is now revisiting the havens of Emathia and his
native Pallene ; him both we Nymphs revere, and the aged sire Nereus
himself ; for the seer knoweth all, what is, what has been, what is being
brought near, and is hereafter to arrive ; so, I ween, the will of Neptune
is, whose monstrous herds and misshapen sea-calves he tends beneath
the flood. Him, my son, you must first make prisoner with fetters, that
he may expound to you all the source of the disease, and make the
issue happy. For without force he will not give you any instructions,
and you will not be able to sway him by intreaty ; bind your prisoner
tight with hard force and fetters ; within these his stratagems will at
last be foiled and fruitless. I myself, when the sun has kindled his
scorching mid-day heat, when the herbage is parched, and the shade

is now most welcome to the herd, will guide you into the aged seer's retreat, whither when weary he retires from the waves, so that you may easily assail him when lying asleep. But when you have seized him, and hold him with your hands and chains, straightway manifold forms will seek to baffle you, and figures of wild beasts ; for he will suddenly become a bristly boar, and a fell tiger, and a scaly dragon, and a lioness with tawny neck; or will give forth a fierce roar of flames, and so strive to slip away from the fetters, or melt away into fleeting water, and so make his escape. But the more he shall turn himself into all kinds of shapes, the more do you, my son, strain tight the binding fetters, until he change his form, and become such as you saw him to be, when he closed his eyes at the beginning of his sleep.

415—452. Cyrene sheds ambrosia over her son, which inspires him with god-like vigour for his undertaking. The cave of Proteus is described, and how he is forced by Aristaeus to tell the cause of his trouble.

So she speaks, and sheds abroad an odorous stream of ambrosia, with which she steeps all the body of her son ; so a sweet effluence breathes from his smoothened hair, and vigour apt for enterprise passes into his limbs. There is a mighty cavern, scooped out in the side of a mountain, whither many a wave is driven by the wind, and parts into retired creeks, a right safe roadstead oft for mariners surprised by a storm; within, Proteus is wont to shelter himself with the barrier of a huge crag. Here the nymph stations the youth in a lurking-place away from the light ; she herself, shrouded in mists, stands at a distance apart. Now the devouring dog-star, that scorches the thirsty Indians, was blazing in the sky, and half the circle of the flaming sun was spent; the herbage was withering up, and the rays were baking down to the mud the hollow river channels, all heated in the dry throats of their stream; when Proteus came along, hastening from the waves to his accustomed cave ; about him the watery people of the vasty deep splash all around in sport the bitter spray. The sea-calves stretch themselves in sleep in different spots of the shore : the god himself, as oft upon the hills the guardian of the stall, when evening brings the steers back from pasture to their homes, and lambs make keen the hunger of wolves that hear their bleatings, sits down on a rock in the midst, and tells their number. Aristæus, so soon as he is given an opportunity to assail him, almost without allowing the aged seer to compose his weary limbs in slumber, rushes forward with loud shout, and seizes him with fetters as he lies. He, on his side, not forgetful of his own craft, transforms himself into all the wondrous shapes that are ; fire, and a dreadful beast, and a running river. But when nought of artifice finds him means of escape, vanquished he returns to his proper form, and speaks at last with human voice : " Why, who was it, most audacious of youths, that bid you visit my mansion ? Or what seek you from me ?" he says. The other in reply : " Thou knowest, Proteus, thou knowest of thyself, and none can deceive thee in aught; but cease thou to attempt to practise deceit. In obedience to injunctions of the gods I have come, to seek from thee an oracle to repair my broken fortunes." So much he spoke. In reply the seer, at last constrained by force, rolled on him eyes fierce-sparkling with grey light, and gnashing his teeth in wrath, opened his lips to speak the oracles of fate.

453—506. Proteus says that Eurydice, in trying to escape from Aris-taeus, was killed by a serpent's bite, and that the vengeance of Orpheus is the cause of the disaster that has befallen Aristaeus. The story of the descent of Orpheus to hell.

Be sure it is the anger of a deity that vexes you ; great are the crimes you expiate ; 'tis Orpheus, unhappy, though all guiltless, who wakes against you this tide of vengeance, if it be not stayed by Fate, and is filled with deep wrath for the loss of his bride. 'Twas she who, while with headlong speed she fled from you through the river, she, a maiden doomed to die, who saw not before her feet the fell hydra, the watchful tenant of the bank, in the high grass. So the sisterhood of the Dryads, her playmates, filled with their cry the mountain-tops ; the peaks of Rhodope were loud with the wail, and the heights of Pangæus, and the martial land of Rhesus, and the Getæ, and Hebrus, and Attic Orithyia. He, with his hollow shell consoling the sickness of love, sang of you, sweet bride, by himself on the desert shore ; of you when day was dawning, of you when it was passing away. He even entered the jaws of Tænarus, the deep portal of Dis, and the grove all darkened with gloomy horror, and visited the powers of the dead, and their awful king, and the hearts that know not what it is to be touched by the prayers of men. Then, stirred from the lowest abodes of Erebus, the shadowy phantoms passed along, and the spectres of them that had left the light, thick as the myriads of birds that dive into the shelter of the leaves, when night-fall, or a wintry shower, chases them from the hills,—matrons and husbands, and the bodies of valiant heroes reft of life, boys and unwedded girls, and youths laid on the funeral pile before their parents' eyes ; whom all around the black ooze and squalid reeds of Cocytus, and the marsh unlovely with its sluggish wave, enchain, and Styx confines with the nine circles of his stream. Nay, the very mansions and inmost chambers of Death were charmed, and the Furies, their locks entwined with lurid snakes ; and Cerberus held agape and fixed his triple mouth, and the blast allowed to rest Ixion's whirling wheel. And now, retracing his steps, he had surmounted every peril, and his restored Eurydice was approaching the upper air, following behind him, (for this condition Proserpine had imposed,) when sudden frenzy seized the unwary lover, pardonable indeed, were pardon known to Hell ; he paused, and looked back upon his own Eurydice, just on the confines of the day, unmindful, alas ! and vanquished in resolve. In that moment all his toil was lost, and his covenant with the ruthless monarch broken, and thrice the thunder-crash was heard to roll across the pools of Avernus. " What is this wildness of frenzy," cried she ; "what is it that has undone my hapless self, and you too, my Orpheus ? Lo, the cruel Fates a second time summon me back, and slumber shrouds my swimming eyes. And now farewell ; I am forced away, mantled round by a world of darkness, and reaching forth to you my nerveless hands, alas, not now your bride !" She ended, and in an instant vanished far away, like smoke that mingles with the fleeting air, and never saw him more, while again and again he vainly grasps at the darkness, and often essays to speak ; nor did the ferryman of Orcus any more permit him to pass the barrier of the marsh. What was he to do? Twice bereft of his bride, whither could he resort? With what lament could he melt the gods below, with what tones could he touch those powers? She, indeed, already cold, was sailing in the Stygian bark.

507—527. *The fate of Orpheus.*

They tell that he, full seven successive months, beneath a towering crag by desolate Strymon's wave, wept ever, and rolled forth these woes beneath the caverns cold, taming tigers, and charming oaks to follow his song ; so the nightingale lamenting beneath the poplar shade mourns her lost young, whom the ruthless churl has marked, and dragged the fledgelings from the nest ; but she weeps all the night, and perched upon a bough still renews her piteous strain, and fills the regions all around with sorrowful laments. No love nor any wedlock swayed his soul. Alone he used to roam the fields of northern ice, and snowy Tanais, and plains ever wedded to Rhipæan frosts, mourning his Eurydice forced away, and the fruitless gifts of Dis: by this tribute the Thracian matrons deemed themselves disdained, and so mid the sacred rites of the gods and the nightly orgies of Bacchus they tore the youth in pieces, and o'er their broad plains strewed his mangled limbs. Then too, while his native Hebrus carried down the midst of its rolling flood his head, rent from the marble neck, the voice and chilled tongue of themselves called " Eurydice, ah, hapless Eurydice !" as the spirit ebbed away; all along the stream the banks replied "Eurydice!"

528—558. *Cyrene directs her son to sacrifice four oxen to the Nymphs, and leave the carcases in the sacred grove till the morning of the ninth day: he follows her instruction, and finds the bodies of the oxen alive with bees, which collect in a swarm on the top of a tree.*

So Proteus spoke, and with a bound plunged into the depth of the flood ; and where he plunged, from beneath the eddy he dashed into circles the foaming wave. But not so Cyrene; for straightway she addressed her anxious son : " My child, you may lighten your heart of its load of gloomy care. This is the whole course of the malady ; hence it comes that the Nymphs, with whom she used to tread the measure in the lofty groves, have sent destruction on your bees. Do but humbly present your offerings, craving their forgiveness, and do homage to the gentle Napææ ; for in answer to your prayers they will grant you grace, and unbend their angry will. But first I will tell you in order what is to be the manner of your supplication. Select four choice bulls, goodly in form above the rest, which now in your herds graze upon the heights of green Lycæus, and as many heifers, whose necks have never felt the yoke. For them set up four altars near the stately shrines of the goddesses, and shed from their throats the sacrificial blood, and so leave the bodies of the steers within the leafy grove. Afterwards, when the ninth dawn has duly shown its rising beams, you are to send Lethæan poppies as funeral gifts to Orpheus, and sacrifice a black ewe, and visit again the grove. With a slaughtered heifer you must do homage to appeased

Eurydice." Without delay he straightway hastes to fulfil his mother's instructions ; he comes to the shrines, rears the appointed altars, leads forth to sacrifice four choice bulls, goodly in form above the rest, and as many heifers, whose necks have never felt the yoke. Afterwards, when the ninth dawn has duly ushered into heaven its rising beams, he sends the funeral gifts to Orpheus, and visits again the grove. Here it is that they behold a miracle, sudden and wondrous to tell, bees breaking through the melted bodies of the oxen, and buzzing throughout the hollow of the belly, and swarming tumultuously in the sides now burst, and trailing in endless clouds, and in a moment on a tree-top uniting their stream, and hanging in a cluster down from the bending boughs.

559—566. *The conclusion of the Georgics.*

So have I been singing of the tillage of fields, and the tending of herds, and of trees, while by deep Euphrates mighty Cæsar flings the bolts of war, and in his conquering course dispenses law throughout the willing nations, and even now aspires to tread the path to heaven. I, Virgil, at that time reposed in the lap of sweet Parthenope, plucking the flower of the studies of inglorious ease; I who warbled shepherds' sportive lays, and bold in youth sung of you, Tityrus, beneath the canopy of your spreading beech.

INTRODUCTION TO THE ÆNEID.

VIRGIL in the Eclogues had described pastoral life amidst the homes of the rude shepherds, but presently he came forth from the woods into the neighbouring fields of the farmers, lastly he was known as the poet of war and religion and policy. As he had before his eyes the city which was the mistress of the world, a city of marble, filled with temples and palaces, enjoying peace both from foreign wars and civil disturbances, as he beheld the closed gates of the mystical Janus, it was natural he should be filled with the desire of celebrating the divine origin of the great republic. But when he who had been enabled to give such perfection to the Georgics as to make them as finished a poem as ever had been written found his days suddenly cut short, it was natural that a poet so fastidious in the structure of his verses should direct that his unfinished poem should be committed to the flames. And yet, though the Æneid bears some marks of an unfinished production, one can hardly agree with Richter that Virgil was right to condemn his epic to the fire, if of the poem, as in the case of Hercules on mount Œta, only the mortal part of it, that is, the hero, Æneas, had been reduced to ashes, while the immortal part, the episodes and descriptions, had been preserved; still less would most readers admit the criticism of Niebuhr that the poem was from the beginning to the end a misconceived idea. For almost as much as the Homeric poems are the representation of the heroical life of Greece, almost as in Dante we have a living record of mediæval faith and opinion, so has the Æneid been justly called "The Imperial Poem," "The History of Rome," "The Mirror of the Glory of the Great Republic." The splendour of its diction and the grandeur of its rhythm fully answer to the majesty of the mighty empire. There is a stately march in the verses, which corresponds to the steady progress of the republic of Rome.

Now this, which appears to be the very heart and soul of the Æneid, the poet never forgets. Thus at the very opening of his subject he tells us that his purpose is to shew the origin "of the long glories of majestic Rome." Mention is made almost directly of the great rival city, whose harbours faced the distant mouths of the Tiber. It is to prevent the foreseen ruin of her beloved Carthage that the queen of heaven labours to keep the wanderers from their destined Italy. Jove himself in verses that are more majestic even than the average tone of the Æneid unrolls the fates, and predicts the day when after many generations peace shall be restored to the world, and the impious Fury be chained within the barred gates of war. As Troy is sinking into flames, the spirit of its hero Hector and the ghost of Creusa point to a city whose walls are to be eternal, from whose temples the celestial powers shall never depart. The Trojan prince through his many wanderings is consoled and encouraged by the voices of gods and men, which all bid him onwards go to Italy. He is supposed to institute the Actian games, which Augustus celebrated after the battle of Actium. He sojourns at the city, where love would fain keep him from glory. It is that very city whose love was to turn to deadly hate. He cannot rest there, for the mandates of heaven bid him still onwards go, lest Italy should be defrauded of her destined empire. The spirit of Dido is kindled by the thoughts of her great descendant, the mightiest enemy Rome ever had, who though he could not destroy the unconquerable city, yet brought her to the very verge of ruin. In the games on the shores of Sicily the Trojan boys go through the evolutions of a sham fight, in which is portrayed the so-called game of Troy, often celebrated by Augustus in the Circus of Rome. Æneas descends to the Elysian fields chiefly to allow the poet to describe the future glories of the long catalogue of the great men of Rome, among whom those of the house of Cæsar hold an especial place. When the hero landed at last on the shores of Italy, portents and oracles had already predicted his arrival, as of one from whom was to spring the Roman race. From heroes, both among the followers of Æneas, and among the Italians who warred against the stranger, the poet is careful to tell us were descended some of the great houses of the republic. The Trojan chief visits the seven hills, the site of Rome, and passes through rural scenes, which some day would be built over by the busy streets and splendid temples of the imperial city. On the divine shield of Æneas are represented not the Homeric battles, fields, vineyards, rustic dances, but the events of Roman history; and in the centre the battle of Actium and the triumph of Augustus, so that the unconscious hero bears on his shoulder the fame and fortunes of his descendants. At the end of a poem in which due honour is given to Italian valour, Juno, the unrelenting enemy of Troy, consents to cease from further persecution on receiving the promise that the name of Troy is to perish, that Latium is still to be Latium, "and Rome's immortal majesty remain."

Now perhaps it may only be a fancy that finds Cleopatra in Dido, Antony in Turnus, Agrippa in Achates; that sees, in Sinon and the marsh, Marius hiding himself in the morass of Minturnæ; that compares Drances with Cicero, and Priam's death with the murder of Pompey the Great: but Turnus on the ramparts of the camp is the representation taken from Ennius of Cocles on the bridge, for Ennius' Annals was a national poem, even as the Æneid was; Minos in the infernal regions is the Roman prætor or judge; the battles and camps of the Æneid are Roman; Virgil cares not for anachronisms, he will not tie himself down to the Homeric form; in this national poem we have the Roman banquet, the Roman funeral, the Roman augury, the Roman ambassadors; throughout it all is the Roman feeling, the perseverance, the stateliness, the attention to details, the vigour and dulness that alike marked the Roman. This is especially the case in the religious part of the poem. The author of the *Christian Year* has said that, next to Sophocles, Virgil is the most religious of the poets of heathenism. The word religious is ambiguous, and it would be difficult to agree with this opinion, if the word religious is taken in its usual sense. But if by religion is meant a belief in fate, then it is quite true that the Æneid is the epic of destiny. We might take as a motto for it Virgil's own line thus rendered by Dryden:

> *But ah ! what use of valour can be made,*
> *When heaven's propitious powers refuse their aid?*

No Stoic dissertation can set forth the power of fate more determinately. Neither Juno, nor Carthage, nor love, nor sword, nor fire, nor sea, nor the fears of his own comrades, can stop the course of fate. The vigorous Turnus contends in vain against destiny :

> *The foes that him affright are heaven and Jove.*

The Trojan prince is careful to appease the gods, he is observant of every detail and formula of religion, he is quick to catch the meaning of heaven from the omens of words, from the flight of birds, from the entrails of victims. In this also he is set forth as a type of the true Roman.

Virgil has lately been called "an untruthful poet, one who walks by lamplight, one who does not sing from the heart, nor to the heart." If Virgil's object was to sing of the foundation of the Roman empire, and by an anachronism, which he is at no pains to conceal, to give to the characters of his epic the Roman form and thought, then he has done this most accurately and truthfully. Virgil commented on by Servius is full of trustworthy information to the antiquarian and historian. Neither is it true to say that "the first thought of Virgil was the emperor and court around the throne, the second the elaboration of his verse." It is of course true that the insipid and unreal character of Æneas is the prime fault of the poem, and that Æneas is modelled on the character of Augustus. But Augustus may reasonably have appeared to the poet not merely as an emperor, nor had Augustus a court in the sense which the word court conveys to modern ears. Virgil may have reasonably regarded Augustus as the restorer of peace and order to the distracted republic, and his poem may have been toned throughout, not "to a spirit of courtier-like adulation," but to a love of national glory. Homer and Virgil were both national poets. They both represent the character of the nation to which they belong. But the Greek nature was buoyant, energetic, lively, diversified; the Roman was staid, persevering, monotonous; hence the difference in the two poets, hence no doubt there is a dulness in nearly all the characters of the Æneid. The same will apply to the supernatural part of the two poems. In the Iliad the gods are capricious, passionate, noisy, tumultuous; their meetings are like the excited assemblies of the populace of Greece in the agoræ of their cities; in the Æneid the gods are more like the senators of Rome; they deliberate with earnestness and strong feeling, at times with angry vehemence, and yet with solemnity and grandeur, as those to whom was committed the government of a great empire. In the Iliad individual feeling is far better expressed; in the Æneid the power of a community is more clearly portrayed.

But the Æneid is free from the great fault of the Iliad, which is unfairness to the Trojans. For Virgil has a feeling for the Trojan settler, and for the Italian native ; for it is the union of these two races which will one day make a people superior in arms and religious observances to any other nation. That there is no adulation in Virgil's poem we cannot say; nor can we deny that if Augustus had been other than what he was, the Æneid might have been in part free from its greatest fault ; but that

"Augustus was dearer to Virgil than his country," is what we have no right to say. Again that Virgil elaborated his verse is plain enough in itself, and is expressly mentioned by ancient writers; sometimes this is over-done, frequently there is an exaggeration of expression, which in part spoils the effect, and now and then almost borders on the ridiculous; but it is a great thing to have finish of style, it is a great point that the rhythm on the whole should so well express the thought. There is in Virgil—unless the great majority of those who have loved his writings be wrong—a continued appeal to the heart; he does sing from the heart and to the heart; there is in him a great tenderness of feeling, something better and more charming than mere Roman virtue or morality; that he excels in pathos, as Homer in sublimity, is the old opinion; and it is surely the right one. This pathos is given at times by a single epithet, by a slight touch, with graceful art by an indirect allusion; this tenderness is more striking as contrasted with the stern Roman character, and with the stately majesty of the verse; the poet never becomes affected or sentimental; he hardly ever offends against good taste; he knows where to stop; he is excellent in his silence as well as in his speech; Virgil, as Wordsworth says, is a great master of language, but no one can really be a master of language unless he be also a master of thought, of which language is the expression. Many are the faults of the Æneid; there is hardly any great poem that has so many; it wants the unity of the Iliad and the Odyssey; sometimes it is too long, then again too short; it is often languid and deficient in fire; scarcely any of the characters in it are happily drawn; the latter six books are inferior to the first six, a fault which it has in common with *Paradise Lost*, but one from which the Iliad is quite free, for it gathers force as it goes on; the Æneid has more faults than the epic of Tasso, though fewer than the Lusiad of Camoens. But if it be true that the faults of this poem be so great, great indeed must be the merits which, in spite of these faults, have made it the study and delight of so many centuries, gaining for it an admiration which some years ago seemed to be on the decline, but which is now perhaps, though more discriminating, yet almost as high as ever. From the Æneid there are more familiar quotations than from the Georgics; though the Georgics are far more faultless, yet particular passages of the Æneid contain finer poetry. Descriptions of scenery and rural life are more touching when interspersed with the events of war and contrasted with sorrow and death, than when they form the direct part of the poem. In the latter books of the Æneid, though on the whole much inferior to the earlier ones, these allusions are more affecting; and when the poet has landed his hero on the shores of Italy, it almost seems as if the poet himself gladly returned to the description of the woods and rivers, and of the customs and manners of his native land; as if once more he was not so much the imperial poet of the republic, as the bard who wandered amidst the scenery of his childhood.

BOOK I.

1—11. THE INTRODUCTION. *The Invocation of the Muse.*

ARMS and the man I sing, who was the first to come from the Trojan shore to Italy and the Lavinian coasts, the exile of fate: many were his wanderings by land, much was he tossed over the deep by the constraint of the heavenly Powers, through the unforgiving wrath of cruel Juno; many too in war were his sufferings, whilst he was founding the city, and bringing his gods into Latium; whence came the Latin race, and the Alban fathers, and the walls of lofty Rome.

O Muse, relate to me the causes, tell me, in what had her will been offended, or what moved her indignation, that she, the queen of heaven, forced a man so renowned for piety, through the course of so many mishaps, to meet with so many toils. Can heavenly minds feel such resentment?

12—33. *The reason of Juno's unrelenting hatred against the race of Troy.*

There was an ancient city, colonists from Tyre possessed it, Carthage by name, confronting in the far distance Italy, and the mouths of the river Tiber, rich in wealth, rugged in the spirit of war: this town Juno is said to have cherished more than any other land, and to have preferred it even to Samos; here were her arms, here her chariot; that this should be the ruling city of the world, would the fates perchance allow it, even in those early days did the goddess intend, and foster the purpose in her heart. Yet she feared, for she had heard that a race was to be derived from Trojan blood, destined in days to come to overthrow the towers of the Tyrian settlers; hence she had heard should come a people ruling far and wide, glorious in war, who would destroy the empire of Africa; that thus the fates were moving the cycle of events. The child of Saturn, dreading this, remembering too the old wars which she had been the foremost of the gods to wage against Troy in the cause of her beloved Argos: not yet also had the cause of her wrath, and her fierce resentment faded from her soul: deep stored in her heart remains the judgment of Paris, and the wrong done to her slighted beauty, and the hated race, and the honours bestowed on the ravished Ganymede. By these thoughts fired with rage to crown her fear, she ever drove far from Latium, and tossed o'er the whole main the Trojans, the remnant left by the Greeks and pitiless Achilles; so during many a year wanderers were they, pursued by the fates o'er every sea. So vast a work it was to found the Roman race.

34—49. *Juno complains that she alone of the heavenly beings is powerless against a mortal man.*

Scarcely out of sight of the land of Sicily were they speeding their sails out to sea, in high spirits were they, as they dashed up the foaming brine with their brazen keels; when Juno nursing an eternal wound within her breast, thus to herself began: "What, am I to desist from my purpose, as one defeated, and am I unable to turn back from Italy the king of the Trojans! The fates, I suppose, forbid me. Why, could Pallas burn the fleet of the Greeks, and drown the mariners

in the deep sea, all for the guilt and frenzy of one man, Ajax son of
Oïleus? With her own hands did she hurl Jove's rushing lightning
from the clouds, she scattered their ships, she lashed up the seas with the
winds; as he gasped out flames from his transfixed breast, she caught
him in the whirlwind, and impaled him on a jagged rock: but I, who tread
with stately pace, the queen of heaven, the sister-wife of Jove, I with one
single nation have warred for many a year. And will any one then
worship the divinity of Juno any longer, or humbly place on her altars
the homage of sacrifice?"

*50—80. The description of the cave of Æolus. Juno begs a boon of
the god of the winds. He professes his willingness to do as the queen
bids him.*

As the goddess in her burning soul still pondered thoughts like these,
she reached Æolia, the home of storms, a region big with blustering
blasts. Here king Æolus in his dreary cavern restrains under his command the struggling winds and the roaring storms, and curbs them with
the bonds of his prison-house. Chafing thereat, his subjects, whilst the
mountain murmurs mightily, rage about the bars of the dungeon: on
his lofty citadel sits Æolus, his sceptre in his hand, he tames their
passions, and controls their rage; did he not, then straightway sea and
land, and heaven's vault they would bear along in their rushing career,
and sweep them all through the breezy air. But the almighty Father
put them aside in dark dens, through dread of this, and on the top above
he placed the mass of mountains high, and appointed them such a king,
as knew how, even as he was bidden, by fixed laws either to tighten or
loosen the reins of power. To him then Juno in suppliant guise thus
addressed these words: "Æolus, (for thee the father of gods and king
of men has appointed both to calm the waves, and again to lift them
with the wind,) a nation, whom I hate, sails o'er the Tuscan sea; all
Ilium and their conquered gods to Italy they bear; strike strength into
the winds, sink and o'erwhelm their ships, or drive them far apart, and
scatter their bodies o'er the sea. I have twice seven nymphs of surpassing beauty; of all these Deiopea is fairest in form; her will I unite
to thee in sure wedlock, and grant her to thee as thy wife for ever, that
in return for such a favour as this, she may pass all her years with thee,
and make thee the father of a lovely race." Æolus says thus in reply:
"Thy work, O queen, is to discover what thou choosest; it is my duty
with zeal to perform what thou dost command. Thy gift to me is all
this kingdom which I have, and this my sceptre, thou makest Jove my
friend, thou grantest me a seat at the feast of the gods, and causest
me to be lord of storms and tempests."

*81—123. A storm bursts forth. Æneas laments that he has not fallen
by a nobler death beneath the walls of Troy. His fleet is scattered.
One ship sinks before the eyes of the prince.*

He spoke, and turned the point of his spear, and pushed on its side the
hollow mountain; and lo! the winds, as though in formed line, rush
forth where a passage is allowed them, and blow with a blast across the
world. In an instant they swoop upon the sea, and East, and South,
and gusty South-west together lash up the whole main from its lowest

depths, and roll to the shore huge billows. Then follow the shouts of the sailors, and the creaking of the cables. Suddenly the clouds rob the eyes of the Trojans of sky and light together ; sable night broods o'er the deep. The poles thunder, and the firmament glitters with frequent flashes, and all nature threatens the mariners with instant death. Straightway the limbs of Æneas are relaxed with a chilling horror; he groans, and raising his clasped hands to the stars, he utters words like these : " O blessed, ever blessed they, whose lot it was before their sires' eyes beneath Troy's lofty walls to die ! O bravest of the Grecian race, son of Tydeus ! why could not I fall on the plains of Ilium, and breathe out my life beneath your hand ? There lies valiant Hector slain by the spear of Æacides, there was slain stout Sarpedon, there Simois bore swiftly beneath his stream and rolled along so many shields and helmets and bodies of the brave."

As he uttered such complaints, roaring from the North came a squall, striking the sail full, lifting the waves to heaven. The oars are shivered, then the prow swings round, exposed to the waves is the side of the ship ; close in a mass comes on it a precipitous mountain-billow. Some of the ships hang on the crest of the waves ; beneath others the yawning water lays bare the ground between the ridges of the sea ; the surging flood rages mingled with sand. Three galleys the South wind has caught, and whirls towards the reefs ; the Italians call these rocks, that stand in the midst of the waves, "The Altars," a huge chine that overtops the sea; three ships the East wind forces into the shallows and quicksands, (a piteous sight,) and dashes them into the shoals, and shuts them in with a bank of sand. One galley, in which sailed the Lycians, and trusty Orontes, before the chieftain's eyes a mighty sea strikes from above on the stern ; forth is dashed out and rolled into the sea the helmsman; whilst thrice in the same place the billow whirls the ship, and drives it round and round, and the devouring eddy swallows it in the sea. Scattered here and there they are seen floating in the wide water ; then are seen the arms of the men, planks, and Trojan wealth, strewed over the waves. And now the storm had mastered the stout ship of Ilioneus, and that of brave Achates, and that in which sailed Abas, and that in which was aged Aletes ; loosed were the fastenings of the ribs of the vessels, and they all admit the deadly deluge, and gape with many a chink.

124—156. *Neptune calms the storm. He sends back the winds to their prison-house. Nature is once more tranquil according to the will of the god.*

Meanwhile Neptune perceived that the deep was embroiled with dreadful roar, and that a storm had been let loose, and that the still water beneath was broken up from its lowest pools; greatly was his wrath stirred at the sight, and looking out o'er the main, he raised his head in serene majesty over the summit of the waves. He sees the fleet of Æneas dispersed o'er the whole sea, the Trojans o'erwhelmed by the billows and the wreck of heaven. Full well he discerned the devices and passions of his sister Juno. Eurus and Zephyr he summons to him, then thus he speaks: " Can such confidence in your race possess you, ye winds, that ye have come to this, to dare to mingle earth with heaven without my sanction, and to raise such mountains on the main? Whom I—but 'tis better far to calm the disturbed waves.   Hereafter with far different punishment shall ye atone for sins against me.   Tarry not, but fly, and tell my message to your king; not to him was given the lordship of the sea nor the dread trident, but to me by lot.   He holds the savage rocks, the homes of you winds, O Eurus; in that hall let Æolus bluster, there let him reign, when he has closed the dungeon of the winds."

So speaks the god, and quicker than he speaks he smooths the swelling seas, and scatters the collected clouds, and restores the day.   Cymothoe and Triton together lend their help, and push the ships off the jagged rocks; he himself heaves them with his trident, and opes the vast quick-sands, and calms the water's surface; and lightly with his wheels glides o'er the crests of the waves.   As oft we see, when in a great people arises suddenly a tumult, and the ignoble crowd rage angrily; presently brands and stones begin to fly; their fury finds them arms; but presently, if they chance to see a man dignified by piety and virtues, they are silent and stand by with listening ears; he guides their souls by his words, and soothes their passions.   Thus all at once is hushed the roaring of the sea, as soon as the Father looking out o'er its surface, and borne onwards through the cloudless sky, guides his steeds, and as he flies, loosens the reins to speed his gliding car.

157—179. The weary Trojans come to a land-locked harbour. Seven ships alone are collected.

The toil-worn crew of Æneas strive to reach in straight course the nearest shore, and turn towards the coast of Africa.   Within a long recess there is a spot; an island forms a harbour by its jutting sides, whereby each wave coming from the main is broken and divides, as it enters the deep creeks.   On either side are huge rocks, and twin cliffs which tower frowning towards the sky, beneath whose peaks the water's surface far and wide lies safe and still; behind, a canopy of woods with quivering tops, and a dark grove with tangled shades overhangs the scene.   Full in front beneath is a cave with pendent rocks; within is fresh water, and seats of natural stone; this is the home of the Nymphs. Here there is no need of cables to hold the weary ships, no anchor fastens them with hooked bite.   In this bay Æneas takes refuge with seven ships collected out of his whole fleet: and with an earnest longing for the land the Trojans come on shore, and win the welcome sand, and stretch their limbs drenched with brine on the beach.   And first Achates struck a spark out of a flint, and nursed the fire in leaves, and put around dry fodder, and quickly fanned the flame into a blaze in the touchwood.   Then they bring forth the gifts of Ceres, though damaged by the water, and the implements of Ceres, weary with their misfortunes; yet they prepare to parch the rescued corn with the fire, and bruise it with a stone.

180—222. The Trojan prince mounts a rock. He shoots seven deer. He consoles his disheartened comrades. They refresh their bodies with food, their souls with conversation.

Meanwhile Æneas climbs a rock, to gain a far-extending view over the open sea, in hopes of seeing somewhere the tempest-tossed ships of

Antheus, and the Phrygian gallies; or Capys' vessel, or the arms of
Caicus in the high-raised stern. Vessel in sight was there none: he
sees before him three stags straying on the shore; they are followed by
their whole herd behind, and the winding line feeds along the valleys.
Here he stopped, and seized in his hand the bow and swift arrows,
the weapons carried by trusty Achates; he lays low the leaders themselves first, who bore on high their tall heads with branching antlers,
and with his arrows drives them before him, and throws into confusion
all the crowding throng of deer amid the leafy woods. And he ceases
not, till he stretches on the ground seven huge stags, a successful hunter,
one for each ship. Then he returns to his harbour, and distributes
them among all his comrades. Next he gives out the wine, with which
generous Acestes had laden the casks on the Sicilian shore, the hero's
gift to the departing mariners; then with these words he soothes their
sorrowing hearts:

"My comrades, ye who know we are not unversed in ill ere now, ye
who have endured worse things than these; God will grant an end even
to this. You drew near Scylla's raging bounds, and the cliffs whose
caverns roar; you too by experience know the rocks of the Cyclops:
recall your spirits, and dismiss sad fear; perchance the day will come,
when the memory even of this will be a pleasure. Through various
mishaps, through sundry risks and chances, our course is to Latium;
there the fates point to quiet resting-places; there heaven allows that
the kingdom of Troy once more shall rise. Endure hardness, and
reserve yourselves for better days!"

Such were his words: sick at heart with a weight of care, hope in his
looks he feigns, deep in his soul his grief he stifles. They busy themselves about the quarry for the coming feast: some strip the skins off the
ribs, and lay the carcases bare; others cut them up, and fix them
quivering on the spits; others set caldrons on the shore, and put fire
beneath. Then with food they recruit their strength, and, stretched
along the grass, fill themselves with good old wine and rich venison.
When hunger was appeased by their feast, and the banquet o'er, with
many words they express their regret for the friends they have lost,
wavering between fear and hope, should they believe them still alive, or
suffering their final doom, and no longer able to hear the voice that
calls on them. Above the rest does pious Æneas mourn in his soul
the fate of brave Orontes, then that of Amycus, and the cruel lot of
Lycus, and valiant Gyas and valiant Cloanthus.

223—253. *In heaven Venus complains to her father Jove of promises
unfulfilled and the wanderings and calamities of a pious race.*

Now this was ended, when Jove from the summit of the sky
looked down on the sea filled with flying sails, and the level lands,
and the shores, and the broad expanse of nations, and as he gazed, he
took his stand on the peak of heaven, and rested his eyes on the realms
of Africa. And there, as he revolved such cares within his soul, Venus
sadder than was her wont, with her bright eyes bathed in tears, addressed
him thus: "Oh thou who rulest with eternal sway the world of men and
gods, and frightest them with thy thunders, what sin so heinous can my

son Æneas, or the Trojans have committed against thee? many are
the deadly losses they have suffered; yet still against them the whole
universe is closed on account of Italy. And yet surely I had thy word,
that from this race should come the Romans, in the cycle of years; yes,
from this race, even from the restored line of Teucer, should come rulers
to hold sea and land in universal sway; what change of mind now alters
thy will, O Father? With this promise I for my part oft consoled myself
for the fall of Troy, and its sad ruin, as I balanced the fates in opposing
scales. But now the same fortune persecutes these men already harassed
by many a woe. Mighty monarch, what end dost thou set to these
toils? Antenor, escaping from the very heart of the Greeks, has been
able to penetrate even to the bays of Illyria, and safely to pass beyond
the inmost realms of the Liburnians, and the fountain of the Timavus;
whence through nine sources, roaring like a mighty mountain, it bursts
forth broad as the sea, overflowing the fields with its waters that sound
like the deep main. Yet here he founded the town of Padua, and gave
his Trojans a settled home, and his name to the nation, and set up
the arms of Ilium; now reposing in perfect peace he rests from his toils.
But we thine own offspring, to whom thou promisest heaven's citadel,
have lost our ships, (oh cruel lot!) and are abandoned to gratify the
wrath of one goddess, and are kept far from the Italian shores. Is this
the reward of piety? is this the way thou restorest us to our empire?"

254—296. *Jupiter briefly unrolls the fates from the war of Æneas in
Italy to the happy age of Augustus Caesar, when wars shall cease,
and the gates of Janus be closed.*

On her smiled the sire of men and gods with that look with which
he calms the sky and storms, and gently pressed his daughter's lips;
then thus he speaks: "Spare thy fears, Lady of Cythera; fixed and
immovable are the fates of thy children according to thy desire: thou
shalt behold the city and promised walls of Lavinium; aloft shalt
thou bear to the starry sky the noble Æneas: my purpose altereth
not. Know then that he—for I will declare the fates, since this is
the care that torments thee, and will unroll the latter pages of
mysterious destiny—he shall wage a mighty war in Italy, and crush
the warlike tribes, and impose laws on the nations, and build walls,
until the third summer sees him reigning in Latium, and the third
winter season is passed since the conquest of the Rutulians. But the
boy Ascanius, now surnamed Iulus—Ilus was his name, so long as
Ilium stood in regal power—shall complete a reign of thirty full years
in the cycle of months, and transfer his rule from its seat at Lavinium,
and strongly fortify Alba Longa. Here, from this time forth for three
hundred entire years, the throne shall be filled by the race akin to
Hector. till the priestess-queen Ilia shall bear to Mars her twins.
Then Romulus, rejoicing in his helmet of the tawny skin of his nurse,
shall succeed to the government of the race, and found the walls of
Mavors, and call the people Romans from his own name. To them
no bounds of realm, no term of years I set; an endless empire I
appoint them. Nay fierce Juno, who now keeps sea, earth, heaven in
turmoil through her fear, will change her purpose to a better course,

will unite with me and cherish the Romans, as lords of the world,
the nation that wears the toga. Such is my pleasure. As ages glide
along, a time will come, when the house of Assaracus will oppress
in bondage Phthia and glorious Mycenæ, and lord it over conquered
Argos. There shall be born one, Trojan in his noble origin, Cæsar,
so great as to bound his empire by the ocean, his renown by the
stars, of the Julian house, a name descended from great Iulus. The
day will come when thou shalt welcome him in heaven, laden with
the spoils of the East, and shall put away thy fears; he too shall be invoked with vows. Then shall the rough age lay aside wars, and soften;
ancient Honour and Vesta, Quirinus united with his brother Remus
shall give forth laws; the dread gates of war shall be closed with
fast iron bars; within shall unnatural Fury, seated on savage arms,
and with hands bound behind by a hundred brazen knots, roar dreadfully with blood-stained mouth."

297—304. *Mercury is sent down to Carthage to inspire queen Dido with*
kindly feelings towards the wanderers.

He spoke, and sends Maia's son down from on high, that the
lands and newly founded city of Carthage may be open to welcome
the Trojans, lest Dido, ignorant of fate's behest, drive them from her
coasts. The god flies through the world of air, steering his course with
the oarage of his wings, and swiftly alights on the shores of Africa.
Soon he does what he is bid, and the Carthaginians lay aside their
fierce feelings; for so God wills; most of all does the queen receive a
peaceful soul towards the Trojans, and a kindly mind.

305—334. *Æneas in a forest meets his mother, disguised as a huntress.*
The pious prince knows the stranger is more than mortal.

But pious Æneas throughout the night pondered many a thought, and
as soon as the genial light of day was granted, determined forth to go,
and explore the strange lands, to find what coasts the wind had driven
him to, who possessed it, men or beasts, (for he sees all uncultivated,)
and then to carry back to his comrades the report of his search. Under
a vault of woods, and beneath a hollow rock, he hides his fleet, shut in
on every side by the tangled darkness of trees; he himself goes forth,
Achates alone attends him, in his hand he brandishes two javelin shafts
pointed with broad steel. He met his mother in the midst of the forest;
she had the look and dress of a virgin, and wore the arms of a virgin,
either of Sparta, or such an one as Thracian Harpalyce, when she tires
her steeds, and outstrips in her course the swift Hebrus. For on her
shoulders, in huntress' guise, she had slung a light bow, her tresses she
let the winds play with; bare was her knee, in a knot she had gathered
the flowing folds of her robe. Before they spake, she said, "Ho, young
men, tell me if perchance you have seen one of my sisters wandering
here, girt with a quiver and the skin of a dappled lynx, or with cries
pursuing close the flight of a foaming boar."

Thus spake Venus, and thus Venus' son began in answer: "None of
thy sisters have been heard of or seen by me, oh! by what name shall
I call thee,—virgin? for thy countenance is not mortal, and the tones of
thy voice are more than human: ah, thou art a goddess surely; but

whether Phœbus' sister, or one of the race of Nymphs, I know not ; give
us thy grace, and whoever thou art, lighten our toils, and instruct us
under what climate of heaven we are, to what regions of the world we
have been tempest-tossed ; ignorant of the people and the country, we
are wanderers, driven hither by the blasts and mighty billows. Many
a victim shall fall by my hand in front of thy altars."

335—371. *Venus disclaims the honour. She tells him the tale of Dido's
wrongs, and her flight, and of her new city and kingdom. She in
. return asks who he is.*

Then said Venus : " I confess I do not claim such honours as these.
With the maidens of·Tyre it is the custom to wear a quiver, and to bind
high on our legs a purple buskin. You see a Punic kingdom, people of
Tyre, a city of Agenor's line ; but the country is African, a race that it is
hard to encounter in war. Dido holds sway here, she came from the
city of Tyre, she fled from her brother. Long is the tale of her wrong,
long are its details, but I will follow the chief events of the history. She
had a husband, by name Sychæus, who was the richest owner of land in
all Phœnicia ; strong was the passion with which hapless Dido loved him ;
to him her father had betrothed the maiden, and united her in the
first auspices of wedlock. But the kingly power of Tyre was held by
Pygmalion, a man in wickedness more savage than all others. Between
these two there came a furious strife. The king with stealthy sword
slays Sychæus unawares by impious craft before the altar, for he was
blinded by the love of gold, and recked nought of his sister's affection ;
and long hid the deed, and with many a crafty pretence, and idle hopes
mocked the loving wife sick at heart. But unsummoned came in her
dreams the spectre of her unburied husband ; he lifted up his countenance
wan in wondrous-wise, and revealed the cruel altar, and showed his
own breast transfixed with the steel, and laid bare all the dark guilt
of the house ; then counsels her to hasten her flight, and to go forth
from her country, and unburies from the earth ancient treasure to help
her on her way, an untold mass of silver and gold. Roused by these
revelations Dido prepared to fly, and collected comrades. There flock
together those who felt towards the tyrant either cruel hatred or keen
fear : ships by chance stood ready ; these they seize and load with gold ;
the wealth of avaricious Pygmalion is borne over the deep main ; a
woman led the exploit. So they reached the place where you will now
behold mighty walls and the rising towers of the new town of Carthage ;
and they bought a plot of ground named Byrsa from the event, for they
were to have as much as they could enclose with a bull's hide. But you,
whoever are you, or from what coasts are you come, or whither do you
hold your course ? " As she asked the questions, he sighed, and drew his
voice deep from his breast.

372—386. *Very briefly the son of Venus tells his fortune.*

" O goddess, if I were to go back to the first beginning, and tell the
tale throughout, and thou hadst leisure to hear the story of our disasters,
before I had ended, Vesper would close Olympus, and lay the day to rest.
From ancient Troy, (perchance the Trojan name has reached your ears.)
over distant seas have we been driven ; by one of its random chances

the storm has brought us to the African coast. I am the pious Æneas, who rescued from the foe my household gods, and in my fleet carry them with me; I am known by fame above the sky. Italy I seek, my true fatherland; my race is drawn from sovereign Jove. With twenty ships I embarked on the Phrygian main, my goddess-mother pointed out the way; given to me were the fates that I followed. Scarce seven ships, and they shattered by waves and wind, now remain; I myself, unknown, in want, am a wanderer over the deserts of Africa, an exile from Europe and Asia." Venus would allow him to complain no more, but broke in with her speech into the midst of the story of his sorrows.

387—417. The goddess draws a happy omen from augury. As she disappears, she is revealed to him in glory. He goes onwards enshrouded in a mist.

"Whoe'er you are, I cannot believe that you breathe the air of life, an object of hatred to the heavenly Powers, seeing that you are come to this Tyrian town. Only go on in your way, and proceed hence to the palace of the queen. For see, I announce to you the return of your comrades, and the recovery of your fleet, now borne into a safe harbour by the change of wind, unless my parents vainly professed the art when they taught me augury. Behold those twelve swans in joyful line, whom just now Jove's bird stooping from the region of the sky threw into confusion in the open firmament, but now they seem in a long extended row either to be choosing, or having chosen to be gazing downwards on their ground. As they returning sport with flapping wings, and gird the pole with their circling flock, and give forth their song; even so your ships, and your youthful comrades either are safe in the port, or are just entering its mouth with full sail. Do but onwards go, and as the path leads you, so guide your steps."

She spake, and as she turned to go, her rosy neck shone forth in beauty, and her ambrosial locks breathed from her head celestial fragrance; down to her feet at once flowed her robe; and by her gait was revealed the true goddess. He recognized his mother, and followed her as she fled with these words: "Why art thou also cruel, and why so often mockest thou thy son with empty phantoms? Why am I not allowed to unite hand with hand, and hear and reply in real words?" Thus he upbraids her, and walks onwards to the walls. But Venus, as they went, shrouded them with a dark cloud, and the goddess threw around them a thick cloak of mists, that no one might see or touch them, or trouble them with delays, or ask the reason why they came. She herself in mid air departs to Paphos, and glad of heart revisits her own shrines, where is a temple in her honour, and where a hundred altars smoke with Sabæan frankincense, breathing with the fragrance of garlands ever fresh.

418—440. Description of the building of Carthage. The Carthaginians are busy as bees. The prince is invisible.

Meanwhile they hastened on the way where the path guides them. Presently they mounted a hill, which hangs steep over the city, and looks down from its summit on the opposite towers. Æneas admires the mass of buildings, that lately were but Numidian huts; he wonders at the gates and the din, and the paved streets. Eagerly the Tyrians ply their

work; some carry on the walls and build a massive citadel, and with their
hands roll up stones; part choose the site for houses, and mark it out
with a furrow. They appoint laws, and choose magistrates and a reverend
senate. Here some are digging a harbour; whilst there others are laying
the deep foundations of a theatre, and hewing from the quarries huge
columns, the tall ornaments of a stage that will be there. As when in
early summer o'er the flowery meads beneath the sun the busy bees are
at work, when forth they lead the full-grown young of their race, or when
they pack their liquid honey, and fill their cells full of sweet nectar, or
receive the burdens of those that come in, or form a martial line, and
drive forth from their hive the drones, a lazy tribe; hotly glows the work,
and the sweet-scented honey is fragrant with thyme. "Happy people,"
says Æneas, "your walls already rise;" and he gazes up at the pinnacles of
the city. On he goes shrouded by a mist, (miraculous to relate,) passing
through the midst, and mingles with the throng, unseen by all.

441—493. *In the centre of the city is a grove, wherein is a temple, and on
its walls pictures of the wars of Troy. Æneas is comforted at the sight.*

In the centre of the city grew a holy grove, luxuriant in foliage, in
which place first the Phœnicians, who had been tossed by the waves and
whirlwind, dug up an omen, pointed out to them by queen Juno, the head
of a spirited steed; for by this sign it was revealed that the nation would
be glorious in war, and gain their substance easily through many an age.
Here to Juno's honour Sidonian Dido was raising a great temple,
enriched with gifts, consecrated by a divine presence: bronze was the
threshold to which the steps ascended, with bronze were the beams
fastened, the hinge creaked on doors of bronze. It was in this grove
first that an unlooked-for sight came before the stranger and calmed his
fears; it was here first that Æneas ventured to hope for deliverance, and
despaired less of his shattered fortunes. For whilst he surveys each
object in the great temple, as he waits for the queen, whilst he thinks with
wonder of the fortune of the city, and admires and compares the various
workmanship of the artists, and the labour of their hands, he beholds the
battles of Troy in all their details, the son of Atreus, and Priam, and
Achilles fierce to friend and foe alike. He stopped at the sight, and with
tears said: "What place, Achates, what country in the world is not by
this time full of our disasters? See there is Priam; even here virtue has
its due reward, tears are shed for misfortune, and mortal woes move
the heart. Away with your fears; this fame of us will bring you some
deliverance." So he speaks, and feeds his soul on the unreal picture,
groaning oft, whilst he bedews his cheeks with floods of tears. For he saw
represented there, how warring round Troy in one part the Greeks were
flying, the Trojan youth pressed them hard; in another part fled the
Phrygians; Achilles with plumed helmet pursued them close in his
chariot. In the next picture he sees, with eyes filled with tears, the tents
of Rhesus whose canvas was white as snow, these were made defenceless
by their first sleep, and the son of Tydeus, covered with the blood of a
great slaughter, was pictured as making havoc of them, and driving off
the fiery steeds to the Grecian camp, before they had tasted the fodder
of Troy, or drank the streams of Xanthus. In another picture might be

seen Troilus flying ; he had lost his arms, unlucky boy, a poor match to
meet Achilles ; he is borne along by his horses, and lying on his back
clings to the empty car, yet still he holds the reins ; his neck and locks
are trailed along the ground, and the dust is marked with his inverted
spear. Meanwhile to the temple of unfriendly Pallas were seen going the
matrons of Ilium with dishevelled hair, and bearing the sacred robe, in
suppliant guise and sad, beating their breasts with their hands: the
goddess with averted look seemed to keep her face fixed on the ground.
Thrice round Ilium's walls had Achilles dragged Hector, and now he was
selling his lifeless body for gold.   Then indeed deep was the sigh the
chieftain gave from forth his heart, as he beheld the spoils and chariot,
and the body too of his friend, and Priam holding up his unarmed hands.
He knew himself too mingling in fray with the Achæan chiefs, and the
troops of the dawn, and the armour of swarthy Memnon.   Penthesilea
raging in the fight leads the bands of the Amazons armed with crescent
shields, glowing with courage in the midst of thousands ; her breast is
exposed, she is girt with a golden belt, a female warrior, a maiden who
dares to engage in battle with men.

494—519. *While he gazes, the queen comes with her retinue.   Then are*
introduced his lost comrades.

While these sights seem so wondrous to Dardan Æneas, while he stands
as one stupefied, and remains fixed in continuous gaze, the queen Dido,
surpassing in beauty, comes in state to the temple, attended by a great
company of youths.   As on the banks of Eurotas or over the ridges of
Cynthus Diana leads her dances, a thousand mountain-Nymphs follow
her and throng around ; she wears her quiver on her shoulder, and as she
steps along o'ertops all the goddesses ; Latona's heart with silent joy
rebounds ; such was Dido, so did she gaily pass along through the
midst, intent on the work and on the glory of the empire that was to be.
Then at the door of the goddess' house, beneath the central dome of the
temple, girt with armed men and supported on her lofty throne, she took
her seat.   There she administered laws and statutes to her subjects, and
divided in equal shares the portions of the work, or chose them by lot ;
when on a sudden Æneas sees approaching amidst a great concourse
Antheus and Sergestus, and valiant Cloanthus, and the other Trojans,
whom the dark storm had scattered o'er the main and driven far away
to distant coasts.   Astonished were both the chieftain and Achates
too, smitten with feelings of joy and fear at once ; eagerly did they desire
to join hand with hand ; but the event, not yet understood, confuses
their souls.   They hide their presence, and under the cloak of the hollow
cloud look to see what their comrades' fortunes were, on what shore they
had left their ships, why they all come: for from each ship advanced a
chosen band, to pray for the queen's grace, and, amid loud cries, they
were entering the temple.

520—560. *Ilioneus, their spokesman, tells who they are, their course, the*
storm, their wishes.

As soon as they were admitted, and freedom of speech granted before
the royal throne, Ilioneus, the eldest of them all, thus began with calm
dignity of speech : " O queen, to whom Jove has granted to found a new

city, and with righteousness to curb wild tribes, we Trojans, a wretched band, borne by winds o'er every sea, pray to you; do you protect our ships from cruel fires, spare a religious race, and with kindly feelings look on our fortunes. · We come not with the sword to devastate the African homes, or to plunder, and carry spoil to the shore; our hearts have no such spirit, nor have the conquered such insolence. There is a land, the Greeks have called it Hesperia, 'tis an ancient realm, mighty in war, rich in its fruitful soil; there dwelt Ænotrian men; now 'tis reported their descendants have named the nation Italian after the leader Italus. Hither was our course, when suddenly arose o'er the billows stormy Orion, and bore us to hidden shallows far away, carried by wanton winds o'er the waves, as the surge mastered us, and o'er inaccessible rocks scattered us; hither, a poor remnant, we have swum to your shores. What race of men can this be? or what land so barbarous as to be the home of such conduct? We are denied the welcome even of the sand; they stir up war, and forbid our settling even on the very edge of the shore. If you reck nought of the human race, and despise mortal arms, yet believe that heaven forgets not right and wrong. A king we had once, Æneas by name, in justice, piety, and arms, second to none, a hero, whom, if the fates still spare, if he breathes the air of heaven, and has not yet sunk to the cruel shades, there is no fear of your ever repenting that you were the first to provoke to kindness. There are too cities in the regions of Sicily, and tilled fields, and a prince of Trojan descent, illustrious Acestes. Suffer us to draw up on shore our fleet shattered by the winds, and from the forests to frame new planks, and strip the leaves and fashion oars; so that, if we be permitted on the recovery of our king and comrades to sail for Italy, we may gladly make for Italy and Latium; but if that trust be gone, and the deep sea of Africa holds thee, good father of thy people, and the hopes formed of Iulus are now no more, that at least we may make for the Sicilian waters, and a home ready for us, from whence we came hither, and may return to prince Acestes." So spake Ilioneus; with one consent all the children of Dardanus shouted assent.

561—578. *Dido modestly replies in words of kind encouragement.*

Then spake Dido briefly, casting her eyes down to the ground: "Free your hearts from fear, Trojans, away with your cares. Necessity, and the new estate of my kingdom force me to such a course, and bid me protect my territories with guards all round. Who can be ignorant of the race of the people of Æneas, and of the city of Troy, its heroism and heroes, and the blaze of such a war as that? We Phœnicians wear not hearts so utterly unfeeling, not so far removed from the city of Tyre does the sun yoke his horses. Should you choose to sail for great Italy and the fields of Saturn, or prefer the country of Eryx and prince Acestes, I will send you hence under the guard of my aid, and help you with my means. Or should you wish to settle together with me in this realm, lo! the city I am founding, 'tis yours; draw up your ships on shore; I will put no difference between Trojan and Tyrian, but count all alike. And would to heaven your king himself, driven by the same wind, were here, even Æneas. I will do my part, and trusty men will I send through all my coasts to see if he has been cast on shore, and is a wanderer in any forest or city of mine."

579—612. *The mist dissolves. Æneas appears in the light. He cannot fully express the thanks of his grateful soul.*

These words raised the spirits of brave Achates and father Æneas; and long they had been eager to burst forth out of the cloud. First Achates addresses Æneas: "Goddess-born, what thought now rises in your soul? You see that all is safe, your fleet saved, your comrades recovered. One only is wanting, he whom in the midst of the waves our own eyes saw sink; all the rest agrees with thy mother's word." Scarce had he said this, when suddenly the encircling cloud parts, and clears into the open sky. There stood Æneas, and suddenly shone forth in beauty amid the clear light; godlike his face and shoulders; for his own mother gave him graceful flowing locks, and the brilliant complexion of youth, and inspired his eyes with joyous lustre: as when art adds grace to ivory, or when silver and Parian marble are set in yellow gold. Then thus he addresses the queen, and appearing on a sudden before all, un-looked for, thus he speaks: "I, whom you seek, am present here, even Æneas of Troy, saved from the Libyan waves. O you, who alone have showed pity for the unutterable woes of Troy, who welcome in your city, in your home, us, the remnant escaped from the Greeks, worn out by all our troubles by land and sea, in need of all things, 'tis not in our power to pay you due thanks, Dido, nor can all the race of Dardanus do this, which is scattered everywhere in the wide world. May the gods, if any Powers above regard the benevolent, if there be any righteousness in heaven and earth, if any conscience to teach us what is right, may they give you the reward you deserve so well. What age so joyous as to bear you? What parents so great as to beget so noble a child? As long as rivers run into the sea, as long as shadows on the mountains traverse the valleys, as long as the pole feeds the stars, so long shall your honour and name and renown be had in remembrance, to whatever lands I am summoned." Thus he spake, and with his right hand grasped his friend Ilioneus, with his left Serestus, then the others, brave Gyas, and brave Cloanthus.

613—642. *Dido welcomes him into her palace. She prepares a splendid banquet.*

First at the sight of the hero was amazed Sidonian Dido, then at the thought of his great sufferings; and thus she spake: "What fortune pursues you ever, goddess-born, through so many hazards? What force of fate drives you to such savage shores? And are you then that Æneas, whom to Dardan Anchises the beauteous goddess of love bore by the stream of Phrygian Simois? And indeed I too can remember Teucer's coming to Sidon, when driven from his country's coasts, to win a new kingdom by aid of Belus: my father Belus was then laying waste rich Cyprus and held it under his victorious sway. Even from that early time I knew the story of the fall of the Trojan town, and your name and the princes of the Pelasgian race. Wherefore come, ye youths, take refuge under our roofs. Me too through many a disaster a fortune like to yours has tossed, and at length willed that I should rest in this land. Not ignorant of ill, I learn to aid the wretched." Thus she speaks; withal she conducts Æneas to the royal palace, withal proclaims a public sacrifice in the temples of the gods. Meanwhile with no less zeal she sends to his comrades at the shore twenty oxen, a hundred bristly chines of bulky boars, a hundred fat lambs with their dams, joyous gifts for the festal day. But the house within is furnished with the splendour of princely pomp, and in the central hall they make ready the banquet; skilfully wrought are the coverlets of bright purple, on the tables is massive plate, and embossed in gold the brave exploits of their sires, a long series of feats, passing through many a hero from the earliest origin of the ancient race.

643—656. *Æneas sends for his son Iulus.*

Æneas, for the natural love of a father would not let his heart rest, sends forward Achates to go swiftly to the fleet, he bids him bear the presents to Ascanius, and bring the boy to the city. All a parent's love and care is settled on Ascanius. Gifts besides he bids him bring, rescued from the ruins of Troy, a robe stiff with figures in gold, and a veil whose hem was embroidered with saffron acanthus; once were they worn by Grecian Helen; she brought them with her from Mycenæ, the day that she sailed to her unhallowed marriage; these were the wondrous gifts of her mother Leda; further, he was to bring a sceptre once borne by Ilione, the eldest of Priam's daughters, and a necklace of pearls, and a crown with blended gems and gold.

657—696. *Venus is full of anxiety. She substitutes Cupid for Ascanius.*

But the Lady of Cythera ever plans in her heart new frauds, new designs, how Cupid transformed in face and look might come in the stead of sweet Ascanius, and by the gifts inflame the queen to frenzy, and insinuate love's fire into her veins: and this, because she dreads the faithless house, and Tyrians double-tongued. The thoughts of Juno's wrath harass her, and as night draws on her fears return. So with these words the goddess addresses winged Love: "My son, my strength, my great power alone, my son who scornest the thunderbolts of the sovereign Father which he hurled against Typhœus, to thee I come for help; a suppliant, I pray for thy divine aid. How thy brother Æneas o'er the sea, and round all the shores is tossed by the hate of persecuting Juno, to thee is well known; oft hast thou grieved with my grief. Him now Phœnician Dido detains, and keeps him with her by blandishment of speech, and I suspect how Juno's welcome will end; Juno will not be inactive at such a crisis of fortune. Wherefore I purpose to anticipate her with my craft, and to encircle the queen with such a flame of love that she may not change through the influence of any god, but be possessed by a passion for Æneas as strong as his mother's love. How thou mayest effect this, now hear my plan: the princely boy, summoned by his loving father, is making ready to go to the Sidonian city; he is my dearest care; he is to bring gifts rescued from the deep and the flames of Troy. Him will I cast into a deep sleep, and on the heights of steep Cythera, or on the ridges of Idalium in some sacred shrine will I conceal him, lest by any means he should know our plot, or come in our way. Do thou counterfeit his looks for one night, I ask no more, and thyself a boy assume the boy's familiar face, so that when Dido right joyously receives thee in her bosom amidst the royal banquet, and flowing cups of wine, when she embraces thee and imprints sweet kisses, then thou mayest breathe secret fire, and beguile her with love's poison." Love is obedient to the words of his dear mother—his wings he doffs, and gladly imitates the gait and steps of Iulus. Then Venus bathes the limbs of Ascanius in calm sleep, and lulls him in her lap, and so the goddess carries him aloft to the high groves of Idalium, where soft marjoram, breathing forth its blossoms, with sweet shade embraces the boy. Thus came then Cupid, obedient to his mother's word, and bringing the royal gifts, delighted to follow Achates as a guide.

697—722. *Amidst the splendour of the feast Cupid insidiously infuses passion into the bosom of the queen.*

When he comes, the queen has already beneath the splendid tapestry reposed herself on her golden couch, and taken her place in the centre. Presently father Æneas, and with him the Trojan youth, meet at the banquet, and recline on purple coverlets. The attendants pour water on their hands, and serve the bread in baskets, and bring napkins smooth to the touch. There are fifty female servants within, whose duty it is to prepare the stores in long array, and with fire to light the sacred hearths: there are a hundred other maidens, and as many waiting-men of equal age, whose task it is to load the tables with the viands and set there the cups. Likewise the Tyrians in numbers flocked to the joyous halls, invited to recline along the embroidered couches. They admire the gifts Æneas gave, they admire Iulus, and the glowing locks of the god, and his feigned words, the robe, and the veil embroidered with saffron acanthus. Above them all the ill-fated Phœnician queen, doomed to a coming curse, cannot satisfy her soul; and as she gazes, so she kindles with love, and the boy and the gifts alike affect her heart. The god first embraced Æneas, and clung round his neck, and gratified to the full the affection of his pretended father; then to the queen he goes. All her eyes, all her soul on him are fastened; and again and again Dido fondles him in her lap; little did she guess, how dread a god was resting on her hapless self. He meantime forgot not his mother, the goddess of the fountain Acidalia; but little by little essays to blot out the remembrance of Sichæus, and with a living passion to preoccupy a heart long dead to love, and a soul to which passion has grown strange.

723—756. *The libation, and invocation to the gods. The song and music of Iopas. The queen asks many a question touching Troy; she begs of her guest to tell of the fall of Ilium, and of his wanderings.*

When the first pause in the banquet came, and the tables were removed, they set the great goblets, and crown the wine with chaplets. A hum of voices passes through the rooms, and their words roll along the spacious halls; from the fretted roof of gold hang down the burning lamps, and night gives place to flaming torches. Hereupon the queen called for a heavy bowl, set with stones of price and bright with gold; this she filled with unmixed wine; Belus had often used it, and all the descendants of Belus; then was there silence in the halls: "Jove," said she, "for thou, they say, givest laws to hosts and guests, may it be thy pleasure to make this day auspicious to the Tyrians, and to those who come from Troy; may our children still remember this day. Be present too, Bacchus, who makest man's heart glad, and Juno to bless us. And you too, O Tyrians, graciously honour this company." She spoke, and on the table poured the offering of the flowing wine, which when done, she first graced it with her lips ; then with a challenge to Bitias gave the cup. He eagerly drained at once the foaming goblet and swilled himself with the flowing golden cup. After him it passed to the other paladins. On his golden harp long-haired Iopas sings aloud the lore taught him by great Atlas. His lay is of the wandering moon, and of the sun's eclipses ; whence sprang the race of man and the beasts of the field ; whence come the showers and lightning ; of Arcturus too he sings and rainy Hyades, and the twin Bears ; why the wintry suns haste so to dip themselves in the ocean, or what delay obstructs the slow-paced nights. The Tyrians oft repeat their applause, the Trojans follow their lead. Likewise with varied talk did hapless Dido prolong the night, deep were the draughts of love she ever drank ; many a question did she ask touching Priam, many touching Hector ; at one time what was the armour in which came Aurora's son, then of what kind were the steeds of Diomede, then how mighty was Achilles. "Nay come," said she, "my guest, and pray tell us from their first beginning of the stratagems of the Greeks, and the misfortunes of your countrymen, and your own wanderings ; for this is now the seventh summer that carries you a wanderer o'er every land and sea."

BOOK II.

1—13. *The preface to the story of the fall of Troy.*

All were hushed, and fixed their gaze in close attention : then father Æneas thus began from his lofty couch : "Ineffable, O queen, is the sorrow you bid me revive ; how the Greeks utterly destroyed the power of Troy and her woeful realm, and the sad sights I have myself beheld, and whereof I have formed a large portion. What Myrmidon or Dolopian, or what soldier of the hardy Ulysses could refrain from tears in telling such a tale? and now dewy night is speeding down the slope of heaven, and the setting stars invite to sleep. But if you have such deep desire to learn our disasters, and in a few words to hear the story of the death-struggle of Troy, although my soul shudders at the recollection, and ever shrinks from it in sorrow, I will begin.

13—57. *The device of the wooden horse. While the Trojans debate what course to take, Laocoon warns them to beware of a Greek stratagem, and hurls his spear at the horse.*

The leaders of the Greeks, worn with war and baffled by fate, when so many years were now gliding past, build, with the aid of the divine skill of Pallas, a horse as huge as a mountain, and form the sides of interlacing planks of fir ; they pretend that it is a votive offering for their safe return : such is the general rumour. In it, in the hollow flank, they secretly enclose the picked warriors they have chosen, and fill full the vast caverns and belly with armed soldiers. In sight lies Tenedos, an island well known by fame, rich and powerful, so long as the realm of Priam lasted, now a mere bay, and an unsafe anchorage for ships ; hither they proceed, and conceal themselves on the desolate shore. We supposed they had gone quite away, and that the wind was wafting them

to Mycenæ. Therefore all the land of Troy frees itself from its long
sorrow. The gates are opened ; it is a pleasure to go and view the Doric
camp, and the deserted stations, and the forsaken coast. Here the troop
of the Dolopians, here savage Achilles pitched his tent ; here was the
station of the fleet ; here they used to fight in the field. Some view with
amazement the pernicious offering to the maiden Minerva, and wonder at
the huge size of the horse ; and Thymœtes is the first to urge that it
be drawn within the walls and placed in the citadel ; whether it were
through treachery, or whether the fate of Troy was already bringing
on this end. But Capys, and those minds that possessed a better
purpose, advise us either to throw down into the sea the thing that
was a craft of the Greeks, and a gift that we distrusted, and to put fire
under it and burn it, or to pierce and explore the hollow recesses of the
womb. The giddy multitude is split into opposite factions. Then it is
that foremost, before all the rest, followed by a great crowd, Laocoon
eagerly runs down from the height of the citadel, and from afar he cries :
" My hapless citizens, how has so wild a frenzy seized you? Do you
believe that the enemy have sailed away ? or do you think that any
Grecian gifts are free from fraud? Is such your knowledge of Ulysses?
Either the Achæans are enclosed and concealed in this frame, or this is
an engine wrought against our walls, intended to spy into our houses and
come down upon our city from above, or there is some hidden deceit ;
trust not the horse, ye Trojans. Whatever it is, I fear the Greeks even
when they bring gifts." So he spoke, and hurled his mighty spear with
impetuous force against the flank and belly of the creature with its curving joints. It stuck fast and quivered, and as the womb received the
shock, the caverns sounded hollow and uttered a groan : and if such had
been the divine destiny, if our minds had been free from infatuation, he
had prevailed on us to mangle with the sword the lurking-place of the
Argives, and Troy would now be standing, and thou wouldst still remain,
O lofty citadel of Priam !

57—104. *A Greek, who had surrendered himself prisoner, is brought
   before Priam. He says his name is Sinon, and that he has been
   ruined by the resentment of Ulysses.*

Lo, some Dardan shepherds meanwhile came, dragging to the king
with loud shouts a youth whose hands were bound behind his back, who,
though they knew him not, had without compulsion put himself in their
way as they approached him, in order to effect this plan, and open Troy
to the Greeks, being confident in soul, and prepared for each event, either
to work out his craft, or to submit to certain death. From all directions
the youth of Troy, in their desire to see the sight, rush crowding round,
and are all eagerness to mock the captive. Now receive an example of
the craftiness of the Greeks, and from one deed of wickedness, learn what
they all are. For when he stood in the midst of the gazing throng,
confused, unarmed, and surveyed with his eyes the Phrygian ranks :
" Alas," he says, "what land, what sea can now receive me ? or what course
in this extremity is left to my wretched self ? for not only have I no place
anywhere among the Greeks, but even the Dardans also are my enemies,
and inflict on me a bloody punishment." By this lamentation our feelings

were altered, and every thought of violence was checked. We encourage him to speak, to tell us of what blood he is sprung, or what story he brings, what he, now captive, has to trust to. He, when at length his fear was removed, makes this speech : " I certainly will declare to you, O king, the whole truth, whatever may be the consequence," he says ; "and I will not deny that I am by birth a Greek; this I say first ; and if Fortune the wicked goddess, has fashioned Sinon to misery, she shall not fashion him to falsehood and deceit. If perchance by hearsay the name of Palamedes, the descendant of Belus, has at all reached your ears, and his story of famous renown, whom the Pelasgi on a false charge, though innocent, on a monstrous information, because he used to oppose the war, condemned to die, (they grieve for him now that he has left the light), my father, being poor, sent me here to the war from my early years, as his comrade and kinsman by blood. As long as he kept his kingly power firm and unimpaired, and was powerful in the conferences of the kings, we too bore some name and distinction. After that through the malice of Ulysses the misleader, (I speak of well known facts) he left the upper world, I dragged on my days in persecution, amid obscurity and sadness, and with my own heart resented the misfortune of my guiltless friend. And in my madness I did not hold my peace, and vowed that if any chance brought it to pass, if ever I returned a conqueror to my native Argos, I would be his avenger, and by my words I aroused fierce enmity against me. From this time began my ruinous downfall, from this time Ulysses always continued to alarm me by new charges, to scatter equivocal rumour among the multitude, and, knowing my purpose, to seek for means to attack me. And indeed he did not rest, until by the agency of Calchas—but yet, why do I uselessly unroll these bitter recollections? or why do I linger, if you account all Achæans to be in one class, and that name is enough for you to hear? This instant take vengeance upon me ; this Ithacus would wish, and the sons of Atreus would purchase at a high price."

105—144. *Sinon tells how the oracles of Phœbus commanded the Greeks to ensure a prosperous voyage home by a human sacrifice; and that he was fixed upon as the victim by the artifice of Ulysses; but made his escape.*

Then indeed we long to inquire and ask the causes of his ruin, ignorant of such a depth of wickedness, and of Greek craft ; quaking with fear he proceeds, and speaks with feigned feelings : " The Greeks often wished to leave Troy, and set about their retreat, and depart, wearied with the length of the war; (and would that they had done so !) as often the inclement fury of the sea kept them on land, and the wild winds alarmed them in the act of starting. Especially, just at the time that this horse formed of maple-beams was standing here, black thunder-clouds roared all through the firmament. In our bewilderment, we send Eurypylus to inquire of the oracle of Phœbus, and he brings back from the sanctuary this terrible response : "With the blood of a slaughtered maiden ye appeased the winds, when first, O Greeks, ye came to the coast of Ilium ; by blood you must seek the power to return, and the sacrifice, to be favourable, demands an Argive life." As soon as this utterance came to the ears of the multitude, their souls were struck with horror, and a cold shudder thrilled through the marrow of their bones, doubting whose doom fate decrees, whom Apollo requires. Hereupon Ithacus with loud clamour drags into the midst Calchas the seer ; he demands what this will of heaven is. And already many had often warned me of the schemer's cruel crime, and had silently discerned what was coming. Twice five days the other remains silent, and shutting himself up refuses by speaking to deliver or expose to death anyone. Scarcely, at last, forced by the loud outcries of Ithacus, he breaks silence by agreement, and dooms me to the altar. All assented, and what each had feared for himself, they endured when diverted to the destruction of a single wretch. And now the dreadful day had come ; for me the sacrificial preparations were being made, and the salted meal, and fillets to place about my brows ; I snatched myself from death, I confess, and broke my bonds, and in a muddy marsh I lay hid all night concealed in the sedge, while they were setting sail, if perchance they would have sailed. And now I have no hope of seeing my old fatherland, nor the children I love, and the parent I long to see, at whose hands perhaps they will even require satisfaction for my escape, and make their miserable death the expiation of this fault of mine. Wherefore by the gods above us and the powers that take cognizance of truth, by whatever unviolated honour, if such there be, still anywhere survives among men, pity such cruel troubles, pity a soul that suffers what it does not deserve."

145—198. *In answer to Priam, Sinon declares that the Greeks have constructed the horse as a propitiatory offering to Pallas, and that by receiving it within their walls, the Trojans may conquer their enemies. His story is believed.*

To these tears we grant him his life, and pity him besides. Priam is the first to bid that the man be released from his manacles and tight fetters, and thus speaks in friendly words : "Whoever you are, from this time forward lose and forget the Greeks ; you shall be ours ; and explain to me truly this that I ask you : to what end have they set up this horse of enormous bulk? Who first suggested it? or what is their object? What religious purpose does it imply? or what engine of war is it?" He ended. The other, fully furnished with craft and Pelasgian wile, lifted towards the stars his hands set free from bonds : " You, ye eternal fires, and your inviolable divinity I take to witness," he says ; "you, ye altars and accursed swords from which I fled, and ye consecrated fillets, which I as a victim wore, it is no crime for me to annul the allegiance I have sworn to the Greeks ; it is no crime for me to hate the men, and bring all things to light, whatsoever they keep secret ; nor am I bound by any of my country's laws. Only do you abide by your promise, and do thou, O Troy, preserve faith with thy preserver, if I shall bring true tidings, if I shall make you a large return. All the hope of the Greeks, and their confidence in undertaking the war, rested on the help of Pallas. Howbeit, since the time when impious Tydides, and Ulysses, the contriver of crimes, having adventured to tear away from the holy temple the fateful Palladium, when they had slain the guards of the summit of the citadel, carried away the sacred image, and with bloody hands dared to touch the virgin fillets of the goddess, from that time the hope of the Greeks began to melt away and to slip from them and be carried backwards : their energy was shattered, the mind of the goddess was turned away from them.   And Tritonia gave the proof of this by no uncertain prodigies.   The statue had scarcely been placed in the camp, when glittering flames kindled in the upraised eyes, and salt sweat ran through the limbs, and the goddess herself (wondrous to tell) thrice sprung from the ground, bearing both her shield and quivering lance.   Straightway Calchas pronounces that they must begin a retreat across the sea and that Pergama cannot be destroyed by Argive weapons unless they seek for new auspices from Argos, and bring back afresh the favour of Heaven, which they had carried away with them over the sea in their curved vessels.   And now, since wafted by the wind they have made for their native Mycenæ, they are providing the means or war and seeking to make the gods their comrades, and they will traverse the sea again, and be here unexpectedly.   So Calchas expounds the omens.   By his advice they have set up as an atonement for the Palladium, for the wrong done to the divinity, this image, to expiate the dreadful sacrilege. However, Calchas bid them raise this mass to so vast a size formed of a framework of oak, and build it up to heaven, that it might not be taken in by the gates, or drawn within the walls, nor guard the people under the shelter of the old faith.   For he said that if your hand had done violence to the gift of Minerva, then utter destruction—which boding may heaven first turn upon himself!—would befal Priam's empire and the Phrygians ; but that if by your hands it went up into your city, Asia, without waiting to be attacked, would come, bringing a mighty war to the walls of Pelops, and that that doom would await our descendants."   By means of such deceptions and the craft of the perjured Sinon, the state-ment was believed, and those men were caught by wiles and forced tears, whom neither Tydides nor Thessalian Achilles, nor ten years, nor a thousand ships subdued.

199—249.   *The terrible death of Laocoon and his sons.   The Trojans open their walls, and drag the horse into the city.*

Hereupon another sight, greater and far more fearful, is presented to us hapless wretches, and affrights our benighted minds.   Laocoon, appointed by lot to be the priest of Neptune was about to slaughter a huge bull at the wonted altars.   But lo, coming from Tenedos over the tranquil deep, (I shudder as I relate it) a pair of snakes with endless folds lie along the main, and together make their way to the shore ; their breasts reared up amid the waves and their bloody crests o'ertop the surge, the rest of the body makes a trail in the sea behind it, and winds along in a rolling coil the endless length of the back ; a sound is heard as the sea is lashed into foam.   And now they had reached the fields, and with their burning eyes suffused with blood and fire, licked with quivering tongues their hissing mouths.   We at the sight flee away bloodless with fear ; they in unwaver-ing line go up to Laocoon ; and first, each serpent encircling the tiny bodies of his two sons twines around them, and with its fangs preys upon their wretched limbs ; afterwards they seize upon himself, as he comes up to help with weapons in his hand, and enchain him with their enormous

spiral wreaths, and now having twice encompassed his waist, having twice
wound their scaly backs about his throat, they o'ertop him with the head
and towering neck. He at the same time struggled with his hands to
tear apart the knots, his fillet steeped in clotted gore and black venom;
at the same time he lifts to heaven frightful cries; like the bellowings of
a wounded bull when it has escaped from the altar, and dislodged from
its neck the ill-directed axe. But the pair of dragons glide in flight to
the top of the temple, and make for the citadel of cruel Tritonis, and hide
themselves beneath the feet of the goddess and the circle of her shield.
Then indeed terror unfelt before steals through the frighted hearts of all,
and they say that Laocoon has paid the righteous penalty of his crime,
seeing that he has violated with his lance the holy frame, and hurled
against its side his sacrilegious spear. With one voice they cry that the
image must be drawn to its temple, and the divinity of the goddess intreated. We cleave the walls, and lay open the battlements of the city.
All apply themselves to the work, and place beneath the feet rolling
wheels, and stretch over the neck bands of flax. The fatal engine climbs
the walls, big with arms. Around it boys and unwedded girls chant sacred
songs, and delight to take in their hands the rope. It ascends, and
threatening glides into the heart of the city. O my country! O Ilium,
home of gods, and Dardan battlements renowned in war! Four times,
just in the threshold of the gate, it stood still; and four times the arms
rang loud in the womb; still we press on, unthinking, and blinded with
frenzy, and set the inauspicious monster in the sacred citadel. Then too
Cassandra opened her lips to speak the doom that was to be, her lips, by
heaven's command, never believed by the Trojans. We, unhappy men,
for whom that day was to be the last, overspread with garlands the
shrines of the gods all through the city.

250—267. *In the night the Greeks sail back from Tenedos. Sinon opens
the horse, and Troy is stormed by the enemy.*

Meanwhile the sphere of heaven moves round, and night rushes up from
the ocean, wrapping in her universal shade both earth and sky and the
craft of the Myrmidons; the Trojans are stretched in silent rest throughout the town; sleep clasps their weary limbs. And now the Argive host
was advancing in naval array from Tenedos, making for the well-known
shores amid the friendly silence of the moon, when the royal ship suddenly shot forth the signal flame, and Sinon, protected by the partial
doom of heaven, unbolts the bars of pine, and sets free the Greeks
imprisoned in the womb. The opened horse restores them to the light,
and joyfully come forth from the hollow frame Thessander and Sthenelus
foremost, and accursed Ulysses, slipping down by the hanging rope, and
Acamas and Thoas and Neoptolemus the descendant of Peleus, and in
the front Machaon and Menelaus, and Epeus himself, the builder of the
deceit. They assault the city buried in sleep and wine; the guards are
slain, and throwing open the gates they admit all their comrades, and
combine with themselves the host of their partisans.

268—297. *The ghost of Hector appears to Æneas and tells him the doom
of Troy.*

'Twas the hour when the first slumber of suffering men begins, and

steals on right welcome by the grace of God; lo, as I slept, before my eyes
Hector full of sorrow seemed to stand and shed a flood of tears, as if
dragged along by the car as once he was, and blackened with bloody
dust, and his swollen feet pierced through with thongs. Ah me, how sad
he looked! how much changed from that Hector who came back arrayed
in the spoils of Achilles, or when he hurled Phrygian flames against the
Grecian ships! Wearing as he did a squalid beard and hair clotted with
blood, and all that multitude of wounds that he received around the walls
of his native city. I, weeping too, seemed to anticipate the hero by
addressing him and uttering words of sorrow : "O light of Dardania,
O surest hope of Troy, what is it that has kept you away so long? O
Hector, long expected, from what region do you come? How gladly we
behold you in our utter exhaustion, after many a death among your
people, after the various woes of the host and of the city! What cause
has shamefully marred the calm brightness of your face? Or why do
I see these wounds upon you?" He answers nought, nor heeds my vain
inquiries; but heaving deep-drawn sighs from the bottom of his breast:
"Alas, flee, goddess-born," he says, "and escape from these flames. The
walls are held by the enemy; Troy from its very summit is sinking into
ruins ; you have fulfilled your duty to your country and to Priam; if
Pergama could be protected by a strong hand, it would have been protected by this of mine also; Troy entrusts to you her rites and her
household gods ; these take to share your destinies, for these search out
the mighty city, which you shall set up at last, when you have wandered
over all the sea." So he says, and in his hands brings forth the image
of mighty Vesta with her fillets, and the undying fire from the secret
sanctuary.

*298—369. Æneas awakes, and finds that the city is in flames. He is
met by Pantheus, the priest of Apollo, and other Trojans. They
resolve to sell their lives dearly.*

Meanwhile the town is filled with tumultuous woe in all directions.
And although the mansion of my father Anchises was retired from
view by its secluded situation and its shadowing trees, still louder and
louder grow the sounds, and the terror of battle comes close upon
us. I am startled from sleep, and mount up to the highest point of
the sloping roof, and take my stand with keenly listening ears. As
when the flame lights upon the standing corn, when the winds are
raging, or a mountain torrent with its rushing stream devastates the
fields, devastates the smiling crops and the toils of the oxen, and drags
down the forests with headlong force ; the shepherd stands amazed
and perplexed as he catches the sound from the lofty summit of a
rock. Then indeed the truth is evident, and the stratagem of the
Greeks revealed. Already the mansion of Deiphobus throughout its
length and breadth has fallen into ruins, as the god of fire prevails ;
already the house of my neighbour Ucalegon is burning ; far and wide
the Sigean channel gleams with the blaze. There arises the cry of
men and the clang of trumpets. Distractedly I take my arms ; and
in taking them I have no adequate method ; but my spirits yearn to

muster a troop for battle. and to hasten to the citadel with my comrades ; frenzy and rage give me reckless resolution, and methinks it were glorious to fall fighting.

But lo, Pantheus, escaped from the weapons of the Greeks, Pantheus the son of Othrys, the priest of Phœbus in the citadel, with his own hands drags along the sacred vessels, and his vanquished gods, and his little grandson, and distractedly comes running to my door. "How stands the fortune of the state, Pantheus? What stronghold are we to seize?" Scarce had I spoken the words, when with a groan he answers thus : "Troy has reached her final day and her inevitable hour. We Trojans are no more ; Ilium is no more, and the mighty renown of the Teucri : relentless Jove has transferred all power to Argos ; the Greeks lord it in the city they have fired. The horse, erect in the heart of the town, pours forth from its height armed men, and Sinon, now a conqueror, insolently flings the flames abroad. Some are crowding in at the double gates, all the thousands that ever came from proud Mycenæ ; others with their weapons have barred the narrower streets in fronted ranks ; the sharp sword with glittering blade is drawn and fixed, prepared to kill ; the guards in the passage of the gates hardly attempt a contest, and resist in aimless war." By such words of the son of Othrys and by the will of heaven, I am carried into the flames and the fight, whither the fell fury of battle, whither the din calls me, and the clamour that goes to the sky. Comrades join me, Rhipeus, and Epytus mighty in arms, presented by the moonlight, and Hypanis and Dymas, and cluster to my side, and the young Corœbus, the son of Mygdon. He in those days had chanced to come to Troy, fired by frantic love for Cassandra, and as a son-in-law brought aid to Priam and the Phrygians, ill-fated, not to have listened to the promptings of his raving maiden. When I saw that they formed a band, and were bold for battle, I to incite them further, begin in these words : "Warriors, hearts in vain most valiant, if you have a determined desire to follow one of desperate daring, you see what is the state of our fortunes ; the gods by whom this realm stood fast, have all departed from it, and left the sanctuaries and shrines ; haste to succour a city that is set on fire ; let us die, and rush into the thickest of the fight. To despair of being saved by any means is the only means of safety for the vanquished." So the spirit of the warriors is heightened to frenzy. Thereupon like ravening wolves in a dark mist, when the audacious rage of hunger drives them reckless forth, and the cubs they have left wait for them with dry jaws, we make our way through weapons, through foes, to no uncertain death, and constantly press on to the centre of the city ; black night hovers round us with her dark vault. Who in words could describe fully the carnage, the deaths of that night, or be able with tears to match our troubles? An ancient city is falling, whose sovereignty has lasted many a year ; helpless forms in vast numbers are stretched on all sides, both throughout the streets and throughout the houses, and the hallowed thresholds of the gods. Nor from the Trojans only is exacted the penalty of blood ; sometimes to the hearts of the vanquished also valour returns, and the victorious Greeks fall. Everywhere is cruel woe, everywhere is panic and death in many a shape.

370—437. *Æneas and his party are at first successful, but fortune soon turns against them, and the band is slain or scattered. Æneas reaches the palace.*

Androgeos first, accompanied by a large troop of Greeks, comes to meet us, believing in his ignorance that we are a body of his countrymen, and without challenge, accosts us with friendly words : "Haste, my men ; why, what slothfulness has kept you back so long? others are spoiling and plundering the burning Pergama ; you are only just now marching from the tall ships." He spoke ; and in a moment— for indeed no reply that he could trust was given him—he perceives that he had fallen into the midst of foes. He was amazed ; and checked and drew in both step and voice. As one who unawares treads upon a snake on the ground in thorny brambles while he struggles along, and flees back from it with sudden start, as it rises up with growing rage, and with its azure throat dilating ; like him Androgeos, struck with terror at the sight, began to retreat. We rush upon them, and encompass them with our arms, and cut them down in all directions, ignorant of the ground, and seized with fright. Fortune assists our first effort. And hereupon Corœbus, exulting in the success and in his high spirit : "My comrades" says he, "let us follow where fortune points the way to safety, and where she shows herself gracious ; let us change our shields, and fit ourselves with the accoutrements of the Greeks. Whether it be craft or valour, who would ask in dealing with a foe? They shall give us arms themselves." When he had thus spoken, he proceeds to put on the shaggy helmet and the handsome and conspicuous shield of Androgeos, and girds to his side the Argive sword. So does Rhipeus, so Dymas too, and all the warriors joyfully ; each man arms himself with the newly-taken spoils. We make our way mingled with the Greeks, by the help of a divinity not our own, and in many a close conflict we engage amid the darkness of the night, many a Greek we send down to Orcus. Some flee in disorder to the ships, and at full speed make for the security of the shore ; some in shameful terror again climb the gigantic horse, and hide themselves in the well-known womb. Alas, no man may rely at all on heaven against its will. Lo, the virgin daughter of Priam, Cassandra, was being dragged by her loosened hair from the temple and sanctuary of Minerva, straining to the sky her burning eyes in vain, her eyes, for fetters confined her tender hands. The infuriate mind of Corœbus endured not this sight ; and he threw himself to certain death into the midst of the troop. We all follow him together, and make an onslaught with serried ranks. Here it is that first we are overwhelmed by missiles of our own countrymen from the lofty top of the temple, and a piteous carnage commences through the form of our armour and the mistake caused by our Grecian plumes. Then the Greeks, with a groan of rage at the rescue of the maiden, crowding from all sides attack us, Ajax fiercest of all, and both the sons of Atreus, and all the army of the Dolopians ; as sometime, when a hurricane bursts forth, opposing

winds meet in conflict, both Zephyrus and Notus, and Eurus rejoicing
in the horses of the East ; the forests creak, and Nereus, all foaming,
wields his furious trident, and wakes the waters from their lowest
depth.   All those, too, whom in the darkness of night amid the gloom
we had routed by our stratagem, and driven through the whole city,
appear ; they are the first to recognize the imposture of our shields
and weapons, and mark the incongruous sound of our speech.   Thereupon we are crushed by numbers ; and Corœbus first by the hand of
Peneleus, is stretched beside the altar of the goddess mighty in battle ;
Rhipeus also falls, who was above all others the most just among the
Trojans, and the strictest observer of right ; Heaven willed otherwise ;
both Hypanis and Dymas perish, pierced through by their countrymen ;
nor did your great piety nor the garland of Apollo shield you as you
fell, O Pantheus.   Ashes of Ilium, and thou, last fire of my people,
I take you to witness, that in your wreck I shunned not the weapons
nor any encounter with the Greeks, and that, should it have been my fate
to fall, my hand had earned my death.   After that, we were parted by
force, Iphitus and Pelias with me, of whom Iphitus was beginning to feel
the weight of age, and Pelias slow of foot through a wound dealt by
Ulysses ; straightway we were called by the din to the palace of Priam.

   438—468. Description of the conflict in defence of Priam's palace.
   Here it is that we behold a mighty contest, as if all the other fights
had no existence anywhere, as if none were dying in all the city beside ;
so fierce a contest we behold, and the Greeks rushing to attack the roof,
and the doorway blocked up by the mantlet that is brought against it.
The scaling-ladders are fixed to the walls, and even close to the door-
posts they struggle up the steps, and with the left-hand meet the missiles by the protection of their shields, with the right grasp the battlements.   Against them the Dardans pluck up towers and the topmost roofing of the houses ; with these missiles they prepare, at the
point of death, to defend themselves ; for they see the end : and gilded
beams they tumble down, the lofty splendour of their ancestors of yore ;
others with drawn swords have barred the doorways below ; these they
guard in close array.   Our courage is renewed to succour the dwelling
of the king, and relieve the warriors by our assistance, and furnish
fresh vigour to the vanquished.   There was a threshold, and a concealed door, and a clear communication with the several parts of Priam's
palace, and an entrance placed secretly at the back, by which ill-
fated Andromache, while the realm endured, used often to pass un-
attended to her father and mother-in-law, and bring to his grandsire
the child Astyanax.   I make my way up to the highest point of the
sloping roof, whence the hands of the hapless Trojans were hurling
their unavailing missiles.   Having assailed all round with iron levers,
at the point where the highest floor allowed us to make it totter at the
joining, a tower that stood with sheer descent, and with its topmost
roof raised up towards heaven, (whence all Troy used to be seen, and
the ships of the Greeks, and the Achæan camp,) we wrenched it from
its deep foundations, and forced it forward ; down in sudden fall it
brings the crashing ruin, and far and wide it lights upon the Grecian

ranks. But others take their place, nor meanwhile does the shower of stones or of any sort of missiles abate.

469—505. *At last Pyrrhus bursts in, resistance is soon at an end, and the palace is destroyed.*

Just in front of the court, and in the entrance of the gate, Pyrrhus proudly fights, glittering in arms of brassy gleam ; as when into the light an adder, fed on poisonous herbs, whom the cold of winter kept swollen underground, now all new, its slough cast off, and shining in youth, rolls along with breast erect its slimy length, towering to the sun, and shoots out its quivering three-forked tongue. At the same moment the giant Periphas, and the driver of the horses of Achilles, the armour-bearer Automedon, at the same moment all the men of Scyros, press into the palace and hurl incessantly flames to the roof. He himself among the foremost has seized a double axe, and is breaking through the solid entrance, and tearing away from the hinges the brass-bound door, and already he has cut through the planks, and hewn out a breach in the stout oak, and made a huge opening with yawning mouth. The palace within appears to view, and the long halls are disclosed ; the inmost chambers of Priam and of the old kings appear to view, and they see armed men standing in the entrance of the gate. But the interior of the house is in a tumult of groans and piteous confusion, and the vaulted mansion from end to end is loud with the wail of women ; the clamour strikes the golden stars. Then trembling matrons wander through the vast palace, and tightly clasp the door-posts and print kisses upon them ; Pyrrhus follows close with his father's fury ; neither bolts nor even guards can stand against him ; the door totters beneath repeated blows of the battering-ram, and the door-posts are knocked from the hinges and fall to the ground. Force finds a way ; the Greeks flocking in violently open out a passage, and cut down the foremost, and crowd the space everywhere with soldiers. Not with such force a foaming river, when it bursts its embankments and rushes forth, and overwhelms with its flood the mounds that stand in its way, pours in a mass furiously over the fields, and all across the plains carries away herds and stalls together. With my own eyes I saw Neoptolemus mad with slaughter, and both the sons of Atreus in the entrance of the palace ; I saw Hecuba and her hundred daughters-in-law, and Priam among the altars polluting with his blood the fires that he himself had hallowed. Those fifty bridal chambers, that large promise of grand-children, those door-posts, proudly adorned with barbaric gold and spoils, fell to the ground ; the Greeks are masters where the fire fails.

506—558. *The history of Priam's death. His headless body lies on the shore.*

Perhaps you may also inquire what was the fate of Priam. So soon as he beheld the downfall of his captured city, and the doors of his mansion torn away, and the foe in the very heart of his inmost chambers, he uselessly arrays his shoulders that tremble with years in the armour his old age had long disused, and girds on his powerless sword, and, sure to perish, is rushing into the crowded ranks of the enemy. In the heart of the palace and beneath the open firmament of heaven, there stood a great altar, and near it a very ancient bay-tree, leaning over the altar, and embracing the Penates in its share. Here Hecuba and her daughters were sitting about the altar in vain, like doves driven downward by a black tempest, cowering together, and clasping the images of the gods. But as soon as she saw Priam himself wearing youthful arms : " What resolve so frantic, my most unhappy husband, has impelled you to gird yourself with these weapons ? " she says ; " or whither are you blindly rushing ? It is not such help, nor such defenders as those that the hour needs ; no, not if my Hector himself were here. Retreat hither at last ; this altar will protect us all, or you will die with us." So she spoke, and received the old king to herself, and set him in the sacred place. But lo, escaped from the murderous hand of Pyrrhus, Polites, one of the sons of Priam, through missiles, through foes, flees along the length of the colonnades, and, wounded though he is, traverses the empty halls ; him Pyrrhus fiercely presses hard in act to strike ; and now, now, he grasps him, and is upon him with his lance; at last, at the moment that he came to view, before the eyes and face of his parents, he fell down, and poured out his life in a torrent of blood. Hereupon Priam, although he now lies in the midst of death, yet does not refrain himself, nor spare his voice and wrath : " Nay, may the gods," he cries, " if there be any kind Power in heaven, to watch such deeds, render you all the thanks you deserve, and yield you your due reward, for such a crime, for such a sacrilege, you who have forced me to see before my face the death of my son, and have defiled with the sight of his murder his father's eyes. But that hero, Achilles, whose son you falsely say you are, was not like you towards his enemy, Priam ; but respected the rights and sanctity of his suppliant, and gave up to the tomb the lifeless body of Hector, and sent me back to my realm." So the old man spoke, and hurled his feeble forceless spear, which was at once repelled by the ringing brass, and ineffectually dropped from the outermost fold of the shield. To whom Pyrrhus : " Then you shall carry this news, and go as a messenger to my father Pelides ; be sure to tell him the story of my fell deeds, and of the degeneracy of Neoptolemus. Now die:" as he said this, he dragged him even to the altar, all trembling, and slipping in the blood shed in torrents by his son, and twined his left hand in his hair, and with his right drew aloft his glittering sword, and buried it up to the hilt in his side. This was the end of Priam's fortunes; by this departure it was his lot to be borne away, while he beheld Pergama burnt with fire and sunk to ruin, he, once proudly great in so many nations and countries, the monarch of Asia. He lies upon the shore a huge trunk, and a head torn from the shoulders, and a corpse without a name.

559—623. *The despair of Æneas. He sees Helen attempting to hide herself in the temple of Vesta. In his anger, he resolves to kill her, but is checked by Venus, who bids him save his family from the ordained destruction of Troy.*

But then it was that dread shuddering first fell around me ; I was

horror-struck; the form of my beloved father came into my mind, as I saw
the king, his equal in age, panting out his life beneath a cruel wound;
my desolate Creusa came into my mind, and the destruction of my house,
and what might have chanced to my little Iulus.   I look back, and gaze
around, to see what numbers are about me.   All have left me through
utter weariness, and have flung their bodies down to the ground or dropped them exhausted into the flames.   And now indeed I was the only one
left, when I descry the child of Tyndareus lurking within the temple of
Vesta, and silently hiding herself in the sacred shrine.   The bright blaze
throws a light upon her, as she paces about, and casts her eyes hither and
thither over everything.   She, with dread foreseeing the enmity of the
Trojans against her for the overthrow of Pergama, and the punishment
the Greeks would inflict, and the wrath of the husband she had deserted,
she, Troy's common Fury and her country's, had concealed herself, and
was crouching among the altars like a thing abhorred.   A flame blazed
up in my soul; indignation prompts me to avenge my falling fatherland,
and exact the penalty of her crimes.   " Shall it be that this woman shall
with impunity see Sparta and her native Mycenæ? and pass along, a
queen, in the triumph she has won, and behold both her husband, and her
family, her parents and her children, attended by a train of Trojan women,
and Phrygian handmaids?   And this, when Priam is slain with the sword,
when Troy is burnt with fire, when the Dardan shore has so often reeked
with blood?   Not so.   For although there is no glorious renown in the
punishment of a woman, and the victory possesses no praise, yet I shall
be praised for having blotted out an abomination, and exacted a well-
deserved penalty; it will be a pleasure to have filled my soul with the fire
of revenge, and satisfied the ashes of my people!"   Such words were
springing from me, and I was borne along by my frantic design, when my
gracious mother revealed herself to my sight, never before so clear to my
eyes, and through the darkness beamed in perfect light, apparent goddess, both in beauty and in majesty such as she is wont to be seen
by the dwellers in heaven, and caught me by the hand and checked
me, and added these words besides from her rosy lips: " My son, what
is this anguish so great, that wakes the wildness of your wrath?   Why
are you maddened with rage? or whither has vanished your affection for
me?   Will you not first see, where you have left your father Anchises,
worn with age? whether your wife Creusa is still alive, and your son
Ascanius? all of whom the Grecian ranks range around on every side,
and unless my guardianship were placed to prevent it, the flames would
now have swept them away, and the sword of the enemy drunk their
blood.   It is not the detested beauty of Laconian Helen, or Paris, that
is the subject of your blame ; it is Heaven, relentless Heaven, that overthrows this mighty empire, and brings down Troy from her summit to the
ground.   Behold (for every cloud which by its veil now dims your mortal
sight as you gaze, and lies damp and dark around you, I will take away ;
dread not any bidding of your parent, nor shrink from obeying my commands), here, where you see the mounds thrown into ruin, and rock rént
away from rock, and eddying smoke mixed with dust, Neptune is shaking
the walls and the foundations displaced by his mighty trident, and is over-

throwing all the city from its base. Here Juno, more cruel than any, is the first to occupy the Scæan gates, and, girt with the steel, summons in her fury the array of her allies from their ships. Now Tritonian Pallas, behold her, has taken her stand on the height of the citadel, gleaming with the tempest, and her fierce Gorgon. The Father himself supplies the Greeks with spirit, and successful vigour; even he himself excites the gods against the Dardan warriors. Haste your flight, my son, and make an end of your struggle. Everywhere I will be with you, and will place you safely within your father's threshold." She ended, and hid herself in the thick shades of night. Dreadful faces appear to view, and the high divinities of heaven fighting against Troy.

       624—633. *Æneas beholds the utter wreck of the city.*

Then it was that all Ilium seemed to me to be sinking down into flames, and Troy built by Neptune to be overthrown from its very foundations; even as when, on the height of the mountains, labourers press on with rival zeal to cut down from the roots an ancient ash, hewn around with the steel, and with repeated blows of the hatchet; it ever threatens to fall, and quivering nods the foliage on its tossing top, until by degrees quite vanquished with blows, it heaves aloud its last groan, and, torn away from the crag, brings down a ruinous mass. I descend, and with God for my guide, make my way unharmed amid flames and foes; the missiles make room for me, and the flames retreat.

634—678. *Æneas goes back to his home, and tries to persuade his father to escape. Anchises refuses, and is determined to perish with the ruin of Troy.*

And when I had now arrived at the door of my father's dwelling, and my old home, my sire, whom before aught else I had been desiring to convey to the heights of the mountains, and above aught else had been striving to reach, refuses, now that Troy is utterly destroyed, to prolong his life, and to endure exile. "Do you, I pray you," he says, "whose blood is in the perfect glow of youth, and whose vigour is sound and strong in all its firmness, do you devise your flight. As for me, if they who dwell in heaven had willed that I should continue to live, they would have preserved for me this abode. It is enough and more than enough, that I have beheld one destruction, and survived the capture of the city. Speak the last words to my body, laid just as it is, just as it is, I pray you, and depart. With my own hand I will find my death; the enemy will take pity upon me, and come for my spoils; slight is the loss of a grave. Long have I lived through lingering years, hateful to heaven and useless, since the time when the father of the gods and king of men blasted me with the breath of his thunderbolt, and scathed me with his fire." So he continued to speak, and remained resolved. We, to stay him, shed many a tear, both my wife Creusa, and Ascanius, and all his family, intreating that he, the father, would not ruin himself and all our fortunes, nor lend his weight to the doom that was pressing us down. He refuses, and abides in the same purpose and in the same spot. I begin to rush back into the fight, and in utter misery wish for death: for what device, or what chance was now afforded us? "Did you imagine, my sire, that I could quit my dwelling leaving you behind, and did a

word so dreadful fall from my father's lips? If it be the will of heaven
that nought be left of so great a city, and this purpose is settled in your
soul, and it is your pleasure to add to the downfall of Troy both yourself
and your family, a door lies open for such a death; and presently Pyrrhus
will be here, fresh from the flowing blood of Priam—Pyrrhus, who butchers
the son before the eyes of the father, the father at the altar. Was it
to come to this, your bearing me away, my gracious mother, through
weapons, through foes, that I might behold the enemy in the inmost
chambers of my house, and that I might see Ascanius, and my father,
and Creusa beside him, one slaughtered in the blood of the other? Arms,
ye men, bring me arms! their last day invites the vanquished. Give me
back to the Greeks; suffer me to revisit and renew the battle. Truly we
will not all die to-day unavenged." Immediately I began again to gird
on my sword, and was fitting and inserting my left-hand into the handle
of my shield, and was rushing out of the house. But lo, clasping my feet
in the doorway my wife clung to me, and held up to his father the little
Iulus. "If you are departing to certain death, carry away us also with
yourself into all that can happen; but if you ground upon experience
some hope in resorting to arms, first guard this house. To whom is the
little Iulus, to whom is your father, and to whom am I, once called your
wife, abandoned?"

679—704. *A favourable omen changes the resolution of Anchises.*

Such were the cries she was uttering, and filling with her lamentation
all the dwelling, when there suddenly appears a prodigy wondrous to tell.
For while held in the hands, and between the faces of his sorrowful
parents, lo, a light crest of fire seems to shed a gleam from the crown
of the head of Iulus, and, with harmless touch, to lick his wavy locks, and
play about his temples. We, struck with terror, begin to tremble in fear,
and try to dislodge the flame from his hair, and to quench with water
the holy fire. But father Anchises joyously lifted his eyes to the stars,
and stretched to heaven his hands and voice: "Almighty Jove, if any
prayers can move thee, look upon us; this is all we ask; and if our piety
deserves it, then grant us thine aid, O Father, and ratify this omen."
Hardly had the old man spoken thus, when with sudden crash it thundered on the left-hand, and a star gliding from the sky through the gloom
shot along, trailing its torch-fire with a flood of light. We observe it,
after floating above the topmost height of the roof and marking its track
in heaven, manifestly burying itself in the forest of Ida, then in a long
line its furrow sheds a gleam, and all the region round is filled with
sulphurous smoke. Hereupon it is that my father is overcome, and raises
himself toward the sky, and makes his prayer to the gods, and does
obeisance to the sacred star. "Now, now, there is nothing to delay me:
I follow, and am with you, where you lead me. Ye gods of my country,
preserve my family in your keeping; preserve my grandson. From you
is this augury; and on your will Troy rests. I, for my part yield, and do
not, my son, refuse to go as your companion."

705—729. *Æneas with his family prepares to abandon Troy.*

He ended; and now the conflagration is heard more distinctly throughout the town, and the fierce tide rolls nearer. "Then come, my dear

father, rest upon my neck; I will support you on my shoulders, and such a toil will not oppress me; whatever shall be the issue of our fortunes, we will both have one common peril, one safety. Let the little Iulus be my companion, and Creusa follow our footsteps at a distance. You, ye servants, give your attention to what I shall say. As you go out of the city, there is a mound and an unfrequented temple to Ceres, and near it an old cypress, preserved through many a year by the reverence of our forefathers. To this one station will we come from different points. You, my father, take in your hand the sacred vessels and the household gods of our country. For me to handle them is a crime now that I have come away from so bloody a strife and from recent carnage, until I have purified myself with running water." So I spoke, and over my broad shoulders and my neck that was to bear him I spread as a covering the hide of a tawny lion, and take my burden on my back; the little Iulus clings round my right hand, and follows his father with unequal steps; my wife comes behind us. We travel through the darker paths; and me, whom lately no showers of missiles could move, nor Greeks closely banded in mass against me, now every breath of air affrights, every sound alarms, bewildered as I am, and trembling alike for my companion and my burden.

730—794. *In the hurried flight to the gates, Creusa is lost. Æneas rushes back, and seeks for her in vain through the burning city. At last her phantom appears, and says she has been taken from him by the will of Heaven. She foretells his wanderings, and the establishment of his kingdom in Italy, and then vanishes from his sight.*

And now I was drawing nigh to the gates, and seemed to have safely passed through all my journey, when suddenly the trampling sound of many feet seemed to reach my ears; and my father, looking on through the gloom, cries: "Flee, flee, my son; they are close upon us." I descry rushing shields and flashing arms. Here it was that some unfriendly Power confused and bereft me of my senses in my panic. For while at speed I keep along the unfrequented parts, and diverge from the familiar line of the road, alas, to my sorrow, my wife Creusa was snatched from me by destiny (whether she stopped, or wandered from the way, or sat down through weariness, I know not), and has not been since restored to my eyes. And I did not look back for her whom I had lost, or turn my thoughts to her, before we arrived at the mound and holy abode of ancient Ceres; here at last, when all were assembled, she alone was missing, and disappointed her companions, and her son and husband. Who was there that I did not accuse, both among gods and among men, or what more cruel calamity did I see in all the city? Ascanius, and my father Anchises, and the Penates of Troy I commit to my comrades, and conceal them in the hollow of a valley, I myself begin to go back to the city, and gird on my shining arms. It is my resolve to meet anew all chances, and traverse again all Troy, and a second time expose my life to perils. First I go back to the walls and the dark portals of the gate, by which I had started from the city, and wearily trace my foot-prints, as I journey back through the gloom, and mark them with my eye. Everywhere horror fills my soul, withal the very stillness frights me. After that, I make my way back to my house, fondly thinking that perchance she might have wandered thither. The Greeks had burst into it, and occupied the whole mansion. In a moment the devouring fire is whirled by the wind to the height of the roof; the flames mount above it, the tossing blaze rages up to heaven. I go on, and revisit Priam's palace, and the citadel. And now in the empty colonnades, in the sanctuary of Juno, the appointed sentinels, Phœnix and accursed Ulysses, were keeping watch over the plunder. Hither from all parts the treasure of Troy, snatched from the burning shrines, both the tables of the gods, and bowls of massy gold, and captured vestments are brought and piled together. Boys and trembling matrons in long ranks stand around. Venturing moreover to send cries vaguely through the gloom, I filled the streets with clamour, and in my sorrow, with repeated shouts, again and again vainly called upon Creusa. As I was seeking her, and unceasingly raving through the houses of the city, the hapless phantom and shade of Creusa herself appeared to me before my eyes, and her form larger than I had known it. I was amazed, and my hair stood up, and my voice clung to my throat. Then she thus began to address me, and to remove my cares by these words: "What avails it to give way so far to frenzied grief, my sweet husband? these events happen not without the will of heaven; nor is it permitted you to convey hence Creusa as your partner, nor does he, the monarch of Olympus, allow it. Distant exile awaits you, and a vast expanse of sea must you plough, and you will come to the land of the West, where Lydian Tiber flows with gentle current between the wealthy fields of men. There a smiling fortune, and a realm, and royal bride are provided you. Drive away your tears for your loved Creusa; I shall not behold the haughty abodes of the Myrmidons or Dolopians, or go to be a slave to Grecian matrons; I, a descendant of Dardanus, and the daughter-in-law of the goddess Venus; but the mighty mother of the gods keeps me still in these coasts. And now farewell, and preserve your love for our common son." When she had spoken these words, she left me, while I wept, and wished to say much more, and faded into thin air. Thrice I then attempted to throw my arms about her neck; thrice the phantom, vainly grasped, fled from my hands, as unsubstantial as the winds, and in all points like a fleeting dream.

795—804. *Æneas finds that his followers have increased to a numerous band. At daybreak he begins his retreat, and carries his father to the mountains.*

Thus it is that I return to my comrades when the night is spent. And here I find with astonishment that a vast number of new companions have flocked to join me, both matrons and husbands, a band of men assembled for exile, a piteous throng. They have come together from all parts, with resolve and means prepared to go to settle in whatever lands I please to lead them to over the sea. And now the morning-star was beginning to rise over the topmost ridges of Ida, and was bringing in the day; and the Greeks blocked up and held the entrances of the gates, and no hope of aid was given us. I retreated, and, taking up my father, journeyed towards the mountains.

BOOK III.

1—12. After the destruction of Troy Æneas builds his fleet, and sails forth an exile from his native land.

AFTER it was the pleasure of the gods to destroy the kingdom of Asia, and the nation of Priam, though guiltless, and when Ilium had fallen from its high estate, and all Neptunian Troy was still smoking from the ground; we are driven as exiles by the auguries of the gods in search of distant homes and desert lands, and we build our fleet just beneath Antandros and at the foot of the mountains of Phrygian Ida, doubtful as to whither the fates would bear us, where they will let us settle; and we collect a company. Scarce had the summer begun, and my father Anchises often bid me unfurl my sails to destiny; when with tears in my eyes I abandon my native shore, and the harbour and the plains where Troy was once, but now no more. Forth am I borne an exile into the deep, with my comrades, and son, and Penates, and great gods.

13—48. He comes to Thrace, but when he would build his city, blood flows from the stem of a tree, and a melancholy voice bids him leave the polluted shore.

Some distance off lies the peopled land of Mavors with its broad plains; the Thracians till it; once reigned there fierce Lycurgus; there was an ancient friendship between Thrace and Troy, and a common worship, so long as fortune remained the same. Hither I am borne, and on the winding shore build my first walls; but unkind were the fates when I landed; and I call the citizens Æneadæ, a name formed from my own.

I was sacrificing to my mother, the daughter of Dione, and to the other gods, to be auspicious to the works I had begun, and to the heavenly king of the dwellers in the sky I was offering a sleek bull on the shore. Perchance hard by was a mound, on the summit of which grew plants of cornel, and myrtles bristling with a thicket of spikes. I drew near, and tried to pluck the green stems from the ground, to deck the altar with leafy boughs, when lo! I see a dreadful prodigy, wondrous to relate. For from the first tree, whose roots I tore up and plucked from the ground, there trickle drops of black blood, and pollute the earth with gore. A cold shuddering convulses my limbs, and my chilled blood curdles with religious awe. Again too I try to tear up a second tough twig, and to probe to the bottom the hidden mystery; and again from the bark of a second shoot flows black blood. Many thoughts passed through my mind, and I worshipped the Nymphs of the country, and father Gradivus, the patron of the fields of the Getæ, that they would deign to duly bless the sight, and remove what boded ill. But when with greater effort I pluck at the third stalk, and with my knees struggle against the sandy ground, then—shall I speak, or forbear?—a lamentable groan is heard from the depths of the mound, and the utterance of a voice is wafted to my ears: "Æneas, why do you tear a wretched being? 'tis time to spare the buried; yes, spare to pollute your pure hands. I am no stranger to you; Troy bore me, nor does such gore trickle from a mere stem. Alas! fly from this cruel land, fly from a shore of avarice. Lo! I am Polydorus.

Here am I pierced, and an iron crop of weapons covers me, and has grown o'er me with pointed shafts." Then indeed my heart was cold with distracting dread, I was as one amazed, my hair stood on end, my tongue clave to the roof of my mouth.

*49—68.   The story of the murder of Polydorus.   They appease the unquiet
ghost of their countryman by a solemn funeral.*

This was that Polydorus whom once, together with a great mass of gold, unhappy Priam had secretly trusted to be brought up by the king of Thrace, in the days when he began to distrust the arms of Troy, and saw the city hemmed in with close blockade.   The Thracian prince, when the strength of the Trojans was broken, and Fortune had turned her back, sided with Agamemnon's power and his victorious arms; he burst all holy ties; Polydorus he murders, and gains his gold by violence.   To what do you not drive mortal hearts, thou cursed thirst of gain?   Now when my terror left my soul, I relate the prodigies that heaven had revealed, first to my father, then to the chosen chieftains of my people, and ask them what they thought.   All judge alike; they bid me depart from the guilty shore, for one may not stay where hospitality is violated, and they tell me to let the winds waft away my fleet.   So first we pay to Polydorus the funeral rites; the ground is heaped on high to make a mound; to his spirit altars are raised, saddened with dark-coloured fillets and gloomy cypress, and around stand the daughters of Troy with locks unloosed in due form.   We pour o'er the tomb cups foaming with warm milk and bowls of consecrated blood, and lay his soul at rest in the grave, and with loud voice wake his spirit with the last words of farewell.

*69—120.   They sail to Delos.   In answer to prayer Apollo bids them
seek their ancient mother, and promises their descendants an universal
kingdom.   Anchises interprets the oracle as pointing to Crete.*

Then, as soon as ever we could trust the deep, and the winds gave us calm waters, and the breeze with a gentle rustling invites us to the main, my comrades launch our ships, and crowd the shores.   Forth we sail from the harbour, lands and cities recede from view.   In the midst of the sea lies a sacred island, most dear to the mother of the Nereids and to Neptune, god of the Ægean, which the grateful archer-god, as it floated round the coasts and shores, bound to lofty Myconos and Gyaros, and granted that it should be fixed and inhabited, and scorn the winds.   Hither I am borne; the island kindly welcomes us weary sailors in a safe port.   We land and do homage to Apollo's town.   King Anius, king at once of men and priest of Phœbus, comes to meet us, his temples were crowned with fillets and holy bay; in Anchises he finds an old friend.   We unite hands in welcome, and enter beneath his roof.

The temple was built of ancient stone; there I worshipped, saying: "Grant us, god of Thymbra, a settled home, for we are weary, grant us walls, and a lasting race, and an abiding city; preserve a second citadel of Troy, and save a remnant rescued from the Greeks and pitiless Achilles. Whom are we to follow?   Whither dost thou bid us go?   Where to settle our home?   Father, give us an omen, and inspire our souls."   Scarce had I spoke, when suddenly all around seemed to shake; the thresholds, and the holy bays, and all the hill about quaked, and the tripod rumbled from the opened shrine. We bend our knees, and sink to the ground, and a voice is borne to our ears: "Ye hardy children of Dardanus, the same land which first bore you from the stock of your sires, will welcome you again on your return in its fruitful richness of soil. Search diligently till you find your ancient mother. Here shall the house of Æneas lord it over all lands, and there shall reign sons of sons, and they who shall spring from them." So spake Phœbus; and mingled with the tumultuous murmurings rose the sound of a great joy, and all enquire what were the walls he spoke of, whither Phœbus calls the wanderers, where he bids us return. Then spoke my father, as he thought over the histories of men of old: "Listen, ye chieftains," said he, "and learn your hopes; in the midst of the open sea lies Crete, an island sacred to great Jove, where is a mount Ida, and the cradle of our race; they dwell there in a hundred great cities, very fruitful are these realms; whence the first father of our race, if I rightly recall what I have heard, Teucer, first came to the coast of Rhœteum, and chose a place for his kingdom. Not yet was standing Ilium or the citadel of Pergamus; they used to dwell there in the low valleys. Hence came the mother of the gods who inhabits mount Cybele, and hence the bronze cymbals of the Corybantes, and the grove of Ida; hence came the invisible secrecy of mysteries, and the yoked lions were harnessed to the chariot of their queen. Come then, and whither the will of Heaven guides, thither let us follow; let us propitiate the winds, and sail for the realms of Gnosus. They are not far distant; if only Jove will befriend us, the third morning will see our ships moored on the coast of Crete." So he spake, and offered due sacrifices on the altars, to Neptune a bull, a bull to thee, beauteous Apollo, a black lamb to the storm, a white lamb to the favouring Zephýrs.

121—146. *Æneas sails to Crete. A pestilence wastes his people.*

A report flies abroad that the chieftain Idomeneus has been driven forth and left his ancestral realm, that the shores of Crete are deserted, the houses freed from our foe, and their abodes left and abandoned. We sail from Ortygia's port, and fly o'er the main, passing by Naxos whose ridges are haunted by the revels of Bacchus, and by green Donyza, by Olearos, and marble Paros, and the Cyclades scattered o'er the water, and we coast through channels thickly sown with islands. The shouts of the sailors arise as they vie with each other in many a task; my comrades bid us make for Crete, the land of our forefathers. A wind freshening at our stern follows us in our course, and at length we are wafted to the ancient shores of the Curetes. So then with eager haste I build the walls of my wished-for town; I call it Pergamea, my people are pleased with the name, and I encourage them to love their houses, and raise their citadel with lofty roofs. And now our ships had been but just hauled upon the dry beach, our youth were busy on marriages and tillage, I gave them lands and settled their homes: when suddenly a wasting plague fell on our bodies, for heaven's atmosphere was poisoned, and wretched was the blight that visited vineyards and crops, and deadly was the season. They left dear life, or dragged their limbs in disease; Sirius too parched the fields with drought; the herbage pined for lack of rain, and the mildewed corn

withheld our food. Back again my father bids me cross the main once
more to Apollo's oracle at Delos, and entreat his grace, praying, what end
would he give to our weary fortunes, whence he bids us essay to find
help in our misery, or whither bend our course.

147—191. *At night the household gods appear to the hero, and tell him
not Crete, but Italy was meant. Anchises then recalls Cassandra's
prophecy.*

'Twas night, and sleep possessed all creatures on the earth : the holy
images of the gods and Phrygian Penates, whom I had brought with me
from Troy, rescued from the midst of the burning town, seemed to stand
before my eyes, as I lay asleep; clearly I saw them in the strong light,
where the full moon poured through the casement of the windows : then I
thought they thus spoke to me, and thus calmed my fears ; "What Apollo
would tell you if you landed at Delos, here he reveals, and lo, before you
ask him, sends us to your threshold. When Troy was set on fire, we
followed you and your arms ; with you for guide, in your ships we traverse
the swelling waves ; yes, and we will raise your children hereafter with
glory to the stars of heaven, and give empire to the great city. Do you
raise mighty walls for men of might, nor shrink from the long labour of
your course. This is not the shore the god of Delos spake of ; Crete is
not the land he bid you settle in. There is a region, the Greeks have
named it Hesperia, the land of the West ; 'tis an ancient land, mighty in
war, fruitful in soil ; once dwelt in it the Œnotrians ; now fame reports
that the descendants call it Italy from the name of their prince Italus :
here is our own abiding home ; hence Dardanus sprang, and father
Iasius, the author of your race. Rise with haste, and gladly report our
words to your aged father; put aside all doubts; tell him to search for
Corythus and Ausonian lands, for Jove denies you the Cretan fields.
Astonished at the vision and the heavenly words—I could hardly call
that sleep, I rather seemed to know their looks face to face, their locks
with fillets bound, and countenances as of life ; then o'er my body
spread a clammy sweat—I spring from my bed, and raise my uplifted
hands and voice to heaven, and cast upon the hearth my purest gifts.
This homage of religion done, I gladly tell my father all, and keep back
no detail. At once he found the error of the doubtful race, and the
ambiguous parentage, and owned he had been misled by a strange mistake touching these ancient lands. Then he says, "My son, persecuted
by the fates of Ilium, Cassandra alone foretold these fortunes in the
future. Now I remember, she predicted such a destiny to our race,
and oft she spoke of Hesperia, oft of Italian realms. But who could
then have thought that Teucer's race should come to Hesperian shores,
or who would then listen to what Cassandra prophesied? Now let us
yield to Phœbus, and warned by the god follow a better course." So he
says; with one consent we gladly obey his words. We abandon this
home likewise, and, leaving a few behind, we set sail, and in our hollow
ships speed o'er the wide main.

192—218. *Overtaken by a storm, they are driven to the Strophades.*

When our vessels had stood out to sea, and no land could now be seen,
with only deep and sky around, then o'er my head gathered a dark

cloud of rain, bearing with it gloom and storm, and the wave ruffled beneath the darkness. Straightway the winds roll the waters, and mighty seas arise; we are scattered and tossed o'er the wide flood. Stormy clouds envelope the light of heaven; misty darkness robs us of the sky; oft flash the lightnings from the riven clouds. We are forced out of our course and wander in unknown waters. Even Palinurus says he cannot distinguish between day and night in the sky, and has lost his course in the midst of the waves. Three whole days of twilight through the murky mist we are wanderers o'er the main, and as many starless nights. On the fourth day at last rising land is descried, the distant mountains open to view, and the curling smoke is seen to roll upwards. Our sails are furled; we ply our oars; without delay our sailors with effort in their work whirl the foaming water, and sweep o'er the azure deep. So I am saved from the waves, and the shores of the Strophades first receive me. Strophades they are called by a Grecian name, islands rising in the wide Ionian sea; where dwells dread Celæno, and the other harpies, since the day that the house of Phineus was closed, and through fear they left their former tables. There is not a more baneful monster than these, nor has a fiercer pest sent by the wrath of the gods risen from the waters of the Styx. Fair are their faces as of maiden's form, but foul and filthy is their trail, and talons they have for hands, and looks always pale from craving hunger.

219—267. *The Harpies pollute the banquet of the Trojans, who attack them with arms.   Then Celaeno predicts that in sore stress of famine they shall eat their own tables.   The prayer of Anchises.*

Hither we are borne and enter the harbour; and lo! spread o'er the plains we see joyous herds of oxen, and flocks of goats o'er the grass without a keeper. We rush on them with weapons, inviting the gods, and Jove himself to share the spoil; then along the winding shore we raise our couches, and begin to feast on the sumptuous banquet. But suddenly with horrible descent from the mountains the harpies are upon us, and with frightful cries they flap their wings, and snatch the meat and pollute it with loathsome touch; dread too was the screech that accompanied the sickening smell. Again, in a retired spot secluded beneath a hollow rock, enclosed around with the shaggy shade of trees, we dress our tables, and again light the fire on the altars. Again, from a different quarter of heaven, and from their dark hiding-place, the noisy flock hovers round the spoil with taloned feet, polluting with their mouths the feast. I bid my comrades seize their arms, for we must wage war with the cursed race. They do as they are bid, and cover with grass the swords they place along the ground, and hide their shields in ambush. So when the monsters fly down, uttering their cries along the winding shore, from a high cliff Misenus gives the signal with his hollow horn of brass. On rush my comrades, and essay a strange fight, striving to wound with weapons the unclean birds of the sea. But they feel no blows on their feathers, nor wounds on their backs, and with swift flight soar aloft, and leave behind the half-eaten prey, and their disgusting trail. Yet one is still left perched on a lofty rock, Celæno, a prophetess boding ill, and utters these words from her breast: "What!

war for slaughtered oxen, and slain steers, true children of Laomedon?
what! war are you ready to wage, and do you drive the unoffending
harpies from their native realm? Hear then these words, and store them
deep in your souls: what the Almighty Father foretold to Phœbus, and
Phœbus Apollo declared to me, that I to you, I, the eldest of the furies,
reveal: Italy is the object of your course; invoke the winds, to Italy you
will come, and you will be allowed to enter the harbour: but you shall
not wall the town the fates will grant, till first an accursed hunger, and
the wrong done to us by this attack, force you to grind with your teeth
your half-eaten tables." She spake, and back to the woods she fled borne
on her wings. Then the blood in my comrades' hearts chilled and
stiffened with sudden awe: their courage fell; with arms no more, but
now with vows and prayers they bid me demand pardon, be they goddesses, or be they hellish and unclean birds. And father Anchises, standing on the shore with outspread hands, invokes the great Powers of heaven,
and solemnly promises offerings in return for the aid he asks; saying:
"Ye gods, avert these threats; ye gods, avert such a calamity; be propitious, and deliver the pious." Then he bids us at once unloose our
cable from the shore, and let out the coils of the cordage.

268—293. *They sail on past the island; at Actium they celebrate*
games as did Augustus after the battle of Actium; then they go on to
Buthrotum.

The winds spread wide our sails; we are borne over the foaming waves,
whither breeze and helmsman invite our speeding course. Presently in
the midst of the flood is seen woody Zacynthus, Dulichium and Same,
and Neritos with steep crags; we shun the rocks of Ithaca, where Laertes
reigned, and we curse the country which reared cruel Ulysses. Presently
too, the storm-capped peaks of mount Leucate open to our view, and
Apollo, the sailor's dread. Weary we sail for this point, and come into
the harbour of the little town; our anchors are cast from the prows; the
sterns are drawn up on shore.

So having gained at length the land beyond our hopes, we purify ourselves in homage to Jove, and kindle altars, and pay our vows, and on
the shores of Actium celebrate the games of Troy. My companions
strip, and, smeared with slippery oil, join in their national wrestling-match.
It pleases us to think that we have passed safely by so many Greek
cities, and held our course through the midst of so many foes. Meanwhile, the sun completes the circle of the full year, and icy winter
roughens the waters with northern blasts. A shield of hollow brass,
which mighty Abas once wore, I hang on the face of the doors, and
mark my act with this verse: "This armour Æneas took from the victorious Greeks." Then I bid them leave the port, and take their seats on the
rowers' benches. My comrades with a will strike the sea with their oars
and sweep its surface. Quickly we lose sight of Phæacia's lofty heights,
and coast along the shores of Epirus, and sail into the Chaonian harbour,
and draw near to the steep city of Buthrotum.

294—355. *Æneas meets Andromache at Buthrotum. She tells him that*
Helenus is now king of the land.

A rumour past belief here fills our ears, that Helenus a son of Priam was king o'er Grecian towns, and had obtained the wife and sceptre of Pyrrhus of the race of Æacus, and that Andromache had passed once more to a Trojan husband. I was amazed, and with strange anxiety my heart was fired to address the hero, and hear the story of so wondrous a fortune. I advance from the harbour, and on the shore leave my fleet ; when, as it chanced, in front of the city, in a holy grove by the stream of a counterfeit Simoïs, Andromache was offering her solemn yearly feast, and gifts of mourning to her husband's ashes, and called on Hector's spirit at a mound, which on the green sward she had consecrated to be a cenotaph, and had dedicated two altars which made her tears ever flow. As soon as she saw me coming, and Trojan arms around, frenzied and scared by the wondrous prodigy, her form stiffened as she looked, the warmth of life forsook her limbs, she swoons, she falls, and hardly at length after a long time she speaks : " Is this a real appearance, is this a living messenger that comes, O goddess-born? are you alive? or if the kindly light of life be gone, tell me, where is Hector?" She spake, and shed a flood of tears, and with her cries she filled the space around. As thus she raves in grief, I find no words, and hardly can reply, and troubled scarcely speak with broken words : "'Tis true I live, and drag my life through all extremity of woe ; doubt not, lady ; no phantom do you see. Alas ! what lot overtakes you, fallen from such a high estate of marriage? or what change of fortune visits you, worthy of your former life? Can Hector's wife still stoop to wedlock with Pyrrhus?" With downcast look and humbled voice she spake : " O only happy maiden out of all Priam's daughters, doomed at an enemy's tomb beneath the lofty walls of Troy to die! you did not endure the choice of any lot, nor in captivity drew near the bed of a victorious lord. But I, from my country's flames borne o'er distant seas, had to endure the insolence of Achilles' son and serve that haughty youth ; in slavery I bore a child ; he afterwards courted Hermione of Leda's race, and sought a Spartan marriage, and passed me over to Helenus, as slave with slave united. For Pyrrhus off his guard Orestes waits in ambush ; for his heart raged with a strong passion for the wife that he was robbed of, and he was ever driven on by the furies of his guilty race ; and so he murders Pyrrhus at the altar of his father. By the death of Neoptolemus a part of his kingdom passed to Helenus by right, and Helenus named the realm Chaonian, and called all the land Chaonia from Chaon of Troy, and built a new Pergama, and placed this city named Ilium on the hills. But you, what winds, what fates have wafted your course hither? or what god hath brought you unconsciously to our shores? what of your boy Ascanius? is he still alive? does he still breathe the air? You once had such a son in Troy. Does the boy still regret his mother's loss? And does such a father as Æneas, such an uncle as Hector stir his soul to the valour of his sires, and to a manly spirit?" Such words she uttered with many tears, and ever encouraged her sorrows, weeping all in vain ; when lo! from the walls the hero Helenus, Priam's son, comes with a long retinue ; he recognises his countrymen, and gladly leads them to his palace, with many a tear interrupting each word.

Onwards I go, and find a little Troy, and a second Pergama, a copy
of the great one, and the dry bed of a stream which bore the name
of Xanthus, and I embrace the threshold of a Scæan gate.   The Trojans
too at the same time enjoy themselves in the friendly city.   The king
entertained them in his spacious corridors.   In the centre of the hall
they poured libations of wine, and on golden platters put the meat-
offerings to the gods, holding goblets in their hands.

356—373. *Æneas asks the seer Helenus to reveal the fates to him.*

Day after day passed on, and the breezes woo our sails, and the
canvas is filled by the swelling wind : with these words I address the
seer, and ask him these questions : "Child of Troy, interpreter of
heaven's will, you who feel the inspiration of Phœbus, who know the
tripods and bays of the lord of Claros, and understand the stars, and the
language of birds, and the omens drawn from their prophetic flight,
speak, I pray—for favourable auguries have told me all my course, and
all the gods with one consent reveal their will that I should make for
Italy, and essay to reach that remote land : one only prophet, the harpy
Celæno, forebodes a strange and unutterable portent, and denounces the
fell wrath of the gods, and speaks of unclean hunger—tell me, friend, what
dangers I should first avoid ? or by what guidance I may hope to vanquish
toils so great ?"   Then Helenus first sacrificed steers in due form, and tries
to gain a blessing from the gods, and unbinds the fillet of his holy head,
and to thy threshold, Phœbus, he leads me with his own hand, full of
many a religious doubt ; and then from his inspired mouth the priest
utters these prophecies.

374—462. *Helenus in a long speech tells the prince he must seek the
    further shore of Italy, he must avoid Scylla and Charybdis, appease
    Juno, and visit the Cumaean Sibyl.*

"Goddess-born, a well-grounded faith assures us that you sail o'er the
deep under the greatest auspices, even so does heaven's king appoint the
allotted fates, and roll the changing cycle of events : such is the order of
their course ; of many things some few will I unfold in my speech, that
more safely you may traverse strange seas, and rest at last in an Italian
port ; the remainder the fates forbid that Helenus should know, and
Saturnian Juno stops my speech.   First then as to Italy, you imagine
that it is near, and in your ignorance are ready to enter at once its
neighbouring harbours ; but distant is the access, inaccessible through
distant tracts of lands that divide you from it.   First must you bend your
oar in Sicilian waves, and traverse with your fleet the surface of the
Ausonian sea, and approach the lake of Avernus, and Ææa, the isle of
Circe, before you can build a settled city in a safe land.   I will tell you the
signs ; do you store and keep them in your mind : when in the days of
your anxiety you shall find by the stream of a retired river a huge sow
lying under the oaks of the bank with a litter of thirty young, resting
on the ground, a white mother with white pigs round her teats ; that is
the spot of your city, that shall be your settled home and rest from your
toils.   Nor trouble yourself to dread the eating of your table in future
time ; the fates shall find a way, and Apollo come to your call.   But
avoid these nearer lands, and this coast of Italian shore, which nighest

to us is washed by the tide of our sea; in all these towns dwell malignant
Greeks. Here the Narycian Locri have built their walls, and Cretan
Idomeneus occupies with arms the Sallentine plains; here is that town
of Philoctetes, Mclibœa's prince, little Petilia resting on its wall. Further,
when your fleet has crossed the sea, and is moored, and you build your
altar, and pay your vows on the shore, then veil your locks, and wrap
yourself in purple cloak, lest amidst the holy fires in the worship of the
gods, a hostile face intrude, and trouble the omens. This custom in
religion let your comrades keep; do you yourself observe the same; to this
holy form let your devout descendants ever be faithful. Further, when you
depart hence, and the wind bears you nigh to Sicilian land, and the straits
of narrow Pelorus begin to open to your view, then make for the land to
the left, and for the sea that lies to the left, long though the circuit be;
avoid the shore and waters to the right. These lands were once torn
asunder with violent rent, and mighty convulsions—so great the changes
length of time can effect—they tell how they started asunder, and though
either land was then one and continuous, yet in the midst the main came
rushing, and with its waves cleaved the Italian coast from Sicily, and
divided fields and cities by a new shore, and flowed between them with
a narrow tide. Scylla guards the right side, merciless Charybdis the left;
and in the lowest eddies of her whirlpool thrice she sucks her huge waves
into the abyss, and again each time shoots them on high, and lashes the
starry heavens with the waters. And Scylla in her dark lurking-place
a cavern confines, oft thrusting forth her mouth, and drawing the ships on
her rocks. Above she has a human face, with beauteous breast a woman
to the waist, but ending in her savage form a monster of the deep, with
dolphins' tails and womb of wolves in one. 'Tis better far to traverse the
utmost point of Trinacrian Pachynus, though with delay, and turn your
winding course all round, than once to have seen misshapen Scylla
within her dreary cave, and the rocks re-echoing to the watery hounds.
Further, if in Helenus be any insight, if to the seer faith be due, if Apollo
fills his soul with revelations of truth, there is one thing, goddess-born,
yes, one thing above all else that I would foretell, and repeat it oft, and
warn you of it again, and again; great is the goddess Juno, above all
others adore her divinity, to Juno chant your vows with willing heart,
mighty lady is she, yet win her to yourself with supplications and gifts:
thus at last you will prevail, and start for the Italian coasts after you
have left Sicily. Now when borne to this shore you draw near to the city
of Cumæ, and its holy lakes, and Avernus with its roaring woods, you will
see the frenzied prophetess, who in the depths of her rocky cave foretells
the fates, and trusts her marks and tokens to leaves. Whatever burdens of her prophecy she writes upon leaves, she arranges in order,
and abandons them shut up in the cave. They remain steady in their
place, nor depart from their order. And yet if the hinge should turn,
and the light wind blow upon them, and if the opened door once disturbs the light leaves, she never troubles herself to catch the letters as
they flit in the rocky cave, nor to recover their proper place, or unite the
verses of her prophecy. So men depart without an answer, and shun the
shrine of the Sibyl. But here count you no loss of time so precious,

(however much your comrades chide, and your voyage urgently invite your sails into the main, though you might fill your sheets with favouring winds,) as not to draw near to the prophetess, and with prayers ask for her oracle. Pray her to prophesy herself, and graciously to speak and open her mouth. She will tell you of the nations of Italy, and of coming wars, and unfold the manner in which you may eschew or endure every toil, and to your prayer she will grant a prosperous voyage. So far am I allowed to warn you with my voice. Go, hasten hence, and by your deeds exalt Troy on high even to the skies."

463—471. *The gifts of Helenus.*

Now when the seer had said this with friendly speech, he next commands gifts of weighty gold and carved ivory to be carried to the ships, and stores in the hulls massive plate, and caldrons of Dodona, coat of mail fastened with hooks and triple twine of gold, and the peak and flowing plume of a splendid helmet, the armour that Neoptolemus once wore. There were gifts too to suit my father. To these he adds horses and their grooms. He supplies us with new rowers, he furnishes my comrades too with arms.

472—505. *Andromache's sad parting with Æneas. Host and guest interchange kind offices, and engage for future friendship.*

Meanwhile Anchises often bade us hoist the sails of our fleet, lest we delay, when we have a wind to waft us. Him the seer of Apollo addresses with much respect: "Anchises, deemed worthy of the noble union with Venus, charge of heaven, twice rescued from the fall of Troy, lo! before you lies the land of Italy; haste to reach it with your sails; and yet you must pass by this nearer shore, and sail over the sea. Distant is the part of Italy which Apollo reveals. Go," said he, "happy in your son's affection. Why do I longer hinder you, and by my speech delay the rising breeze?" With no less zeal Andromache, sorrowing at the last moment of parting, brings robes embroidered with tissue of gold, and for Ascanius a Phrygian cloak, nor yields to her husband's gifts, and loads him with the presents of the loom, and thus she speaks: "Receive these tokens, my boy, and may they be to you as memorials of my work, and bear witness to Andromache's lasting love, who was Hector's wife, O you who alone are left to call Astyanax to mind. Such were his eyes, such his hands, such the look he wore; and now his age were yours, and as you, so would he be growing to man's estate." As I parted from them, I spake to them, while tears gushed forth: "Farewell, and happy live, your fortune is completed; we are summoned from one fate to another. You have gained your rest, no surface of the sea need by you be ploughed, nor need you seek Italian fields which ever seem to fly. You see the city of Xanthus, and a new Troy built by your own hands, under better auspices, as I pray, a city less exposed to the Greeks. If ever the day comes when I enter the Tiber, and reach the fields along its banks, and behold the towers granted to my race, hereafter we will unite cities related and people akin in Epirus and in Italy, and make them both one Troy; for they have one author Dardanus, and have had one common misfortune. Let that charge remain to our descendants."

506—567. *The pilot waits for a clear sky. The next morning they sa-*
lute Italy. Happy omens attend them. They pass the towns of Italy
till they come to Sicily.

We speed along the main close to Ceraunia, whence is the passage to
Italy, and the shortest voyage o'er the waves. Meantime the sun sets,
and the mountains are shaded with night. We throw ourselves on the
bosom of the wished-for land close to the water, choosing by lot who
should guard the oars, and all along the dry beach we rest our weary
bodies; soft sleep bedews our limbs. Nor yet had Night, led by the hours,
mounted to the zenith of her sphere, when active from his bed rose Palinurus, and explores every breeze, and with listening ears tries to catch the
gale; he observes all the stars together gliding o'er the silent sky, Arcturus and the rainy Hyades, and the twin Bears, and carefully notes Orion
with his belt and sword of gold. When he sees all nature settled in the
calm sky, he gives a shrill signal from the stern; we start our fleet, and
essay our voyage, and spread the flying sails. And now Aurora had put
the stars to flight, and just begun to blush, when in the distance we see the
misty hills, and low coast of Italy. Achates is the first to shout "Italy!"
Italy my comrades salute with joyous shouts. Then my father Anchises
crowned a great bowl with a chaplet, and filled it with unmixed wine, and
called on the gods, as he stood on the tall stern: "Ye gods, lords of sea
and earth and storms, give us a smooth course, and an easy wind, and
blow with propitious gales." The breezes we prayed for freshen, and
the harbour is seen to open as we draw nearer, and a temple of Minerva
appears on the heights. My comrades furl their sails, and turn their
prows to the strand. The harbour by the force of the eastern wave is
scooped into the shape of a bow: the jutting rocks are sprinkled with
briny foam: sheltered is the bay itself; the towering crags slope their
sides as with double wall; and the temple is retired from the shore.
Here on the green sward I saw the first omen, four horses white as snow
feeding on the spacious plain. And my father Anchises said, "'Tis war,
thou stranger-land, that thou dost offer; for war are horses armed, and
this herd threatens war. And yet, for all that, these steeds at times
will often submit to the chariot, and underneath the yoke in concord
bear the bit. So there is hope of peace." Then we pray to the holy
power of Pallas, who clasheth arms, for she first received us in triumph;
and in front of the altars we veil our heads with Phrygian cloak; and by
the warnings of Helenus which he specially gave, we burn to Argive
Juno the offerings we were told to pay. Then without delay, no sooner
are our vows fulfilled, than we turn to sea the horns of our sail-clad yard-
arms, and flee from the homes of the Grecian race, and the fields we
distrust. Hence is descried Tarentum's bay; the town belongs to the race
of Hercules, if report tells true. Over against it rises the Lacinian
goddess, and the towering crags of Caulon, and Scylacæum, that wrecks
the mariners. Here, rising in the horizon from the Sicilian flood, Ætna
is descried; and from afar we hear the moaning of the main, and the
lashed cliffs, and the breakers roaring to the shore; the shallows surge,
and the sand is thrown up by the swell. And my father said: "No doubt
this is that dreaded Charybdis, and these the cliffs, these the frightful

rocks that Helenus warned us of. Save yourselves, my comrades, and ply in time your oars." They did as they were bid; and Palinurus was the first to turn his creaking prow to the waters to the left; for the left made all our crew with oars and sails at once. We are lifted to the heavens on the crested wave, and again we sink to the lowest shades, as the wave descends. Thrice did the cliffs roar amidst the rocky caverns, thrice did we see the foam dashing up, and the starry skies dripping.

568—587. *They pass by the mountain Ætna. The description of a volcano. A gloomy night.*

Meanwhile, the wind and sun leave us weary mariners at once, and ignorant of our course we drift to the coast of the Cyclops. The harbour is sheltered from the approach of winds, unmoved in its broad bay; but hard by thunders Ætna with dreadful ruinous crash, and sometimes hurls forth on high a murky cloud smoking with pitchy whirlwind and red-hot embers, and raises balls of flame, and licks the starry pole; again ofttimes it lifts and belches forth rocks and the entrails of the torn mountain, and masses with a moan the melted stones on high, and surges from its lowest depths. Fame says Enceladus' form scorched by the thunderbolt is overwhelmed by this mighty pile, and that huge Ætna placed above him breathes forth flames from its bursting furnace ; and as often as the giant turns his weary side, as oft does all Sicily awake with rumbling roar, and the heavens are veiled with smoke. All that night long, under the covert of the woods we endure monstrous portents, but cannot see the causes of that noise. For the constellations gave no light, and the pole was not bright with its starry firmament ; but there were clouds o'er the dark heaven, and the still dead of night hid the moon in a mist.

588—611. *Achemenides, the comrade of Ulysses, a piteous object, begs mercy of the Trojans.*

The following day was just rising with its early dawn, and Aurora had scattered from the sky the damp shades, when suddenly from the woods is seen to come forth the strange form of an unknown man, wan with extreme leanness, and clad in wretched garb, who lifts his suppliant hands towards the shore. We turn and look. Frightful was his squalor, his shaggy beard hung down, his garment had thorns for clasps ; and yet in other things he was a Greek, one who had once been sent to Troy in his country's arms. Now when he saw at a distance the Dardan dress, and Trojan armour, for a while, terrified at the sight, he stood motionless and checked his steps ; then to the shore hurrying rushed with tears and prayers ; "By the stars," he said, "I adjure you, by the gods above, by the light and breath of heaven, O Trojans, take me hence ; lead me to any lands, I care not what; this will be enough. I know that I was one of the sailors of the Grecian ships, nor do I deny that I attacked in war the Trojan gods. For which, if such be the injury of my crime, tear my limbs and scatter them o'er the waves, or drown me in the deep sea. If I am to perish, it will be a comfort to perish by human hands." He spoke, and embraced our knees, and prostrate still to our knees he clung. We encourage him to declare who he was, and whence sprung, and then to reveal to us what fortune pursued him. My father Anchises himself, without delay, gives his right hand to the youth, and comforts his heart with a ready pledge.

612—654. Achemenides tells the tale of Ulysses and Polyphemus, already told by Homer.

He lays aside his fear at last, and thus he speaks: "Ithaca is the country whence I come, I was the companion of ill-fated Ulysses; my name is Achemenides, my father Adamastus was poor; would to heaven I had been content with my fortune and stayed at home; but for Troy I set out. Here my comrades, while in haste they flee from the cruel abode, forgot and left me in the dreary den of the Cyclops. 'Tis the home of putrid gore, and bloody food; 'tis dark within and vast: its giant master strikes the stars with his head—ye gods, deliver the earth from such a monster, 'tis hard to bear his sight, and none can address him with speech. He feeds on the entrails and black blood of his victims. I saw with mine own eyes how he grasped in one hand two of our company, and as he lay supine in the middle of his den dashed them against a stone, and the dabbled hall swam with gore; I saw him chew their limbs streaming with matter and black blood, while their joints still warm quivered beneath his teeth. Yet he suffered for his sin; for Ulysses could not brook such wrongs, nor did the prince of Ithaca forget his nature in such a crisis of events. For, as soon as, glutted with meats, and stupid with drink, he rested his drooping neck, stretched o'er his den with monstrous length, and belched forth foul gore, and pieces of food together with bloody wine, as he lay asleep, we prayed to the mighty gods, and each our duty chose; then all at once on every side pour upon him, and with a sharpened weapon bore his eye so huge, his single eye deep set beneath his scowling forehead, of form and size like to a Grecian shield, or the sun's shining disk; and so at last with joy avenge our comrades' ghosts. But fly, ye wretched men; yes, fly, and from the shore your cables cut at once. Dire is the form and huge the size of Polyphemus in his hollow cave, when he pens his fleecy flock, and milks their udders; but, as great and dire as he, are a hundred monstrous Cyclops; who dwell up and down along these winding shores, and wander on the lofty mountains. Thrice have the horns of the moon been filled with light, all which time I drag on my life in the woods amongst the lonely lairs and haunts of the wild beasts, and from a rock in the distance I see the huge Cyclops, and tremble at the tramp of their feet, and the roar of their voices. A poor, sorry living, berries and stony cornels, the boughs supply; I pluck the herbs and gnaw their roots. As I looked all around, this was the first fleet I sighted drawing to the shores. To this I surrender myself, let it turn out to be whate'er it may, content to have escaped this monstrous race. I rather choose that you should destroy my life with any kind of death."

655—691. The monster Polyphemus is seen. The Trojans save the Greek and fly out to sea. They remember the counsel of Helenus, and sail southwards.

Scarce had he spoken, when on the summit of the mountain we see Polyphemus himself, the shepherd in the midst of his sheep, moving along with mighty bulk towards the well-known shore, a monster horrible, misshapen, huge, bereft of the sight of his eye. The trunk of a

pine guides his feet with the effort of his hand, and steadies his steps ;
his fleecy sheep follow him : they were his only pleasure, and solace in
his woe. When he has reached the deep waves and come to the sea, with
the water he washes the flowing blood from the hollow of his lost eye,
gnashing his teeth, and moaning, and stalks through the water quite
out to sea, and, for all that, the waves did not yet wet his tall sides.
We hurry and hasten our flight far from thence, having taken on board
the suppliant who well deserved our help, and quietly cut our cables ;
forward we bend, and sweep the water's face with emulous oars.   He
heard the noise, and to the sound of the splash directed his steps. But
when he could in no wise reach us with his hand, nor keep pace in
pursuit with our flight through the Ionian waves, he raises a mighty
shout, at which the sea and all its billows shook, and far into land the
Italian country was terrified, and Ætna rumbled in its winding caverns.
Thereby was roused the race of Cyclops forth from the woods and from
the lofty mountains, and they rush down to the harbour, and crowd the
beach.   We can descry the brothers of Ætna standing there in impo-
tent rage, each with his frowning eye, bearing their lofty heads towards
heaven, a dreadful conclave; as when with lofty tops towering oaks, or
spiry cypresses are seen to rise, the tall wood of Jove, or the grove of
Diana.   Keen fear drives us in haste to uncoil our ropes, and to fill
our sails with any favouring winds. On the other hand, the injunctions
of Helenus warn us against Scylla and Charybdis ; unless our crews
can hold their course straight on between these two in the narrow space
that saves from death, we determine to sail back.   When lo ! sent to
our aid the north wind came blowing from the point in the strait at
Pelorus.   I am wafted past the mouth of Pantagia with its natural rocks,
and the bay of Megara, and Thapsus lying low.   These shores were
pointed out by Achemenides, companion of ill-fated Ulysses, as he coasted
once more back along the scene of his wanderings.

692—715. *Sailing along Sicily Æneas comes to Drepanum, where his
father Anchises dies.*

Stretched in front of the Sicanian bay lies an island over against
Plemmyrium washed by many waves ; men called the place of old
Ortygia.   Fame says that hither Alpheus, river of Elis, forced his hidden
way beneath the sea, who now through the mouth of thy fountain,
Arethusa, mingles with the waves of Sicily.   We do as we are bid,
and pay homage to the great divinities of the place ; and next I pass
the rich soil by marshy Helorus.   After that, we sail close to the high
cliffs and jutting rocks of Pachynus, and Camarina is seen in the distance, a place the fates forbad should ever be moved, and the plains
of Gela, and great Gela itself named from its river.   Next steep Acragas
shows its giant walls ; it once reared spirited steeds.   And thee I leave,
Selinus city of palms, for heaven gives us breezes ; and coast along by
the shallows of Lilybæum with their dangerous hidden rocks.   Then the
harbour and joyless shore of Drepanum receive me. Here I, who have been
driven by so many storms of the sea, lose, alas ! my father Anchises, my
comfort in every care and calamity ; here, best of fathers, thou didst
abandon thy weary son ; alas, in vain hadst thou been rescued from

such great dangers. Nor did the seer Helenus, though he warned me of many horrors, nor the fury Celæno predict this sorrow. This was my last toil ; this the goal of my long voyage. As I left this place, the god drove me to your shores.

716—718. *Æneas ends the tale of his wanderings.*

Thus father Æneas, one, in the presence of many listeners, told his tale, and brought before them heaven's decrees and his own voyage. At length he paused, and made an end, and ceased his speech.

BOOK IV.

1—53. *Dido's restless passion. She confides to her sister her love for Æneas, and her scruples. Anna encourages her love, and extols the advantage and glory of an alliance with the Trojans.*

BUT the queen, smitten from the first with deep pain, ever nurses the wound within her veins, and is wasted by a hidden fire. Many a time does the worth of the hero, and many a time does the glory of his descent come back full upon her soul: his looks and words cling fixed within her breast, and pain withholds from her limbs quiet repose. The following dawn was visiting the world with the lamp of Phœbus, and had dispelled from the sky the damp shadow, when thus in distraction she speaks to the sister of her heart: "Anna, my sister, what visions bewilder and appal me? Who is this new guest that has entered our abode? What a hero is he in countenance and bearing! how noble is his spirit and soldiership! I for my part believe, and my conviction is not ungrounded, that he is the offspring of the gods. Baseborn souls their cowardice detects. Alas, by what storms of fate has he been tossed; what wars endured to the end did he recount! Were I not resolved in soul fixedly and immoveably not to consent to ally myself to any one in the bond of marriage, since the time that my first love played me false, and disappointed me by death ; were I not quite weary of the bridal-chamber and the torch, perhaps I had been able to give way to this one weakness. Yes, Anna, I will confess it, since Sychæus my unhappy husband met his doom, and the Penates were sprinkled with a brother's blood, he alone has swayed my feelings, and pressed upon my resolution till it totters. I recognize the traces of my former flame. But I could wish that either the earth would first open from its lowest depths to receive me, or that the Almighty Father would strike me down to the shades with his thunderbolt, to the ghastly shades of Erebus, and the abyss of night, before I violate thee, O Chastity, or annul thy rights. He who was the first to join me to himself has carried away my affections; let him keep them with him, and preserve them in his grave." So she spoke, and filled her bosom with a burst of tears. Anna replies: "Dearer than the light to your sister, will you in sad solitude waste away all through your youth, nor prove the sweetness of children, nor the blessings of love? Think you that ashes and buried spirits of the dead care for that? Albeit no suitors formerly moved you in your sorrow, not in Libya, not before that,

at Tyre; though Iarbas was scorned, and other chiefs, whom Africa rears,
a land enriched with victory, will you fight even against a love that has
pleased you?   And does it not enter your mind in whose lands you have
settled?   On this side the towns of the Gætulians, a race invincible in
war, and the unbridled Numidians hem you round, and the inhospitable
Syrtis; on that a region desolate through drought, and the Barcæi raging
far and wide.   Why should I speak of wars rising at Tyre, and the
threatenings of your brother?   I at least consider that by the authority
of the gods and the favour of Juno the ships of Ilium have been steadily
wafted on this course.   To what grandeur will you see this city rise, and
this realm, my sister, by such a marriage!   With the warriors of Troy on
our side, how mightily will the glory of Carthage be exalted!   Do
but intreat the indulgence of Heaven, and when your sacrifices have
proved propitious, give yourself up to hospitality, and weave a chain of
pretexts for delay, so long as the winter and watery Orion rage in all
their might upon the sea, and his ships are shattered; so long as the
wild sky may not be encountered."

54—89. *Dido strives by sacrifices to win the grace of Heaven to excuse
the breaking of her vow. Her absorbing love for Æneas.*

By these words she filled with the flames of love a soul already kindled, and inspired with hope a wavering mind, and melted away its scruples.   First they visit the shrines, and seek to obtain grace at every
altar; they slay ewes duly chosen, to Ceres the Lawgiver, and to Phœbus,
and to father Lyæus; to Juno above all the rest, for she is the guardian
of marriage ties.   The beautiful Dido herself, holding a bowl in her
hand, pours it out just between the horns of a spotless cow, or before the
eyes of the gods paces beside the rich altars, and solemnises the day
with offerings, and gazing intently upon the opened breasts of the victims,
examines their palpitating vitals.   Alas how ignorant are the minds of
priests!   What can vows, what can shrines do for her in her frenzy?
The stealing flame is incessantly devouring her heart, and her wound un-
uttered lives deep within her breast.   The wretched Dido feels the flame,
and roams all through the city in her frenzy, like a doe shot by an arrow,
whom a shepherd chasing with his weapons has pierced from afar in her
security amid the Cretan forests, and has left there the winged dart un-
wittingly; she in flight ranges through the Dictæan groves and glades;
the fatal shaft is fixed fast in her side.   Now she conducts Æneas with
her throughout the town, and exhibits the wealth of Sidon, and the city
already provided; she begins to speak, and breaks off with her words
half formed.   Now at the decline of day she again resorts to the same
banquet, and again in her madness craves to hear the troubles of Troy,
and again hangs upon his lips as he tells the tale.   Afterwards, when the
guests have separated and the moon in her turn buries her light in gloom,
and the setting stars invite to sleep, in solitude she mourns in her empty
mansion, and throws herself upon the couch that he has left; him she
hears and sees, though she be far from him, and he from her; or linger-
ingly fondles Ascanius on her lap, fascinated by his father's likeness, if
so she can beguile her ineffable love.   The towers that are begun cease
to rise, the young men no longer practise arms or construct harbours and

secure defences for time of war, the works are broken off and suspended, and so are the mighty frowning walls, and the engine raised as high as heaven.

90—128. Juno's stratagem to cause Æneas to set up his kingdom at Carthage, instead of in Italy. Her conversation with Venus.

So soon as the beloved wife of Jove knew that she was possessed by such a curse, and that her reputation was not proof against her passion, the child of Saturn addressed Venus in words like these: "Splendid renown indeed, and magnificent spoils are you winning, you and your boy, a great and glorious name, when one woman is conquered by the craft of two gods. And I am not in the least unaware that through dread of a city of mine you have held in suspicion the hospitality of proud Carthage. But what limit is there to be, or what now can be the object of so keen a strife? Let us rather establish an everlasting peace and a settled marriage. You possess the whole object of your purpose: Dido burns with love, and has felt the passion coursing through her veins. Let us then govern this nation in common, and with equal authority; let us suffer her to own a Phrygian husband for her lord, and to deliver into your hand the Tyrians as her dowry." To her, for she perceived that with a counterfeited object she had spoken, in order to divert to the shores of Libya the empire of Italy, Venus in reply thus began: "Who would be so mad as to refuse such an offer, or to prefer to contend with you in war, if only, as you tell me, success be the sequel of our work? But all in doubt I am driven along by fate, whether it be the will of Jove that one city hold the Tyrians and them who have come from Troy, or if he consents that the nations be united and firmly leagued together. You are his wife, it is your privilege to sound his intention by your prayers. Lead the way; I will follow." Then Queen Juno thus replied: "That task shall rest with me. Now attend, I will inform you in a few words in what way your immediate object can be accomplished. Æneas and the hapless Dido with him intend to go into the forest to hunt, when to-morrow's sun has begun to display his rising, and has revealed the world with his beams. Upon them I will pour down from above a black cloud of rain mingled with hail, while the beaters are busy and are encircling the coverts with their toils, and will wake with thunder the whole heaven. Their attendants shall disperse and be shrouded in thick darkness. Dido and the Trojan chief shall light upon the same cave. I will be present, and if I am assured of your compliance, will unite them in lasting wedlock, and will make her his for ever. This shall be their proper marriage." Cytherea assented without opposition to her request, and smiled as she discovered the craft.

129—172. The hunting party. Dido excuses and openly proclaims her wedlock with Æneas.

Meanwhile Aurora rises and has left the ocean. When it is broad daylight, the flower of the youth pass out from the gates. Nets with wide meshes, snares, hunting spears with broad heads, and Massylian horsemen pour forth, and the keen-scented strong hounds. The princes of Carthage await at the entrance their queen, while she lingers in her chamber, and her steed stands brilliant with purple and gold, and full of spirit champs the foaming bit. At last she comes forth escorted by a numerous suite, with her Sidonian mantle bordered with an embroidered hem; her quiver is of gold, her hair is fastened into a knot with a golden clasp, a golden buckle binds up her purple dress. Likewise both her Phrygian attendants and the joyful Iulus pass along. Æneas himself, beautiful beyond all the rest, joins her troop as her companion, and unites the train. Like Apollo when he leaves Lycia in the winter and the streams of Xanthus, and visits his mother's Delos, and sets up anew his dances, and around the altars in a mass the Cretans and Dryopes revel, and the painted Agathyrsi; he himself steps along the ridges of Cynthus, and with a pliant wreath gracefully confines his flowing hair, and with a circlet of gold entwines it; his weapons rattle on his shoulders. No less lightly than he Æneas went along; grace as bright as his beams forth on his heroic countenance. When they arrived among the high mountains and trackless thickets, straightway the wild goats driven down from the brow of the rock ran along the ridges; in another direction the stags scour over the open plains, and unite in crowded flight their dusty bands, and leave the mountains. But the young Ascanius in the heart of the valleys exults in his spirited horse, and now passes these, now those in his career, and longs for a foaming wild boar to be granted to his prayers among the cowardly herds, or for a tawny lion to come down from the mountains. Meanwhile the sky is filled with tumult and terrible roar; then comes a storm of mingled rain and hail; and the Tyrian attendants in disorder, and the Trojan youths, and the Dardan grandson of Venus have fled to shelter hither and thither throughout the fields. Dido and the Trojan chief light upon the same cave: the torrents pour down from the mountain. Both primæval Earth and Juno that waits upon the bride give the sign: fires flash in the firmament that acknowledges the marriage, and the Nymphs cry aloud on the topmost height. That day was the first that was of death, and the first that was of misery the source; for Dido is neither any longer influenced by a regard for appearance or reputation, nor any longer thinks of a clandestine love: she calls it wedlock; behind this name she screens her frailty.

173—197. *Description of Fame. She spreads abroad the disgrace of Dido, and excites the anger of king Iarbas.*

Immediately Fame begins to traverse the mighty cities of Libya, Fame who is surpassed in swiftness by nothing else that is bad; she grows by her restless motion, and gathers vigour as she speeds along; small through fear at first, presently she exalts herself towards heaven, and stalks along the ground, and hides her head amid the clouds. Her the Earth her mother, exasperated with wrath against the gods, brought forth, as they tell, to be the youngest sister of Cœus and Enceladus, with nimble feet and rapid wings, a monster frightful, huge; who, for every feather on her body, has as many wakeful eyes beneath, (wondrous to tell) as many loud tongues and mouths, as many ears that she pricks up to listen. By night she flies between heaven and earth, through the gloom, with buzzing wings, nor droops her eyelids in soothing sleep; by day she keeps watch, perched either on the very top of a house, or on high towers, and continually terrifies great cities, being as firmly attached to what is false and wrong, as she is a messenger of truth. She at that time began to fill the nations with manifold report, exulting in it, and to repeat alike fact and fiction; how that Æneas has come, sprung from Trojan blood, to whom as a husband fair Dido deigns to be united; that now with one another they are passing the whole length of winter in slothful excess, unmindful of their kingdoms, and enslaved by shameful passion. This the loathed goddess pours abroad into the mouths of men. Straightway she directs her career to king Iarbas, and fires his soul with her words, and piles up motives for his wrath.

198—237. *Iarbas the son of Jupiter Ammon prays to Jove to revenge him for the disdain of Dido. Mercury is bidden to command Æneas to quit Carthage.*

He, the son of Ammon by a ravished Libyan Nymph, set up to Jupiter in his broad realms a hundred vast temples, a hundred altars, and had consecrated the undying fire, the everlasting watcher of the gods, and a ground rich with the blood of victims, and thresholds flowery with various garlands. And he, frantic in soul and fired by the bitter rumour, is said, before the altars, in the midst of the holy gods, to have addressed to Jove many a humble prayer with hands uplifted: "Almighty Jove, to whom the Maurusian people, when they feast on their embroidered couches, now pour out in homage the libation of wine, dost thou behold this? or is it without cause that we dread thee, my father, when thou hurlest thy thunderbolts? and do aimless flashes flash amid the clouds terrify our souls, and tumultuously roar at random? A woman, who, when wandering in our territory, founded at a price a little town, to whom we granted a strip of coast for cultivation, and whom we made the lady of the land, has rejected marriage with us, and has received into her realm Æneas for her lord. And now that Paris, with his effeminate train, his chin and oiled hair bound up with the Mæonian turban, enjoys his plunder; we bring gifts to temples which are thine forsooth, and guard a glory which is nothing." As he was uttering such prayers, and clasping the altars, the Omnipotent heard him, and directed his eyes to the royal walls and the lovers forgetful of their better fame. Then he thus addresses Mercury, and gives him this commission: "Go now, my son, summon the Zephyrs, and downward glide upon thy wings, and address the Dardan chief, who now loiters in Tyrian Carthage, and regards not the cities granted him by fate, and carry down my command through the fleet breezes. His beauteous mother did not promise us that he would be such as this, nor is it with this purpose that she has twice rescued him from the warriors of Greece; but she promised that it would be he who would rule Italy, big with empire, and fierce in war, who would hand down a race from the ancient blood of Teucer, and bring all the world beneath his sway. If the glory of such high fortunes has no power to stir him, and he does not for himself, for his own renown, take in hand the task, does he, being a father, grudge his Ascanius the citadel of Rome? What are his plans? or with what expectation does he linger among a hostile people, and regard not his Ausonian progeny, and the Lavinian fields? Let him set sail; this is all; let this be our message."

238—295. *Mercury's flight to earth. He first lights on Mount Atlas; from thence he proceeds to Carthage, and delivers to Æneas the command of Jove. Æneas with reluctance begins secretly to prepare for his voyage.*

So he spoke; the other made ready to obey the mandate of his mighty sire; and first he fastens on his feet the winged sandals all of gold, which bear him soaring on his wings, either over sea or land, as swiftly as the rushing blast. Next he takes his wand; with it he summons forth from Orcus pale spirits, others he sends down to gloomy Tartarus; he gives sleep, and takes it away, and unseals the eyes from death; strong in its power he drives the winds before him, and stems the stormy clouds; and now, as he flies along, he descries the crest and steep sides of hardy Atlas, who props the heaven on his top, Atlas, whose piny head, ever encircled with black clouds, is lashed by wind and rain; snow pours down and covers his shoulders; besides, torrents flow headlong down the old man's chin, and his beard is bristling and stiff with ice. Here first Cyllenius, poised on even pinions, paused; hence with all his force he shot straight downward to the sea, in semblance like a bird, which round about the coast, and about the rocks where fish abound, flies low close to the surface of the sea. Even so the child of Cyllene, as he came from his maternal grandfather, flew along between earth and sky, cleaving his way between the sandy shore of Libya and the winds. As soon as ever he reached on his winged feet the mean suburbs of the city, he beholds Æneas laying the foundation of fortresses and rebuilding houses: the sword he wore was starred with yellow jasper, and the mantle that hung down from his shoulders blazed with Tyrian purple, a gift which wealthy Dido had wrought, and interwoven the warp with golden thread. At once he accosts him: "Is it you that now are laying the foundations of proud Carthage, and in your fondness for a wife are building up a splendid city? Alas, forgetful of your realm and fortunes! The ruler of the gods himself sends me down to you from bright Olympus, he who sways by his will heaven and earth, he himself bids me carry these commands through the fleet breezes; what are you planning? or with what expectation do you idly loiter in the land of Libya? If the glory of such high fortunes has no power to stir you, and you do not yourself, for your own renown, take in hand the task, regard the rising fortune of Ascanius, and the promise of Iulus your heir, to whom the realm of Italy and the land of Rome belong by right." When Cyllenius had uttered these words, he left the sight of man while the words were still on his lips, and vanished from the eyes far away into fleeting air. But Æneas straightway was struck speechless with amazement at the sight, and his hair stood on end with horror, and his words were stifled in his throat. He longs to flee away, and leave the land he loves, awe-struck at so high a warning and the divine command. Alas what is he to do? with what address can he now dare to try to conciliate the frantic queen? what opening can he adopt? And now hither now thither he swiftly de-

spatches his divided mind, and hurries it in various directions, and
continually whirls it through everything. As he balanced his plans,
this seemed to be the best; he summons Mnestheus and Sergestus
and the valiant Serestus, and bids them silently equip the fleet, and
muster their comrades to the shore, and get ready their arms, and
disguise the motive for the change of scheme: he himself meanwhile,
since the good Dido is in ignorance, and cannot imagine that so deep
a love can be broken off, will try to discover the means to approach
her, and the times when she can be addressed most gently, and the
method proper for his object. Quickly all with joy obey his order, and
haste to execute his commands.

296—361. *Dido at once detects the purpose of Æneas. She intreats him
not to forsake her. Æneas pleads the inexorable command of Jove.*

But the queen divined his craft, (who can deceive a lover?) and from
the first surmised the coming storm, distrusting even perfect safety. The
same impious Fame brought her news that the fleet was being equipped,
and preparations made for a voyage. Bereft of sense she raves, and fired
with madness rushes wildly all through the city, like a Thyiad roused by
the moving of the sacred mysteries, when the cry of Bacchus is heard, and
the triennial orgies goad her to frenzy, and Cithæron by night invites her
with its din. At length she anticipates Æneas by accosting him with
these words: "Did you think, traitor, that you could even disguise so
great a crime, and leave my land in silence? Does neither my love, nor
the hand you gave me once, nor Dido doomed to die by a cruel death,
keep you back? Moreover are you constructing a fleet in the winter
season, and hastening to sail over the deep while the winds are at the
height of their rage, hard-hearted? Why, if you were not trying to reach
lands that belong to others, and a home that you know not, and if old
Troy were standing, would your fleet set out for Troy over a boisterous
sea? Is it I whom you fly from? By these tears of mine and your own
plighted hand, since by my own act I have left nothing else to my
wretched self, by our union, by the marriage we have entered upon, if
I have deserved well of you in aught, or anything of mine has been dear
to you, pity my sinking house, and, if there is still any room for prayer,
cast aside your resolve, I entreat you. You are the cause that the tribes
of Libya and the chiefs of the Numidians hate me, that my Tyrians are
disaffected. You too are the cause that my chastity is lost, and former
reputation, by which only I could have risen to the stars. To whom do
you give me up, me at the point of death, my guest? For this name is
all that remains of that of husband. Why do I pause? Is it till my
brother Pygmalion demolish my walls, or the Gætulian Iarbas carry me
away captive? If only I had become the mother of any child by you
before your flight, if some little Æneas were playing in my palace, who,
after all, might reflect you in his countenance, I am sure I should not
think myself utterly captive and desolate." She ended: he through the
warning of Jove kept his eyes still unmoved, and with an effort confined
his pain within his heart. At last he makes a short reply: "I will never
deny, O queen, that you have fully merited the utmost that you have the
power of reckoning in words; and I shall not be sorry to remember

Elissa as long as I remember my own self, as long as the breath of life rules these limbs. I will speak shortly as the subject demands. I neither thought to conceal this my flight clandestinely (do not imagine it), nor did I ever hold forth a husband's torches, or enter into such an alliance as this. Would fate allow me to lead my life according to my own choice, and settle my troubles at my own pleasure, I would make the city of Troy my dwelling above all others, among the dear remnant of my people; the proud palace of Priam should still stand, and my hand should have founded for the vanquished a second Pergama. But now it is mighty Italy that Grynean Apollo, it is Italy that the Lycian oracles have bade me strive to reach: here is my love, here is my country. If the citadel of Carthage and the sight of a Libyan city charm you a Phœnician, why after this are you jealous, if Trojans settle in Ausonian land? We too have a right to seek out a foreign kingdom. Me the troubled phantom of my father Anchises, whenever night shrouds the world with her damp shadows, whenever the fiery stars arise, warns in sleep, and terrifies; me my young Ascanius grieves, and the wrong done to one I love, whom I am defrauding of the realm of Italy, and the fields given by fate. Now too the interpreter of heaven, sent by Jove himself (I call to witness both divinities), has brought me commands through the fleet breezes; with my own eyes I saw the god in full light entering the city, and drank in his words with these ears. Cease to kindle by your complaints both yourself and me: it is not by choice I follow Italy."

362—392. *Dido bursts into an agony of passionate reproaches.*

All through this speech she views him with averted looks, rolling her eyes hither and thither, and surveys him from head to foot with silent gaze, and thus breaks forth in rage: "Neither was a goddess your mother, nor Dardanus the founder of your race, traitor! but Caucasus bristling with rugged rocks begot you, and Hyrcanian tigresses gave you suck. For why do I disguise my feelings? Or for what deeper insults do I curb myself? Has he sighed at my weeping? Has his look relented? Has he been subdued to tears, or pitied his lover? What shall I say first, what next? Surely, surely, neither mighty Juno, nor the Father, the son of Saturn, behold these deeds with impartial eyes. There is no true honour in the world. Cast out upon the shore, destitute, I took him to myself, and madly established him in a share of my kingdom. I saved his lost fleet, I rescued his comrades from death. Alas! I am driven along fired by furies. *Now* the diviner Apollo, *now* the Lycian oracles, *now*, too, sent by Jove himself, the interpreter of heaven bears through the breezes his horrible, commands. No doubt such a task belongs to the gods above, no doubt such a care troubles their tranquillity. I neither try to hold you here, nor refute your words; go, follow your Italy, wafted by the winds, make for your kingdom o'er the waves. I at least hope, that if righteous deities have any power, you will drain the cup of retribution amid the rocks, and often call upon the name of Dido! With black fires I will pursue you, though I be far away; and, when cold death has separated my limbs from my spirit, my shade shall be with you wherever you are. You shall receive your punishment, wicked one! I shall hear it, and the story of it will come to me through the depths of hell." With these words she suddenly breaks off her speech, and, sick with sorrow, shuns the daylight, and turns away, and withdraws herself from sight, leaving him full of hesitation through fear, and essaying oft to speak. The maidens take her up, and bear back her lifeless limbs to her marble chamber, and lay them on the couch.

393—449. Æneas continues to prepare his fleet for the voyage. Dido again and again implores him to stay. She begs her sister to beseech him to remain at least for a short time; but Anna's intreaties are fruitless.

But pious Æneas, though he longs to soothe and comfort her sorrow, and to divert her pain by his words, often sighing, and staggered in resolution by strong love, nevertheless begins to execute the commands of heaven, and revisits his fleet. Then indeed the Trojans set themselves to the work, and launch the lofty ships all along the shore. The keel is careened and floated, and they bring leafy oars, and unshaped timber from the forests, in their eagerness for flight. You might observe them in the act of departing, and flocking out from all quarters of the city. Even as when ants, mindful of the winter, ravage a huge heap of corn, and store it up in their abode, the black troop moves across the plains, and over the grass they incessantly carry in the plunder along the narrow way; some with all their force push on with their shoulders mighty grains of corn, some keep the line together, and punish the slothful; the whole path is alive with the work. What was then your feeling, Dido, when you discerned such a sight, or what sighs did you heave, when from the height of your citadel you saw before you the long line of the shore full of life, and beheld the whole surface of the sea beneath your eyes made tumultuous with such loud clamours? Wicked love, what is there to which you do not drive the hearts of men? She is driven to resort again to tears, again to strive to win him by intreaty, and humbly to surrender her pride to love, lest she leave any course untried, and so die in vain. "Anna, you see the busy haste all along the shore; already the sail invites the gales, and the mariners in their joy have wreathed the sterns with garlands. I, since I have been able to look forward to so cruel a blow, shall also be able to endure it, my sister. Nevertheless, perform this one kindness for me, Anna, in my misery; for that traitor used to court the friendship of you alone, to intrust to you his inmost feelings; you alone knew to what means and at what times he was most easily accessible; go, my sister, and humbly address my haughty enemy; I did not conspire at Aulis with the Greeks to destroy the Trojan people, or send a fleet to Pergama; nor have I torn from the grave the ashes or the spirit of Anchises, that he should refuse to allow my words to enter his deaf ears. Whither is he recklessly rushing? Let him grant this last gift to his hapless lover: let him wait for an easy flight, and winds to waft him. I no longer ask for our former marriage, in which he has played me false, nor that he be deprived of his fair Latium, and forsake his kingdom; I crave nothing but time, a space for my frenzy to abate, wherein my fortune may teach me whom she has vanquished to mourn. I beg of you this last kindness, pity your sister; and, if you grant it me, I will repay you with the interest of my death." Such were the intreaties she used to make, and such the lamentations her unhappy sister bears and bears again to him. But he is not melted by any lamentations, nor listens compliantly to any addresses; fate stands in the way, and heaven stops the unmoved ears of the hero. Even as when Alpine blasts strive one against another to tear up an oak vigorous in its ancient strength, blowing upon it now from this point, now from that, a creaking is heard, and, as the trunk is shaken, the foliage deeply strews the ground; the tree itself clings to the crag, and as far as it lifts its top to the air of heaven, so far does it extend its root to hell. Just so, the hero is beaten upon by incessant intreaties from every point, and feels the pain keenly in his mighty heart: his resolve remains unshaken; the tears that fall are vain.

450—473. *Dido's despair. Her presages of death.*

Then it is that hapless Dido, distracted by fate, prays for death; she loathes to look upon the vault of heaven. To make her more determined to fulfil her design, and leave the light, she saw, when she was laying her gifts on the altar of burnt incense, (a frightful thing to tell,) the holy water growing black, and the wine, as she poured it out, turning into unclean gore. She revealed this that she had seen to no one, not even to her sister. Moreover, there was in her mansion a marble temple to her former husband, which she used to cherish with wondrous homage, and garland it with fillets of snowy wool and festal foliage. Hence she plainly seemed to hear the solemn speech and summons of her lord, when gloomy night was mistress of the world; and oft she heard the solitary owl on her high station give forth the sad sepulchral strain, and prolong her lingering lamentable cry: and moreover many a prediction of ancient prophets affrights her with its awful warning. In her dreams Æneas himself savagely drives her frantic before him; and ever to be left all alone she seems, ever to be journeying without a companion on an endless way, and seeking to find her Tyrians in a desolate land. Like as Pentheus in his madness sees the troops of the Eumenides, and a twofold sun, and a double Thebes rise to view; or as the son of Agamemnon, Orestes, driven over the stage, when he flees from his mother armed with firebrands and deadly serpents, and the avenging furies sit in the threshold.

474—503. *Dido, by disguising her purpose, persuades Anna to prepare the funeral pile.*

Therefore when she has taken the frenzy to her bosom, overpowered by misery, and doomed herself to die, she works out with her own heart the time and the means, and, addressing her speech to her sorrowing sister, conceals her purpose by her looks, and wears upon her brow the serenity of hope: "I have discovered a plan, congratulate me, my sister, to give him back to me, or release me from my love for him. Near the ocean that binds the earth, and near the setting sun, lies the remotest spot of Ethiopia, where mightly Atlas upholds upon his shoulder the revolving heaven studded with burning stars; a priestess from hence, a Massylian by nation, has been pointed out to me, the keeper of the temple of the Hesperides, who used to give feasts to the dragon, and guarded the holy boughs on the tree, sprinkling the food with dewy honey and sleepy poppy. She professes to release by charms whatever minds she pleases, but upon others to inflict cruel pains, to stay the current of rivers, and turn back the courses of the stars; and she calls up by night the spirits of the dead. You may perceive the earth rumble beneath your feet, and the ash-trees come down from the mountains. I take to witness, my dear sister, the gods, and thee, and thy sweet self, that unwillingly I arm myself with magic arts. Secretly erect, I pray you, a funeral pile rising toward heaven in the inner court of my house, and upon it let them lay the arms of the man, which the impious one left hanging in the chamber, and all he once wore, and the marriage-bed, the scene of my ruin; it is my pleasure to destroy all that reminds me of the wicked man, and the priestess so instructs me." Thus she speaks, and is silent; pallor withal overspreads her countenance. Nevertheless, Anna does not believe that she is hiding death behind her strange rites, and does not realise such a pitch of frenzy, or fear anything worse than happened at the death of Sychæus. Therefore she prepares what is asked for.

504—521. *Dido dresses the funeral pile.*

But the queen, when, in the retirement of her dwelling, the pile has been built up on high, huge with pine-brands and fagots of the ilex, strews garlands over the spot, and crowns it with funeral foliage: on the top she lays all that was his, and the sword that he left, and his image, on the couch, knowing well that which was to be. The altars are set up around, and the priestess with loosened hair loudly invokes the three hundred gods, and Erebus, and Chaos, and the threefold Hecate, the chaste Diana of triple countenance. She had also poured out sprinklings of water which pretended to be of the fount of Avernus, and downy plants that hold the milk of black poison are sought for, cut with brazen shears by moonlight, and the love-charm is sought for that is torn away from the forehead of a colt at its birth, and seized before the dam can take it. She herself, with holy meal and holy hands, beside the altars, with one foot stripped of its sandal, in flowing dress, with death in view, invokes the gods, and the stars that know the will of fate: next, she prays to every power that justly and mindfully keeps watch over lovers ill-matched in their union.

522—553. *In the silent night Dido is restless with grief and frenzy.*

'Twas night, and weary bodies throughout the world were enjoying quiet repose, and the woods and wild waves had sunk to rest; at the hour when the stars are in the midst of their circling course, when every field is still, when beasts and painted birds, both those that haunt the wide waters of the mere, and those that dwell in the savage thickets of the country, hushed in sleep beneath the silent night, soothed their sorrows and their hearts that had forgot their troubles. But not so the Phœnician wretched in soul; and never does she sink to sleep, or take in the night with eyes or bosom; her pain redoubles, and her love again swells up and surges, and she is swayed by a mighty tide of passion. Thus then she begins, and so she ponders with her own heart; "Now what am I about? shall I, now that I am scorned, go back, and court those that were my suitors, and humbly beg for marriage among the Numidians, though I have already so often disdained them for husbands? Shall I then follow the fleets of Ilium, and obey the utmost that the Trojans command? Shall I do so because they are glad to have been once relieved by my help, and gratitude for a past deed is still cherished in their memories? But suppose that I were willing; who will let me do so, or receive in his haughty ships my hateful self? Alas, lost one, are you so ignorant, and do you not yet realise the treachery of the race of Laomedon? What next? Shall I, all alone, accompany the exulting mariners in flight? Or shall I, encircled by my Tyrians, and the whole force of my people, bear down upon them, and again force over the sea the men whom I could scarcely tear away from the city of Sidon, and shall I bid them unfurl their sails to the winds? Nay, die, as you deserve, and drive away your sorrow with the sword. It is you, that, overpowered by my tears, it is you, my sister, that first loaded me in my frenzy with these ills, and exposed me to my enemy. And I was not permitted to pass a blameless life, like a wild creature, free from wedlock, and to leave such cares untouched! My faith has not been kept, the faith I pledged to the ashes of Sychæus." Such was the outburst of wailing that she uttered from her heart.

554—583. *Warned by Mercury, Æneas suddenly sets sail.*

Æneas on his high poop, being now resolved to start, was lying asleep, all things being now duly prepared. To him the form of the god, as he returned in the same guise, was presented in sleep, and a second time seemed thus to warn him, in all points like to Mercury, both in voice, and bloom, and auburn hair, and the youthful beauty of his limbs: "Goddess-born, can you still sleep on in such a crisis, and are you so mad as not to discern the immediate perils that encompass you, nor to hear the favourable breezes blow? She is planning within her heart craft and accursed crime, now determined to die, and is waking the tossing tides of passion. Do you not flee hence with headlong speed, while there is yet space to speed away? Soon you will behold the sea surging with ships, and fierce firebrands blazing, soon you will see the shore glowing with flames, if the dawn find you lingering in this land. Come now, break off delay. A thing fickle and changeable ever is woman." So he spoke, and melted into black darkness. Then it is that Æneas, struck with alarm at the sudden apparition, tears himself from sleep, and urges his comrades to the utmost: "Speedily awake, my warriors, and set yourselves to row; swiftly unfurl the sails, Lo, a god, sent from the height of heaven, again spurs us on to flee away in haste, and cut the twisted cables. We follow thee, holy divinity, whosoever thou art, and again with gladness obey thy command. May'st thou be with us, I pray, and aid us with thy grace, and send into the sky propitious stars." He spoke, and snatches from the scabbard his flashing sword, and strikes the hawsers with the naked blade. All are at once possessed with the same ardour; they hurry and hasten; the shore is deserted; the sea is hidden beneath the fleet, with vigour they dash up the foam, and sweep the dark blue sea.

584—629. *Dido descries the fleet of Æneas as it sails away. She breaks out into a passion of rage, and prays that Carthage may ever be the foe and the scourge of Italy.*

And now Aurora, as she left the saffron couch of Tithonus, was just beginning to shower fresh light upon the world. The queen, as soon as ever she saw the first whitening streak of dawn, and the fleet moving onward with level sails, and perceived that the shore and harbours were quite deserted by the mariners, again and again striking violently her beauteous breast, and tearing her auburn hair: "O Jove," she says, "shall this man, this foreigner, escape, after he has mocked my realm? Will ye not arm with speed, and pursue him from all parts of the city, and others at once draw down the ships from the dockyards? Begone, fetch me firebrands quickly, give me weapons, ply your oars. What am I saying? or where am I? What madness makes my purpose change? Unhappy Dido! Do your impious deeds come home to you now? They should have done so at the time that you gave him your sceptre. Behold the truth and honour of him, who, they say, carries with him the household gods of his family; of him who bore upon his shoulders his father worn with age. Had I not the power to drag him away and tear his body in pieces and strew it o'er the waves? Could I not have slain with the sword his comrades, nay, Ascanius himself, and served him to form a feast at his father's table? But the chance of battle would have been doubtful. It would: whom could I, doomed to die, be afraid of? I could have carried fire into his camp, and filled his decks with flames, and utterly destroyed both son and sire and all the race; then with my own hand would have added myself to the number. O Sun, who visitest with thy fires all the deeds of earth, and thou, Juno, who art the expounder and the conscious witness of these pains of love, and Hecate, that art invoked with cries by night at the crossways throughout the cities, and ye avenging Furies, and ye, guardian gods of dying Elissa, receive these words, and direct your well-deserved wrath against evil deeds, and hear my prayers. If it must be that his abhorred self reach the harbour, and swim to land, and if thus the fates of Jove require, if this be determined and fixed, still, harassed by the war and hostility of a bold nation, driven from his land, torn away from the arms of Iulus, may he beg for help, and behold the shameful deaths of his people; and may he not, when he has submitted to the conditions of an unequal peace, enjoy his kingdom or the prosperity he longs for; but fall before his time, and lie unburied on the open shore. This is my prayer, these my last words I pour out with my blood. Then do ye, O Tyrians, persecute with hatred his descendants, and all the future race, and send this as an offering to my ashes. Let there be no love and no league between the nations. Arise, some avenger, from my bones, to chase with fire and sword the Dardan settlers—now—hereafter—at any time, when strength shall be given. I pray that shore may be against shore, sea against sea, army against army: may both they that live now and their posterity be enemies."

630—705. *The story of Dido's death.*

So she spoke, and continually turned her thoughts in all directions, seeking how most speedily to break off from her the light she hates. Then in few words she addressed Barce the nurse of Sychæus; for her own was lying in black ashes in her old fatherland: "Dear nurse, bring hither to me where I stand my sister Anna; tell her to haste and sprinkle her body with river-water, and bring with her the prescribed victims and propitiatory offerings ; in such manner let her come : and you yourself shade your brow with the sacred fillet. It is my purpose to perform the sacrifice to Stygian Jove, which I have duly entered upon and prepared, and to put an end to my woes, and consign to the flame the funeral pile of him that is the offspring of Dardanus." So she speaks ; the other hastened her steps with an old woman's officiousness. But Dido, all trembling, and wild with her savage task, rolling her blood-shot eyes, and with her quivering cheeks interspersed with hectic spots, and pale at the approach of death, rushes through the doorway of the inner portion of the palace, and, full of frenzy, mounts the lofty pile, and unsheathes the Dardan sword, a gift that had not been asked for such a purpose as this. Hereupon, when she had viewed the Trojan dresses and the well-known couch, after pausing awhile in tears and thought, she threw herself upon the bed, and spoke her last words : "Ye dear adornments, so long as fate and heaven allowed, receive this spirit of mine, and release me from these woes. I have lived my life, and finished the course that fortune assigned me, and now great will be my phantom that will pass beneath the earth. I have set up a glorious city, I have seen the walls that I have built myself, I have avenged my husband, I have exacted retribution from my hostile brother—happy, alas too happy, if only the Dardan ships had never reached my shore!" She spoke; and with her lips pressed upon the couch, "Shall I die unrevenged? But yet let me die," she says ; "thus, thus it is my joy to descend into the darkness. Let the cruel Trojan drink in with his eyes the sight of this fire from the deep, and carry with him the omens of my death." She ended ; and with such words still on her lips, her attendants see her fallen upon the blade, and the sword reeking with gore, and her hands bespattered with it. A cry goes up to the height of the halls ; Fame rushes wildly through the frighted city. The houses resound with wailings and groans and the shrieks of women ; the sky reechoes with loud laments. Just as if Carthage or ancient Tyre had been stormed by the enemy, and was sinking altogether into ruins, and the furious flames were rolling through the dwellings of men and the temples of the gods. Aghast was her sister when she heard it ; and all distracted as she hurries along, disfiguring her face with her nails, and her bosom with her fists, she rushed through the throng, and cries to her dying sister by name : "Was this your purpose, my sister? Did you assail me with guile? Was it this that the funeral pile you asked for, this that the fires and the altar were to bring me? What shall be my first lament in my desolation? Did you scorn to have your sister for your companion in death? You should have invited me to the same doom ; the same pang dealt by the sword and the same hour should have despatched us both. Did I really build the pile with these hands, and solemnly summon the gods of our country, in order to be cruelly away from you when lying like this? You have destroyed yourself and me, my sister, and your subjects, and the senators of Sidon, and your city. Bring water for her wound ; I will wash away the blood, and if there still remains any last fluttering breath, I will catch it with my lips." So she spoke, and had reached the top of the lofty steps, and throwing her arms around her swooning sister, clasped her in her bosom with sighs, and strove to stanch with her dress the black gore. The other, after trying to lift up her heavy eyes, sinks back again ; the sword fixed deep grides within her breast. Thrice rising, and resting on her elbow, she lifted herself up ; thrice she rolled back upon the couch, and with swimming eyes sought to find the light in the height of heaven, and, when she found it, sighed. Then almighty Juno, in compassion for her long agony and painful departure, sent down Iris from Olympus to release the wrestling spirit, and the limbs that are entwined around it. For inasmuch as she was perishing neither by nature nor by a deserved death, but miserably before her time, and fired by sudden frenzy, Proserpine had not yet taken from her head the yellow lock, and consigned her life to Stygian Orcus. Therefore Iris flies down through the sky, all dewy on her saffron wings, trailing in the light of the opposite sun a thousand various hues, and takes her stand above her head ; " I by command bear away this lock holy to Dis, and release you from this body." So she says, and with her hand severs the lock : and in a moment all warmth has fled away, and life faded into the winds.

BOOK V.

1—34. *The flames of the funeral pile of Dido are an evil omen to the Trojans on the deep. Stormy weather warns them to turn aside to Sicily.*

MEANWHILE Æneas was now in his mid-course o'er the sea, firm in his purpose, and was cutting through the dark waves ruffled by the north wind, and looked back on the walls, which were now bright with the fires of the funeral pyre of unhappy Dido. Unknown was the cause which had lighted so great a flame ; but the thought how cruel are the pains of a strong passion when violated, and the knowledge of what a frenzied woman can do, cause the minds of the Trojans to pass through sad forebodings. When the vessels were out at open sea, and no land met the sight any more, but sea everywhere, and sky everywhere, o'er his head there gathered a dark storm of rain, bringing with it gloom and foul weather, and the wave ruffled beneath the darkness. Then spake the pilot Palinurus himself from the lofty stern : "Alas! why have such clouds o'ercast the sky ? What dost thou threaten, father Neptune ?" He spake, and at once bids them reef the sails and labour at their strong oars, and sidewards turn the sails to meet the wind, and speaks thus : " Noble Æneas, not if Jove himself would give me the warrant of his word, could I hope to reach Italy in such weather. The winds have changed, and roar across our course, as they rise from the lowering sunset, and the air is thickening into clouds. Nor have we strength to struggle in the teeth of the wind, or make head against it. Since Fortune prevails, let us even obey, and turn our course to her bidding. Far off cannot be, I imagine, the trusty shores of your brother Eryx, and the harbour of Sicily, if only I am duly mindful, when I again note the stars, before observed." To him said pious Æneas : " I too all along have known that the winds will so have it, and see that in vain you try to make head against them.

Shift your sails, and turn your course. Can there be a land more pleasant to me, or one to which I would rather direct my weary ships, than that which holds my friend, Dardan Acestes, and in its bosom embraces the bones of my father Anchises?" So said he; they made straight for the harbour; the favourable west-winds fill their sails, swiftly o'er the swelling sea is borne the fleet, and at last they gladly turn to the familiar shore.

35—41. Æneas is hospitably received by Acestes.

But at a distance on the summit of a lofty hill Acestes wonders at the coming of the friendly ships, and hastes to meet them : roughly was he dressed, armed with javelins, clad in the skin of an African bear ; him a Trojan mother had borne to the river Crimisus. He was not unmindful of his sires of old, and welcomes them on their return, and gladly entertains them with rustic wealth, and consoles the weary mariners with friendly supplies.

42—71. As it is the anniversary of the funeral of Anchises, his son declares he will celebrate games in honour of his memory.

When the bright morrow put the stars to flight at the early rising of the sun, Æneas summons his comrades from the whole shore to a meeting, and speaks from the eminence of a mound : "Noble children of Dardanus, descendants of the mighty gods, the months have run their course, and the year's circle is completed since the day that we committed to the earth the remains and bones of my parent, the seer, and dedicated the altars of grief. And now, unless I am mistaken, the day is at hand, which I shall always keep as a day of sadness, always as one to be much observed ; it was heaven's will, we must submit. This day I would keep, if I were an exile in the African Syrtes, or overtaken by a storm in the Grecian sea, or if I were in the very heart of Mycenæ, yet would I perform my annual vows, and duly solemnise the day by processions, and load the altar with its proper gifts. Now by no will of mine we are come even to the ashes and bones of my father, I cannot think without the purpose and providence of heaven, and have been wafted hither and entered a friendly harbour. Come then, and with one consent let us gladly celebrate this worship; let us invoke the winds; and so may my father will, that, when I have founded my town, I may year by year offer these sacred rites to him in a consecrated temple. Acestes of Trojan race gives you for every ship two heads of oxen according to the number of vessels ; invite to your feasts the Penates of your country, and those worshipped by our host Acestes. Further, when the ninth morn raises its genial light for mortals, and with the beams of the sun reveals the world, then I will propose for the Trojans first a contest of swift-sailing ships ; and he who is strong in the foot-race, and he who bold in strength bears himself better than others, either to throw the dart or shoot with light arrows, and if there be one who dares to engage with the cestus of ox-hide, let them altogether be present, and expect to receive the prizes earned by victory. See that you all eschew ill-omened words, and crown your brows with leaves."

72—103. As they worship the spirit of Anchises, a harmless snake glides over the altar. It is perhaps the familiar spirit of the father of Æneas.

He speaks, and puts around his temples a wreath of his mother's myrtle. Helymus does the same, the same Acestes ripe in years, the same does the boy Ascanius, the rest of the youth follow. Then from the council went the hero to the mound, with many thousands, in the centre of the great crowd that attended. And here he duly pours in libation two bowls full of unmixed wine, two of new milk, two of the blood of the victims; and scatters bright flowers, and thus he speaks: "Hail, holy parent, the second time hail, ye ashes, which I again revisit in vain, and thou soul and shade of my sire. For heaven did not suffer me to have you with me in my search for the coasts of Italy, and the fields the fates give us, and Ausonian Tiber, whate'er that stream may be." He finished his speech, when from the depth of the holy tomb came gliding a serpent, which with huge length trailed seven coils, seven folds; gently round the tomb it went, passing lightly o'er the altar: blue were the streaks on its back, but bright spots of gold made its scales to blaze like fire ; as when in the clouds the rainbow casts a thousand colours of various hue from the opposite sun. Amazed at the sight was Æneas. The serpent with long trail crawling between the bowls and polished cups just tasted the meats, and harmless slunk back beneath the shelter of the tomb, and left the altars where he had fed. Encouraged by this the hero renews the offer-ings to his father, which he had begun ; he knew not whether to think this to be the Genius of the place, or the attendant spirit of his sire ; two sheep he sacrifices according to the rites, as many swine, as many steers with sable backs; and oft he poured wine from the bowls, inviting the soul of great Anchises and the spirit freed from Acheron. Moreover, his comrades, each according to their ability, with cheerful mind offer gifts, they load the altar, and sacrifice steers ; others in order set the caldrons, and, stretched along the grass, beneath the spits place hot burning coals, and roast the entrails.

104—123. *The names of the ships and captains of the vessels that start in the race.*

And now the long-expected day was come, and the steeds of the bright god ushered in the ninth morn with unclouded light, and rumour and the name of famous Acestes had roused the neighbouring people; they crowded the shore with joyous company, for they had come partly to see Æneas' men, and partly were prepared to enter the lists. There first, before the eyes of all and in the centre of the circus, are placed the gifts; sacred tripods, and chaplets of green leaves, and palms, the victor's prize, and arms, and robes dyed with Tyrian purple, a talent of gold and a talent of silver; then the trumpet from the centre of the mound with its notes proclaims the opening of the games. First enter the contest four ships chosen from the whole fleet, fairly matched with their heavy banks of oars. Swift was the Pristis which Mnestheus pro-pels with his spirited crew; (soon would he be Mnestheus of Italy ; from his name are called the house of Memmius :) huge was the Chimæra, huge its bulk, which Gyas commands ; it seems like a floating town; it the Dardan youth impel with triple tier of rowers ; in three banks rise the oars: next Sergestus, from whom the house of Sergius has its name, is

borne in the mighty Centaur; whilst in the dark-blue Scylla comes
Cloanthus, from whom you are descended, O Roman Cluentius.

124—243. *The course, the swiftness of the ships, the various chances of
the race, the hard won victory of Cloanthus.*

In the distance out at sea is a rock facing the foaming beach; at times
it is submerged and buffeted by the swelling waves, when the stormy
north-westers hide the stars; in calm weather it is quiet, and rises
above the still sea with level surface; a station where the cormorants
most delight to bask. On it father Æneas placed the goal of the race,
a green leafy oak as a mark for the mariners, and a point whence they
might know when to turn home, and to bend round in the circuit of the
long course. Then they choose their places by lot; and the captains
themselves standing on their sterns are seen from afar glittering in the
beauty of gold and purple; the youthful crew are crowned with wreaths of
poplar leaf, stripped are their shoulders, and glitter with streaming oil.
They take their seats on the benches, their arms are stretched on the oars;
intently they wait for the signal; throbbing excitement and straining
passion for renown draw the blood of their bounding hearts. But the
moment the clear-toned trumpet gave forth its notes, all at once shot
forth from their starting-places; the shout of the mariners strikes the
sky; their arms are drawn to their breast, the sea is turned up, and
lashed into foam. They plough up their furrows in time; all the water's
surface is opened and dashed up by the oars, and three-headed prows.
Not so rapid in the two-horsed race are the chariots, when they scour the
plain, and pouring from the starting-point rush forward; not so eagerly
do the charioteers urge the yoked steeds, and shake their waving reins,
while they hang forward to give their lashes force. Then the whole forest
re-echoes to the applause, and to the shouts and zealous cries of the
backers, the shores shut in by woods repeat the sound, the hills are struck
and the clamour rebounds. Gyas takes the lead, and in the front skims
o'er the waves amidst the confusion and the shouting; next Cloanthus
follows close; he was better manned, but his bulky boat clogged his
speed. Next to these, at equal distance, the Pristis and the Centaur
strive to pass each other and gain the foremost place. At one moment
Pristis gains, then the Pristis is beaten and passed by the great Centaur,
again they are both level, and shoot forward with prows abreast, cutting the briny waters with their long keels. And now they neared the
rock, and were close to the turning point, when Gyas, foremost in the
race, victor in the midst of the billows, thus charges with loud voice his
pilot Menœtes: "Why so far to the right, pray? hither turn your course,
hug the rock, let your oar blades graze the cliffs to the left: let others stand
out to sea." So said he. Menœtes feared the hidden reefs, and turns his
prow towards the deep waters of the open main. "What do you so far
out? steer for the rocks, Menœtes," again shouted Gyas to recall him:
and lo! he looks back and sees Cloanthus close to his stern, in possession of the water near the rock. So Cloanthus, between the galley of
Gyas and the roaring rocks, just shaves the island in his course to the
left, inside Gyas, and suddenly passes the leader, and leaves the goal
behind, and now he is in safe waters. Then great was the anger and

fury in the young man's heart; tears flowed down his cheeks, he forgot his own honour, his comrades' safety, and pushed headlong from the high stern into the sea the dastard Menœtes. Himself as pilot takes his place at the helm, he himself is steersman, and exhorts his men, and turns the rudder to the rock. But heavily rose at length and scarcely from the deep water Menœtes; for he was old, and he was dripping in his drenched clothes: he swam to the surface of the rock, and sat down on the dry stone. As he fell in, the Trojans laughed; they laughed at the swimming pilot, they laugh as he vomits from his breast the briny water. Hereupon a joyous hope kindles in the heart of the two rearmost, Sergestus and Mnestheus, that perhaps they might pass the lagging Gyas. Sergestus first gets the foremost place, and nears the rock; and yet he is not leading by the whole galley's length, he is leading by half a length, half his ship the rival Pristis overlaps with her beak. But Mnestheus paces the deck, and in the midst of his comrades exhorts them, saying: "Now, now, ply your oars, ye that once were comrades of Hector, ye whom in the last fortunes of Troy I chose for my followers; now put forth that strength, that spirit which ye once shewed in the African quicksands, and in the Ionian sea, and in the running waves of Malea. I Mnestheus aim not now to gain the prize, nor strive for victory; and yet, if only!—but let those win, to whom Neptune appoints success; to return the last of all would be shameful: my friends, succeed as far as to avoid this, and prevent such foul disgrace." They strain with all their might, and bend to their oars; mighty are the strokes with which the brazen ship quivers, the water slips away beneath; then short of breath they pant, their limbs shake, their lips are parched; sweat courses in rivulets all o'er their frames. Chance, rather than their efforts, brought to the men the honour they coveted. For Sergestus, eager even to frenzy, turns his prow towards the rock, taking the inner side, and enters the dangerous channel, and there the unlucky captain stuck on the jutting shelves. The rocks were shaken with the shock, the oars dashed against the pointed coral, and broke with a crash, the prow was driven in, and motionless there it hung. At once rise the rowers, and loud are their shouts as they stop; quickly they get out their iron-bound pikes, and sharp-pointed poles, or pick up their broken oars floating in the flood. But joyful is Mnestheus, his success gives him fresh energy, swiftly he plies his bank of oars, and invokes the winds, and makes straight for the waters which flow to the shore, and runs o'er the open main. So a dove, when suddenly scared in her cave, (for her home and beloved nest is in the hollows of the porous stone,) is borne forth in flight towards the fields, and in terror flaps her wings loudly in her dwelling, but soon she glides in the calm sky, and skims on her liquid way, nor so much as moves her swift wings. Thus speeds Mnestheus, and thus the Pristis of her own accord flies, and cleaves the water at the end of her course; the way of the boat bears it as it skims along. And first he leaves Sergestus behind, struggling on the high rock, in the shallows, while in vain he calls for aid, and essays how best to run with broken oars. Then he follows hard on Gyas and the boat Chimæra of huge bulk; it must needs lose, for it has no pilot. Cloanthus alone remains, and that too close to the end of the race; Mnestheus pursues him, he strives with all

his might, he presses him hard.　Thereupon the shouts redouble, and all
unite with zeal to encourage the pursuer, the air resounds with the
tumult.　The one crew would be ashamed did they not keep the glory
that was theirs, and the honour they had won, they would barter life for
victory; the others success animates; the thought is father to the power.
And perchance with beaks exactly matched they had divided the prize; but
Cloanthus stretched out both his hands to sea, and poured forth earnest
prayers, and called upon the gods to hear his vows. "Ye gods, whose empire is on the main, o'er whose waters I now run, gladly will I on this shore
place before your altars a white bull, binding myself by my vow, and will
throw its entrails into the briny billows, and pour flowing wine." He spake,
and his words were heard deep down beneath the waves by all the choir of
Nereids and of Phorcus, and by the virgin Panopea; and father Portunus
himself with mighty hand pushed the galley in its course.　It swifter than
wind or flying arrow speeds towards land, and is safe in the deep harbour.

244—285.　*Æneas gives prizes to the captains of each ship.*

Then Anchises' son, having summoned all in due form, bids the
herald with loud voice declare Cloanthus conqueror, and crowns his temples with a wreath of green bay, and commands them to choose as gifts
three steers for each ship, and wine; and gives them a weighty talent
of silver to carry away.　To the captains themselves he adds special
presents: to the conqueror he gave a cloak with tissue of gold, round
the hem of which in deep hue ran Melibœan purple with a double wavy
edge; on it was embroidered the princely boy, who on leafy Ida hotly pursues at full speed with his dart the swift stags; keen hunter he seemed,
like to one panting for breath; Jove's armourbearer soaring up from Ida
bore him aloft with his talons.　The old guardians of the prince in vain
stretch their hands to the stars, and the hounds bay fiercely towards
heaven.　But he whose merit gained the second place, to him next the
hero gives a coat of mail; it was fastened with clasps, and had a triple tissue
of gold; the chieftain himself had stripped Demoleus of it, when he was
conqueror on the banks of swift Simois beneath lofty Ilium; the captain
is to have it to wear, an ornament and defence in battle.　Scarcely could
the servants, Phegeus and Sagaris, bear the corslet with its mazy twine,
as they carried it with effort on their shoulders; and yet, in days of
old, Demoleus clad in this drove before him as he ran the straggling
Trojans.　As the third prize the hero gives a pair of bronze cauldrons,
and bowls of highly wrought silver, embossed with figures.　And so they
all now had their gifts, and proud of their presents were seen to go,
their temples bound with purple ribbons, when, with much effort cleared
from the cruel rocks, with oars lost, disabled and crippled, with one tier,
Sergestus brought along his galley, in forlorn plight amidst the mocking
crowd.　So oft a snake has been surprised on the causeway of a road;
a brazen wheel has passed over it obliquely, or with heavy blow some
traveller has left it crushed and half dead; in vain it tries to escape, trailing its long body; in its upper coils it is still fierce, its eyes glare, it raises
itself, and lifts its hissing neck; its lower part, disabled by the wound,
still clogs its speed, as it struggles with its knotty tail, and twists itself
into its own folds.　Such was the oarage with which the galley slowly

moved; and yet it hoists its canvas, and enters the harbour's mouth with full sails. Æneas gives Sergestus the promised present; for the prince is thankful that the ship is saved, and his comrades rescued from the sea. So he gives him a slave, skilled in the work of the loom, Minerva's art; she came from Crete, her name was Pholoe, she had two sons at her breast.

286—361. *The footrace. The mutual affection of Nisus and Euryalus. Nisus loses the race himself, but wins it for his friend. Æneas is again generous beyond his promises.*

So, this contest ended, pious Æneas goes to a grassy plain, which hills with winding woody vales enclosed on every side, in the midst of which was the circus of a theatre; the hero of many thousands went in the centre of the company, and took his seat on a raised throne. Here, if there were any who perchance would contend in the rapid race, their hopes he stirs by rewards, and proposes prizes. So there came from all sides to run Trojans mingled with Sicilians, Nisus and Euryalus foremost, Euryalus distinguished by beauty, in the flower of his youth; Nisus famed for his loving affection for the boy; then followed next Diores, a prince of the noble race of Priam; after whom came Salius and Patron together; whereof one was an Acarnanian, the other of Arcadian blood, of the people of Tegea; next appeared two Sicilian youths, Helymus and Panopes, trained in the forests, the attendants of old Acestes; many besides, whose fame is buried in obscurity. Then, in the midst of them, Æneas thus spake: "Hear my words with goodwill, and gladly give them heed. Not a man of this list shall depart without a gift from me; to each will I present two Cretan arrows with points of polished steel, and an axe to carry, whose figures are of silver. To all alike there shall be this same reward: the three first shall receive prizes, and have their temples bound with wreaths of grey olive. Let the first winner receive a horse adorned with trappings; the second an Amazonian quiver full of Thracian arrows, round which is twined a belt of broad gold, and a clasp fastens it with neatly-shaped jewel; the third must go away contented with a Grecian helmet." So he spoke; they choose their places; and when they hear the signal, in an instant they scour the course, and leave the starting-point behind: they pour forth like storm-clouds, at the same moment they mark the goal with their eyes. Foremost takes the lead, and far ahead of all the runners Nisus springs forward, swifter than the winds or winged thunderbolt. Next to him, but next with a long interval, follows Salius; then a space is left between, and third runs Euryalus; and Euryalus is followed by Helymus; and then close to Helymus lo, Diores flies along, and with his foot almost treads on the heel of Helymus, pressing on his shoulder, and were there but more of the course left, he would shoot forward and pass him, or leave the contest undecided. And now they were nigh to the end of the course, and exhausted drew close to the winning point, when in the slippery blood down falls Nisus, unlucky wight; for it so happened some steers had been slain, and the blood poured forth had drenched the ground and green grass. Here the youth, all but a triumphant winner, could not steady his steps, but stumbled on the ground which he pressed, and forward he fell just in the filthy slime, and in the blood of the victims. Yet he forgot not Euryalus, he remembered the love he bore him. For he put himself in the way of Salius, as he rose amid the slippery ground; and Salius tumbled and lay in the thickened sand. Forward springs Euryalus, a winner by his friend's aid, and holds the foremost place, and flies along amidst the applause and clamour that befriends him. Next follows Helymus, and then Diores, who now wins the third prize. Hereupon the whole assembly of the great theatre, and the presence of the elders in the front row, is filled with the noisy clamours of Salius; the prize was wrested from him by a trick, he demands that it be restored. The feeling of all supports Euryalus, and his tears that become him well, and merit that shews more pleasantly in a fair form. Diores backs him, shouting with loud voice: for he has gained a prize, and in vain has attained the third reward, if the first gift is restored to Salius. Then said father Æneas: "Your rights remain unchanged to you, my lads, and the order of the prizes is altered for no one; but I may be allowed to shew my pity for the bad luck of my friend who is free from fault." So speaking, to Salius he gives the huge hide of an African lion ponderous with shaggy hair, and paws o'erlaid with gold. Then said Nisus: "If such prizes are given to the vanquished, and such pity to the fallen, what gifts will you give equal to the merits of Nisus? due to my deserts is the first prize, but the same unkind fate baffled myself and Salius." And as he spake, he shewed his face and limbs disfigured with the wet slime. The good father laughed at him, and bid them bring forth a shield, the workmanship of Didymaon, taken down from the holy door of Neptune's temple, a spoil of the Greeks. With this noble gift he honours the excellent youth.

362—425. *The third contest, the boxing match. Dares plays the braggart. Entellus, though old in years, encouraged by Acestes, takes up the challenge.*

Next when the race was ended, and he had bestowed all the gifts, "Now," says he, "if anyone has courage and a ready spirit in his breast, let him step forth, and put up his arms with his hands bound with the gauntlet." So he speaks, and proposes two prizes for the fight; for the conqueror a steer with horns gilded, and wreathed with fillets; a sword and noble helmet to console the conquered. Without delay, forthwith Dares shews his face, a man of huge strength, and rises amidst the loud applause of the crowd: he was the only man who used to contend against Paris. He too at the grave, where lies mighty Hector, smote the conqueror Butes of gigantic size, who coming forward vaunted himself of the race of Amycus of Bebrycia; but Dares stretched him in the agonies of death on the yellow sand. Such was Dares, who first raised his towering head for the fight, displaying his broad shoulders, tossing his arms alternately forward, striking the air with blows. A champion is sought to meet him; but no one out of all that crowd dares to encounter the man, or to bind the cestus on his hands. So then Dares in high spirits, imagining that all kept aloof from the contest for the prize, stood before Æneas, and without further delay he there with his left hand held the bull by the horn, and thus he speaks: "Goddess born, if no one dares to venture on the fight, what end is there to standing here? how long am I to be kept dangling here? Order the gift to be brought forth." At the same time all the Trojans shouted applause, and bade that the promised prize be given to the man. Hereupon Acestes severely chid Entellus, who chanced to be sitting next to him on the bank of green sward: "Entellus, in days of old you were the bravest of heroes, but 'tis bootless now, if thou art so tame as to allow such a glorious prize to be carried off without a contest? where is now the god who trained you, your master, Eryx, of whom you have boasted oft to us in vain? where now your fame spread through all Sicily, and those spoils that are hanging in your halls?" He in answer said: "It is not my love of fame and glory that is gone, driven away by terror; but rather that my blood is chilled and dulled by the deadening power of age, and my strength is past its prime and is lifeless in my limbs. If I had but the youth I had in days of yore, that youth in which that braggart fellow exults, if I had but that, I should not have waited for a prize or that fine steer, to enter the lists; indeed the gifts I nothing reck." He spake, and straightway threw into the ring a pair of gauntlets of gigantic weight; in these was brave Eryx wont to bear his hands to the fight, and bind upon his arms the tough hide. The minds of all were thereat amazed; for in those gauntlets the huge hides of seven bulls were stiff with lead and iron stitched in. Above all others Dares himself is amazed, he draws back and declines the fight; and the noble son of Anchises tries their weight and turns in his hand the huge twisted thongs of the gloves. Then the old man uttered these words from his breast: "What, if anyone here had seen the cestus with which Hercules himself was armed, and had witnessed the fatal battle on this very shore? These were the arms which your brother Eryx wore of old: you may see even now the stains from the blood and scattered brain: in these he stood up against mighty Hercules; to use these was I trained, while a more generous blood supplied me with strength, before envious old age had sprinkled both my temples with grey hairs. But if Dares of Troy declines to use these our arms, and such be the judgment of pious Æneas, and Acestes, who urges me to this contest, approves of it, let us make the fight fair: for your sake I waive the gauntlets of Eryx, lay aside your fear, and do you take off your Trojan cestus." He spake, and from his shoulders threw back his double cloak, and stripped the huge joints of his limbs, his huge long and brawny arms, and took his stand a giant in the midst of the arena. Then the father of his people, the son of Anchises, brought forth gauntlets of equal size, and bound the hands of both with fairly matched gloves.

426—484. *The combat. Entellus proves victorious. Æneas gives prizes to both the boxers.*

Straightway either combatant took his stand rising on tiptoe undaunted, lifting his arms upwards into the air. Standing at their height, they draw their heads far backwards to escape the blows, and mingle hands with hands, and provoke the fight; the one was the better man in quickness of foot, and relied on his youth, the other strong in limbs and giant size : but his stiff knees tremble and totter, and a painful panting breath convulses his sides.   Many are the fruitless blows which the combatants aim at each other, many echo on their hollow sides, or sound loudly on their chests ; often do their hands play round the ears and temples, their cheeks rattle under the heavy thumps.   Heavily stands Entellus, and steady with one single effort just eludes the blows, only by moving his body, and by the quickness of his eye.   But Dares is like one who attacks a lofty city with engines of war, or in arms beleaguers a fort on the mountain, and tries this and that approach, and skilfully surveys all the ground and presses the place hard with varied assaults, but all in vain.   Entellus rises to strike a blow, and shews his right hand, and lifts it on high ; the other foresaw the descending stroke, and slipped aside, and with active body instantly withdrew.   Entellus wasted his strength on the air, and untouched by blow, of himself, with heavy frame fell heavily at once to the earth with huge weight, as oft a hollow pine torn from its roots falls suddenly either on Erymanthus, or on lofty Ida.   Then rise with zeal for their champion both the Trojans and men of Sicily : the shouts rise to the sky ; first up runs Acestes ; the old prince pities his old friend, and raises him from the ground.   The hero, not dispirited nor daunted by his fall, with fresh vigour returns to the fight ; passion kindles his strength, shame and the consciousness of merit give fire to his force ; and furiously he drives Dares headlong o'er all the plain ; redoubling his blows with either hand in turns.   Delay there was none ; no respite ; as thick the strokes as the hailstones, when a storm rattles on the roofs ; even so, with blow close upon blow, did the hero ever with both his hands batter and pound Dares.   Then father Æneas would not suffer his fury to go further, and forbad Entellus to rage in the fierceness of his wrath, and put an end to the fight, and rescued weary Dares, and thus speaks : " Unhappy man !   How could such madness possess your soul ?   Do you not feel your strength ill-matched, and heaven opposed ?   So yield to God."   He spoke, and with his word separated the combatants.   His faithful comrades bear to the ships Dares, as his weak limbs shake, and as he tosses his head on either side, and vomits from his mouth clotted gore and teeth mingled with the blood : when called, they receive the sword and helmet ; the prize and bull they leave with Entellus.   Then the conqueror, with spirits high overflowing, proud of the bull, said thus : " O goddess born, and ye Trojans, learn, what strength I had in my frame when young, and from what a death ye save and rescue Dares."   He spoke, and stood confronting the bull, which stood there, the prize of the fight ; then drew back his hand, and directed the hard cestus just between the horns, rising to the blow, and dashed the glove on the bones, and smashed the brains.   Laid low, lifeless, quivering, falls on the ground the ox.   He o'er the body utters these words : " This is a better life that I offer to thee, Eryx, as a substitute for Dares : here victorious I lay aside my cestus and my art."

485—544.   *The fourth contest, the trial of archery.   A dove is fastened to a high mast.   The first archer hits the mast, the second cleaves the*

string, the third shoots the bird when free in the air. The arrow of
Acestes catches fire in the sky, an omen of future events.

This done, straightway Æneas invites any who may be willing to
contend with swift arrows, and offers prizes ; and with his own stalwart
hand raises a mast from the galley of Sergestus, and fastens on high to
the lofty pole a fleet dove with a cord tied round it, as the mark for their
arrows' point. The archers flock together ; then a brazen helmet receives
the lots thrown into it ; and first before all comes forth the turn of Hip-
pocoon, son of Hyrtacus ; his backers applaud ; next comes the name of
Mnestheus, he who just now was victor in the race of ships, Mnestheus
crowned with wreath of green olive ; third was Eurytion, your brother,
O glorious Pandarus, who once when commanded to disturb the treaty
did first shoot your arrow into the Grecian host. Acestes' name remained last at the bottom of the casque ; Acestes ventured, though old,
to essay young men's work. Then did the archers with stalwart strength
bend their curved bows, each as he best could, and draw the arrows from
their quivers ; and first through the sky from the twanging string did the
arrow of the youthful son of Hyrtacus cleave its way, whizzing through the
light air ; on it flies ; it is fixed in the wood of the confronting mast.
The mast shook thereat, and the terrified bird fluttered her wings,
while all around sounded with loud applause. Next keen Mnestheus took
his stand, and drew his bow, and aimed high, then at the same moment
directed eye and arrow ; and yet the unlucky archer failed to hit the
bird itself with his arrow ; he cut the knot and linen bands, which fastened the foot of the bird suspended from the lofty mast : the dove fled
speeding towards the air and dark clouds. Then quickly did Eurytion,
for from the first he had his bow ready, and his arrow on the string, call
upon his brother to hear his vows ; and he takes his view of the dove
which was now rejoicing in the open firmament, and as it was flapping its
wings he pierces it beneath the dark cloud. Down it falls lifeless, and
leaves its spirit amid the stars of heaven, and, as it descends, brings with
it the arrow fixed in its body. Acestes alone was left, and he had lost the
prize ; yet he shot his shaft into the air aloft, for the father of the people
displayed at once his skill and twanging bow. Thereupon a sudden
prodigy appears, destined to prove a mighty presage ; a great result
shewed its truth, and seers alarmed the world, as they foretold that the
omen pointed to a distant time. For as the reed flew, it caught fire in
watery clouds, and marked its course by flames, and, as it consumed, vanished into thin air ; so often shooting stars fall from the heaven, and as
they fly trail behind them their length of hair. Amazed were Sicilians
and Trojans, and doubtful in their minds, and prayed to the heavenly
Powers ; nor did great Æneas refuse the omen, but embraced Acestes,
who was glad at the sight, and loads him with noble gifts, and speaks
thus : " Accept these presents, my father ; for the great king of Olympus
shews by these auspices his will that you should receive a special reward.
You shall have the gift which once belonged to my aged sire himself,
a goblet graven with figures ; Cisseus of Thrace once gave it to my father
Anchises, a noble gift, that he should receive it as the memorial and
pledge of his affection." Thus he spake, and binds his temples with a

wreath of green bay, and proclaims Acestes as first victor above all the
rest. Nor did good Eurytion envy him for the prize by which he was
preferred, though Eurytion alone had brought the dove down from the
height of heaven. With the next gifts he is honoured who cut the line,
with the last he who hit the mast with the flying arrow.

545—603.　*The game of Troy. Augustus loved this game. The evolutions of the Trojan boys are like the intricacies of the Labyrinth, or the
gambols of dolphins. So end the games.*

But father Æneas, the games not being yet ended, summons the son
of Epytus, the guardian and companion of the boy Iulus, and thus speaks
into his trusty ear : "Go quickly," he says, "and say to Ascanius, that if he
has his boyish troop ready with him, and has arranged the manœuvres of
his horses, he should lead forth his companies in honour of his grandfather, and display himself in arms." He himself commands that all the
people who had poured into the long circus withdraw, and leave the
plain open. Forth ride the boys, and in a line before the presence of
their sires shine on their curbed steeds ; as they pass along, all the youth
of Sicily and Troy admire and applaud. All have their hair closely
bound in due form with a wreath of trimmed leaves ; each bears two
darts of cornel wood tipped with iron shaft ; some on their shoulders wear
polished quivers ; on the upper part of their breast there passes o'er the
neck a pliant necklace of twisted rings of gold. There are three troops
of riders, and each company has a captain riding ; each captain is followed by twelve boys, who glitter in the divided band, under leaders
of equal age. The first troop of boys in high spirits was led by a little
Priam bearing the name of his grandsire ; he was your noble son, Polites,
destined to give a new race to Italy ; he rides on a Thracian steed,
piebald with white spots ; the pasterns of its forefeet were white, white
was the forehead it shewed when it pranced on high. The second was
Atys, whence the Latins of the Attian house drew their descent ; a little
boy was Atys, loved in his boyhood by the boy Iulus. The third was Iulus,
the fairest of all in form ; he rode on a Sidonian steed ; beauteous Dido
gave the horse as a memorial and pledge of her affection. The rest of the
youth are borne on Sicilian steeds, the gift of old Acestes. The Trojans welcome with applause the youths, whose hearts flutter with excitement ; with
joy they gaze on them, and recognize in them the likeness of their ancestors. When the boys had ridden in high spirits round the whole circuit
of the spectators before the eyes of their relations, then with a shout the
son of Epytus gave the expected signal, cracking his whip. They rode
about in equal divisions, and broke up into three parts, separating their
troops, and, when summoned back again, they wheeled round and charged
with lances levelled in rest. Then other courses backwards and forwards
do they begin, facing one another with a space between, and intertwined
circle after circle, whilst they wage in arms the likeness of battle ; and
sometimes they expose their backs in flight, sometimes they turn their
darts in a charge, or march together in peaceful line. As 'tis said in the
days of old, the Labyrinth in lofty Crete had a path woven with dark walls,
and a puzzling bower full of doubt with a thousand zigzag ways, where
a maze, hard to discover and hard to retrace, confused the marks set by

him that would trace it. So the sons of the Trojans at a gallop interlace
their courses, and weave in sport a maze of flight and combat; like dolphins, who, as they swim through the watery main, cleave the Carpathian
or Libyan sea, and play through the waves. This manner of exercise
and these games Ascanius first repeated, whilst girding with walls Alba
Longa, and taught the Prisci Latini to celebrate them, even as he himself when a boy, and the Trojan youth with him, had learnt them; the
Albans taught them to their children; from them in succession mighty
Rome received the games, and retained the ancestral custom; and even
now the game is called Troy, and the boys are called the Trojan troop.
Thus far were the sports celebrated in honour of the holy sire.

604—699. *But sorrow follows mirth. Juno sends down Iris, who, taking
a human form, fills the Trojan matrons with a weariness of their
endless voyagings. They set fire to the ships. Æneas hastens to
the shore. In answer to the prayer which he offers in his extremity
Jove sends rain. The fleet is saved.*

But here first Fortune changed, and was fickle to her faith. Whilst
they pay these annual rites to the tomb by various games, Juno,
daughter of Saturn, sent Iris from heaven to the Trojan fleet, breathing winds to help her flight; many were Juno's plans, and she had
not yet glutted her ancient hate. The messenger, the maiden goddess,
hastened on her way along a rainbow of a thousand colours; seen by no
man down she speeds swiftly along her path. At once she sees the great
throng, and surveys the shore, and sees the harbour lonely, and the
fleet unguarded. But far away on the lonely beach the Trojan women
apart were weeping for the loss of Anchises, and all together were
ever gazing on the main, and still they wept. "Alas! what seas, and
how much ocean still remains for us weary women!" So did they all
say. What they pray for is a home; they are tired of toiling o'er the
deep. So Iris, not unskilled in mischief, throws herself into the midst,
and lays aside the face and robe of a goddess; she becomes like Beroe
the aged wife of Doryclus of Tmarus; for she was once of famous race,
and had children now no more; thus transformed, the goddess mingles
with the Trojan matrons. "O wretched women," she said, "whom Grecian
hands did not drag to death by the sword beneath your country's walls!
Unhappy race, for what destruction does fortune reserve you? The
seventh summer is now in its fall since the destruction of Troy, whilst
we are borne o'er seas, o'er all lands, o'er many an inhospitable rock,
measuring the stars in our course, whilst o'er the mighty main we
pursue Italy that ever flies from us, and are tossed by the billows.
Here are the territories of Eryx your prince's brother, here is Acestes
for a host; who forbids our founding walls, and giving our citizens a
town? O my country, and ye Penates in vain rescued from the foe,
will no walls ever be called Trojan again? shall I see nowhere a new
Xanthus and Simois like the rivers Hector once loved? Come then,
and with me burn these unlucky ships. For during my sleep the
phantom of the prophetess Cassandra seemed to put in my hand
burning torches: said she, 'Here look for Troy, here is a home for
you.' The time is come to act; delay not to obey such clear portents;

see here are four altars of Neptune; the god himself supplies us
with brands and courage to use them." She spake, and first of all with
fury seized the burning torch to destroy the ships, and lifted her hand
on high, and with an effort brandished the flame, and hurled the brand.
Inflamed are the minds and amazed the hearts of the daughters of
Ilium. Here one, of all the company the eldest, Pyrgo by name, nurse
to many princes, sons of Priam, thus spoke: "Matrons, this is no Beroe
before us, this is no Trojan wife of Doryclus: mark the proofs of a
beauty more than human, mark her glowing eyes; see how she breathes,
what a countenance, what tones of voice she has, what a gait as she
walks. I myself at the beginning of the rites parted from Beroe, and
left her sick, grieving that she alone was absent from the pious duty,
and could not pay to Anchises due offerings." So she spake. But the
matrons, perplexed at first with eyes of evil import gazed at the ships,
and were divided in doubt between their fond love of the land where
they were safe, and the kingdom whither they were called by Heaven's will: when suddenly the goddess rose through the sky with
poised wings, and cleft her way on the wide arch of a rainbow.
Then indeed amazed at the portents, and driven by frenzy, they raise
an universal cry, and bring the fire from the hearths in the houses;
while some rob the altars, and throw together leaves and twigs and
brands. As a horse speeding with slack reins, so rages Vulcan o'er the
benches and the oars and the painted sterns of fir. Eumelus bears
the news to the tomb of Anchises and the seats of the theatre, that
the ships are set on fire; they look round, and with their own eyes
see the dark ashes rise in a cloud. And foremost of all Ascanius, just
as he was leading the evolutions of the riders, even then on his steed
keenly rides towards the fleet now in confusion; his frightened guardians could not stop him. "What," cried he, "is this strange madness in you? what now, what is your purpose, alas! my wretched
countrywomen? no hostile ships, no unfriendly fleet you burn, you burn
your own hopes. Look at me, I am your own Ascanius." He took off
and threw down his helmet before him, which he wore when he was
waging in sport the mimic war. Thither hastens Æneas too, and the
Trojan bands together. But the matrons fly scattered along the shore
hither and thither, and steal away to the woods or any caverns they can
find; they repent of their attempt, and hate the light, and their heart
is changed, and they know their friends again, and the spirit of Juno
is cast forth from their souls. But not on that account did the flames
of the conflagration lay aside their untamed fury: beneath the damp oak
smoulders the tow, breathing forth a slow column of smoke, and the fire,
spreading gradually, devours the keels, and destruction makes its way
down the whole hull of the ships: in vain is the strength of the heroes,
and the streams of water poured on the flames. Then pious Æneas
tore his garment from his shoulders, and called on the gods for help,
and lifted up his hands: "Almighty Jove, if thou dost not yet utterly
hate all the Trojans to a man, if the mercy thou usedst to shew of old
still regards human woe, grant, Father, that the fleet may escape from
the flames even now, and rescue the slender hopes of Troy from doom:

or do thou, (which alone is left for me,) with the blow of thy thunderbolt strike me down to death, if such are my deserts, and here destroy
me with thy own right hand." Hardly has he uttered this prayer,
when a shower is poured forth, and a murky storm rages unrestrained,
and with the thunder the steep hills tremble, and the level plains;
down rushes from the whole sky a tempestuous deluge, pitchy black
with rain and cloudy south-winds; the water from the sky fills the
ships; the half-burnt planks of oak are drenched; until all the fire
is put out, and all the ships, except four, are saved from destruction. ·

700—718. *Nautes counsels Æneas to leave the old and fainthearted in
Sicily.*

But father Æneas, shocked at the sad misfortune, hither and thither in
his breast ever ponders mighty shifting cares; should he settle down in
Sicilian fields and forget his destiny, or should he strive to reach Italian
coasts. Then aged Nautes, a man whom above all others Tritonian
Pallas had taught, and made him renowned for deep lore—such were the
answers Pallas oft gave him, that he might know what the mighty wrath
of heaven portended, or what the fated chain of events required. And so
he then comforted Æneas with these words, and thus began: "Goddess
born, whither the fates draw us on, or draw us back, thither let us follow;
come what may, by bearing we can vanquish all our fate. You have a
friend in Trojan Acestes of the race of the gods; take him as a partner in
your counsels, a willing sharer in your cares; to him entrust those who
are too numerous, now you have lost these ships, and those who are tired
out by your great enterprise, and your fortunes; pick out the aged, and
matrons weary of the sea, and whoever you have with you a feeble and
timorous throng; let them find their town in this land, for they are now exhausted. They will call the city Acesta by a name derived from your friend."

719—745. *The spirit of his father appears in a vision of the night, and
gives the same advice, and further tells him to come and see him in
Elysium.*

His spirit was stirred by this counsel of his old friend, and then indeed
is his mind distracted by every care. And dark night had mounted in its
car to the summit of the heaven; when it seemed to him that from above
glided down the phantom of his parent Anchises, and suddenly uttered
these words: "My son, once dearer to me than life, so long as life
remained, my son, persecuted by the fates of Ilium, by Jove's command
I come hither; Jove from thy fleet drove the fire, and at last looks on
you with pity from the height of heaven. Obey the advice, for it is very
good, which old Nautes now gives; the chosen youth, hearts of courage,
take with you to Italy. A hardy race, roughly trained, has to be subdued
by you in Latium. Yet first approach the nether home of Dis, and
through deep Avernus go to meet me, my son. For, believe me, impious
Tartarus holds not me, nor the sad shades of death, but I dwell in Elysium amid the pleasant companies of the good. Hither will guide you
the holy Sibyl, when you have shed the blood of many black cattle.
Then shall you learn all your line, and your destined city. And now,
farewell; damp night rolls onwards in her central course; and soon will
the cruel rising sun breathe on me with his panting steeds." He spake,

and vanished like smoke into the thin air. Æneas said : "Whither rushest thou so soon? Whither dost thou hurry? From whom fleest thou? or who tears thee from my embrace?" He spake, and awakens the dying embers and the slumbering fire, and humbly worships the Lar of Pergamus, and the inmost shrine of ancient Vesta, with holy cake of meal, and censer full of frankincense.

746—761. *Sergesta is founded; a temple to Venus is built on Eryx.*

Straightway he sends for his comrades; and specially for Acestes, and tells them what is Jove's command, and the counsel of his dear father, and what is now his own settled purpose. They quickly close with his plan; nor does Acestes decline to do what he enjoins. They enrol the matrons in the new town, and part with those who wish to stay behind, souls that have no craving for high renown. They themselves repair their benches, and replace the oaken planks of the ships, which the flames had half consumed; they make for their vessels new oars and cordage; a scanty band, but hearts of valour vigorous in war. Meanwhile Æneas marks the city's walls with a plough, and apportions the houses by lot; he bids this be a second Ilium, and these places a new Troy. Trojan Acestes delights in his kingdom, and solemnly inaugurates his forum, and gives laws to his chosen senators. Then on the summit of mount Eryx a sacred shrine, which seems near the stars, is founded to Venus of Idalia, and a priest is appointed, and a holy grove of wide extent planted round the tomb of Anchises.

762—778. *The feelings of the matrons are changed. They sorrow when Æneas sets sail.*

And now all the people had feasted during nine days, and due offerings paid on the altars; the sleeping winds had laid the waves to rest, and the wind blowing fresh invites them again to the deep. Loud is the lamentation heard along the winding shore: they linger in mutual embraces night and day. And now the very matrons, the very men, to whom the face of the deep seemed so rough, and its very deity intolerable, are willing to go, and bear every toil of voyage. Them good Æneas comforts with friendly words, and with tears commends to his kinsman Acestes. He next bids three bullocks to be sacrificed to Eryx, a lamb to the Tempests, and that the cable of each ship be loosened in succession. He himself with his temples bound with leaves of trimmed olive, standing apart on the prow, holds in his hand a bowl, and casts the entrails into the briny waves, and pours the flowing wine. A wind rising from the stern speeds them on their way. With emulation his comrades lash the sea, and sweep its surface.

779—824. *Venus begs Neptune to give the fleet a safe passage. Neptune promises safety to all but one. The sea is calm, and the god attended by his retinue of Tritons and Nereids.*

But Venus meanwhile distressed by care addresses Neptune, and utters these complaints from her breast: "Juno's fierce wrath and unrelenting heart force me, Neptune, to descend to the humblest prayers. For no length of time, no piety can appease her, nor will she bend to Jove's command, or to the fates, and cease from troubling. Not content with utterly destroying the city out of the very heart of the nation of Phrygia by her

cruel hatred, nor with dragging it through every suffering, she still persecutes the remnant of Troy, the very ashes and bones of the ruined race.
Let her find out, if she can, good reasons for such fury. Thou thyself
canst bear me witness what a tumult she lately stirred up in the African
waters. She mingled every sea with the sky, in vain relying on the storm
of Æolus. The realm in which she thus dared to act was thine. So
wickedly she hath driven to frenzy the matrons of Troy, and foully burnt
the ships of the Trojans, and by the loss of the fleet has forced them to
leave comrades on a strange land. For the rest of the voyage I pray, permit them to sail safely o'er the waves, permit them to reach Laurentian
Tiber, if my prayers are lawful, if those walls are granted by the fates."

Then the son of Saturn, the lord of the deep sea, thus spake: "There
is every right, Lady of Cythera, for thee to trust in my realm, from it thou
derivest thy race; I deserve too thy faith. Often have I checked its fury,
and the mighty rage of sky and sea. Nor less on land, as I can call
Xanthus and Simois to witness, has been my care for thy son Æneas.
That day when Achilles pursuing the terrified bands of Troy dashed them
against the walls, and consigned to death many thousands, and the rivers
choked with corpses roared as with grief, and Xanthus could not find his
way, and roll his stream out into the sea; on that day Æneas met the
strong son of Peleus; the odds of strength and gods were against thy
son; but I rescued him in a hollow cloud, and that, though I wished to
level to the ground the walls of perjured Troy built by my own hands.
Now also the same purpose continues mine; away with fear. Safe will
he reach the harbour of Avernus, as thou wishest. One only will there be,
whom he will lose in the flood and miss; one life will be given as an atonement for many." When with these words he had calmed the breast of
the goddess, and given her joy, the Father yokes his horses to his chariot
of gold, and puts in the mouth of his steeds the foaming bits, and with
his hands slackens all the reins. Lightly flies the god o'er the surface of
the level sea in his azure car. The waves subside, and beneath the
thundering axletree the swelling plain of the waters lies smooth, and the
stormy clouds fly from the firmament. Then the manifold forms of his
retinue are seen, huge monsters of the deep, and the ancient band of
Glaucus, and Palemon son of Ino, and the nimble Tritons, and all the
host of Phorcus; the left side of the chariot is held by Thetis, and Melite,
and the maiden Panopea, and Nesæe and Spio and Thalia and Cymodoce.

*825—871. The god of Sleep brings drowsiness over the eyes of the faith-
ful Palinurus. He falls into the sea. Æneas turns pilot himself,
sorrowing for his lost comrade.*

Here the mind of Æneas long anxious is thrilled by the soothing
vicissitudes of joy: he bids all the masts quickly to be raised, and on the
sailyards the sails to be stretched. All at once veered the sheet, and
loosened the bellying canvas to right, to left; at once they all turn up and
down the tall ends of the sailyards; favouring breezes bear the fleet along.
Foremost before them all Palinurus led the close line; with an eye to him
the rest were bid to direct their course. And now damp night had just
reached the centre of its course in the heavens; the sailors stretched on
their hard seats beneath the oars had relaxed their limbs in quiet repose;

when lightly from the stars of the sky glided down the god Sleep, and parted the dusky air, and separated the shades of night, flying straight to you, Palinurus; to you he brought a fatal sleep, and yet you did not deserve this: on the high stern the god took his seat, in shape like Phorbas, and uttered these words: "Palinurus, son of Iasus, the sea of itself bears on the fleet; steadily blow the breezes; the hour is meant for repose. Rest your head; and let your weary eyes steal from toil. I myself for a short time will do your duty for you." To whom Palinurus speaks, scarcely raising his eyes: "Would you bid me not know the look and calm waves of the tranquil sea? Would you have me believe in such a monster? Why indeed should I trust Æneas to the treacherous gales, I who have been so often deceived by the cheats of a serene sky?" So he said, and holding fast and clinging to the helm, he never let go his hold, and kept gazing up to the stars. When lo! the god waves o'er his temples a bough drenched with Lethe's stream, and, as he lingered, relaxed his swimming eyes. Hardly had the sudden slumber just unnerved his limbs, when Somnus, leaning over, broke off part of the stern, and pushed helmsman with his helm headlong into the waves; in vain the pilot called often on his comrades. The god flew as a bird soaring into thin air. But not the less the fleet speeds safely on its course o'er the face of the sea, and according to the promise of Neptune is borne securely on. And now, driven onwards, it was just nearing the cliffs of the Sirens; once they were hard to pass, and on them bleached the bones of many men; there hoarsely roared the rocks resounding with the restless sea: when the father of his people observed that his ship had lost its pilot, and floated uncertainly; and so with his own hands he guided it o'er the waves all night long, while still he often groaned, for shocked was his soul at his friend's sad fate: "Alas! too much did you believe the sky and tranquil deep; unburied will you, Palinurus, lie on an unknown coast."

BOOK VI.

1—33. *Æneas lands in Italy at Cumæ, and goes to consult the Sibylline oracle. Description of the sculpture on the doors of the temple of Apollo.*

So he speaks with tears, and gives his fleet the reins, and in time glides in to the Eubœan shores of Cumæ. Seaward they point the prows; then with biting tooth the anchor makes fast the ships, and the curving keels fringe the beach. The throng of youths spring forth with ardour on the strand of Italy; some search for the seeds of flame that lie hidden in the veins of flint; some scour the woods, the tangled haunts of wild beasts, and shew the streams they have discovered. But pious Æneas goes towards the citadel which high Apollo commands, and the distant cell of the awful Sibyl, a vast cavern; for her mighty mind and soul the Delian seer inspires, and reveals the things that are to be. Presently they enter the groves of Trivia, and her golden house. Dædalus, as tradition tells, when fleeing from the realm of Minos, having dared on rapid wings to trust himself to the sky, along the unwonted path floated on to the cold North; and at last, poised in air, rested above the Chalcidian citadel. Restored to earth here first, he dedicated to thee, O Phœbus, the oarage of his wings, and founded a mighty temple. On the panels of the door is wrought the death of Androgeos; next, the people of Cecrops, bidden to pay as a yearly tribute (oh piteous doom!) the bodies of seven of their sons: the urn is set; the lots are drawn. On the opposite side the land of Crete, rising out of the sea, forms the counterpart; here is portrayed the cruel passion for the bull, and the craft of Pasiphae's love, and the mixed issue, and the Minotaur, the offspring of double shape, the record of accursed wedlock; here is described that famous bewildering mansion, and the maze that cannot be disentangled: albeit Dædalus, through pity for the queen's deep passion, himself made clear the puzzle and windings of the house, guiding with a thread the darkened steps of Theseus. You too, Icarus, would fill a large place in so great a master-piece, did grief allow it. Twice he had essayed to work out in gold your fall; twice sank the father's hands.

33—55. The Sibyl arrives, and bids Æneas to sacrifice, and leads him into the temple. She feels the inspiration of the god.

And so they would have gone on to survey closely all things in succes-sion, had not Achates, who had been sent on before, now arrived, and with him the priestess of Phœbus and Trivia, Deiphobe the child of Glaucus, who thus speaks to the prince: "This hour does not call for sights like those; now it were best to sacrifice seven bullocks of a herd that never felt the yoke, and as many ewes duly chosen." When she had thus addressed Æneas, (and his men delay not to perform the offering she commands,) the priestess summons the Trojans into the lofty temple. The vast side of the rock of Cumæ is hewn out into a cavern, whither a hundred broad approaches, a hundred doorways lead; from whence spring as many cries, the responses of the Sibyl. They had reached the entrance, when says the virgin: "It is the time to inquire your destinies; the god! behold, the god!" While thus she spoke before the portal, all at once her look and her colour were changed, her locks became disor-dered; then her bosom heaves, and wildly swells her heart with frantic rage; and her stature seems larger, and her voice sounds not like a mor-tal's; for she is breathed upon by the spirit of the god, now closer to her. "Do you delay to make your vows and prayers, Trojan Æneas?" she says; "do you delay? For indeed the mighty mouths of the awe-struck mansion will not unclose till then." So she spoke, and held her peace. An icy shudder thrilled through the strong nerves of the Teucri, and their prince pours out his prayer from the bottom of his heart.

56—97. The prayer of Æneas. The prophecy of the Sibyl.

"Phœbus, who didst ever pity the distressful struggles of Troy, who didst point the Dardan shaft and hand of Paris against the body of Æa-cides, so many seas that encompass mighty lands have I sailed into with thee for my guide, and have reached the far remote Massylian tribes, and the fields the Syrtes fringe; now at last we grasp the shores of ever retreating Italy; thus far only may a Trojan fortune have followed us! It is now meet for ye also to spare the people of Pergama, all ye gods and goddesses, against whose pleasure Ilium stood, and the high renown of Dardania. And thou, most holy prophetess, thou that foreseest coming fate, grant me (I ask a kingdom that is but due to my destinies,) that in Latium the Teucri may settle, and the wandering gods and persecuted divinities of Troy. Then to Phœbus and Trivia I will set up a shrine of massy marble, and ordain holydays in the name of Phœbus. Thee too a solemn sanctuary awaits in our dominions; for there I will deposit thy oracles and fateful mysteries uttered for my people, and will consecrate chosen ministers to thee, propitious Power. Only commit not thy responses to leaves, lest they fly away in disorder, the sport of rushing winds; chant them thyself, I entreat thee." So he ended the words of his mouth. But the prophetess, not yet tamed to the will of Phœbus, raves furiously within her cave, striving to throw off from her bosom the mighty god; so much the more he strains her maddened mouth, curbing her wild heart, and fashions her by his control. And now the hundred vast entrances of the mansion open of their own accord, and carry to the outer air the response of the prophetess: "Hail, you that at last have finished the dread dangers of the sea! But more grievous perils on land remain. Into the realm of Lavinium the children of Dardanus shall come; release your bosom from this anxiety; but they shall also wish that they had never come. Wars, horrid wars, I see, and Tiber foaming with torrents of blood. You will not be without a Simois, or a Xanthus, or a Doric camp; a second Achilles is already provided for Latium, himself too goddess-born; and Juno will nowhere be absent, but ever arrayed against the Teucri; whilst you, in your distress and need, what nations of Italy, or what cities, will you not humbly supplicate? Again a stranger-bride, again a foreign marriage, shall cause the Trojans such a world of woe. Yield not you to your troubles, but march more boldly to meet them, in the path your fortune shall permit you. Your first road to safety, though you little think it, shall be opened to you from a Grecian city."

98—123. Æneas replies, and begs for the help of the Sibyl in his errand to the shades.

In these words the Cumæan Sibyl from her shrine chants her awful riddles, and makes the cave re-echo, shrouding truth in darkness; such is the curb Apollo shakes in her frantic mouth, and such the goad he works within her breast. So soon as her frenzy is abated, and her raving lips are hushed, thus begins the hero Æneas: "No form of trouble that arises, O maiden, is to me strange or unlooked for; all things I have foreknown, and gone through already with my own heart. One thing I pray: since here is said to be the door of the king of hell, and the gloomy pool where Acheron overflows, may it be my fortune to pass into the sight and presence of my dear father; teach thou the way, and unlock the sacred portal. He it was whom I, through flames and a thousand pursuing spears, bore away on these shoulders, and rescued from the midst of the foe: he, the partner of my voyage, feeble though he was, dared with me to face all the seas, and all the frowns of ocean and sky, beyond the strength and portion of old age. He too it was, who with prayers used to enjoin upon me humbly to address thee, and visit thy threshold. Both son and father pity, propitious Power; for thou canst do all things; and it is not in name only that Hecate has made thee mistress of the groves of Avernus. If Orpheus could summon the spirit of his bride, strong in his Thracian lyre and tuneful strings; if Pollux ransomed his brother by dying for him in turn, and so often goes and comes back along the path,—why should I speak of mighty Theseus, why of Alcides? my descent also is from sovereign Jove."

124—155. *The Sibyl instructs Æneas to find the golden bough, that will be his safeguard in his journey. She tells him of the death of one of his comrades.*

In such form was he praying, and clasping the altar, when thus the prophetess began to speak: "O you that are sprung from the blood of gods, Trojan son of Anchises, easy is the descent of Avernus; night and day lies open the door of gloomy Dis; but to retrace your footsteps, and safely reach the upper air, this is the task, this the struggle. But few, the children of the gods, whom righteous Jove has loved, or their glowing virtue has exalted to heaven, have had the power. All the tract that lies between, forests possess, and Cocytus encircles, as it glides along with dark meandering. But if your mind has such deep desire, so great a passion, twice to float upon the Stygian flood, twice to view black Tartarus, and it is your pleasure to throw yourself into the mad endeavour, learn the duties you must first perform. There lurks in a shady tree a bough, all golden both in leaf and pliant twig, an offering dedicated to the Juno of hell; this all the grove conceals, and dim dells of shadow shut it in. But no man is permitted to enter the hidden parts of the earth, but he who has plucked from the tree its offspring with the golden leaves. Fair Proserpine has ordained that this shall be brought to her, her own peculiar offering: when the first bough is rent away, another all of gold succeeds, and the branch breaks into foliage of a like metal. Therefore search aloft with your eyes, and, when you have found it, duly pluck it with your hand; for it will of itself willingly and easily come away, if destiny invite you; otherwise, you will not be able by any force to subdue it, nor to rend it away with the hard steel. Besides, there is the body of your friend lying lifeless (alas, you know it not), and polluting with death all the fleet; while you are inquiring for oracles, and lingering in our portal. First commit him to his place of rest, and lay him in the grave. Bring black victims; let them be your first propitiatory offering. So at last you will view the Stygian groves, and the realms to which the living may not pass." She spoke, and closed her lips in silence.

156—178. *The story of the death of Misenus.*

Æneas goes on his way, with fixed gaze and sorrowful countenance, leaving the cave, and with his own heart ponders the issues he cannot see. With him journeys his faithful Achates, and paces on, possessed with equal grief. Many things they discussed in various talk with one another, who was the lifeless comrade, what the corpse to be buried, that the prophetess spoke of: and so soon as they arrive, they see Misenus stretched on the dry shore, cut off by an undeserved death, Misenus, son of Æolus, whom no other man surpassed in mustering warriors, and kindling the soul of battle with his note. He had been mighty Hector's comrade; by Hector's side he fought the battle, conspicuous by his clarion, and his spear as well. After victorious Achilles had stripped the chieftain of life, the valiant hero had made himself the companion of Dardan Æneas, following no lower fortune. But at that time, while he makes the surface of the sea ring with his hollow shell, and with his note challenges the gods to contest, Triton in jealousy (if the tale deserve belief,) surprised the warrior, and plunged him in the foaming waves amid the rocks. Therefore all were wailing around with loud cries, the pious Æneas above the rest. Then without delay they hasten to perform the bidding of the Sibyl, and work with all their power to pile up with trunks of trees the altar of the dead, and to raise it high towards heaven.

179—211. *They go into the forest to gather wood for the funeral pile. There Æneas sees and plucks the golden bough.*

They go into an ancient wood, the lofty coverts of the wild beasts; down comes the pitch-pine, the ilex resounds beneath the stroke of the hatchet, and beams of ash and oak easy to cleave are split with wedges; they roll in from the hills mighty mountain ashes. Æneas also, in the midst of a work so busy, leads the way by inciting his comrades, and girds on weapons like their own. And thus he muses with his own sad heart, gazing on the boundless forest, and prays in these words: "O that that golden bough would now reveal itself to us in this great wood! For the prophetess told all your story, alas, too truly, Misenus." Scarce had he so spoken, when it chanced a pair of doves came flying through the sky, close beneath the eyes of the warrior, and settled on the green turf. Then the great hero recognises his mother's birds, and joyfully makes his prayer: "Be ye my guides, I beseech, wherever my path may lie; and speed straight your flight into the groves, where the wealthy bough o'ershadows the fruitful soil; and do thou, I pray, fail not my doubtful fortunes, my goddess-mother." So he spoke, and stayed his steps, observing what omens they bring, whither they proceed to take their flight. They, as they feed, advance on the wing only so far as the eye of one who follows them can keep within its vision. Afterwards, when they arrive at the jaws of noisome Avernus, they fleetly rise upward, and gliding through the clear air, both together settle in the wished-for spot on the top of the tree, whence through the boughs the gleam of gold flashed forth distinct. As in the woods amid the wintry cold with strange foliage the misletoe is wont to bloom, which its own tree does not bear, and to encircle with its yellow shoots the rounded trunks; such was the look of the leafy gold in the dark ilex; so the foil crackled beneath the gentle breeze. At once Æneas grasps and greedily breaks away the clinging bough, and bears it within the dwelling of the prophetic Sibyl.

212—235. *The funeral and monument of Misenus.*

And not the less the Trojans meanwhile wept for Misenus on the shore, and brought the last gifts to the unthankful ashes. First they build up a huge pile, rich with fagots of pine and planks of oak, the sides of which they intertwine with gloomy foliage, and set up in front funereal cypresses, and dress it on the top with glittering arms. Some quickly bring warm water, and caldrons bubbling with heat, and wash and anoint the body of the cold dead. A mournful cry is raised. Then they lay out upon the couch the limbs o'er which they have duly wept, and cast above purple robes, his well-known garments. Some raised on their shoulders the great

bier, and, according to the rite of their forefathers, held with averted eyes
the torch they applied. The heaped offerings of incense burn; so do
the meat-offerings, and the bowls of streaming oil. When the ashes
had sunk, and the flame died out, they washed with wine the remains
and thirsty embers, and Corynæus covered with a brazen urn the gathered
bones. He too thrice bore to his comrades all around clear water,
sprinkling them with light dew from the branch of a fruitful olive, and
purified the warriors, and spoke the farewell words. Next pious Æneas
places over him a tomb of ponderous mass, and the tools of the hero's
trade, both oar and trumpet, beneath a towering hill, which now after
him is called Misenus, and keeps the name throughout the ages for ever.

236—263. *Æneas offers sacrifice at the entrance of the cave that leads
to hell. Encouraged by supernatural signs, he and the Sibyl begin
the descent.*

When these duties are performed, he carries out with haste the instructions of the Sibyl. There was a cavern, deep and huge with its vast
mouth, craggy, sheltered by its black lake and forest gloom, o'er which
no birds might speed along unharmed; such an exhalation, pouring from
its black jaws, rose to the vault of heaven; wherefore the Greeks named
the spot Avernus. Here the priestess first sets for sacrifice four oxen with
sable backs, and slowly pours the wine upon the brow, and plucking the
topmost bristles just between the horns, lays them upon the hallowed
fires, to be the first offering; calling aloud on Hecate, a queen in heaven
and in hell. Others apply the knife to the throat and catch in basins the
warm blood. Æneas himself slays with the sword a ewe lamb of black
fleece to the mother of the Furies, and her mighty sister; and to thee,
O Proserpine, a barren cow. Then to the Stygian monarch he inaugurates
an altar by night, and lays upon the flames whole carcases of bulls, pouring rich olive oil over the burning entrails. But lo, just before the earliest
rays of the rising sun appeared, the ground began to rumble beneath
their feet, and the woody ridges to be stirred, as the goddess drew nearer
and nearer. "Away, I pray you, away, ye uninitiated," the prophetess
exclaims aloud, "and withdraw from all the grove; and do you enter on
the path, and quickly draw your sword from its sheath; now you need
courage, Æneas, now resolve of soul." So much she spoke, and full of
frenzy darted into the open cave; he keeps pace with his guide, as she
goes onward, with no timorous steps.

264—267. *The invocation.*

"Powers, who possess the realm of spirits, and ye, silent shades,
and ye, Chaos and Phlegethon, regions hushed in universal night, may
I be allowed to utter the things I have heard; may it be granted me,
by your will, to unfold truths buried in the deep of the earth and in
darkness."

268—294. *The dwellers in the entrance of the gate of hell.*

Dimly they went along beneath the lonesome night, through the
gloom, and through the empty mansions and unsubstantial realms of
Dis; such is the journey in the woods through the glimmering moonlight, beneath the unkindly beam, when Jove has buried the sky in
gloom, and black night has robbed the world of its colour. Just before

the porch, and in the opening of the jaws of Orcus, Grief and Avenging Pains have set their couch; and there ghastly Diseases dwell, and joyless Old Age, and Fear, and Hunger that impels to crime, and squalid Want, forms fearful to view, and Death, and Toil; next Sleep, Death's own brother, and the bad Delights of the mind, and War fraught with doom, in the threshold before the eye; and the iron chambers of the Furies, and maddening Discord, her snaky hair entwined with bloody wreaths. In the midst an elm, shadowy, vast, spreads out its boughs and aged arms, which common rumour says that cheating Dreams possess for their abode, and fasten beneath every leaf: and moreover many various forms of monstrous beasts are there, the Centaurs make their stalls in the entrance, and the Scyllas of twofold shape, and hundred-handed Briareus, and the huge beast of Lerna, with its terrific hissing, and Chimæra armed with flames, the Gorgons, and the Harpies, and the shape of the phantom with triple body. Hereupon Æneas, alarmed with sudden panic, hastily seizes his sword, and presents against them as they come the naked edge; and had not his sage companion warned him that those were unsubstantial disembodied spirits, flitting about within the hollow phantom of a shape, he would have rushed upon them, and idly struck asunder shadows with the steel.

295—336. Description of Charon, and the dead conveyed in his boat. The fate of the unburied.

Hence begins a way which leads to the waters of Tartarean Acheron. This flood, all turbid with its muddy stream and dreary rapids, rages along, and belches forth into Acheron all its sand. A grim ferryman guards the waters of this river, Charon, hideous in his squalor; for on his chin there lies a huge mass of untrimmed gray hair, his eyes are fixed and fiery, a filthy cloak hangs down from his shoulders by a knot. With his own hands he works the boat along with a pole, and manages the sails, and is always conveying to the shore the dead in his murky bark, old as he now is; but fresh and vigorous is the old age of a god. Hither all the throng was rushing in a tide towards the bank, matrons and husbands, and the lifeless bodies of valiant heroes, boys and unmarried girls, and youths that were laid·on the funeral pile before their·parents' eyes; thick as the leaves fall to the ground in the forests, when the autumnal cold begins; or thick as the birds come in crowded flight to land from the high sea, when the cold season drives them across the deep, and sends them into sunnier lands. There they stood, intreating to be the first to pass across, and ever stretched forth their hands with longing desire for the farther shore. But the surly boatman admits now these, now those; but others he thrusts to a distance, and keeps away from the brink. Æneas, for he wondered and was amazed at the tumult, "Tell me, maiden," he says, "what means the thronging to the stream? Or what is it the spirits require? Or by what distinction are some compelled to leave the bank, while others sweep with the oar the lurid pool?" To him the aged priestess thus in few words replied: "Offspring of Anchises, authentic child of Heaven, you behold the deep flood of Cocytus, and the marsh of the Styx, by whose divinity the gods fear to swear and not keep their oath. All this crowd that you behold is forlorn and unburied; that ferryman is Charon ; these, who are borne upon the flood, have been interred. And he is not allowed to convey them between the dreadful banks, and across the roaring stream, before their bones have been laid in their place of rest. A hundred years they roam, and flit about these coasts ; then at last they are received, and visit again the pool they long to win." The son of Anchises paused, and stayed his steps, full of thought, and pitying in soul their hard lot. There he observes all sorrowful and destitute of the rites of death, Leucaspis, and the captain of the Lycian fleet, Orontes ; whom, both at once, when on their voyage from Troy across the tossing deep, Auster overwhelmed, plunging in the water ship and crew as well.

337—383. *Palinurus tells Æneas the story of his death. The Sibyl consoles him, by predicting the honours that are to be paid him in the country where he perished.*

Lo, the pilot Palinurus came along, who late, in the voyage from Libya, while he watched the stars, had fallen from the stern of the ship, and been tumbled into the midst of the waves. Æneas, when he had hardly recognised him full of sorrow in the thick darkness, was the first to address him thus : "Which of the gods was it, who snatched you from us, Palinurus, and sunk you in the midst of the main? Tell me, I pray. For Apollo, though I never before found him a deceiver, deluded my soul by this one oracle, in that he foretold that you would be unharmed by sea, and reach the Ausonian shores. Is this indeed his faithful promise?" The other in reply ; "Neither did the tripod of Phœbus deceive you, prince, Anchises' son, nor did a god plunge me in the deep. For in headlong fall I dragged down with me the rudder, wrenched away by mishap, with rude violence; the rudder, which I, its appointed guardian, was holding steadfastly, and guiding the ship's course. By the savage seas I swear, that I conceived no such great fear for myself, as for your ship, lest, stripped of its helm, and violently bereft of its master, it might not live, while such a sea was rising. Three winter nights the South wind wildly bore me on the water, across the boundless main ; scarcely, on the fourth dawn, as I raised myself upward, I caught sight of Italy from the surface of the sea. By slow degrees I swam towards land ; soon I should have gained safe ground ; had not the ruthless race, while I was weighed down in my drenched garments, and striving to grasp with crooked hands the rough points of a crag, attacked me with the sword, and in their ignorance thought me a prize. Now I lie at the mercy of the waves, and the winds ofttimes cast me on the shore. Wherefore by the pleasant light of heaven, by your father, I beseech you, and the promise of your rising Iulus, rescue me from these woes, unconquered prince : either cast earth upon me yourself, (for you have the power to do it,) and again repair to the port of Velia ; or now, if there be any means, if the goddess that gave you birth shews you any, (for not without the will of Heaven, I ween, you are about to sail o'er streams so dread, and the Stygian pool,) lend your hand to your hapless pilot, and carry me with you across the flood, that in death I may repose in a tranquil place of rest, at least." So had he spoken, when the priestess thus begins : " Whence comes it, Palinurus, that you feel a longing so unlawful? Will you, unburied, view the waters of the Styx, and the Furies' grim stream, and unbidden approach the bank? Cease to hope that divine destiny can yield to prayer. But receive into your memory my words, the consolation of your hard fortune. For your bones the neighbouring tribes, far and wide throughout their cities, compelled by signs from Heaven, shall propitiate, and set up a mound, and to the mound shall bring due offerings, and the place shall keep for ever the name of Palinurus." By these words his cares are cleared away, and his grief for awhile driven from his sorrowing heart ; he is pleased with the land that is to bear his name.

384—416. Charon, awed at the sight of the golden bough, carries Æneas and the Sibyl across the Styx.

And so they proceed to accomplish their journey, and draw nigh to the river. And the boatman, when, from the spot where they stood, he marked them, from the Stygian flood, coming onward through the silent grove, and turning their steps towards the bank, thus, before they spoke, encountered them with these words, and challenged them besides : " Whoever you are, who advance in arms to our stream, say now wherefore you come, there, from that place, and check your step. This is the world of Shades, of Sleep and slumberous Night; it is forbidden to convey the bodies of the living in the Stygian bark. Truly it brought me no joy that I admitted into my boat Alcides on his journey, and Theseus, and Pirithous, sprung from gods though they were, and of might invincible. The former violently pursued the sentinel of hell from the throne of the monarch, to bind him, and dragged him trembling hence ; the latter attempted to force away our queen from the bridal-chamber of Dis." In reply to this the Amphrysian prophetess shortly answered: " With us there is no such stratagem; refrain your passion; nor do our weapons intend force ; let the monstrous doorkeeper in his cave fright with his ceaseless bark the bloodless shades; let chaste Proserpine abide within her uncle's portal. Æneas of Troy, renowned for piety and valour, descends, to meet his sire, to the deepest gloom of Erebus. If the sight of such high piety has no power to move you, still (she discloses the bough which was hidden in her dress,) acknowledge this bough." And no more than this she spoke. The other, viewing with astonishment the awful gift of the fateful stem, which he beheld after a long space of time, turns to land his sable vessel, and draws nigh to the bank. Next he thrusts out other spirits, who were sitting along the length of the benches, and clears the gangways; withal he admits into the hull the great Æneas. The crazy craft groaned beneath the weight, and through its leaks let in a flood of marshy water. At last on the other side of the stream he lands in safety prophetess and hero on the unsightly mire and gray sedge.

417—425. The Sibyl stupefies Cerberus with a cake of drugged honey and wheat.

These are the realms huge Cerberus makes ring with the barking of his threefold jaws, reposing his enormous bulk in the cave that fronts the ferry. To him the prophetess, seeing that the serpents of his neck begin to bristle, throws a cake stupefying with its honey and drugged wheat. He, opening wide in ravenous hunger his three throats, snaps up the proffered morsel, and, sunk upon the ground, relaxes his monstrous back, and stretches his huge carcass throughout the length and breadth of the cavern. Æneas gains the passage while the sentinel is buried in sleep, and rapidly surmounts the bank of the flood o'er which there is no return.

426—439.   *The inhabitants of the first regions of hell.*

Straightway cries are heard, and wailing loud, and the spirits of infants weeping in the entrance of the door, whom, without sharing the sweets of life, and torn from the breast, the day of doom swept away, and plunged into untimely death. Next to these are they that were condemned to die on a false charge: and these abodes are by no means assigned without allotment, without a judge; Minos rules the scrutiny, and shakes the urn; he convokes the conclave of the silent dead, and learns their lives, and the charges brought against them. The regions that come next in order are filled by a sad company, who, without guilt, have been the authors of their own death by violence, and sick of the light of day have flung away their lives. How ready they would be now, to endure beneath the height of the sky both penury and hard struggles! The law of Heaven forbids, and the unlovely marsh with its joyless flood binds them in, and Styx hems them round with nine circles of its stream.

440—476.   *The Mourning Fields.   Æneas sees Dido, and tries in vain to soothe her.*

Not far from hence the Mourning Fields are shewn, spreading on every side; such is the name by which they call them. Here they whom cruel love has wasted away with pining pain, are concealed in secluded paths, and covered all round by a myrtle grove; not even in death do their woes desert them. In these regions he descries Phædra, and Procris, and Eriphyle full of grief, pointing to the wounds dealt by her cruel son, and Evadne, and Pasiphae; in company with them Laodamia goes along, and Cæneus, once a youth, a woman now, and again transformed by fate into her original shape. Among them Phœnician Dido, fresh from her wound, was wandering in a vast wood: the hero of Troy, so soon as he stood nigh her, and recognised through the gloom her dim figure—even as in the beginning of the month one sees, or thinks he sees, the moon uprising through the clouds—shed tears, and addressed her with the tenderness of love: "Hapless Dido, were then the tidings true which came to me, that you had perished, and sought with the sword your final doom? Alas, was I the cause of your death? By the stars I swear, by the gods above, and by whatever bond of honour exists in the depth of the earth, unwillingly, O queen, I retreated from your coast. But the command of Heaven it was, which now compels me to travel through these shades, through regions overgrown with mould, and through the abyss of night, that forced me by its behests; and I could not believe that I should by my departure bring you such deep woe as this. Stay your steps, and withdraw not yourself from my view. Why do you flee from me? This is the last time Fate allows me to speak with you." By such words Æneas strove to soothe her soul, burning with wrath though she was, and glaring gloomily, and drew tears from his eyes. She, turning from

him, kept her looks fixed on the ground, and was no more melted by the
words he essayed to speak, than if she were a solid rock of flint, or a
Marpessian crag. At length she hurried away, and disdainfully fled back
into the shady grove, where Sychæus, her former husband, sympathises
with her woes, and requites her with equal love. And not the less Æneas,
shocked at her hard calamity, follows her far along her path with his tears
and his pity.

477—493. *The abode of the heroes. The Greeks are scared at the sight
of Æneas.*

Then he sets himself anew to perform the journey assigned him.
And presently they reached the farthest fields, the secluded fields,
haunted by those renowned in war.   Here Tydeus meets him, here
Parthenopæus famed in fight, and the pallid form of Adrastus; here
the children of Dardanus, o'er whom many a lament had been wafted
to heaven; for they fell in battle; and he sighed as he discerned
them all in long array, both Glaucus, and Medon, and Thersilochus,
Antenor's three sons, and Polyphœtes holy to Ceres, and Idæus, still
keeping his car, still his arms.   Right and left the spirits surround him
in crowds; and it is not enough to catch one sight of him; it is their
joy still to linger near him, and walk with him side by side, and learn
the reasons of his coming.   But the princes of the Greeks and the
battalions of Agamemnon, as soon as they saw the warrior, and the
armour flashing through the gloom, began to quiver in boundless panic;
some turned their backs in flight, as of yore they hurried to the ships;
some strive to raise a feeble cry; the shout attempted mocks their straining lips.

494—534. *Among the heroes, Æneas meets Deiphobus cruelly mangled.
Deiphobus relates how he was murdered on the night Troy was
taken.*

And now he saw Deiphobus, Priam's son, with all his body mutilated,
his face cruelly mangled, his face and both his hands, and his temples
robbed and bereft of the ears, and his nostrils lopped away by a shameful stroke.   It was even with difficulty he recognised him, as he trembled
and cowered, and tried to conceal the marks of his monstrous torture:
and Æneas, before he spoke, in well-known accents accosts him:
" Deiphobus, mighty in arms, descendant of the ancient blood of Teucer,
whose will has inflicted upon you a punishment so cruel? Who has
been permitted to treat you so outrageously? Rumour told me that
you, on the night of our doom, tired with the slaughter of a host of
Greeks, sank down upon the mingled mass of carnage.   I myself then
set up in your honour an empty barrow on the Rhœtean coast, and with
solemn cry thrice called on your spirit. Your name and arms mark
the spot; I was not able, my friend, to see your body, and lay you,
when I departed, in our native soil." The son of Priam replies:
" Nought by you, my friend, has been left unperformed; you have fulfilled every duty to Deiphobus, and to the phantom of his corpse. But
my fate it was, and the pernicious wickedness of the Spartan woman,
that plunged me into these calamities; these are the keepsakes she has
left me. For you know how we spent the night of our doom, amid

deluding joys; and it must be that you remember it only too well. When the fateful horse with a bound o'erpassed the lofty walls of Pergama, and brought in its teeming womb an armed battalion, she, in feigned religious dance, led around the city the Phrygian women raising the bacchanal cry; she herself in their midst held a mighty firebrand, and called in the Greeks from the height of the citadel. At that time I, unhappy man, was within my bridal-chamber, worn with cares and weighed down with sleep; and as I lay, repose, sweet and deep, and the very image of quiet death, lay heavy upon me. Meanwhile my worthy wife clears the house of all its arms, and had filched away from beside my head my trusty sword: she invites into the dwelling Menelaus, and opens to him my door, no doubt hoping that that would be a great gift in the eyes of her lover, and so might be blotted out the shame of her past misdeeds. Why do I prolong my tale? They break into the chamber; withal the son of Æolus, the instigator of crimes, joins the band. Ye gods, repay the Greeks that outrage, if with pious lips I pray for vengeance! But come, tell me in your turn, what fortunes have brought you hither, a living man. Is it driven by wanderings on the deep you come, or at the bidding of Heaven? or what other chance constrains you to visit the sad and sunless abodes, the regions of disorder?"

535—547. *At the bidding of the Sibyl, Deiphobus departs.*

During this exchange of talk, Aurora on her rosy chariot had already traversed half the span of heaven in her etherial course; and perhaps they would have prolonged such converse through all the allotted time; but the Sibyl at his side warned and shortly addressed him: "Night is fast coming on, Æneas; we waste the hours in weeping. This is the point, where the way divides into two branches: the right is that which runs beneath the battlements of mighty Dis; along it lies our road to Elysium: but that on the left inflicts on the bad their punishment, and conducts them to Tartarus, the home of impiety." Deiphobus in answer; "Let not thine anger rise, great priestess: I will depart; I will fill my place in the number of the shades, and return to the darkness. Go then, go, glory of our land, enjoy a better fate than mine." He spoke, and with the words on his lips turned his steps away.

548—561. *Æneas inquires the meaning of a dreadful prison-house on the left of the path.*

Æneas suddenly looks round, and beneath a rock that lies on the left sees battlements extended wide, surrounded with a triple wall, and encircled by a rushing river with waves of torrent fire, Tartarean Phlegethon, that rolls down its channel rattling rocks. Opposite stands the gate of ponderous size, with pillars of solid adamant; so that no mortal might, nay, not the dwellers in the sky, are strong enough to throw it down in war; up towards heaven stands the iron tower; and in her seat Tisiphone, with robe girt up and stained with blood, guards the porch by night and day, a sleepless sentinel. Hence are clearly heard groanings and the sound of the cruel scourge; next clanking iron, and dragging chains. Æneas stopped, and stood still, affrighted at the din. "What forms of crime are these? Tell me, maiden. Or what are the heavy punishments they feel? What means this wail so loud, that rises to the sky?"

562—627.   *The Sibyl describes Tartarus and its inhabitants.*

Then thus the prophetess began to speak : "Illustrious captain of the Trojans, no one that is holy may tread the threshold of the wicked ; but Hecate, when she made me mistress of the groves of Avernus, herself taught me the divine punishments, and guided me through all the scenes. Cretan Rhadamanthus is lord of these kingdoms, kingdoms most severe ; and scourges guilt, and hears its story, and compels men to confess the commission of those crimes, which in the upper world, exulting in a fruitless craft, they delayed to atone for till the late hour of death. Tisiphone, the avenger, armed with her whip, unceasingly lashes the shuddering criminals, and taunts them withal, and with her left hand brandishing her grim serpents, summons her ruthless sisterhood. Then at last, with a horrid sound of the grating hinge, the awful doors fly open. See you the form of the watcher that sits in the porch? the shape that guards the threshold? The Hydra, still more fierce, that monster with the fifty black and gaping mouths, has its dwellingplace within. Then Tartarus itself yawns with sheer descent, and stretches down through the darkness, twice as far as the eye travels upward to the firmament of heaven. Here the ancient brood of earth, the Titan warriors, struck down by the thunderbolt writhe in the bottom of the pit. Here I also saw both the sons of Aloeus, enormous frames, who essayed to tear down by force the mighty heaven, and thrust out Jove from the realms on high. I saw Salmoneus too, enduring the cruel punishment that overtook him while he imitated the fire of Jove and the noise of Olympus. He, drawn by four horses, and waving his torch, throughout the nations of Greece and the heart of the city of Elis went in triumph, and claimed to receive divine homage. Fool! to strive, with car of brass and trampling steeds of horny foot, to counterfeit clouds and darkness and the inimitable bolt ! But the Almighty Father from amid thick thunderclouds hurled his shaft, no firebrands he, nor smoky pinewood blaze, and smote him headlong down with the tremendous blast. Likewise one might see Tityos also, child of Earth the universal mother, he whose body lies stretched o'er full nine acres ; and the fell vulture with crooked beak, feeding on his imperishable liver, and vitals fruitful with punishment, gropes for its meal, and makes its dwelling deep within his breast, and no respite is allowed to the entrails that ever grow afresh. Why should I mention the Lapithæ, Ixion, and Pirithous? over whose heads is hanging a black crag, every moment about to slip, and looking like a rock in act to fall : lofty festal couches glitter with golden feet, and before their eyes a banquet is spread in kingly sumptuousness : at their side reclines the eldest of the Furies, and forbids them to lay their hands on the feast, and springs up, brandishing her torch, and cries with voice of thunder. Here they who hated their brethren, while life lasted, or struck their father, or entangled their client in a web of fraud, or who gloated by themselves over riches they had found, and gave no share to their friends, (who are they that form the largest throng,) and they who were slain for their adultery, and they who followed impious arms against their country, and scrupled not to break allegiance to their lords, in close prison await their punishment. Ask not to learn what is the punishment they expect, or in what guise of pain or in what doom they are engulphed: some roll along a huge stone, and hang with outstretched limbs upon the spokes of wheels; unhappy Theseus sits and will sit there for ever; and Phlegyas in his depth of woe warns the world, and with loud cry speaks his counsel through the gloom; 'Warned by me, learn righteousness, and not to scorn the gods.' One sold his country for gold, and placed over it a tyrannous master; for a price he made and unmade laws; another forced his daughter to be his bride, and formed a forbidden wedlock: all dared to attempt monstrous crime, and gained the object of their daring. Not if I had a hundred tongues, a hundred mouths, and a voice of steel, could I comprise in words all the shapes of wickedness, or run over the names of all the punishments."

628—636. *Æneas deposits the bough in the gateway of Pluto's palace.*

When the aged priestess of Phœbus had uttered these words, "But now come," she says, "hasten on your way, and perform the offering you have undertaken: let us make speed; I descry the battlements reared by the furnaces of the Cyclops, and the gates with their archway that fronts us, where the precepts we have received bid us deposit this gift." She ended; and advancing side by side along the shadowy path, they hurry o'er the ground that lies between, and draw nigh to the door. Æneas gains the entrance, and sprinkles his body with fresh water, and hangs up the bough in the threshold opposite.

637—659. *Elysium; its inhabitants, and their pastimes.*

When at length these duties were completed, and the offering prescribed by the goddess performed, they came to pleasant places, and the smiling lawns of happy groves, and the homes of the blessed. Here a bright sky robes the fields with fuller radiance and with dazzling light; and they know their own sun, their own stars. Some exercise their limbs on grassy wrestling-grounds; in sport they contend, and struggle on the yellow sand: some mark the measure with their feet, and sing songs. Likewise the holy Thracian bard, in his flowing dress, keeps time to the music with the seven separate notes of the voice; and strikes them now with his fingers, now with his ivory quill. Here is the ancient progeny of Teucer, a beauteous race, valiant heroes, born in better years, both Ilus, and Assaracus, and Dardanus the founder of Troy. From a distance he views with wonder the visionary arms and chariots of the heroes. Their lances stand fixed in the ground, and all about their steeds unharnessed are feeding o'er the plain. The delight in chariots and arms they had when living, the care they took to feed their glossy steeds, attends them undiminished now they are laid in earth. Lo, he observes others to right and left along the grass, banqueting, and chanting in chorus the joyful Pæan, amid the fragrant grove of bay-trees, whence to the world above the full-flowing stream of Eridanus rolls onward through the forest.

660—678. *Musaeus directs the Sibyl to Anchises.*

Here the company of those who met their wounds in fighting for their fatherland, and they who were holy priests, while this life lasted, and they who were pious bards, and spoke things meet for the ear of Phœbus, or who gave life refinement by the arts they discovered, and they who by their good deeds won the gratitude of others; all these have their brows encircled with snowy fillets. Them, as they crowded round, the Sibyl thus addressed, Musæus before the rest; for the largest throng make him their centre, and to him look up, as he stands above them with towering shoulders: " Say, blessed spirits, and you, excellent bard, what region, what spot, contains Anchises? For his sake have we come hither, and floated o'er the vast rivers of Erebus." Then to her the hero thus in few words replied : " No one has a fixed abode ; we dwell in the shady woods, and haunt the couches that the river-banks afford, and the meadows that the fountains freshen. But do ye, if such is the object of your hearts' desire, pass over this ridge; and presently I will set you down on a gently sloping track." He spoke, and passed on before them, and from the height points out the shining fields: after that, they leave the summit of the hill.

679—702. *The meeting of Æneas and Anchises.*

But father Anchises, deep within a verdant vale, was surveying with studious thought the spirits now shut up, and destined to pass into the light above; and chanced to be reviewing all the array of his people, and his beloved descendants, and the fates and fortunes of the heroes, and their characters and deeds of might. And he, when he saw Æneas advancing across the grass to meet him, eagerly stretched forth both his hands, and tears streamed down his cheeks, and his words started from his lips: " Have you come at last, and has the affection your sire has looked for o'ercome the difficult way? Am I allowed to gaze upon your face, your own, my son, and to hear and utter in reply familiar words? I of myself was concluding in soul and conceiving that so it was to be, as I measured the seasons of time ; and my study has deceived me not. A pilgrim o'er lands how many, and seas how fierce, tempest-tossed by perils how dread, do I welcome you, my son! How much I feared lest the realm of Libya might work you woe!" He in reply : " Your phantom, my father, your sad phantom it was, that often came before me, and compelled me to take my way to this portal: my fleet lies moored on the Tuscan brine. Suffer me to clasp your hand in mine; suffer me, my father, and withdraw not yourself from my embrace." As thus he spoke, he bedewed his face with a flood of tears. Thrice he then essayed to throw his arms about his neck; thrice the phantom, vainly grasped, fled from his hands, as unsubstantial as the winds, and in all points like a fleeting dream.

703—723. *The river of Lethe, and the spirits who drink its waters.*

Meanwhile, in a retired vale, Æneas views a secret grove, and woods with rustling brakes, and Lethe's stream that drifts along beside those quiet homes. About it unnumbered tribes and nations hovered; even as when in the meadows the bees, beneath the cloudless summer sky, settle on flowers of various hue, and swarm round the white lilies; all the field is loud with the hum. Æneas is startled at the sudden sight, and inquires the cause he cannot tell; what yonder stream may be, or who the men that throng its banks in crowd so great. Then father Anchises: "Souls, to whom by fate a second body is due, drink beside the wave of Lethe's flood the waters of indifference and a long forgetfulness. These spirits I have long desired myself to tell you of, and shew them to your gaze, and read the catalogue of this line of my children, that with me you may rejoice the more in your discovered Italy." "O my father, can it be imagined that any spirits pass from hence aloft to heaven above, and return again to the cumbrous body? Whence have the hapless souls so unblest a longing for the light?" "I will tell you myself, my son, and keep you not in perplexity." Anchises takes up the tale, and expounds each truth in order.

724—751. *Anchises expounds the doctrine of the Soul of the Universe.*

"First, the sky, and earth, and watery plains, and the moon's bright sphere, and Titan's star, a Spirit feeds within; and a Mind, instilled throughout the limbs, gives energy to the whole mass, and mingles with the mighty body. Thence springs the race of men and beasts, and the lives of winged fowl, and the monsters Ocean bears beneath his marble floor. Those seeds have fiery soul and heavenly birth, so far as irksome bodies clog them not, and earthy limbs and members fraught with death do not blunt their vigour. Hence is the source of their fears and desires, their griefs and joys; and they catch no glimpse of heaven, in gloom imprisoned and a darksome cage. Nay, even when life has left them with its latest ray, still every ill and all the plagues of the body do not utterly pass out from the wretches, and it must needs be that many defilements long-contracted grow deep into their being in wondrous wise. Therefore they suffer a probation of punishment, and pay the full penalty of past misdeeds; some hung aloft are exposed to the viewless winds; from some the taint of guilt is washed away beneath the boundless flood: we suffer each his own ghostly penance: after that, we are released, to range through the wide spaces of Elysium, and possess the happy fields, a scanty band: till a long course of time, when the full cycle is complete, has purged away the long-contracted stain, and leaves pure the etherial essence, and unadulterated fire of heaven. All these, when they have travelled round the circle of a thousand years, God summons in mighty throng to the river of Lethe, that so, forgetful of the past, they may go back to visit again the vault of the sky, and begin without reluctance to return to the body."

752—787. *Anchises shews Æneas the royal line of his descendants down to Romulus.*

So spoke Anchises, and conducts his son, and with him the Sibyl, into the midst of the groups and noisy crowd, and takes his stand upon a mound, whence he can scan them all as they front him in long array, and learn their features as they come towards him. "Come now, I will rehearse in my speech the renown that henceforward is to attend the sons of Dardanus, the descendants of the Italian line that are to be, glorious spirits, and fated to pass into our race; and will teach you your destinies. He whom you see, the youth that leans upon a pointless lance, his lot it is to hold a station nearest to the light above; he will be the first to rise to the upper air with a mixture of Italian blood, Silvius, an Alban name, your last child, whom late in time your wife Lavinia to you in your old age shall bear in the woods, to be a king and sire of kings, by whom our race shall be lords in Alba Longa. He that comes next is Procas, the pride of the Trojan people, and Capys, and Numitor, and he that shall reflect you in name, Silvius Æneas, alike in piety and arms renowned, if ever Alba receive him for her king. What youths are there! see, what mighty vigour they display, and bear brows shaded with the civic wreath of oak! These for your posterity shall build Nomentum, and Gabii, and the city of Fidenæ; these shall place upon the mountains the fortress of Collatia, Pometii, and the stronghold of Inuus, and Bola, and Cora. These shall then be names: the lands are nameless now. Moreover the child of Mavors shall become the companion of his grandsire, even Romulus, whom of the blood of Assaracus his mother Ilia shall bear. See you how a double crest is settled on his head, and his father himself already marks him with his own glory for a tenant of the sky? Observe, my son, he will be the author, beginning from whom that farfamed Rome shall bound her empire by earth, her pride by heaven, and, one within herself, encompass with her wall seven embattled heights, blest in her line of heroes; even as the Berecynthian mother, with her crown of towers, is borne in her car throughout the cities of Phrygia, exulting in her progeny of gods, embracing her hundred descendants, all denizens of heaven, all possessors of the lofty skies.

788—807. *The glory of the Julian line, and the praise of Augustus.*

Now hither bend the gaze of both your eyes, regard this clan, and your own Romans. Here is Cæsar, and all the posterity of Iulus, that is to pass beneath the vault of heaven. This, this is the hero, who oft you hear is promised you, Augustus Cæsar, of deified Cæsar's race, who shall establish in Latium a second time the golden age, throughout the fields where Saturn once was king: beyond the Garamantæ and beyond the Indians he shall extend his empire: there lies a land without the bound of the constellations, outside the pathway of the year and the sun, where Atlas, bearer of the sky, upholds upon his shoulder the circling heaven studded with fiery stars. At his foreseen approach, even now the Caspian realms and the land of Mæotis quake to hear the responses of the gods, and the mouths of sevenfold Nile are in a tumult of terror. Not even Alcides traversed so large a space of earth, although he pierced the hind with feet of brass, and brought peace to the groves of Erymanthus, and made Lerna tremble with his bow; nor he, the conqueror, who manages his car with reins festooned with vine-leaves, Liber, when he drives the tigers down from the towering peak of Nysa. And are we still slow by prowess to spread our power, and does fear forbid us to settle in the Ausonian land?

808—853. *The kings of Rome, and heroes of the republic. The panegyric of Rome.*

But who is he yonder, that bears the sacred things, distinguished by his boughs of olive? I begin to discern the hoary locks and chin of the king of Rome, who first shall establish the city upon the foundation of law; he, sent from the humble Cures, and a poor land, to sovereign sway. To him in course Tullus will succeed, who shall break the repose of his country, and wake to arms the lazy warriors, and the troops to whom triumphs have grown strange. Close to him follows the somewhat boastful Ancus, even at this very time too much pleased with the breezes of the people's breath. Choose you also to see the Tarquin kings, and the proud spirit of Brutus the avenger, and the fasces he recovered? He is the first that shall acquire the consular command, and the ruthless axes; and he, the father, shall in the cause of fair freedom summon to punishment his sons, who strive to wake another war. Unhappy man! However posterity shall deem of such an action, love of his country shall prevail, and the boundless passion for renown. Moreover, behold yonder the Decii, and the Drusi, and Torquatus with his ruthless axe, and Camillus bringing back the standards. They again, whom you see glittering in like arms, united spirits now, and so long as they are buried in darkness, alas! how fierce a war shall they wage with one another, if they reach the light of life, what battles and carnage shall they create! The father-in-law coming down from the rampart of the Alps, and the citadel of Monœcus; the son-in-law with all the East in battle array to meet him! Do not, my children, do not make such wars familiar to your souls, nor point your power and might against your country's heart; and do you be the first to refrain, you who trace your descent from the sky; fling from your hand the darts, my own child! Yonder hero shall triumph over Corinth, and guide to the height of the Capitol his victorious car, made famous by Achæan slaughter; that other shall bring to the ground Argos and Agamemnonian Mycenæ, and the son of Æacus himself, the descendant of Achilles strong in battle, avenging his ancestors of Troy, and the pollution of Minerva's shrine. Who would leave you unnoticed, mighty Cato, or you, Cossus? Who the line of Gracchus, or the two thunderbolts of war, the Scipios, twins in glory, the bane of Libya, and Fabricius, rich in his scanty store, or you, Serranus, sowing in your furrowed field? Whither do ye hurry me all weary, ye Fabii? You are that greatest one of your race, who, singly, by delaying restore our state. Let others with finer touch beat out the breathing brass, (I well believe it;) let them express from marble features that live; let them plead causes better, and with the wand mark out the paths of heaven, and tell the times at which the stars arise : make it your business, Roman, to rule the nations with your sway; let these be your arts; to enforce the maintenance of peace, to spare the submissive, and crush in war the proud."

854—886. *The praise of the two Marcelli. A lament for the younger's early death.*

So said father Anchises, and further speaks to his wondering hearers : "See how Marcellus advances, all glorious in the noblest spoils, and like a conqueror o'ertops all the warriors! He it is who shall set firm the realm of Rome, when shaken by rude commotions in the land; he shall trample down beneath his horse-hoofs the Carthaginian, and the Gaul that wakes the war anew; and a third time hang up the captured arms to father Quirinus." And here Æneas, (for walking with

the hero he observed a youth of surpassing beauty and flashing arms,
but joyless was his countenance, and downcast the gaze of his eyes ;)
" Who, my father, is he that thus accompanies the warrior on his
way? His son, or some one of the mighty line of his descendants?
How loud the applause of his companions around him ! What majesty
in himself appears ! But black night with mournful shade hovers about
his head." Then father Anchises begins with starting tears : " My son,
seek not to learn your people's boundless woe : him fate shall but show
to the world, nor suffer him longer to exist. Too mighty had the Roman
race appeared to you, ye gods of heaven, had these blessings become
its own for ever. How deep the groans of men that famous Plain shall
send up to the mighty town of Mavors ! or what sad obsequies shalt thou,
O Tiber, see, when thou glidest past his new-built sepulchre ! And no
other youth of Trojan blood shall raise to such a height of hope his
Latin forefathers ; nor shall the land of Romulus vaunt herself so high
in any other of her children. Alas his piety, alas his antique honour,
and his hand invincible in war ! No one would with impunity have
advanced to meet him in arms, either when he marched on foot against
the foe, or struck the spurs into the sides of his foaming steed. Alas,
hapless boy ! If it may be that you break through your hard fate,
you shall be a Marcellus. Give me handfuls of lilies ; I would strew
bright flowers, and plenteously, with these gifts at least honour the spirit
of my descendant, and discharge an unavailing duty."

887—901. *Anchises tells Æneas what awaits him in Italy, and dis-*
misses him and the Sibyl through one of the gates of Sleep. Æneas
sails to Caieta.

So they wander all around throughout the whole region, o'er the
broad plains of shadow, and survey everything. And when Anchises
has guided his son through each one of these scenes, and fired his
soul with the passion for future fame, he next relates to the hero the
wars which from this time he must wage, and tells him of the Laurentian
peoples, and the city of Latinus, and how he is to flee or to face each
difficulty.

Twofold are the gates of Sleep ; whereof the one is said to be of horn,
by which an easy exit is granted to the visions of truth ; the other
glittering with the polished whiteness of ivory: but false the dreams
the Powers below send to the world above. There Anchises with these
words then attends to the last his son, and with him the Sibyl, and
dismisses them by the ivory gate : Æneas makes his way to the ships,
and joins again his comrades. Then along the straight line of the coast
he sails to Caieta ; the anchor is cast from the prow ; the sterns are
grounded on the beach.

BOOK VII.

1—24. *The nurse of Æneas dies. Her burial at the promontory of Caieta (Gaëta). The Trojans pass by the shore where Circe dwells, and hear the roaring of the beasts that have once been men.*

You too, Caieta, nurse of Æneas, gave by your death everlasting fame to our shores : even now your honour guards your grave, and, whatever glory it may be, the name marks the resting-place of your bones in the great land of the west. But the pious Æneas having duly performed the last honours, having raised the mound of the tomb, as soon as the deep sea was calm, sails onwards in his course, and leaves the harbour. The breezes freshen as night draws on, nor does the bright moon refuse to light their course ; the deep is brilliant beneath her tremulous ray. Next they coast along the shores of the land of Circe, where the wealthy daughter of the Sun fills her inaccessible groves with the music of ceaseless song, and in her glorious halls burns the scented cedar to give her light by night, and with her shrill-toned shuttle she runs through the finely-spun woof. Hence were distinctly heard the angry roars of lions, as they struggled against their bands, and moaned in the depth of the night, and bristly boars and bears were ramping in their cages, and the forms of huge wolves were howling : all these transformed from human shape the cruel goddess had, by magic herbs, clothed with the faces and bodies of wild beasts. Lest the pious Trojans should suffer such monstrous changes, and lest they should be driven thither, and land on the cursed shore, Neptune filled their sails with favourable winds, and gave them a swift course, and bore them beyond the surging shoals.

25—36. *At morn the sea becomes calm, and the Trojans quietly enter the mouth of the Tiber.*

And now the sea began to blush with the morning rays, and in the lofty firmament saffron Aurora shone in her car of rosy hue : when the winds at once dropped, and every breath of air suddenly subsided, and the oars labour in the lazy water. And here Æneas from the sea beholds a great grove. The Tiber divides it with its pleasant stream, a river with whirling eddies, and yellow with thick sand ; here it bursts forth into the sea ; around and above were birds of various plumage, which haunting the banks and channel of the stream charmed the air with their song, and flew in the grove. The prince bids his comrades turn their course, and put their prows towards the land, and gladly takes shelter in the shaded river.

37—45. *The poet invokes the Muse, as he has come to the second part of his poem.*

Come now, Erato, aid me, and I will set forth the kings and the crisis of events, and the state of ancient Latinum, when first the stranger host moored its fleet on Ausonian coasts. Do thou, goddess, do thou instruct thy bard ; I shall sing of dreadful wars, I shall sing of battle array, and of princes driven by their passions to dreadful slaughter, and of the Etrurian bands, and all Hesperia mustered for fight. A greater order of events arises for my song, a greater theme I essay.

46—106. King Latinus: his daughter Lavinia. Portents of various kinds foretell the arrival of an illustrious stranger, who is to be the son-in-law of the king.

Old was Latinus then, and ruled his lands and cities in long and quiet peace. Tradition tells that he was son of Faunus, and of the Laurentian nymph Marica. Picus was father to Faunus; Faunus goes back to thee, O Saturn, as parent: thou wast the earliest author of the race. Latinus had no son, such was heaven's will, no male issue; he that was born to him was taken away in early youth. One daughter alone maintained the hopes of his home and great house ; she was now of age for marriage, she was of full years to be a bride. Many were the suitors who came from mighty Latium, and all Italy; above all others wooed her Turnus famed for beauty, noble in descent from ancient forefathers ; for him the queen-mother was zealous with strong desire that he should be her son-in-law: but in the way there stood the prodigies of heaven with sundry dreadful signs. A bay-tree grew in the centre of the house in its inmost recess, its leaves were holy, with awe it had been kept for many years. 'Tis said that there father Latinus found it, when he began to build his palace, and himself dedicated it to Phœbus, and from it gave the name Laurentian to the settlers. The highest point of it was possessed by a thick swarm of bees, wondrous to tell, which with a mighty buzz flew through the clear sky ; their feet were intertwined, and lo! a sudden swarm hung from the leafy bough. Straightway said the seer: "We clearly see a foreign hero's advent, a troop from the same quarter comes to the same quarters and lords it over the crown of the citadel." Further, as the maiden Lavinia standing by her father lights the altar-fire with holy torches, she seemed as by a miracle to catch in her flowing locks the flame, whilst all her head-dress burnt with waving fire ; lighted was the hair of the princess, lighted was the crown, with jewels set: enveloped in smoke and wrapped in yellow light she scattered fire through all the palace. They said this was sent a portent dreadful, and marvellous in appearance ; for they predicted illustrious renown and destiny to the lady herself, but that to the nation the omen portended a great war. These prodigies disturbed the king, and so he goes to the oracle of Faunus his prophetic sire, and consults the groves 'neath high Albunea ; which is the greatest of woods, resounding with the murmur of its holy fountain, and breathing forth from its dark shade a strong mephitic exhalation. From this grove the nations of Italy, and all the land of Œnotria look for responses, when in perplexity. Hither the priest brings his gifts, and as silent night draws on, lies on a bed of skins and woos sleep; then he sees many phantoms flitting in wondrous wise, and hears manifold voices, and enjoys the converse of gods, and addresses the powers of Acheron let loose through deep Avernus. Here too at this time father Latinus, coming for oracular response, offered in due form an hundred woolly sheep, and lay raised on their skins and on a bed of fleeces ; suddenly a voice came forth from the deep grove: "Aim not to unite your daughter in Latin wedlock, O my offspring, nor trust the marriage ready to hand ; from abroad will come sons-in-law, who by the children of their blood will raise our name to the stars, grandsons of whose stock will see the universe swayed and ruled beneath their feet, where'er the sun in forward and backward course visits either ocean." This response of father Faunus, and warnings given in the silent night, Latinus does not keep within his lips, but Fame flying far and wide had already carried them round about through the Italian towns, when the Trojan youth moored their ships on the grassy mound of the river's bank.

107—147.   The prophecy of the Harpy Celaeno that seemed so dreadful, is fulfilled by a playful remark of the boy Iulus.   The happy Trojans feel they have reached the goal of their wanderings.

Æneas and the foremost captains and fair Iulus rest their limbs beneath the branches of a lofty tree, and set their meal in order, and place their banquets on cakes of barley meal along the ground; so Jove who had foretold did now advise, and on a ground of grain they pile the fruits of the field.   It chanced that here they had consumed all else, and so the want of food forced them to turn to eat their scanty cakes of grain, and with hands and venturous jaw to invade the circle of the crust, in which the fates were bound, and not to spare the broad squares of cake : "See! our tables now we devour," quoth Iulus ; nor said more in playful joke.   That speech when heard first shewed the end to toil, and no sooner was it uttered by the speaker, than his father caught it from his mouth, and awe-struck at heaven's will stopped his further speech ; forthwith he said : "Hail, O land which the fates owe me, and ye, O faithful Penates of Troy, hail ; here is our home, this is our country.   For my father Anchises, now I recall it to mind, left to me such secrets of fate : 'When, my son, hunger shall force you, driven to unknown shores in the day that your meal is short, to devour your tables, then may you hope for a home after weary wandering, and there remember first to build your houses with your hand, and fortify them with a rampart.'   This then turns out to be the hunger then foretold ; this is the last that awaited us, destined to put an end to our deadly losses.   Come then, and joyfully at the dawning light of the sun let us search what lands these are, who dwell therein, where is the city of the nation, and let us go to explore in different directions from the harbour.   Now pour from bowls a libation to Jove, and with prayers invite my father Anchises, and again set cups of wine on the tables." So he spake, and next he wreathes his temples with leafy bough, and prays to the genius of the spot, and to Earth the first of all the gods, and to the Nymphs, and to the streams as yet unknown ; then he invokes Night, and the rising stars of Night, and Jove of Ida, and the Phrygian mother in due order, and his two parents, one in heaven, the other in Erebus.   Thereupon the Almighty Father thrice in the cloudless sky thundered from on high to the left, and with his own hand shook the cloud glowing with golden rays of light, and displayed it in the firmament.   Hereupon a sudden rumour spreads through the Trojan troops, of the advent of the day on which it was fated they should found their walls.   With zeal they solemnize the feast, and joyful at the mighty omen they set their goblets, and crown their wine with garlands.

148—194. When morning comes orators are sent to Latinus; the camp is fortified. A description of the hardy Italians, and of the simple palace of the king.

As soon as the next day arose, and visited the earth with its early beam, in different directions they search out the city and its territory, and the coasts of the people ; this they learn is the pool of the fountain Numicius, this river is the Tiber, here dwell the brave Latins. Then the son of Anchises orders a hundred orators chosen from every rank to go to the august city of the king ; they were all veiled with boughs of Minerva's tree, and were to bring gifts to the monarch, and to sue grace for the Trojans. There is no delay, they hasten as they are bid, and onwards go with rapid feet. Æneas himself marks out his walls with a shallow trench, and lays the foundations of the place ; and encircles his first settlement on the shore with turrets and a mound after the manner of a camp. And by this time the youths had finished their journey, and now they descry the towers and lofty houses of the Latin town, and draw near to the wall. In front of the town boys and young men in the early flower of life are being trained in horsemanship, and break in horses amid the dust, or try to stretch strong bows, or hurl darts of tough wood with their arms, and challenge one another to run and throw. Then riding forward on his steed a messenger reports to the ears of the aged king that mighty heroes have arrived clad in unknown dress ; the monarch orders them to be summoned within his palace, and takes his seat in the centre on his ancestral throne. A palace august, ample, supported on a hundred tall pillars, stood in the citadel, the royal castle of Laurentian Picus, made awful by its woods and by the religious dread of their forefathers. In this palace the kings with happy omen used to receive their sceptre, and first bear the fasces aloft ; this house of the curiæ was a temple for them, this was the hall for their holy feasts ; in this they slew the ram, and here the fathers used to take their seats at the long tables. Further too, here were the images of their ancient forefathers in succession, carved out of old cedar ; both Italus, and father Sabinus, who first planted the vine, (he still holds his crooked pruning-hook beneath his statue,) and the old god Saturn, and the image of Janus, him of the double forehead ; these all were standing at the vestibule, and other kings from the beginning of the race, and patriots, who for their country had suffered wounds in war. Besides, many suits of armour were hung up on the door, chariots taken in war, bent battle-axes, and helmet plumes, and bulky bars of gates, javelins and shields and beaks, the spoils of ships. Picus himself the tamer of wild steeds sat there with the crooked wand of Quirinus, girt in his short robe, in his left hand he had his oval shield ; whom Circe wooed possessed by passion's power, then struck him with her golden wand, and with her drugs transformed him into a bird, sprinkled with pie-bald colours on his wings. Within such a noble temple of the goddess, seated on the seat of his forefathers, did Latinus summon the Trojans to his presence in the palace, and, when they were admitted, he thus first spake with voice composed.

195—211. *Latinus knows who the strangers are. He gives them a*
kindly reception.

"Sons of Dardanus, your city and race are not unknown to us, and we
have heard of you, who hither o'er the sea direct your course; tell me,
what is your aim? What reason brings your fleet? In need of what
come ye to Italian coast o'er so many dark blue waters? Was it ignorance
of your course, or storms that drove you—such are the many mishaps
mariners meet with in the deep—that you have entered between the banks
of our river, and are now resting in the harbour? Shun not our hospitable welcome, nor be ignorant of us Latins, true children of Saturn,
who are not righteous by constraint of laws, but of our own free will
abide by the customs of the ancient god. And indeed I can remember—
though time the tale obscures—that the old Aurunci so told, how that
from these fields sprang Dardanus, and hence penetrated to the cities
of Phrygia near mount Ida, and to Thracian Samos, now Samothracia
called. He started hence from his Etruscan home at Corythus, and now
the golden palace of the starry firmament receives him on his throne, and
adds to the numbers of the gods by the altars raised to him."

212—248. *Ilioneus the spokesman briefly tells the tale of Troy's disasters,*
their own humble wishes, the fates that they followed, and offers the
gifts of Æneas.

So spake the king, whose words Ilioneus thus followed: "O monarch,
of the glorious race of Faunus, neither has dark storm driven us o'er the
waves, and forced us to take refuge in your land, nor has any constellation
or any shore misled us from our straight course: it was of set purpose
and with free choice of mind that we are all come to this city; we, who
are exiles from that kingdom which once the sun in its journeys from the
lowest line of heaven used to behold the greatest on earth. From Jove
is the origin of our race; in Jove their forefather the Dardan youth rejoice;
from Jove by noblest descent comes our king himself, Æneas of Troy,
who has sent us to your threshold. How great a tempest burst from cruel
Mycenæ, and passed o'er the plains of Ida, by what destinies driven
either continent of Europe and Asia clashed in conflict, the man has
heard, whoe'er he be, whom the farthest land removes by the ocean that
spreads afar, and if there be any, whom the zone of the torrid sun lying
in the midst of the four zones divides from us. From that deluge of
destruction we have been borne o'er the watery waste, and beg for a humble
home for our country's gods, and a harmless strip of land, and air and
water free to all alike. We shall be no dishonour to your realm; nor
will your renown be spread as slight, or the gratitude of such a kindness
ever be forgot; nor will Italy repent of having welcomed Troy in the
bosom of her soil. By the destinies of Æneas and by his right hand of
power, whether in faith and peace, or in war and arms any one has
experienced it, I swear that many are the people, many are the nations—
despise us not, because we come to you bearing in our hands these fillets
before us, and sue with words of prayer—who have courted us, and
wished to unite with us: but the revealed will of Heaven has forced
us by its commands diligently to seek your land. Hence Dardanus is
sprung, hither he returns, and by mighty mandates Apollo is urgent that

we should come to Tuscan Tiber and the holy water of the fountain Numicius. Further, our king sends you gifts, humble tokens of his former fortunes, relics rescued from the fires of Troy. With this golden bowl Anchises used to pour libations at the altars, these did Priam wear, when he summoned his people in due form to give them laws, even this sceptre, and holy tiara, and these robes, the workmanship of the daughters of Ilium."

249—285. Latinus is stirred in his religious soul by the recollection of oracles and omens. He even promises his daughter to the stranger, and sends gifts to the camp.

At these words of Ilioneus, Latinus keeps his face fixed downwards in a steady gaze, and remains motionless in his place, rolling his musing eyes, nor does the broidered purple so much move the king, nor Priam's sceptre so much move him, as are his thoughts centred on his daughter's union in marriage, while he weighs within his soul the oracle of ancient Faunus, saying to himself: "This is that great son-in-law whom the fates portend as coming from a foreign home, summoned to reign here with auspices of equal rule; this is he whose issue will be glorious in merit, one which will by its might take possession of the whole world." At length he gladly says: "May the gods bless our purpose, and their own auguries! I will grant, Trojan, what you wish; nor do I slight your gifts. You shall not, so long as Latinus is king, want the fruitful soil of a rich land, or miss the abundance of Troy. Only let Æneas come hither in person, if such is his desire to know me, if he is eager to be united with me by ties of hospitality, and would have the name of ally; he need not dread the countenance of a friend; part of the peace it will be to touch your monarch's hand. On your part do you now report to your king my mandates: I have a daughter; to unite her to a husband of our race, neither the oracles from the shrine of my father nor many prodigies in the heavens allow; that a son-in-law will hither come from foreign coasts, this is what they foretell awaits the Latins, such as shall raise our name to the stars by his issue. That this is he, the man whom the fates demand, I both believe, and, if my soul presages aught of truth, I hope."

The father speaks, and chooses steeds from all his stud. There were standing three hundred glossy horses in his high stables. Forthwith for all the Trojans he commands that they be led forth in order, wing-footed chargers, caparisoned with purple and broidered housings; golden are the collars that hang suspended from their breasts, of gold are their coverings, yellow gold they champ betwixt their teeth. To his absent guest Æneas he sends a chariot, and a pair of chariot-horses, of heavenly breed, breathing from their nostrils fire, of the race of those which Circe, cunning in works of art, deceiving her father, reared of bastard brood from a mare she introduced. By such gifts and such words of Latinus the men of Æneas elated return riding on their horses, and carry back tidings of peace.

286—322. All seems prosperous, when Juno beholds the hated race safely landed at the mouth of the Tiber. She bursts into a passion of rage. She will move even Hell itself against her enemies.

But lo! the cruel wife of Jove was returning from Argos, the town of Inachus, and was riding in her chariot in mid heaven; and from the sky far off, even from Sicilian Pachynus, she descried Æneas now rejoicing and his Dardan fleet. She sees that they are now founding their houses, that now they trust the land; that they have abandoned their ships. She stopped, as one possessed by fierce passions: then shook her head, and poured forth these words from her breast: "Ah! race I hate, and Phrygian fates that counter run to mine! Could they not fall on the plains of Sigeum? Could not the captured be led captive? Could not the fire of Troy be their funeral pyre? Through the midst of armies in battle array, through the midst of flames they have found a path. But, I suppose, my heavenly powers are wearied out at last and helpless lie, or, my wrath sated to the full, I now can rest. Nay, but I dared to follow them driven forth from their country, and persecuted them o'er the waves, and threw myself in the way of the exiles over the whole sea. I have spent against the Trojans all the powers of sky and sea. How did the Syrtes, or Scylla, or vast Charybdis help me? They wished for Tiber's bed, there are they hidden from danger, they care not now for the ocean or for me. Mars had power to destroy the monstrous race of the Lapithæ; the father of the gods himself surrendered to Diana ancient Calydon, that she might glut her rage. What crime of the Lapithæ or of Calydon deserved so great a punishment? But I, Jove's mighty consort, who could bear to leave nothing untried, luckless as I am; who have turned myself to every device, am vanquished by Æneas! Now if my divine powers be not strong enough, surely I must not doubt to implore the help of any might that anywhere exists: if heaven I cannot bend, then hell I'll wake. Be it so, that I must not keep him from his Latin realm, and Lavinia must be his spouse, and nought can change the fates: yet to put off that day, and to delay such great events, is mine; yet may I exterminate the people of either king. With such a price of their subjects' lives let son and father-in-law buy their union. Blood of Trojans and Rutulians shall be your dowry, maiden; Bellona waits for you, to be your bridesmaid; nor was Cisseus' daughter alone pregnant with a brand, and alone brought forth flames in wedlock; nay, the same to Venus is her own offspring, a second Paris is her son, and funeral torches again are lighted to burn a second Troy."

323—340. *Juno calls up from the lower world the fury Alecto.*

When she had uttered these words the dread goddess descended to earth; she rouses Alecto, worker of woe, from the abode of her accursed sisters, and from the nether darkness; to whose heart baneful wars are dear, passions, plots, and crimes of mischief. Hateful is she even to her father Pluto, hateful is the monster even to her hellish sisters; into so many forms does she change, so dreadful are her shapes, so black the blood of many snakes which she bears. Her Juno inflames with these words, speaking thus: "Virgin daughter of Night, give me this labour with all thy heart, this service, lest my honour or glory be enfeebled and have to give way, and lest Æneas and his friends be able to court Latinus with this wedlock, and occupy Italian lands. Thou canst arm to strife united brethren, and trouble homes with hate; thou canst bring scourges and funeral torches into houses; thou hast a thousand ways, a thousand arts of mischief: stir up thy inventive soul! Tear in sunder the compact of peace, sow seeds of wicked war; let the youth at the same moment wish for and demand and snatch up arms."

341—403. Alecto first fills the heart of the queen with fury against Æneas and the intended marriage. The queen stirs the matrons with a frenzy as of Bacchanalian revellers.

Forthwith Alecto imbrued with Gorgonian poison, first flies to Latinus and the lofty palace of the Laurentian king, and straightway besieges the peaceful threshold of Amata, whom, concerning the arrival of the Trojans and marriage of Turnus, the pains and passions of a woman inflamed to rage. On her the goddess throws one of the snakes from her dark hair, and sends it into her breast, into her inmost heart, that, full of frenzy by this monster, she might confound the whole house. The serpent gliding between her garments and smooth breast, crawls along unfelt, unknown to the maddened queen, breathing into her its snakish breath ; the huge snake transforms itself into her twisted golden necklace, into the ribbon of her long fillet, and entwines itself into her hair, and with slimy coils creeps o'er her limbs. Now whilst the venom in its beginning stealthily glides with flowing poison, and thrills her feelings and wraps her bones with fire, before her soul had yet conceived the flame in its height within her whole breast, in softer tones, after the usual manner of mothers she spake, with many a tear, about her daughter, and the Phrygian marriage : "Is then Lavinia to be handed over as a spouse to houseless Trojans, O father? have you no pity for your daughter or yourself, or for a mother either, whom, when the first wind blows, the perfidious pirate will abandon, and sail out to sea, and carry the damsel off? Was it not even thus that the Phrygian shepherd penetrated to Lacedæmon, and bore Helen the daughter of Leda off to the Trojan cities? What is become of your oath, and religious promise? what of your old regard for your kindred and the right hand you so often pledged to your kinsman Turnus? If what you look for is a son-in-law of descent foreign to the Latins, and that is settled, and the commands of your parent Faunus constrain you, whatever land is free and distinct from our rule, I for my part account as foreign, and so interpret heaven's decree. Indeed to Turnus, if we trace back the early origin of his house, his forefathers are Inachus and Acrisius, and his country in the heart of Mycenæ." When with these words she had in vain tried to work on Latinus, and finds that he is proof against them, and when the maddening mischief of the snake had glided deep into her heart, and pervaded her whole soul ; then indeed the unhappy queen, stirred by mighty portents, infuriated past control, rages through the length and breadth of the city ; as oft a top flies beneath the twisted whip, which boys intent on the game lash in a great circle through an empty hall ; the top driven by the thong is borne along its winding course ; above stand in amazed astonishment the youthful band, in admiration of the whirling top ; the blows give it fresh speed. With course as swift the queen is borne along through the centre of the city amidst the warlike people. Nay forth into the forest she flies, she feigns the inspiration of Bacchus, she ventures on a greater crime, she enters on greater frenzy, and hides her daughter in the woody mountains ; that she might rob the Trojans of their marriage, and delay the nuptial rites ; "Evoë, Bacche!" is her raging cry, "thou alone art a worthy husband for the maiden!" So she shouts. "Indeed for thee," she says, "my daughter carries the waving thyrsus, thee my daughter celebrates in the dance, for thee she nourishes the sacred locks." Fame flies before, and the same frenzy inflames the breasts of the matrons with frenzy, and drives them all together in search of strange homes. They abandon their houses, they bare their necks and hair to the winds. But others fill the sky with tremulous cries, and clad in skins bear wands with vine-leaves crowned. The queen herself in the centre with fury lifts a blazing torch, and sings in her daughter's and Turnus' name the nuptial song, rolling her blood-shot glaring eyes; and sudden fiercely shrieks; "Lo! ye Latin dames, hear me, where'er you be, if in your loving souls there is still any regard for unhappy Amata, if a care for a mother's natural rights still touches your souls, loose the bands of your locks, and with me begin the orgies."

404—474. Next Alecto goes to Turnus. She takes the form of an old priestess. Turnus derides her womanish fears, but the Fury reveals herself in hellish form; the young man springs from his bed full of rage; he rouses the spirit of the Rutulians.

In such wise amidst the forests and desert haunts of wild beasts Alecto drives the queen hither and thither by the stings of Bacchic rage. When she judged she had made fierce enough the first fits of frenzy, and had overthrown the purposes and all the house of Latinus, straightway the baneful goddess rises thence on her dusky pinions to the walls of the daring Rutulian, to the town which is said to have been founded for settlers of Acrisius by Danae, borne fleetly thither by a wafting wind. The town was in days of yore named Ardea by our ancestors, and Ardea still retains its ancient name; but its former fortune is past. Here in his lofty palace in the middle of the dark night Turnus enjoyed quiet sleep. Alecto lays aside a Fury's fierce face and limbs; she is transformed, and takes the countenance of an old woman, and her ugly forehead is furrowed with wrinkles; she appears to have grey hair bound with a fillet, and wreathed with an olive bough; she changes herself into Calybe, the old priestess of the temple of Juno, and rises before the eyes of the young man, and speaks these words: "Turnus, will you be content to waste so many toils in vain, and see your sceptre transferred to Dardan settlers? The king refuses you your bride, and dowry bought by blood, and seeks for a foreigner as heir to his realm. Go to, expose yourself to danger, to meet with ingratitude and scorn; go now, and lay low the hosts of Etruria; shield the Latins with peace. This is the very message which to you lying in placid slumber the almighty daughter of Saturn bids me plainly tell. Wherefore bestir yourself, and glad to take up arms make ready to arm the youth, and to lead them forth from the gates, and slay the Trojan captains, who have made their station in the fair river, and burn their painted ships. The mighty power of Heaven bids you do this. Let king Latinus himself, unless he consents to give you your bride, and obey your words, at length feel and know what Turnus is in arms."

Thereupon the young man, mocking the priestess, thus replies to her speech with these words: "The news of the fleet which has sailed into the

Tiber's stream, has not, as you suppose, escaped my knowledge; do not alarm me with such idle terrors; nor has queen Juno forgotten me. But old age, o'ercome with torpid sloth and barren of truth, troubles you, mother, with idle cares, and mocks you, a priestess, with fancied fears amongst armed kings. Your duty is to guard the images and temples of the gods; leave war and peace to men, war must be waged by men."

At such words as these Alecto burst into fury. Then as the young man spake a sudden tremor seizes his limbs; his eyes grow stiff through fear; so many are the snakes with which the Fury hisses, so dire a form is shewn. Then rolling her eyes of flame, she cast him backward, as he hesitated and sought for words to speak, and high on her head she raised a pair of snakes, and cracked her whip, and uttered these words from her rabid mouth: "Lo! I am she o'ercome with torpid sloth, whom old age barren of truth makes to dote with fancied fears amidst armed kings. Give heed to these words: I am come from the abode of my accursed sisters, in my hand I bear war and death." She spake, and hurled her brand upon the young man, and fixed beneath his heart her torch which smoked with lurid light. A great terror broke his sleep; and a sweat that burst o'er his whole body bathed his bones and limbs. Frenzied he shrieks for arms; he looks for his arms in his chamber and in his halls. The love of the sword and the wicked madness of war rage in his soul, and wrath besides; as when the flame of a fire of twigs roaring loudly is placed beneath the sides of a seething caldron; with heat the waters bubble; within rages the struggling water, steaming and surging high with foam; then the bubbling wave boils over; the thick steam flies to the air. So then he enjoins the chieftains of the youth to violate the peace, and march to king Latinus, and bids arms to be prepared, saying they must guard Italy, and push the enemy from their coasts; that he himself would be found a match for Trojans and Latins united. When he had spoken these words, and called the gods to hear his vows, the Rutulians vie in exhorting one another to arms. One is moved by the noble beauty of the youthful form of the prince, another by his royal forefathers, another by the glorious exploits of his hand.

475—539. *Thirdly, Alecto goes to the woods. A pet deer of the daughter of the ranger of the woods is wounded by Iulus. Then the rustics are enraged. The fiend blows her horn. A battle is fought, and blood is shed.*

While Turnus fills the hearts of the Rutulians with daring spirits, Alecto speeds on her hellish wings towards the Trojans, with new fraud observing the ground, where on the shore fair Iulus is hunting the wild animals with snares and riders. Here the goddess of Cocytus throws in the way of the hounds a source of sudden rage, and fills their nostrils with the familiar scent, that they may pursue a stag in hot chase; this was the first cause of woes, and first inflamed the souls of the rustics for war. There was a stag of surprising beauty with tall antlers, which, snatched from its dam, was reared by the boys the sons of Tyrrheus, and by their father Tyrrheus, who was ranger of the royal herds, and to whom was entrusted the care of the plains far and wide. Taught to obey command was the stag, which their sister Sylvia with much attention would often adorn, twining its horns with pliant garlands, and combed its hair, and bathed it in the pure fountain. It, trained to bear the hand, and accustomed to its master's table, would wander in the woods ; and back again returned of its own accord to the familiar threshold however late the night. As it was wandering far from home, the eager hounds of the huntsman Iulus started it, as it chanced to float down the stream, or cooled its heat on the grassy bank. Ascanius too, fired with the love of noble fame, himself shot an arrow from his bent bow ; nor did the god suffer his hand to miss, and the reed flying with a loud whiz passed through the belly and flanks of the stag. But the wounded animal took refuge within the familiar house, and moaning took shelter in its stall, and all bathed in blood, and like one that begged for pity, with cries it filled the whole house. Sister Sylvia beating her breast with her hands, first prays for aid, and calls together the hardy rustics. They, for the fierce fiend lurks in the silent woods, suddenly appear ; one armed with a brand burnt at the end, another with a heavy knotty club ; what each finds as he searches, that rage makes a weapon. Tyrrheus calls his bands ; it so chanced he was cleaving an oak in four parts with a wedge driven in ; he snatches up a hatchet, he breathes fury. But the cruel goddess from the place of her watch having found the moment for mischief, flies to the steep roof of a hut, and from the top of the thatch she blows to give the shepherd's signal, and on the crooked horn strains her hellish voice, at which forthwith all the wood shook, and the forests echoed from their depths. The sacred lake of Trivia heard the sound from afar ; Nar heard the sound, a river white with sulphureous water, and the sources of the mere Velinus ; and mothers start, and press their infants to their breasts. Then swiftly to the summons, where the dread trumpet gave the signal, from every quarter rush together, with weapons quickly seized, the sturdy tillers of the soil ; moreover also the Trojan youth, to aid Ascanius, pour forth from the open gates of the camp. They fight in battle array. It is come to this, that they contend not in rustic fight, nor with hard clubs or stakes, whose points are hardened in the fire ; but they decide the struggle with the two-edged sword, and the dark harvest of war bristles with drawn weapons, and the brazen armour gleams struck with the sun, and throws the light up to the clouds : as when a wave begins to shew white foam, as the wind rises, little by little does the sea swell, and lifts its waves higher and higher ; at last it rises in a mass to the sky from its lowest depths. Here in the first ranks by a whizzing arrow the youth Almon, the eldest of the sons of Tyrrheus, is laid low ; for the weapon that gave the wound was fixed within his throat, and choked the passage of the flexible voice and the delicate breath of his life with blood. Many fell around, and old Galæsus too, who threw himself between the ranks to speak for peace, in those days of old the most righteous and wealthiest in the fields of Italy ; five bleating flocks, as many herds, were his property, with a hundred ploughs he tilled his farm.

540—571. *The Fury exults in her success, and promises greater things still, but Juno warns her to depart: and the fiend returns to Stygian darkness.*

And thus whilst this battle is being fought in the plains with doubtful issue, the goddess having made good her promise, after she had inaugurated the war with blood, and begun the first fight by death, leaves Italy, and turning her course through the air of heaven, with haughty voice, as one victorious, addresses Juno : " See, for thee discord is complete by baneful war; now bid them unite in friendship, and join in compact, seeing that I have sprinkled the Trojans with Italian blood. Further I will add this to what I have done, if I am assured of thy will : by rumours I will bring neighbouring cities to the war, and kindle their souls with the love of maddening Mars, so that they may flock to help; I will scatter arms over the fields." Then Juno answered : " Of terror and fraud there is more than enough; sown are the seeds of war; they fight hand to hand with arms; chance first put arms in their hands; now fresh blood has stained them. Such a marriage and such a nuptial song may now be celebrated by that noble son of Venus and king Latinus in person. But that thou shouldest wander with more lawless freedom in the air of heaven the mighty Father, the supreme king of Olympus, would not permit. Give place, and quit the field. I, whatever fortune and trouble still remains, myself will guide all." So spake the child of Saturn. The Fury raises her whizzing snakish wings, and flies to her home by Cocytus, and leaves the upper heights of air. There is a place in the heart of Italy beneath high mountains, well known, and told of by rumour in many a land, the valley of Amsanctus; the dark side of a wood hems it in on either hand with thick foliage, and in the centre a roaring torrent resounds o'er the rocks with whirling eddies. Here a dreadful cavern is shown as the vent of cruel Dis, and a mighty gulf, through which bursts Acheron, opening its jaws fraught with pestilence; in it the Fury hides herself, a fiend abhorred, and relieves earth and heaven.

572—600. The shepherds, Turnus, and the matrons demand war. Latinus alone resists, but finding his efforts vain, shuts himself up in his palace.

Nor with less zeal meanwhile does the queen, the child of Saturn, put the last hand to the war. To the city from the field of battle rush the whole crowd of shepherds, bearing the slain with them, the boy Almon, and Galæsus disfigured by his wounds, and implore the gods, and conjure Latinus. Turnus is there, and in the midst of the charge of slaughter, and in the fire of discord aggravates the terror: crying—" The Trojans are foisted into the kingdom, a mongrel brood of Phrygians is mingled with us, I am driven from this door." Then they, whose mothers frenzied by Bacchus bound over the pathless woods in dances, for of no mean power was Amata's name, collected from every quarter meet, and importunately demand war. Straightway with one consent all, against the omen, against the oracles of the gods, with the will of heaven adverse, clamour for unholy war. Eagerly they crowd round the palace of king Latinus. He resists, like an immoveable rock of the sea, like a rock of the sea, when a mighty roaring storm is coming on, which holds itself by its mass amidst many waves blustering around; in vain do the cliffs and crags covered with foam resound on every side, and the sea-weed dashed against the sides is washed back. But when no power was given him to overcome their blind purpose, and events followed the will of cruel Juno; the father of his people often calls to witness the gods, and the air in which there was no divinity to help, and says, "Alas we are shipwrecked by fate, and are borne before the storm! yourselves will pay with your sacrilegious blood the atonement of this guilt, wretched men. You, Turnus, will await the end of your impiety, an awful punishment, and you will worship Heaven with vows, but all too late. For I have gained my rest, and I am quite at the entrance of my haven; a happy death is all I lose." He spake no more, but shut himself in his palace, and abandoned the reins of government.

601—628. *Then Juno opens the gates of War. Italy is excited.*

There was a custom in Italian Latium, which thenceforward in succession of time the Alban towns observed as sacred, in these days Rome the mistress of the world observes, when first they move Mars forth to battle, be it Getæ or Arabs or Hyrcanians against whom they prepare to wage with force tearful war, or to march to India, and press on to the home of the Morning, and claim back from the Parthians the captured standards. There are twin gates of War, such is their name, hallowed by religious awe, and the dread of fierce Mars; a hundred bronze bolts close them, and the eternal strength of iron-plated oak, nor does the guardian Janus ever leave the threshold. Of these gates, when the senate has fully determined on war, the consul, conspicuous in the state robe of Quirinus, and girded in Gabine fashion, with his own hand unbars the creaking threshold; he himself summons to battle; then follow the crowd of youths; and horns of brass breathe forth their hoarse accord. In obedience to this custom, on that day Latinus was bidden to make proclamation of war against the men of Æneas, and to throw open the fatal portals; the father of his people would not so much as touch them, and turning away shrunk back from the ill-omened duty, and hid himself in dark obscurity.

Thereupon heaven's queen, the daughter of Saturn, descended from the sky, and with her own hand pushed the lingering gates, and turned the hinge, and burst open the iron-bound portals of War. In a blaze is Italy, unexcited and unmoved before; some prepare to march o'er the plain on foot; others mounted on tall steeds rage enveloped in clouds of dust; all clamour for arms. Some with fat grease polish their shields, and rub their darts till they shine, and point their battle-axes on whetstones; gladly they carry standards, and catch the notes of the blowing horns.

629—640. *Five great cities prepare war.*

As many as five great cities place anvils, and forge new weapons; Atina, powerful town, and proud Tibur, Ardea, Crustumeri, and Antennæ with her crown of towers. They hollow helmets safely to protect their heads, and weave wicker shields with bosses out of osier; others beat out brazen breastplates or polished greaves of ductile silver. To such an use passes all the honour of the ploughshare and pruninghook, all the love of the plough; they remould the swords of their sires in the furnace. And now the clarions sound the signal; the watchword passes round, the token for the war. One from his hall hastily snatches his helmet;

another yokes his snorting steeds, and takes his shield, and dons his triple coat of mail, and girds on his trusty sword.

641—646. The Muses are invoked to recall the memory of events dim through antiquity.

Ye goddesses, now open Helicon, and wake your song, telling what princes were roused by war, what troops in battle array followed each chieftain, crowding in the plain; with what heroes Italy, a prolific land, flourished even in those early days, with what arms she burned: for you, remember, Ladies, and you can tell what you remember; to us a faint and slight breeze of fame is hardly wafted.

647—654. The contrast between Mezentius and Lausus.

The first to enter war is a warrior fierce from Tuscan coasts, Mezentius, the despiser of the gods; he arms his troops. By his side marched his son Lausus: there was not a fairer man, if you except the form of Laurentian Turnus; Lausus, the tamer of horses, the conqueror of wild beasts in the hunt. A thousand men he leads, in vain they followed from Agylla's town; worthy he was of obeying a better father; Mezentius should not have been his sire.

655—669. Aventinus, the son of Hercules.

Next to these, handsome Aventinus, sprung from handsome Hercules, displays o'er the sward his chariot, conspicuous with the prize of the race, and his victorious steeds; on his shield he bears a badge of his father's labours, a hundred snakes, and Hydra with her belt of serpents; him in the wood of the Aventine Rhea the priestess brought forth in stealthy birth to the regions of light, a woman united with a god, when the conqueror, the hero of Tiryns, having slain Geryon, reached the Laurentian fields, and bathed his Spanish oxen in the Tuscan stream. His men hold javelins in their hands, and warlike pikes for the battle, and fight with the sword tapering in a point, and the Sabine dart. The captain on foot, swinging the huge lion's skin, with frightful uncombed bristles, with its white teeth, which he wore o'er his head, even as he was, entered the royal palace, rough and shaggy, with the Herculean dress fastened round his shoulders.

670—677. Catillus and Coras, the brothers from Tibur.

Next the twin brothers leave the walls of Tibur, Catillus and Coras, keen in fight, Argive youths, and in the front ranks amidst the thick weapons on they come, like as when two Centaurs, born amidst the clouds, descend from the lofty top of a mountain, in swift course leaving Omole, and snowy Othrys ; as on they rush, the great forest gives place, and the bushes yield with loud crash.

678—690. Caeculus, the son of Vulcan.

Nor was the founder of Præneste's town wanting on that day, whom every age has believed to have been born to Vulcan amidst the cattle of the field, and to have been found an infant on the hearth; his name was Cæculus. Him follows a rustic legion from a wide extent of country, both the men who dwell in high Præneste, and those who live in the fields of Juno of Gabii, and by the cold Anio, and on the rocks of the Hernici freshened with streams, those whom rich Anagnia feeds, or you, O father Amasenus. They have not all armour, or shields, or rattling cars, the greater part of them throw balls of blue lead; part carry two darts in their hand, and wear for helmets tawny caps of wolf-skin; bare is the left foot as they march in measure along, a boot of raw hide protects the right.

691—705. *Messapus, the son of Neptune.*

But Messapus, tamer of horses, the offspring of Neptune, who bears a charmed life against death from fire or steel, suddenly summons to arms the tribes that had been long inactive and unexercised in war, and again handles the sword. These form the lines of Fescennium, and the troops of the Æqui Falisci, these hold the heights of Soracte and the fields of Flavinium, and Ciminus, both mountain and lake, and the groves of Capena. They marched in steady array, and sang of their king, as ofttimes snow-white swans amid the watery clouds, returning home from feeding, and uttering musical notes from their long necks; the noise resounds, and the Asian meadow re-echoes far their cries. Nor would any one think that from so long a line a body of armed men was thronging for battle array; but that high up in the air a cloud of noisy fowl was being driven to the shores.

706—722. *Clausus the Sabine, from whom was descended the Claudian house.*

Lo Clausus, leading a mighty troop of the ancient blood of the Sabines, himself worth a mighty troop, from whom now is spread through Latium the tribe and house of the Claudii, from the day that the Sabines were admitted to a share of Rome. Together came the mighty cohort of Amiternum, and the Prisci Quirites, the whole band of Eretum, and all Mutuscæ, olive-bearing town; those who dwell in the city of Nomentum, and the country of Rosea by Velinus, and the rough rocks of Tetrica and mount Severus, and Casperia, and Foruli, and those who live by the stream of Himella; those who drink the Tiber and Fabaris; those whom cool Nursia sent; and the military classes of the state of Hortia, and the Latin people; and those whom Allia divides with its flowing course, stream of unlucky name: as many waves as roll in the African expanse of waters, when fierce Orion sets in the wintry waves; or as in early summer the thick standing ears turn their colour, either in the flat plains of Hermus, or in the yellow corn-fields of Lycia. The shields clash, and the ground trembles, stirred by the tramp of feet.

723—760. *Halesus, Œbalus, Ufens, Umbro.*

Next Agamemnon's son, a natural foe to the Trojan name, Halesus, yokes his steeds, and hurries to the field a thousand warlike men to Turnus' aid; who with mattocks turn the hills of Massicum fruitful in Bacchus' gifts, and those whom from their high hills their Auruncian sires sent, and those near the levels of Sidicinum, and those who leave Cales and every dweller by the Volturnus, river of shoaly fords, and with them Saticula's rough race, and the band of the Osci. Their weapons are neatly-turned javelins, which it is their custom to fasten to a flexible thong of leather. Their left hand a buckler protects; in close combat they use scimitars.

Nor shall you pass untold of in my verses, Œbalus, the son of Telon by the nymph Sebethis, as tradition tells, in the days that he ruled

Capreæ of the Teleboans, now advanced in years ; but the son, dis-
daining his father's realm, even then held in his sway far and wide the
tribes of the Sarrastes, and the plains watered by the Sarnus, and those
who dwell in Rufæ and Batulus, and the fields of Celennæ, and those
whom the walls of apple-bearing Abella look down upon : in Teutonic
fashion they used to throw their darts ; their head-pieces were bark
taken from the oak-tree, of bronze were their glittering crescent-shields,
of bronze each glittering sword.

You too, O Ufens, Nursæ amidst the hills sent to the battle, a
warrior glorious in the renown of successful arms : whose people was
rugged above other tribes, trained to constant hunting in the woods, the
Æquicoli, whose soil was stiff and hard.

Moreover from the Marruvian race came the priest, who on his helmet
wore for a plume the trimmed leaves of a fruitful olive ; he was sent by
king Archippus, bravest of the brave was he, named Umbro ; who
with the charms of song and hand used to shed sleep on the brood
of vipers, and venom-breathing Hydras, and assuaged their rage, and
cured their bites by skill.   But the wound of the Trojan spear-point
he had not power to heal ; vain to help him against the blow were the
chants that lulled to sleep, and the herbs found on Marsian hills.   The
pool of Anguitia wept for you, Fucinus with its glassy pool, the crystal
meres wept for you.

761—782.   *Virbius the son of Hippolytus the friend of the goddess
Diana.*

There marched too to the war the fair child of Hippolytus, by name
Virbius, whom crowned with glory his mother Aricia sent, reared in
the groves of Egeria, round about its marshy shores, where is Diana's
altar rich with gifts and easily appeased.   For they tell the tale, how
that Hippolytus, when he died by the falsehood of his stepmother and
with his blood satisfied the penalty that his father exacted, torn to pieces
by his frightened horses, yet again returned to see the stars of the
firmament and breathe the upper air, recalled to life by Æsculapian
herbs and by the love of Diana.   But the Almighty Father could not
brook that any mortal man should rise from the nether shades to the
light of life, and with his own hand he cast with his thunderbolt down
to the waters of Styx the inventor of so daring a medicine and of such
a skill.   But Trivia, kindly goddess, hides Hippolytus in a retired home,
and entrusts him to the nymph Egeria, and to the retreat of a grove,
where alone and in obscurity he might pass his days amid Italian woods,
and by a change of name be called Virbius.   On this account too,
hoofed horses are kept far from Trivia's temple and hallowed woods,
because on the shore, frightened by the monsters of the deep, they
overthrew the chariot and dashed the youth on the ground.   Yet not
the less for that did his son drive his fiery steeds on the level plain, and
in his chariot rush to the war.

783—802.   *Turnus himself in stature is higher than the rest : his helmet
and shield.*

Turnus himself, warrior of surpassing form, is busy amidst the foremost, holding his arms, taller than the rest by his whole head.   His

lofty helmet crested with triple plume bears aloft the Chimæra, breathing from her jaws Ætnean flames; so much the more does she rage wildly with baneful fires, as the more blood is shed and the battle waxes fiercer. But his polished shield is adorned by Io with her lifted horns worked on gold, she now is covered with bristly hair and has become a heifer, (famous is the subject of the device) and there is the maiden's keeper, Argus, and father Inachus pouring his river from embossed urn. Him follow a cloud of infantry, and the shield-bearing troops throng over the whole plain, and the Argive youth, the bands of Aurunci, the Rutuli and old Sicani, and the battle array of the Sacrani, and the painted bucklers of Labicum; those who till your woods, Tiber, and the sacred shore of Numicius, and cultivate with the plough-share the hills of the Rutuli, and the ridges of Circæi; where Jove of Anxur presides over the fields, and Feronia rejoices in her green grove; where lies the black pool of Satura, and cool Ufens winds its course through the lowly vales, and is lost in the sea.

803—817. *The Volscian Camilla is a warrior-maiden, of miraculous swiftness of foot. All gaze with admiration at the undaunted virgin.*

Last came Camilla from the people of the Volsci: she led a troop of horse, and squadrons drest in glossy brass; a warrior-woman; her woman's hands were not trained to the distaff or basket of Minerva, but the maiden learnt to endure hard warfare, and in speed of foot to outstrip the winds. She would either flee o'er the topmost blades of the untouched corn, and lo! the tender ears were uninjured by the race; or, over the mid sea, hung upon the swelling billow, she would keep on her way, nor wet her nimble soles on the surface of the water. Her all the youth pour forth from house and field to see, and crowding matrons admire and gaze as she passes, open-mouthed with astonishment of soul, marvelling how the regal grace of purple veils her smooth shoulders, how a clasp entwines her locks with gold, how she herself wears Lycian quiver, and pastoral shaft of myrtle tipped with javelin's point.

BOOK VIII.

1—25. *Turnus musters his forces, and sends an envoy to Diomede.*

So soon as from the citadel of Laurentum Turnus raised aloft the sig- nal of war, and with hoarse note his trumpets rang, and so soon as he roused his fiery steeds, and clashed his arms, forthwith men's minds were troubled; withal the whole of Latium leagues together in disordered haste, and the youthful warriors are wild with rage. The foremost chiefs, Messapus and Ufens, and Mezentius the scorner of the gods, from all parts muster their forces, and far and wide strip the fields of their husband- men. Also, Venulus is sent as envoy to Diomede's mighty city, to pray for help and tell him all, how that Trojans are endeavouring to settle in Latium, that Æneas has arrived with his fleet, and is trying to in- troduce his vanquished Penates, and says fate calls him to be king, and that many nations are joining the Dardan hero, and that his name is growing great throughout the length and breadth of Latium. That of what plan this attempt forms the foundation, what result of battle he desires to gain, should fortune attend him, is more clearly seen by Diomede himself than by king Turnus or king Latinus. Such was the course of events throughout Latium. And when the hero of Laomedon's line views all these things, he is swayed by a mighty tide of thoughts ; and now hither, now thither, he swiftly despatches his divided mind, and hurries it in various directions, and continually whirls it through everything. Even as from the brim of a brazen bowl the tremulous watery ray, caught by the sunbeams or the reflection of the sparkling moon, flits through all the regions round about, and in a moment springs aloft, and strikes the ceiling's loftiest point.

26—67. *The river-god Tiber appears to Æneas, and instructs him to form an alliance with Evander.*

'Twas night, and through all the world deep sleep possessed the weary creatures, the tribe of birds and beasts ; when father Æneas, on the river-bank, and beneath the vault of the cold sky, harassed in heart by thoughts of dread war, had laid himself down, and allowed sleep at last to steal over his limbs. To him the genius of the spot in his own shape, Tiber, as an old man, seemed to rise from the pleasant stream amid the poplar bower ; the god was veiled in a hoary robe of fine-wrought flax, and his locks were shaded with a covering of sedge ; then thus he began to address the hero, and remove his troubles with these words : "You that are sprung from the race of the gods, who bring back to us from the hands of the foe the city of Troy, and preserve Pergama for ever, long looked for by the land of Laurentum and the fields of Latium, here is your sure home, your sure Penates ; go not from them, nor be frighted by the threats of war. All the swelling rage and wrath of Heaven has subsided. And presently, before your eyes, that you may not think this the idle coinage of sleep, a huge sow shall lie, discovered beneath the ilex-trees upon the bank, with a litter of thirty young ones, a white sow, resting on the ground, with white pigs about her teats. This shall be the site of your city, there shall be sure repose from your toils : and on that spot, when thrice ten years come round, Ascanius shall found a city, and call it by the noble name of Alba. Now attend, I utter no uncertain prediction ; I will instruct you in a few words by what means you may victoriously despatch the work that must be done at once. On these shores Arcadians, a race that derives its descent from Pallas, who were the comrades and followers of Evander and his standards, chose a site, and built on the hills a city, called Pallanteum from the name of Pallas their progenitor. They ever wage incessant war with the Latin nation ; them attach to your camp as allies, and with them form a league. I myself will guide you between my banks, and straight along my stream, so that in your upward voyage you may with your oars overcome the current that is against you. Come, rise, goddess-born, and when the earliest stars begin to set, duly offer to Juno your prayers, and overcome with humble vows her wrath and her frowns. When you have conquered, you shall pay to me your homage. I am he whom you behold sweeping my banks with plenteous stream, and cleaving the fruitful cornlands, dark-blue Tiber, a river well-beloved by Heaven. Here is my mighty home; my source flows forth from towering cities." So spoke the River; then he plunged into the deep pool, diving to the bottom; night and sleep forsook Æneas.

68—96.   *The prayer of Æneas. He sails up the Tiber.*

He rises, and gazing on the eastern rays of the sun in heaven, in due form holds up water from the river in the hollow of his hands, and pours forth to the sky such words as these: "Nymphs, Nymphs of Laurentum, from whom the rivers take their birth, and thou, father Tiber, with thy hallowed stream, receive Æneas, and at last protect him from peril. Whatsoever be the source, where thy pool contains thee, thou that pitiest our disasters, from whatsoever soil thou flowest forth in all thy beauty, thou shalt ever be duly worshipped by me with homage and with gifts, thou horned river, the monarch of the western waters!   Only be with me, I beseech thee, and more surely ratify thy will!"   So he speaks, and chooses from the fleet a pair of ships, and mans them with a crew; withal he furnishes his comrades with arms.   But lo, a portent, unlooked-for and wondrous to behold, a spotless sow amidst the forest, of the same colour as her white litter, was reposing, and plain to view on the grassy bank: her pious Æneas slays in sacrifice to thee, even to thee, most mighty Juno, and sets her with her brood beside the altar.   On that night, through all its length, Tiber calmed his swelling flood, and flowing backward stood so still with silent stream, that gently he smoothed the face of the waters, like a mere and placid pond, so that the oars moved without an effort.   So with speed they go forward on their voyage; amid cheerful murmur the keel careened glides o'er the shallow stream; and the waters view with wonder, and so does the forest unused to the sight, the shields of warriors flashing afar, and painted hulls floating on the river. They, as they row along, exhaust both day and night, and pass by the long extended windings of the stream, and are shaded by trees of various kinds, and o'er the tranquil surface cleave their way between the green woods.

97—125.   *Æneas meets with Pallas, the son of Evander.*

The blazing sun had climbed to the centre of the arch of heaven, when from a distance they descry walls, and a citadel, and roofs of houses thinly scattered, which now the mighty wealth of Rome has raised as high as heaven; then Evander there possessed his scanty state.   With speed they turn their prows to land, and draw nigh to the city.   It chanced that on that day the Arcadian prince was offering sacrifice in honour of Amphitryon's mighty descendant, and of the gods, in a grove in front of the city.   With him his son Pallas, with him all the flower of the young men, and his poor senate, were offering incense to this hero, and the gore still warm was smoking beside the altars.   So soon as they see the tall ships and the crews gliding to land amidst the shadowy grove, and noiselessly plying their oars, they are alarmed at the unexpected sight, and all forsake their tables, and start up.   Them Pallas dauntlessly forbids to interrupt the sacrifice, and himself catches up a weapon, and flies to meet the strangers, and at a distance from a knoll he cries: "Warriors, what cause has constrained you to explore ways that you know not?   Whither do ye bend your course?   Of what nation are ye? From what home do ye come?   Is it peace that ye bring hither, or war?"

Then father Æneas thus speaks from the lofty stern, and holds forth in his hand a bough of olive, the messenger of peace: " Men of Trojan blood you see, and arms at enmity with the Latins ; men whom they with disdainful war have driven outcasts from their land. We come to find Evander. Take to him these tidings, and say that the flower of the chieftains of Dardania have come, and ask for his forces to join them." At so great a name Pallas was awe-struck and astonished: " Come forth, I pray you, whoever you are," he says, " and speak to my sire face to face, and as our guest enter our abode." Then he welcomed him with the grasp of his hand, and clasped his right hand, and clung to it.

126—183. *Æneas tells Evander of their common ancestry. Evander relates his meeting with Anchises in Arcadia, and promises the Trojans his aid.*

They go forward, and pass into the wood, and leave the river behind them. Then Æneas addresses the king with friendly words: " Best of men of Grecian blood, to whom fortune has decreed that I should pray, and hold forth branches dressed with wreaths, I certainly was not struck with terror, because you were a leader of the Greeks and an Arcadian, and because you were by blood allied to both the sons of Atreus : but it is my own worth and the holy oracles of Heaven, and the kinsmanship of our forefathers, and your renown that is spread over the world, that have united me to you, and made me a willing follower of the force of fate. Dardanus, the first father and founder of the city of Ilium, sprung from Electra the daughter of Atlas, as the Greeks tell the tale, sailed to the land of the Teucri ; strong Atlas begat Electra, Atlas, who supports upon his shoulder the sphere of heaven. Your forefather is Mercury, whom beauteous Maia conceived and gave birth to on the cold peak of Cyllene ; now Atlas, if we trust at all the tradition we have heard, that same Atlas, who bears aloft the stars of the universe, is the father of Maia. So the descent of both of us branches off from one stock. Trusting to these facts, I sent no envoys, and did not essay by means of artifice to form the foundation of a compact with you ; my own self, and my own life, I have voluntarily placed in your hands, and come in suppliant guise to your gate. The same people, the people of Daunus, who persecute you with cruel war, assail us too ; if they expel us, they believe that nothing will be wanting to enable them to bring all Italy utterly beneath their yoke, and to be lords of the sea that washes it above, and of that below as well. Receive and give me your pledge. With us are hearts valiant in war, with us are souls resolved, and a band of warriors proved in action." So spoke Æneas. The other all the time attentively surveyed his face, and eyes, and his whole figure, as he talked. Then thus in few words replies : " How gladly I welcome and recognize you, most valiant of the Trojans ! How I am reminded of the words and voice and countenance of your sire the great Anchises ! For I remember that Priam, the son of Laomedon, when he came to visit the realm of his sister Hesione, on his voyage to Salamis, went on to visit the cold confines of Arcadia. Then the springtime of youth was beginning to clothe my cheeks with downy bloom ; and I viewed with wonder the Trojan princes, I also wondered at the son of Laomedon himself ; but loftier than all

Anchises passed along. My mind glowed with youthful ardour to accost the warrior, and grasp his hand in mine. I ventured to address him, and eagerly led him within the walls of Pheneus. He at his departure gave me a handsome quiver, and Lycian arrows, and a mantle inwrought with gold, and a pair of bridle reins, all of gold, which now my Pallas has. Therefore I unite with you in sign of treaty the hand you ask me to give; and also, as soon as to-morrow's dawn brings back light to the world, I will let you go cheered by my aid, and will assist you with supplies. Meanwhile, since you have come to us as friends, with good will perform with us this sacrifice, which it were a sin to defer, and forthwith make acquaintance with the table of your allies." When these words had been spoken, he orders that the repast and the cups that had been taken away be again set out, and himself arranges the warriors on the grassy seat, and welcomes Æneas as the chief with a couch and the hide of a shaggy lion, and invites him to his maple throne. Then with all speed chosen youths, and the minister of the altar, bring the baked flesh of bulls, and pile upon the baskets the finely-made gifts of Ceres, and serve the wine. Æneas and his Trojan warriors together feast upon the whole length of a chine of beef and the purificatory entrails.

184—279. *Evander explains the signification of the festival his people are keeping. The story of the death of Cacus.*

When hunger was allayed, and the desire to eat satisfied, King Evander says: " It is no idle superstition, born from ignorance of the ancient gods, that has enjoined upon us this established sacrifice, this regular feast, this altar to a Power so high : saved from fearful dangers, my Trojan guest, we institute and perform anew honours well deserved. Now first remark this crag that overhangs the cliff, how masses of stone have been thrown down all about, and the mountain home stands desolate, and the rocks have brought down a ruinous heap. Here was a cave with a mouth that ran back deep within, which the abhorred shape of half-brutish Cacus tenanted, a place impervious to the sunbeams: and ever with fresh slaughter the ground was steaming, and heads of men, ghastly with shocking gore, hung fixed upon the haughty doors. The father of this monster was Vulcan: his were the black fires he used to belch from his mouth as he stalked along in huge bulk. For us, as for others, time brought at last to our longings the help and advent of the god. For the great avenger, made proud by the slaying and the spoils of Geryon of triple form, came here, even Alcides, and was driving hither as conqueror his enormous bulls; the steers overspread the valley and the river too. But Cacus (for his mind was maddened by frenzy), that there might be no crime nor craft that he had not dared or attempted to do, drove away from their stalls four bulls of goodly size above the rest, and as many heifers of surpassing beauty; and, that there might be no footprints turned directly towards his cave, he dragged them thither by the tail, and stole them away with the marks of their journey reversed, and hid them deep in the dark hollow of the rock. To the eye of one who sought to find them, no prints led to the cavern. Meanwhile, as the son of Amphitryon was just removing from their stalls his well-fed herds, and preparing to go away, the steers began to low at setting out, and all the grove was filled with their cries, and noisily they began to leave the hills behind them. One of the steers returned the cry, and lowed within the hollow cave; and, though close shut up, baffled the hope of Cacus. Now it was that the wrath of Alcides furiously blazed forth with deadly gall; he snatches up with his hand his arms, and his oaken club loaded with knobs, and at full speed runs towards the heights of the towering hill. Then for the first time our people saw Cacus trembling and with troubled eyes. Away he flees at once swifter than the east wind, and makes for his cavern : fear winged his feet. No sooner had he shut himself in, and, by breaking the fastenings, dropped down an enormous crag, which was made to hang there by his father's cunning in iron-work, and with that barrier had blocked up and secured the doorway, than lo, the hero of Tiryns was upon him, with fury in his heart ; and as he surveyed every means of approach, rolled his gaze hither and thither, gnashing his teeth. Thrice, boiling with wrath, he traverses all the Aventine hill, thrice he fruitlessly assails the stony portal, thrice in weariness he sits down to rest in the valley. There stood a pointed flinty rock with jagged crags all over, rising up upon the back of the cave, of towering height to view, a fit home for the nests of unholy birds; this rock, as, hanging o'er the ridge, it inclined towards the river on the left, he, pushing hard against it from the right, stirred from its place, and tore away and loosened from its lowest roots; then with sudden shock he drove it forward: beneath that shock all the sky resounds; the banks spring apart, and backward flows the frighted stream. Then the cave, the vast palace of Cacus, stands revealed to sight, and his shadowy den is disclosed from its depths ; just as if beneath some force the earth, yawning open from her depths, were to unlock the mansions of hell, and expose the ghastly kingdoms, hateful to the gods, and the boundless pit were also to be seen, and the spirits of the dead were struck with panic at the entrance of the light. So Alcides from aloft assails with missiles the robber suddenly caught in the light he looks not for, and shut up in his hollow rock, and bellowing with un-earthly roars; and the hero calls to his aid all sorts of weapons, and plies him with boughs of trees and blocks of stone. The other on his part, for in truth there was now no way left to shun the peril, belches forth from his jaws a mass of smoke (wondrous to tell), and shrouds the dwelling in blinding darkness, robbing the eyes of the power to see before them, and gathers within the cave a ball of smoking gloom, and darkness mixed with fire. The soul of Alcides endured it not, and straight down-ward with a bound he cast himself through the fire, where the smoke drove along its thickest tide, and the vast cave surged with pitchy vapour. Amid the gloom he seizes Cacus, as he belches forth his fruitless flames, grappling him with knotty gripe, and with hard grasp strangles him till his eyes start from the sockets, and his throat is drained of blood. Straightway the doors are torn away, and the deadly den disclosed ; and the bulls he had dragged away, and the theft he had disclaimed with oaths, are laid bare to heaven ; and by the feet he is drawn forth, a mis-shapen corpse. Men cannot sate their hearts with viewing the terrific eyes of the half-brutish monster, his features, and his breast all shaggy with bristles, and his jaws where the flames are quenched. From that time

homage has been performed, and posterity have joyfully kept the day ; and
Potitius was the first founder of the festival, and the Pinarian house is the
guardian of the worship of Hercules. He it was who set up this altar in
the grove, which by us shall ever be called greatest, and ever will be
greatest. Wherefore come, ye youths, in discharge of honour due to merit
so high, wreathe your hair with leaves, and present with your hands the
cup, and invoke our common god, and with goodwill offer the wine."
So he spake; whereupon the people veiled their hair with the foliage of
Hercules of double shade, and down the garland hung with leafy twine,
and the right hand was charged with the sacred bowl. All with haste
joyfully pour the libation upon the table, and intreat the gods.

280—305. *The worship and praises of Hercules.*

Meanwhile evening draws nearer, as the sphere of heaven slopes down.
And now the priests, and at their head Potitius, come along, girt with
skins according to custom, and carrying torches. Anew they solemnize
the feast, and bring to the second course welcome gifts, and pile the
altars with laden dishes. Next the Salii draw near to sing around the
kindled altar, their brows bound with poplar wreaths. On one side is the
choir of youths, on the other that of the aged; they in verse chant the
renown and deeds of Hercules ; how with the grasp of his hand he
strangled the earliest monsters his stepmother sent, the two serpents,
how he too o'erthrew in war illustrious cities, both Troy and Œchalia;
how he passed through a thousand difficult toils at the bidding of King
Eurystheus, by the doom of cruel Juno. "It was thy hand, unconquered
Power, that slew the cloud-born Centaurs of twofold shape, both Hylæus
and Pholus: thou didst slay the monsters of Crete, and the huge lion
beneath the rock of Nemea. Before thee the Stygian waters trembled;
before thee the doorkeeper of hell, as he lay in his gory lair upon half-
devoured bones. And no shapes could terrify thee, not Typhœus himself,
wielding his weapons in towering stature; thy presence of mind forsook
thee not, when encompassed by the snake of Lerna with its multitude
of heads. Hail, Jove's undoubted child, thou whose presence is a new
glory to the gods! Both ourselves and thy sacrifice approach with
favouring step." Such are the deeds they celebrate in song: above all
they introduce the den of Cacus, and the monster himself with his breath
of fire. All the grove together re-echoes with the din, and the hills rebound.

306—368. *Evander tells the history of the early inhabitants of Italy, and shews Æneas various places in his city. They enter the dwelling of Evander.*

After that, all the people return to the city, when the religious cere-
monies have been duly performed. The monarch clogged with age went
along, and kept beside him as his companions Æneas and his son, as he
walked, and lightened the way with various conversation. Æneas is
filled with wonder, and rapidly runs his eyes o'er all around ; and is
attracted by various spots, and with pleasure both asks for and is told of
the records left by the men of former times. Then says king Evander,
the founder of the citadel of Rome : "These groves were once haunted
by the gods of the soil, Fauns and Nymphs, and a race of men sprung
from the trunks of trees and hard oak ; they had no rule of life and no

civilisation, and knew not how to yoke oxen, or to store up wealth, or to refrain from wasting what they had won : but lived on boughs and the rude sustenance gained by hunting. Saturn was the first to come from heavenly Olympus, fleeing from the armed power of Jove, and an exile spoiled of his kingdom ; it was he who made into a settled society a people untaught and scattered over the tops of the mountains, and gave them laws, and chose that the land should be called Latium, because in safety he had lain concealed in this region. It was under this king that the golden age existed, of which tradition tells ; in such perfect peace he ruled the realm ; until by degrees crept in a time degenerate and discoloured ; and the frenzy of war, and the passion for gain. Then came the Ausonian bands and the Sicanian tribes, and the land of Saturn often changed its name : then came kings, and savage Thybris of enormous frame, from whom we Italians have since called our river by the name of Thyber ; the ancient Albula has lost its proper name. Me, forced from my fatherland, and exploring the uttermost parts of the sea, almighty Fortune and irresistible Fate settled in these regions ; and the dread warnings of my mother, the nymph Carmentis, drove me hither, and Apollo's divine authority." Scarce had the words been spoken, when straightway he goes on to shew him the altar and also the gate which the Romans call by name the Carmental, an ancient honour paid to the nymph Carmentis, the prophetess of fate, who was the first to predict that the children of Æneas would be great and Pallanteum renowned. After this he points out the vast grove, which valiant Romulus made a refuge anew, and the Lupercal beneath the breezy rock, so called after the Arcadian model of Lycæan Pan. Furthermore he shews the grove of holy Argiletum, and himself attests the spot, and tells of the death of Argus his guest. After this he guides him to the Tarpeian rock, and the site of the Capitol, now all of gold, once a tangled mass of woody thickets. Even then the awful sanctity of the spot used to scare the frighted rustics, even then they shuddered at the grove and cliff. "This wood," he says, "this hill with leafy crown, is haunted by a god, what god it is, is doubtful ; the Arcadians believe they have beheld Jove himself, while many a time his right hand shook the darkling ægis, and stirred the thunder-clouds. You see besides these two towns with ruined walls, remains and records of the men of old. This citadel was built by father Janus, that by Saturn ; the one was named Janiculum, the other Saturnia." So conversing with one another, they drew near to Evander's homely dwelling, and saw the cattle all around lowing in the Roman Forum and the sumptuous Carinæ. So soon as they reached the abode : "This," says he, "is the threshold through which victorious Alcides passed, this is the palace which received him. Dare to scorn wealth, my guest, and fashion yourself also to deserve divinity, and approach our poverty without disdain." So he spoke, and led the great Æneas beneath the roof of his lowly abode, and placed him reclining on a bed of leaves and the hide of a Libyan bear. On speeds the night, and clasps the world with sable wings.   ·

369—406. *Venus persuades Vulcan to assist Æneas. Vulcan's forge.*

But Venus, whose mind was not without reason filled with a mother's fears, and agitated by the threatenings of the Laurentes, and their fell outbreak, addresses Vulcan, and thus begins to speak in her husband's golden chamber, and with her words breathes on him love divine : " So long as the Argive princes were wasting with war Troy predestined to this ruin, and the battlements doomed to fall by hostile flames, I asked not any help for the wretches, I asked not for the armour of your skill and power, nor wished, my dearest husband, uselessly to employ the efforts of yourself or of your workmanship : albeit I owed a deep debt to Priam's sons, and often wept for the painful struggle of Æneas. Now by Jove's commands he has fixed his home on the shores of the Rutulians. Therefore I come a suppliant now, and ask arms of your divinity that I reverence, a mother for her son. You the daughter of Nereus, you the bride of Tithonus had power to move with tears. Behold what nations are leaguing together, what strongholds with their gates barred are whetting the sword against me, and for the destruction of my people." She ended ; and all around with snowy arms the goddess fondles in soft embrace her hesitating lord. He all at once felt the wonted flame, and the well-known warmth passed into his marrow, and shot through his melting bones. Even as when perchance a glittering rent of fire, torn open by the gleaming bolt, shoots through the thunder-clouds with flashing light. His consort, pleased with the stratagem, and conscious of her charms, perceived it. Then speaks the Sire, bound with the chain of everlasting love : " Why do you search so deep for reasons? Whither, Lady, has departed your trust in me ? Had your anxiety been like this, then too had it been in my power to arm the Trojans, nor would the Almighty Father, nor the Fates, have forbidden Troy to stand, and Priam to survive for ten years more. And now, if you intend to wage war, and such is your resolve, all the careful skill in my craft that I can promise, all that can be wrought with iron and molten electrum, all the force of flames and blasts—desist from expressing by your prayers distrust in your power." Such were the words he spoke, and gave the caresses he longed to give, and sinking into the lap of his queen, courted quiet sleep to steal along his limbs.

   407—453. *The making of the armour by the Cyclops of Etna.*

   After that, when the middle stage of night's course was completed, and the first slumber had banished sleep, at the time when the woman, who is compelled to support life by her distaff and the slender earnings of her craft, revives the ashes and smouldering fire, adding the night to her hours of work, and by lamp-light keeps her maidens toiling at a ceaseless task, that she may be able to preserve unstained her husband's bed, and rear her little children ;—like her, and with not less zeal, the lord of fire at that season rises from his soft couch to the labours of his craft. Near the Sicanian shore and Æolian Lipare, an island towers from the sea with a peak of smoking rocks, beneath which a cavern thunders, and the deeps of Etna, hollowed by the forges of the Cyclops ; and hard blows upon the anvils are heard to give forth a noise, and hot bars of Chalybian iron hiss within the caves, and in the furnaces fire pants out its blast : it is the house of Vulcan, and the land is named Vulcania. Hither from the height of heaven the lord of fire then came down. In their dreary cave the Cyclops were forging the iron, Brontes, and Steropes, and

Pyracmon with naked limbs. In their hands was a half-wrought thunderbolt already finished in part;—such as from all the sky the Father hurls
in numbers down on earth; part was still unfinished. Three shafts of
writhen rain, three of watery cloud, they had blended with it, three of red
fire and winged southern wind. Now they were mingling with their work
frightful flashes, and din, and dread, and wrath with its pursuing flames.
Elsewhere with haste they prepared for Mars his car and flying wheels,
with which the god arouses men and whole cities; and with all their
might were finishing the terrific ægis, the armour of angry Pallas, with
serpent-scales and gold, and the twine of snakes, and on the breast of
the goddess the Gorgon's self, with eyes still rolling in her severed head.
"Set all your tasks aside," he says, "and remove the works you have
begun, Cyclops of Etna, and give your minds to this; arms must be
wrought for a valiant hero. Now is the time to use your strength, your
nimble hands, and every lesson of your art. Turn delay to haste." No
more he said; so they with speed all set themselves to the work, and
equally divided the toil. In streamlets runs the brass, and ore of gold,
and piercing steel is melting in the mighty furnace. They begin to shape
a ponderous shield, strong enough by itself to meet all the darts of
Latium, and weld one upon another circles sevenfold deep. Some with
the windy bellows alternately catch and expel the blast; others dip in the
pool the hissing brass; the cavern groans beneath the anvils piled upon
it. They, one after the other, with vigorous force raise their arms in
measure and turn with biting tongs the molten mass.

454—519. *Evander promises to make the Etruscans, who have revolted
     from their king Mezentius, the allies of Æneas.*

While in the coasts of Æolus the Lemnian sire is hastening on this
work, the kindly light, and the morning songs of birds beneath his roof,
call up Evander from his lowly home. The old man rises, and clothes his
limbs with the tunic, and wraps around his soles the Tuscan bandage of
the foot: then to his side and shoulders he buckles his Arcadian sword,
drawing close the panther's hide that hung down upon his left: and likewise a pair of guards, his hounds, go out before him from the lofty threshold, and attend upon their master's step. The hero, mindful of his
words and the service he had promised, went on towards the dwelling
and chamber of his guest Æneas. No less early Æneas came along:
with the former his son Pallas walked in company; with the latter
Achates. When they met, they joined hand in hand, and sat down in
the inmost chamber of the house, and at last enjoyed the conversation
they might now begin. The monarch is the first to speak: "Most mighty
captain of the Teucri (for while you survive I will surely never admit that
the state or realm of Troy is vanquished), to meet so great a name as
yours, my power is but weak for aid in war: on this side we are shut in by
the Tuscan stream, on that the Rutulian presses hard upon us, and sounds
about our wall with clashing arms. But I intend to unite with you mighty
nations and a camp made rich with kingdoms; this means of safety unlooked-for chance presents; hither approach at the request of fate. Not
far from hence lies the site of the city of Agylla founded on an ancient
rock, where once a Lydian race renowned in war fixed its home on the

Etruscan hills. When the people had now prospered for many years, in course of time King Mezentius ruled them with overbearing sway and savage arms. Why should I tell of the horrid massacres, the outrageous crimes of the tyrant? May Heaven keep them in store to fall upon his own head and on his race! Nay, he even used to unite the bodies of the dead with the living, joining them hand to hand and face to face (dire form of torture!) and so, in that miserable embrace, streaming with corruption and gore, he killed them by a lingering death. But his subjects, wearied out at last, take up arms and beset him in his own house, in the midst of his boundless fury; they cut down his supporters, they hurl fire to the roof of his palace. He amid the carnage slunk away, and has sought refuge in the land of the Rutulians, and is protected by the arms of Turnus, his friend. So all Etruria rose in righteous wrath; with arms prompt for war they demand that the king be surrendered to their vengeance. You, Æneas, I will make captain over these thousands; for their ships in crowded squadrons are loud with rage all along the shore, and require that their standards advance. The aged seer keeps them back, pronouncing the will of Fate: 'Mæonia's chosen band of warriors, the flower and soul of men of old descent, ye whom righteous indignation bears against the foe, and Mezentius fires with rage he well deserves, no man of Italy may command so great a nation; choose foreign leaders.' Then the Etruscan array made its camp on this plain, awed by the warnings of heaven. Tarchon himself has sent to me ambassadors with the crown and sceptre of royalty, and delivers to my hands the ensigns of power, bidding me enter the camp, and take under my sway the Tyrrhene realm. But old age, halting with cold and worn with lapse of years, and strength now past the time for deeds of valour, withhold empire from me. I would urge my son to the enterprise, were he not of mixed blood by his Sabine mother, and so derived from her a share of her native land. Do you, whose years and descent are smiled upon by Fate, you, whom the gods require, enter on your career, right valiant captain of Trojans and Italians! Moreover, I will join with you this my son Pallas, my hope and comfort; under your governance let him practise to endure warfare and the hard work of Mars, to observe your exploits, and to look up to you from his early years. To him I will give two hundred horsemen, the flower of our vigorous youth, and Pallas shall bring you as many more in his own name."

520—545. *Venus gives the sign of impending war.*

Scarce had he finished speaking, when Æneas the son of Anchises and his faithful Achates fixed their eyes upon the ground, and with their own sad hearts would have pondered over many a hardship, had not Cytherea given forth an omen in the cloudless sky. For suddenly shot from heaven comes a forky flash, and with it a noise; and straightway all the air seems thrown into a tumult, and the swell of the Tyrrhene trumpet to peal along the sky. They raise their eyes; again and again breaks forth the mighty crash; arms they behold amidst a cloud in a clear quarter of the heaven reddening through the bright atmosphere, and sounding with thunderous clash. Confounded were the hearts of the rest; but the Trojan hero recognized the meaning of the sound, and the promise of his goddess mother. Then he speaks: "Do not indeed, my host, do not ask at all what event these wonders bring; I am summoned: my divine parent forewarned me she would send from Olympus this sign, if war was near at hand, and through the air would convey, to succour me, arms wrought by Vulcan. Alas, what fearful carnage is close upon the wretched Laurentes! Turnus, what a punishment will you suffer at my hands! In what multitudes, O father Tiber, wilt thou roll beneath thy flood shields of men, and helmets, 'and corpses of the brave! Let them call for battle-fields, and break the compacts they have made!" When he had uttered these words, he rose from his lofty throne: and first he wakes afresh the fires that slept on the altars of Hercules, and joyfully approaches the Lar he worshipped yesterday, and the little Penates: Evander and the youth of Troy all in like manner sacrifice ewes duly chosen.

546—584. *Æneas takes leave of Evander. Evander's farewell to his son.*
Afterwards he walks hence to his fleet, and visits again his comrades. Out of their number he chooses the foremost in valour to be his own attendants to the war ; the rest sail down the stream, and idly drift along the favouring flood, to carry to Ascanius news of his state and of his father. Steeds are given to the Trojans who are marching to the Tyrrhene fields : they bring for Æneas one chosen out for himself, covered all over with a lion's tawny hide, that brightly shone with gilded paws. The rumour flies abroad, published at once throughout the little city, that horsemen are going with speed to the home of the Etruscan king. Mothers in their anxiety redouble their vows, and fear comes closer to the peril it dreads, and now the shape of War is larger seen. Then old Evander, clasping the hand of his departing guest, clings to it, with weeping that cannot be satisfied, and speaks to him thus: "O that Jove would give me back the years that are past! Such as I was when close beneath Præneste I laid low the foremost ranks of the enemy, and burnt whole heaps of conquered shields, and sent King Erilus with this right hand to Tartarus. To him at his birth his mother Feronia had given (fearful to tell!) three lives, three sets of brandished arms; thrice he must be laid low in death; yet on that day this hand robbed him of all his lives, and as often stripped him of his arms. I would not now at all be torn from your sweet embrace, my son; and never should Mezentius in contempt for myself, his neighbour, have wrought with the sword so many barbarous murders, have bereft my town of so many citizens. But you, ye gods of heaven, and thou, most mighty ruler of the gods, Jupiter, pity, I beseech you, the Arcadian king, and hear a father's prayers: if your will, if fate keep for me my Pallas safe from harm, if I live destined to see him and be made one with him again, I beg for life; I am willing to endure every hardship. But if, O Fortune, you threaten some unutterable disaster, now, now, I pray, suffer me to cut short my hateful life, while my fears are unfulfilled, while my presage of the future is doubtful, while thee, dear boy, my sole and last delight, I hold in my embrace; and may no fatal message wound my ears." These words at the moment of separation the father poured forth; his servants bore him swooning within the palace.

585—607. *Æneas and his band reach the Etruscan camp.*
And now the troop of horsemen had quite passed out at the open gates,

Æneas among the first, and his trusty Achates; after them the other lords of Troy; Pallas himself in the middle of the train, brilliant with broidered scarf and arms inwrought: such as, when bathed in Ocean's flood, the morning-star, that Venus loves above the other starry fires, exalts in heaven his sacred head and melts the gloom away. Mothers stand trembling on the walls, and follow with their eyes the dusty clouds and the squadrons with their gleaming brass. They all in arms march onward through the thicket by the way that leads them soonest to their goal; a shout is raised, and in close array the horses' hoofs with fourfold trampling shake the crumbling plain. There stands near Cære's stream a mighty grove, held sacred far and wide through the reverence of the men of old; hollow hills shut it in on all sides and encompass the wood with a belt of black fir-trees. Tradition tells that the old Pelasgi, who were the first that ever possessed the Latin lands, dedicated to Silvanus, the god of fields and flocks, the grove and a holyday as well. Not far from hence Tarchon and his Tuscans had placed their camp in a strong position, and from a high hill all the host could now be seen, and had pitched its tents on the open plain. Hitherward Æneas and his band of warriors chosen for battle advance, and refresh themselves and their weary steeds.

608—731. *Venus brings the arms to Æneas. Description of the designs engraven on the shield.*

But Venus, beauteous goddess, amid the clouds of heaven was near at hand, bringing her gifts; and so soon as from afar she saw her son in a secluded valley, and retired from the cold stream, with these words she addressed him, and freely appeared to his view: " Lo, these are the gifts I promised, fashioned by my husband's art; henceforth fear not, my son, to challenge to the fight either the proud Laurentes or the fierce Turnus." So spoke the queen of Cythera, and sought her son's embrace: beneath an oak that stood before them she placed the radiant arms. He, exulting in the gift of the goddess, and an honour so great, cannot satiate his joy, and rolls his gaze over each separate piece. He admires, and poises in his hands and arms the helm's terrific plumes and breathing flames, and the sword, fate's instrument, the corslet of stiff brass, in hue like blood, of massive size, like as when a dusky cloud against the sunbeams glows and shines afar; next the polished greaves of precious metal and refined gold, and the lance, and the ineffable fabric of the shield. There the lord of fire, not unversed in prophecy, nor ignorant of future time, had wrought the fortunes of Italy and the triumphs of Rome; there he had carved every generation of the line that was to descend from Ascanius, and all the wars as in succession they were fought. Also he had wrought the mother-wolf as she lay stretched out in the green cave of Mavors; about her teats the twin boys hung in play, and their dam licked them unterrified; she, bending back the length of her shapely neck, caressed them one after the other, and fashioned their bodies with her tongue. Not far hence he had introduced Rome, and the Sabine women rudely carried away in the assembled crowd of the theatre, when the great games of the circus were performed, and a fresh war straightway springing up between the men of Romulus and king Tatius and his austere Cures. Afterwards the same kings, their mutual conflict laid aside, in arms, and holding bowls in their hands, stood before the altar of Jove, and with the sacrifice of a sow concluded the treaty.   Not far from thence chariots swiftly rushing different ways had torn asunder Metius : (yet, would that you abode by your promise, man of Alba !) and through the forest Tullus dragged along the mangled body of the traitor, and the brambles dripped with dews of blood.   Moreover, Porsena was there, commanding them to receive the banished Tarquin, and hemming the city round with strict blockade ; the sons of Æneas hurried to take the sword for freedom.   Him you might behold like one in the act of wrath, in the act of menace ; because Cocles dared to break away the bridge, and Clælia had burst her fetters and was swimming across the stream.   At the top, Manlius, the guard of the Tarpeian fort, stood before the temple, and kept the lofty Capitol ; and the palace was all rough, freshly covered with the thatch of Romulus. And here a silver goose, flitting in arcades of gold, proclaimed that the Gauls were already in the threshold ; the Gauls were coming close up through the bushes, and grasped the citadel, screened by the darkness and the favour of a gloomy night.   Golden their flowing hair, their dress of gold ; their cloaks are striped and shining ; also, their milk-white necks are circled with collars of gold ; each in his hand brandishes two Alpine javelins, their bodies are protected by their long shields.   Here he had forged the bounding Salii and the naked Luperci, and the crests bound with wool, and the targets dropt from heaven ; holy matrons in their easy cars conveyed through the city the sacred vessels.   Far hence he adds to the work the regions of Tartarus also, the deep portal of Dis ; and the punishments given to crimes, and you, Catiline, as you hang from a frowning rock, and shudder at the glance of the Furies ; and far removed from them, the pious ; and Cato among these dispensing laws. Between these groups the likeness of a swelling sea extended far and wide, all golden : but the blue waters foamed with hoary spray ; and around, dolphins of shining silver swept the main into circles with their tails, and cleft the surge.   In the midst you might behold fleets armed with brass, the conflict of Actium, and all Leucate you might see glowing with the array of battle, and the billows glittering with gold.   On this side Cæsar Augustus, leading into the fight his Italians, with the Fathers and the People, the Penates and the great gods, standing on the lofty poop ; his joyous brows breathe forth a double flame, and on his head is seen his father's star.   In another part, with winds and gods propitious, Agrippa raised aloft leads on the line ; whose brows gleam with the beaks that form the naval crown, proud ornament of war !   On this side Antonius, with his barbaric aid and various arms, victorious from the nations of the Morning and the shore of the Red Sea, brings with him Egypt, and the powers of the East, and the remote Bactrians ; and there follows him (O shame !) an Egyptian wife.   All at once rush on, and the whole surface of the deep begins to foam, convulsed with the long stroke of the oars, and the beaks of triple tooth.   Out to sea they speed ; you would think that Cyclades rooted up were floating on the main, or that high mountains were moving against mountains in battle : on towered ships of bulk so vast the warriors press to the fight.   With

the hand are hurled showers of flaming tow, and shafts with winged steel.
The plains of Neptune are crimsoned with wondrous carnage. In the
midst the queen urges on the host with the cymbal of her native land ;
and not even yet does she descry the two snakes that are behind. The
monstrous shapes of gods of every kind, and barking Anubis, uplift their
shafts against Neptune and Venus and Minerva. Mars, wrought in steel,
rages in the heart of the conflict, and the fell Furies from the sky,
and Discord in mantle rent exulting stalks along, and Bellona follows
her with bloody scourge in hand. Actian Apollo, when he saw the sight,
bent his bow from above ; in dread of him every Egyptian and Indian
and Arabian and Sabæan turned his back in flight. The queen herself
was seen to woo the wafting winds and spread the sails, and loosen all
the shrouds. Her amid the carnage, pallid at the approach of doom, the
lord of fire had figured as borne along by the waves and western wind ;
then, opposite her, the Nile in all his huge extent lamenting, and opening
wide his folds, and with all his robe expanded calling the vanquished
to his dark-blue lap, and the coverts of his stream. But Cæsar, in threefold triumph passing through the walls of Rome, was dedicating to the
gods of Italy an eternal votive gift, three hundred mighty shrines
throughout the whole city. The streets were loud with joy and sports
and shouts. In every temple is a chorus of matrons, in every one an
altar ; slain steers before the altars strew the ground. He himself,
seated in the snow-white portal of fair Apollo, reviews the offerings of the
nations, and duly fixes them to the proud doors ; in long array the
vanquished peoples come along, as various in language, as in fashion
of dress and arms. Here had Mulciber portrayed the Numidian tribe,
and the ungirt Africans, here the Leleges, and Carians, and the Geloni
that bear the bow ; with waves now humble Euphrates flowed along ; and
the Morini, the remotest of men, and the Rhine of double horn, and the
unsubdued Dahæ, and Araxes that spurns a bridge. Such figures
throughout the shield of Vulcan, the gift of his mother, he admires, and
though he knows not the events, is pleased with their pictured shadow,
as he lifts upon his shoulder the fame and fortunes of his descendants.

BOOK IX.

1—24. *Turnus is urged by Iris to seize the opportunity, and attack the
Trojans in the absence of Æneas.*

Now whilst such were the deeds done in a far distant quarter, Saturnian
Juno sent Iris from heaven to daring Turnus. It chanced that then in
the grove of his ancestor Pilumnus Turnus sat in a consecrated dell. To
whom thus spake the daughter of Thaumas, with her rosy lips : "Turnus,
the fortune which to your wishes not one of the gods would dare to
promise, lo ! in the course of events this day offers, though you looked
not for it. Æneas has left his town, his comrades, his fleet ; he has gone
to the realm and home of Palatine Evander. Not content with this, he
has penetrated to the farthest towns, even to Corythus, and there
he arms the bands of Tuscans, the companies of the tillers of the field.
Why linger ? now is the hour to call for your steeds, for your chariot.

Away with all delay, strike the camp with terror, take it by storm. She spake, and raised herself to heaven on her poised wings, and as she fled, drew within the clouds the arch of a mighty bow. The youthful prince knew the goddess, and raised his folded hands to the stars, and followed her flight with these words : " Iris, glory of heaven, who sent thee down to me in thy course from the clouds to earth? whence comes this weather suddenly serene? I see the heavens parted in their centre, and the stars straggling in the sky. Omens so clear I follow, whoe'er thou art, that callest me to arms." Thus having said, he went on to the river, and filled the palm of his hand with water from the surface of the stream, making many a prayer to the gods, and loaded heaven with his vows.

25—76. *The Trojans keep within their camp. Turnus attacks the fleet.*

Straightway all the host marched o'er the open plain, rich in steeds, rich in broidered vests and gold. In the van is Messapus, the sons of Tyrrheus close the rear, in the centre of the line is the general, Turnus. Like as when the deep Ganges rises silently with its seven majestic streams, or when Nile ebbs on the plain with fertilizing waters, and presently sinks within its channel. Here the Trojans view from far a sudden cloud of black dust collecting, and darkness rising o'er the plains. First from the rampart that faced the foe Caicus calls aloud : " What mass, my countrymen, is this, rolling with black gloom? Quickly bring swords, give weapons, mount the walls ; the enemy is upon us ; quit yourselves like men." With loud shouts the Trojans retire through all their gates, they line their walls. Such was the charge of Æneas, wise captain, when he departed, that if in his absence any change of fortune should arise, they were not to venture to put the battle in array, nor to trust the open field, content to keep to the camp, and maintain the walls safe behind the rampart. So, though shame and anger urge them to engage hand to hand, yet they bar the gates, and fulfil his charge, and under arms wait for the foe in their hollow turrets. As Turnus flew forward outstripping the slowly marching line, attended by twenty picked horsemen, so suddenly he is before the town ; a piebald Thracian horse bears the prince, a helmet of gold with crimson crest covers his head. "Youths, will any man join me to be the first against the foe?" "Behold!" he says, and whirling his lance, hurls it into the air, the prelude of the fray, and on his tall steed bounds into the plain. With shouts his comrades take up the challenge, and follow with a cheer that rings with terror; they marvel at the Trojans, how tame their souls, who will not trust themselves to a fair field, nor like men meet them in arms, but keep close within their camp. The prince excited rides round the walls on every side, looking for an entrance where there is none. As when a wolf plots mischief against a full fold, ravening up to the pens in the dead of night, for he has borne the winds and rain ; the lambs safe beneath their dams bleat evermore ; he maddened and restless with rage is ramping against those he cannot reach ; the fury of hunger that has long been gaining strength torments the beast, and his jaws are dry for want of blood. Just so the rage of the Rutulian chief, as he gazes on the walls and camp, glows more and more ; anger burns within his hardy heart, as he thinks how he can attempt an entrance, and what approach would dislodge the enclosed Trojans from their entrenchment, and send them streaming into the plain. The fleet which lay hid close to the camp, guarded all round by a rampart and by the stream of the river, he suddenly attacks ; he calls to his exulting comrades to bring fire, and glowing in spirit fills his hand with a blazing brand. Then indeed they set themselves to the work, encouraged by the presence of Turnus, and all the youth arm themselves with smoking torches. They seize them from the hearths around ; the smoking brand bears its pitchy light, and Vulcan rolls to the stars a mass of glowing ashes.

77—106. But the goddess Cybele had received from Jupiter a promise that the ships of Æneas should be transformed into sea-nymphs.

Tell me, Muses, what god turned from the Trojans the cruel fires? who chased from the ships such fierce flames? Worn with age are the proofs of the fact; but the fame thereof has lasted through years. At the time that Æneas was first building his fleet on Phrygian Ida, and making ready to sail o'er the deep main, 'tis said that the Berecynthian mother of the gods herself thus addressed great Jove : "Grant, my son, to my prayer that which thy dear parent asks in return for the lordship of Olympus. I have a pine-forest, dear to me through many a year ; there was a holy grove on the summit of the heights, whither they used to bring their sacrifices ; dark was it with black pines and the boles of maple-trees : these I gladly gave to the Dardan prince, when he needed a fleet ; but now anxious fear grievously torments me. Relieve my terrors, and let thy parent have so much power with her prayers, that they be not shattered in any voyage, or destroyed in any storm of wind ; let them find it good to have grown on a mountain dear to me." To her replied her son, who sways in their motions the stars of the universe : "My mother, whither wouldst thou call the fates? or what dost thou ask in thy prayer? Can vessels framed by mortal hand have immortal might? Can Æneas securely pass through the insecurity of perils? To what god is such power allowed? Nay but rather, when their toils are past and they reach the end of their voyage, even the Italian harbours, whatever ship has escaped the waves, and carried the Dardan chief to the Laurentian fields, from it will I take its mortal form, and bid it be one of the goddesses of the great sea, in shape like Doto daughter of Nereus, or Galatea, who breast the foaming main." He spake, and ratified his word by the streams of his Stygian brother, by the banks pouring with pitchy torrent and a black abyss, and gave his nod thereto, and with his nod made all Olympus shake.

107—122. When the fated day came the promise was fulfilled.

So then the promised day was come, and the fates had fulfilled the destined hours, when the wrong that Turnus threatened warned the mother of the gods to drive the brands from the holy ships. Here first a strange light gleamed before their eyes, and a great cloud was seen to skim over the sky from the eastern horizon ; the Idæan choir appeared ; then a dreadful voice fell from heaven through the air, and filled the Trojan and Rutulian hosts : "Haste not, Trojans, to defend my ships ; no need to arm your hands ; as soon to burn the seas shall Turnus be allowed, as these my holy trees. Do you go free, go, for ye are goddesses of the

sea; 'tis the will of the mother of the gods." And lo! in an instant the
stern of every ship breaks away its hawser from the bank, and like a
dolphin makes for the depth of the water with its beak plunged in the
stream. From the same depths, (marvellous miracle!) as many brazen
prows as stood by the shore, so many maiden faces rise again, and are
wafted o'er the seas.

123—167. *Turnus is not daunted by portents, which he applies to the
Trojans themselves.*

Aghast were the minds of the Rutulians; even Messapus himself was
terrified, and his horses affrighted; the river Tiber too seems to stay,
roaring hoarsely, and calls back his stream from the sea. But daring
Turnus lost not heart; in spite of all he raises their spirits by his words,
in spite of all he chides his men: "For the Trojans these portents are
meant; thus Jove himself has taken from them their wonted help: their
vessels wait not for our weapons, or for Rutulian fires. So then the seas
are closed to the Trojans, they have no hope of flight; half the world
is lost to them; the land is in our hands; and on it many thousands, even
the Italian nations, are in arms against them. I fear not the fateful
answers of the gods, if there be any the Phrygians boast of as their
champions. Enough has been given to Venus and the Fates in the fact
that the Trojans have landed on the fields of fruitful Italy. I too have
my fates to meet their's, that with the sword I should utterly destroy the
accursed race, since my promised wife is taken from me: nor are the sons
of Atreus alone stung by that wrong, or Mycenæ alone allowed to take
up arms. Ah! but perhaps one ruin is enough. Rather should one sin
have been enough, for they should have learnt utterly to hate almost all
the female sex. A set of men, whose confidence is the breadth of an
earthwork, and to whom the delay that a trench can cause, a slight parti-
tion from death, gives spirits;—have they not seen the walls of Troy built
by Neptune's hand sink into flames? So you, my chosen friends, which
of you is ready sword in hand to tear down the rampart, and with me
to rush into their confused camp? I have no need of Vulcan's arms, or
of a thousand ships, against these Trojans. Forthwith let all the Tuscans
unite with them. They need not fear the shades of the night, nor the
cowardly theft of the Palladium, when the guards at the summit of the
citadel were slain; nor will we hide ourselves in the dark belly of a horse;
in broad daylight, in open field, I am resolved to encompass their walls
with fire. I'll make them know they have not to deal with Greeks and
Pelasgic youth, cowards, whom Hector kept at bay to the tenth year.
Now then, since the better part of the day is spent, for what remains of it,
in joy, my men, refresh your bodies after success, and in readiness look
forward to the fight." In the meanwhile, to Messapus is entrusted the duty
of blockading the gates with the watches of guards, and of surrounding
the walls with night-fires. Twice seven Rutulians were chosen, to watch
the walls with soldiers; and they were each followed by a hundred youths,
whose crimson crests and golden armour gleamed. They keep watch
up and down, and relieve sentries, and stretched on the sward enjoy
themselves o'er their cups, and drain their bronze goblets. The fires
blaze around; the night is passed in wakeful watch and play.

168—175. *The Trojans guard their camp.*

All this the Trojans look down upon from above, from the rampart,
under arms maintaining their high walls; also with anxious dread they
examine their gates, and join the bridges of their bulwarks: weapons are
in their hands. Diligent in command are Mnestheus and Sergestus, keen
in spirit; for them did father Æneas, if perchance danger should summon
them, appoint as leaders of the youths, and guardians of the common-
weal. Along the walls the whole host, dividing the dangers by lot, keep
watch, and in turns actively discharge the duties that fall to each.

176—223. *The episode of Nisus and Euryalus. Their affection. Their generous conversation at the gate of the camp.*

Nisus was guard of the gate, right valiant in arms, son of Hyrtacus;
whom Ida, the hunter's hill, had sent to follow Æneas; quick was Nisus
with the dart and flying arrows; by his side was his companion Euryalus;
there was not a fairer than he among all the men of Æneas, who had put
on Trojan arms; the unshorn cheeks of the boy were just streaked with
the early down of youth. One love the two did feel, together to the wars
they rushed, that night too on guard together did they keep the gate.
Nisus first says: "Do the gods inspire men's souls with this ardour,
Euryalus, or does each man make a god of his own strong passions?
My restless soul even from the first has been bent on entering battle, or
on some great attempt; it cannot brook quiet rest. You see what confidence in their fortunes possesses these Rutulians. Their fires glitter few
and far between; buried in sleep and wine they lie; and all is hushed
around. Next then hear what I plan, and what a purpose rises now in
my heart. That Æneas should be summoned, all, commons and senators
alike, earnestly demand; and that messengers be sent to bring back certain news. If to you they will promise the rewards I ask, for myself the
glory of the deed is recompense enough; I seem to myself to be able to
find a way beneath yonder mound to the walls and towers of Pallanteum."
Astonished was Euryalus, smit with a mighty love of glory; at once he
thus addresses his ardent friend: "Me then can you shrink, Nisus, from
making your partner in deed of danger so extreme? Can I let you go
alone into such peril? It was not so that my father Opheltes, himself
a man of war, trained and bred me amidst the terrors of the Grecian
arms and the trials of Troy: nor such has been my conduct in my com-
panionship with you, since I have followed noble Æneas and the extremity
of fate. Here indeed is a soul that scorns life, which believes that that
honour to which you aspire is cheaply bought therewith." Nisus in
answer said: "I indeed had no such fears of you; 'twere impious so to
think; not so. As I speak the truth, so may great Jove restore me in
triumph to you, or whatever god beholds us here with kindly eyes. But
if any Power (you see how many perils lie in such a hazard), if any
Power, be it chance, or be it god, should hurry me into adversity, I would
have you survive; your youth deserves life better; may there be one to
snatch my body from the fight, or bring it back, and consign it to a grave;
or if our wonted fortune forbid as much as that, at least may pay the
funeral rites to the body, though not found, and honour it with a tomb.
Nor let me be the cause of such a woe to your hapless mother, who alone,

my child, when other mothers did not dare so much, follows you ever, regardless of the walls of great Acestes." The other said : " In vain you weave a chain of idle pleas. My resolve changes not now, nor turns from its purpose. Let us haste," said he. At the same instant he rouses the watch, who relieve them, and take their turn ; he leaves his post, and follows Nisus, as companion ; so both seek audience of the prince.

224—313. *The leaders of the Trojans, and especially Iulus, applaud their generous courage. Iulus promises that the mother of Euryalus shall be to him in the place of Creusa. The two adventurers are armed by the captains of the host.*

All other living creatures through the world by sleep relieved their cares and lulled their hearts into forgetfulness of toil : the foremost leaders of the Trojans, a chosen band of youths, were holding counsel on the highest matters of the state, what should they do, or who should now go as messenger to Æneas. They stand leaning on their long spears, holding their shields, in the centre of the open space of the camp. Then Nisus and with him Euryalus, in haste and alert, beg to be admitted; grave, say they, is the matter, and worth the delay. Iulus was the first to welcome the hastening youths, and bade Nisus speak. Then said the son of Hyrtacus : " Hear, I pray, with impartial minds, ye men of Æneas; nor judge of these our offers from our years. The Rutulians unnerved by sleep and wine are hushed in silence; we have ourselves observed the place for our secret sally, which lies open at the double road from the gate nearest to the sea : there is a break in the watch-fires, and the dark smoke is rising to the stars; if you will allow us to try our fortune, we will go to find Æneas even as far as the towers of Pallanteum ; and soon you will behold him laden with spoils, having made a great slaughter. Nor can we miss our road as we journey; we have seen the distant city while constantly hunting in the dark valley, and traced the bank all along the river." Then spake Aletes grave in years and ripe in wisdom : " Gods of my country, beneath whose eternal guardianship Troy ever is, ye do not then after all intend utterly to wipe out the race of Teucer, else ye had never given us young men of such brave breasts and hearts resolved." He spake, and held the shoulders and hands of both, bedewing his countenance and face with tears. "What reward," said he, "worthy of such virtues can I think of as gifts to you, my friends? The brightest reward of all, heaven and your conscience will give you : the remainder pious Æneas will pay to you forthwith ; and he who has all his life before him, Ascanius, will never forget such great deserts." " Nay I myself adjure you both," so Ascanius takes up Aletes' words, "for in my sire's return lie all my hopes of safety. Yes, you, Nisus, I adjure by the great Penates and Lar of Assaracus, and the central shrine of ancient Vesta; whate'er my fortunes are, whate'er my trust, I put it in your care; recall my sire, restore him to my sight; if I recover him there is nothing sad. I will give you a pair of cups made of pure silver, embossed with figures, which my father took the day he conquered Arisba; and a pair of tripods; two great talents of gold; an antique goblet, the gift of Sidonian Dido. But if it is granted me to take possession of Italy, and obtain the royal sceptre, a conqueror, and to settle the lot of the booty : you saw the horse on which Turnus rides, the arms he wears all golden; that very steed, the shield, the crimson crests, I will exempt from the chance of lot; already they are your prize, Nisus. Further, my father will give you twice six chosen matrons, and captives, and all the goods that each possesses; in addition, the domain of king Latinus. But you, whom my years follow at a nearer distance, a boy, yet deserving reverence, even now I embrace you with my whole heart, and take you as my companion for every risk. In no exploit of mine will I seek glory except with you; be it peace, or be it war, in you I will have the greatest faith in word and deed." To whom thus speaks Euryalus: "That no day may ever prove me unlike this brave beginning, is all I promise, whether fortune fall adverse or prosperous. But above all gifts I would pray you to grant me one boon: a mother I have, of the ancient race of Priam; hapless mother! she lingered not in the land of Ilium, but left with me; she stayed not in the city of great Acestes. I leave her now ignorant of this risk, be it what it may be; I bid her not farewell; Night and your right hand be my witness, that I cannot bear a mother's tears. But do you, I pray, comfort my helpless mother, aid the parent whom I leave. Oh may I have this hope of you; I shall go with greater courage to meet every risk." Moved were their souls, the children of Dardanus shed tears; above the rest the fair Iulus; his soul was touched with that reflection of the love he bore to his own father. Then thus he speaks: "Promise to yourself all that is worthy of your great attempt. Your mother shall be mine, Creusa all but in name; for not little are the thanks due to one who has such a son. Whate'er be the result of this deed, I swear by my life, my father's wonted oath, whate'er I promise you on your return successful, the same shall remain good for your mother and race." So he speaks with tears; at the same time he takes the sword from his side; it was o'erlaid with gold; Cretan Lycaon had wrought it with wondrous skill, and made it to fit its ivory sheath. To Nisus Mnestheus gives the skin taken from a shaggy lion; trusty Aletes changes helmets with him. Forthwith they advance armed; whom, as they go, the whole band of chieftains, young and old alike, escorts with vows. Moreover fair Iulus, who had a soul beyond his years, and the thoughts of a man, gave many a charge to be carried to his father. But the winds scatter them all, and give the idle prayers to the clouds.

314—366. *Nisus and Euryalus slay many Rutulians in the camp, and pass safely through it.*

They go forth and pass the trench, and through the shades of night they make for the camp which is to prove such a deadly foe, yet destined themselves first to be a destruction to many. In confusion, in the midst of sleep and wine, they see the bodies of men stretched o'er the grass, the chariots placed with poles erect on the shore, the charioteers among their reins and wheels, arms and cups of wine, all in medley lying. First thus spake the son of Hyrtacus: "Euryalus, we must do a deed of daring; the occasion calls us; hither lies our way. Do you, lest any troop rise at our rear, be on your guard, and look carefully far around you. I will lay all waste here, and lead you on by a broad passage." Thus he speaks, then hushes his voice; at the same instant he attacks with his sword haughty Rhamnes, who, perchance,

raised high on coverlets, was breathing forth sleep from all his breast,
a king himself, and to king Turnus too his favourite augur ; but fate
by augury he could not drive away.   Three servants lying carelessly
amidst their weapons, and the armourbearer and . charioteer of Remus
he smites, for he came upon them close beneath the chariot, and with
the steel he cuts their drooping necks : next he lops off the head of
their master, and leaves the trunk heaving as the blood flows forth ;
the earth and their beds are warm and drenched with black blood.
Further he slays both Lamyris and Lamus, and young Serranus ; at
many a game had he played that night ; distinguished for the beauty of his
face was he ; he lay his limbs outstretched, o'erpowered by the copious
god, happy if he had continued his games throughout the night, and prolonged them e'en to break of day.   As a famished lion works confusion
through the full fold, when maddening hunger urges him on ; he drags
and devours the feeble flock, struck dumb with terror ; he rages with his
blood-stained jaws.   Nor less the slaughter which Euryalus wrought ; he
too, full of fire, rages through the camp, and comes suddenly on a great
nameless crowd in the centre space, on Fadus too, and Hebesus, and
Rhœtus, and Abaris ; the rest surprised ; but Rhœtus wide awake, and
seeing all ; in his terror he slunk behind a great goblet : he tried to rise,
but full in his breast the Trojan close at hand buried his whole sword ;
then drew it forth again crimsoned with flowing death ; the other pours
forth his life, and as he dies vomits the wine mingled with his blood ;
the conqueror presses forward eagerly on his stealthy work.   And now
he was on his way to the comrades of Messapus ; there he saw the dying
fires were fainting, and the horses tied in careful wise were feeding on
the grass ; when Nisus shortly spoke, for he felt that they were carried
forward with over eager thirst for blood : "Let us desist," quoth he, "for
the unfriendly light draws near.   Of punishment we have taken enough ;
we have made a lane through our foe."   Many are the arms of men finished
with solid silver that they leave behind, goblets too, and fine coverlets.
Euryalus carries off the trappings belonging to Rhamnes, and his belt
with golden studs ; these gifts once wealthy Cædicus sent to Tiburtian
Remulus, they were joined in friendship, though they never met ; Remulus
at his death left them to his grandson ; after his death the Rutulians
gained them by war and battle : these arms Euryalus now snatches up,
and puts them on his valiant limbs, but all in vain.   Then he puts on
Messapus' helmet, light for wearing, adorned with plumes.   Forth from
the camp they go, and strive to reach what seems a place of safety.

367—449.   *The Latin horsemen under Volscens see the helmet of Eury-
     alus glittering in the moonlight.   They surround the wood and take
     Euryalus.   Nisus has escaped.   But finding he has missed Euryalus,
     he returns.   Unable to save his friend, he avenges him and dies.*

Meanwhile the horsemen sent forward from the Latin town were on
their way, whilst the rest of the battalion halts on the plain in battle array :
the cavalry were bringing answers to king Turnus, three hundred were
they, all shielded riders, Volscens was their captain. .And now they were
just nearing the camp, and were coming under the walls, when they see
the two turning a little in their course to the left, and in the glimmering

shades of night the helmet betrayed the thoughtless Euryalus, as it glittered against the moonbeams. It was not seen for nought. From the line shouts Volscens : "Stand, ye men ; what the reason of your journey? who are you in arms? whither going?" They said nothing in answer, but hastened their flight into the forest, and relied on the night. The horsemen throw themselves in their way at the well-known cross-roads on every side, guarding every exit with a ring of watchers. There was a forest of wide extent, shaggy with thickets of dark oak, which close brambles filled throughout ; here and there shone a footpath along the hidden tracks. The darkness of the boughs and the burden of his spoils encumber Euryalus, and fear misleads him from the right direction of the path. Nisus escapes ; and now without a further thought he was safe beyond his foes, even as far as the place afterwards called Alban from Alba's name ; at that time king Latinus had there his lofty stables. The moment that he stopped, and in vain looked back for his friend, who was not there, he said : "Unhappy Euryalus, in what direction have I left you? or whither shall I go to find you?" Again he retraces all the intricate way of the perplexing forest, and tries to trace back again his footsteps carefully observed, and wanders amidst the silent thickets. He hears the horses, he hears the noise, and the sign of pursuers. 'Tis but a short time more, and a shout reaches his ears, and then he sees Euryalus ; him just at that moment the whole band seizes overpowered by the deception of the place and of the night, as suddenly the crowd confounds him ; vain are his many efforts to escape. What could his friend do? by what force of arms should he venture to rescue the youth? Should he rush into the midst of the foe to certain death, and seek a quick and noble death by many a wound? Hastily brandishing his spear with his arm drawn back, he looks up to the moon high in heaven, and thus he prays : "Do thou, O queen, do thou propitious come to aid my effort, thou glory of the stars, thou guardian of the woods, Latona's child ; if ever for me my father Hyrtacus brought gifts to thy altars, if ever I offered more presents from my own hunting, or hung them in thy dome, or fixed them to thy holy roof ; let me confound this troop, and do thou guide my dart through the air." He spake, and with the effort of his whole strength he hurls his spear. Forth flies the lance and cleaves the shades of night, and pierces the back of Sulmo who was looking away, and there it breaks, and while the wood splits, it passes through to his heart. He rolls over, and pours from his breast a stream of hot blood, then is cold in death, while his sides quiver with deep-drawn sobs. The troopers look round every way. Encouraged thereby, lo ! again he poised a second dart from above his ear. While they are bewildered, the spear passes through the temples of Tagus with a whizz, and remains fixed in the pierced brain, and is hot with his blood. Fiercely rages Volscens, but he sees nowhere the man who sent the dart, he knows not whither in his wrath to direct his vengeance. "You, how-ever," said he, in the meanwhile, "with your life's blood shall give me satisfaction for the sins of both ;" then drew his sword, and rushed on Euryalus. Then indeed, as one amazed, frenzied, cries Nisus ; he could not hide himself in the covert any more, or bear such dreadful agony.

"Me! me! here am I, who did the deed, on me turn your swords, ye Rutulians, mine is all the sin; nought could he dare or do; I call heaven above us to witness, and the conscious stars. His only fault was too much love for his unhappy friend." So spake he; but already the sword driven with force has passed through his friend's side, and rends his beauteous breast. Euryalus falls and writhes in death, and the blood gushes o'er his lovely limbs, and his neck sinking down reclines on his shoulder. Even as when a bright flower cut down by the plough languishes in death, or when poppies droop their heads with weary neck, if perchance they are burdened with a weight of rain. But Nisus rushes into the midst; among them all he makes for Volscens alone, on Volscens alone are his efforts bent. Around him the foes collect, they close in fight, they push him back on either side. He presses on with no less zeal, he whirls his flashing sword, until he has buried it full in the shouting Rutulian's mouth, and in the act of death he takes his enemy's life. Then he threw himself on his lifeless friend, pierced with many a wound, and there at last reposed in tranquil death.

O happy pair! if aught my verse can do, no day shall ever take you from the memory of time, so long as the house of Æneas dwells hard by the immoveable rock of the Capitol, and the Father of Rome holds his imperial sway.

450—472. *The Rutulians discover the slaughter in the camp. The Trojans are discouraged by the spectacle of the bloody heads of Nisus and Euryalus.*

The victorious Rutulians, masters of the booty and spoils, bore back to the camp the dead body of Volscens, as mourners. Nor less in the camp was the grief, when Rhamnes was found dead, and so many chieftains killed in one slaughter, with Serranus and Numa too. Great was the crowd that pressed up to their bodies, and to the dying men, and to the place still warm with fresh slaughter, and the copious streams of foaming blood. They knew the spoils, as they spake to each other, and recognised the bright helmet of Messapus, and the trappings recovered with labour that cost so dear.

And now Aurora, leaving the saffron couch of Tithonus, was just beginning to sow her rising light o'er the earth, now did the sun pour forth his beams, now was nature revealed by the day; Turnus rouses his men to arms, with arms himself is clad, and musters the brazen array to the fight; each whets his own rage, though with various talk. Farther, they bear in front those very heads, oh piteous sight! fixed on raised lances, and they follow with loud shouts; the heads were those of Euryalus and Nisus. The hardy men of Æneas on the left side of the walls set their array to face the foe, the right side is guarded by the river, and they maintain the deep trenches, and on the tall turrets stand, but sad in heart; for the faces of their two comrades fixed on the spears in front affected their minds; they were but too well known to their unhappy friends, as they dripped with black blood.

473—502. *The lamentations of the mother of Euryalus.*

Meantime winged Fame flitting through the panic-struck town hurries with her news, and speeds to the ears of the mother of Euryalus. Then suddenly the warmth of life left the limbs of the wretched parent; from her hands fell the shuttle, unrolled was her task. Forth she flew in her misery, and with a woman's shriek, with hair torn, as one frenzied, she rushes straight to the walls, and the foremost ranks; she thought not of men, or of danger, or of darts; then she fills heaven with her wails: "Is it thus I see you, my Euryalus? Could you then, you who were the last comfort of my old age, yes, had you the heart to leave your mother desolate, O cruel son? And when you were sent to such a risk, was not your wretched parent allowed to take a last farewell? Alas, on a stranger land you lie exposed a prey to Latin dogs and birds! Nor have I, your mother, laid you out in death, or closed your eyes, or bathed your wounds, using as a shroud that mantle, which for you I wove in haste, working ever night and day, beguiling the fears of old age with my web. Whither shall I go to find you? or what land now holds your limbs and torn body and mangled form? Is this all, my son, that you can bring me back of yourself? Is this what I followed o'er land and sea alike? Pierce me, O Rutulians, if you have any feeling; on me hurl all your darts, me first slay with the sword; or do thou, great father of the gods, have pity, and with thy thunderbolt send this soul thou hatest beneath Tartarus, since no other way can I break the thread of cruel life." By these wailings were their spirits shaken, sadness and lamentation passes through all, languid is their strength, and spiritless for fight. As she thus kindles the fierceness of grief, Actor and Idæus take her, such were the commands of Ilioneus and of Iulus bathed in tears, and they bear her in their hands within her house.

503—524. *The Rutulians make their first attack on the Trojan camp.*

But the trumpet from afar with its ringing brass gave the warning of its terrific note; a shout follows, the sky re-echoes. Forward hasten the Volsci, advancing the covering of their shields in line; they prepare to fill the trenches and tear down the rampart. Some look for an approach, or with ladders would scale the walls, where the line is broken, and the light shews through the ring of warriors, who stand less thick. To meet this the Trojans pour forth every kind of missiles, and push the foe down with sturdy poles, for they were trained to the defence of walls by the long war of Troy. Stones too they roll down of dangerous mass, in hopes of somewhere breaking through the covered array of men; whilst for all this the assailants gladly endure every chance of war beneath the close shed of shields. And yet they cannot longer hold out, for, where the crowded mass of men presses upon them, there the Trojans roll a huge mass of rocks, there they push it over; which far and wide laid the Rutulians low, and broke up the roof of arms. And now the daring Rutulians care no longer to contend in blind battle, but strive with missiles to drive the Trojans from the rampart. On another side, Mezentius, terrible to view, is seen shaking an Etrurian pine, and throws into the town the smoking flaming brand; whilst Messapus, tamer of steeds, Neptune's son, tears down the rampart, and calls for ladders to scale the walls.

525—529. *The invocation of Calliope.*

Ye Muses, and thou, Calliope, I pray, inspire my song; that I may tell what slaughter, what destruction Turnus wrought; whom each warrior sent down to the shades: do ye with me unfold the mighty scroll of war; for you remember, Ladies, and from your memory can relate.

530—568. *Turnus sets a tower of the Trojan camp on fire, and slays many of their men.*

There stood a tower, high it rose above men's eyes, tall its drawbridges, well placed it was to command the foe; which all the Rutulians strove with all their might to storm, and with their utmost strength and means to level; the Trojans opposed them, and defend it by hurling stones, and standing thick they shoot darts through the hollow loopholes. The first to throw the blazing brand was Turnus, who fixed the flames in its side; the fire fanned by the wind caught the planks, and clung to the burnt doors. Troubled and confused were those within; in vain would they escape from the mischief. Whilst they crowd together and retire back into the part free from the pest of flame, lo! suddenly with its weight down the tower falls, and all the sky resounds with the crash. Half dead, while the huge mass followed upon them, transfixed by their own weapons, or with breasts pierced with splinters of hard wood, down to the earth they came. Hardly did Helenor only and Lycus escape; of these two Helenor was in the springtime of youth, whom for the Lydian king his slave Lycymnia reared in secret, and sent him in forbidden arms to Troy; lightly was he armed with naked sword, he had no glory blazoned on his shield. So when he saw himself amidst the thousands of Turnus' men, and the Latin array on this side, on that side the Latin array, as wild beast, hemmed in by a thick ring of hunters, rages straight against the darts, and knowing well its doom throws itself upon its death, borne with a bound above the hunter's spears; e'en so the youth rushes sure to die into the midst of the foe, and where he sees the weapons thickest, there he goes. But Lycus, swifter far of foot, flying between the foes and the darts reaches the walls, and now he strives to grasp the lofty battlement with his hand, and to clutch his comrades' right hands; him Turnus follows with feet and dart at once, and taunts him thus triumphant: "Fool, did you hope you could escape my hands?" then seizes him as he hangs, and tears him down with a large part of the wall. As when some hare, or swan of snow-white form, is borne aloft by Jove's armour-bearer, who flies on high with crooked talons, or as a lamb lamented by its dam with many bleatings is snatched by the wolf of Mars from the fold. On every side is raised a shout; they onwards charge, and fill the trenches with fagots; others throw blazing brands up to the battlements.

569—589. *The various fortunes of the siege.*

Ilioneus with a rock, the mighty fragment of a mountain, lays low Lucetius, as beneath the gate he comes with torch in hand; Liger slays Emathion, Asilas Corynæus; Liger was good with the dart, Asilas with the arrow that from afar eludes the sight of men. Cæneus kills Ortygius, Turnus the conqueror Cæneus; Turnus kills Itys, Clonius, Dioxippus, Promulus, Sagaris, and Idas standing as a champion on the topmost tower; Capys slays Privernus; him first Themilla's lance had lightly grazed; he thoughtless cast aside his shield, and to the wound his hand applied; then on its feathers the arrow silent flew, his hand was pinned to his left side, and the point buried within gashed the breathing lungs of life with deadly wound. In glorious arms the son of Arcens stood; embroidered was his cloak by needle's point, brilliant did he shine in Spanish dye, conspicuous by his fair face; him his father Arcens had sent, reared in his mother's grove near the streams of Symæthus, where is the altar of Palicus rich with gifts and easily appeased; Mezentius drops his spear, and thrice around his head whirled with the twining thong the whizzing sling, and split open the centre of the skull with full blow from the glowing lead, and stretched him at his length on the deep sand.

590—620. *Numanus taunts the Trojans, contrasting the hardihood of Italians with the effeminacy of Phrygians.*

Then first 'tis said Ascanius aimed a swift arrow in war; up to that time he had but frightened flying beasts; and with his hand laid low valiant Numanus surnamed Remulus, who lately had made his bride the younger sister of Turnus. He, in front of the foremost rank, uttering aloud words worthy and worthless to record, and with his heart swelling at the thoughts of his new royal alliance, stalked up and down, and gave himself out as some great one with his noisy clamour: "Are ye not ashamed again to be cooped up within besieged walls, ye twice captured Phrygians, and to screen yourselves from death behind battlements? See, these are the men who woo our maidens by war! What god, or what madness has driven you to Italy? Here are no sons of Atreus, nor Ulysses wily in words. A hardy race are we from our birth, our infants we carry down to our streams, and harden them in the icy-cold water; our boys rob sleep to hunt, and scour the woods; to tame horses is their sport, and shoot arrows from the bow. Next, our youths patient of toil, and trained to do with short fare, either subdue the earth with hoes, or shake towns with war. Each time of life is worn with the use of iron, and we prick the backs of our steers with the inverted spear; nor does old age that wearies others weaken our strength of soul, or impair our force. Our gray locks we press with the helmet; and ever is it our delight to bear off the newly taken booty, and to live on spoil. As to you, your vests are broidered, dyed with saffron or glowing purple; sloth is dear to your hearts, your pleasure is to indulge in the dance; your tunics have sleeves, your turbans ribbons. Oh! truly Phrygian women are ye; ye are not even Phrygian men; go ye over lofty Dindymus, where the pipe utters the familiar tones of its unequal sound. The timbrels and Berecynthian flute of the Idæan mother summon you thither; leave arms to men, and give up the use of iron."

621—671. *Iulus with an arrow shoots the boaster. Apollo in the form of Butes praises the boy. The Trojans recognise the god, and defend their camp with fresh vigour.*

As he uttered such boastful words, and spake such shameful indignities, Ascanius could not brook him; but turned towards him and from his horsehair string aimed his arrow, and stretching his arms apart stood firm; but first, a suppliant, prayed and vowed to Jove: "Oh! Jove almighty, favour my daring attempt. With my own hands will I bring to thy temple solemn gifts, and place before thy altar a snow-white bullock, as tall as its mother, such as shall begin to butt with its horn, and scatter the sand with its feet." The Father heard his prayer, and from a clear quarter of the heavens thundered on the left; at the same instant twanged the death-dealing bow, and the arrow drawn to the

breast flies with a dreadful whizz, and passes through the head of Remulus, and pierces his hollow temples with its iron point. "Go to," said
Iulus, "mock valour with vaunting taunts. The twice-captured Phrygians
send back this answer to the Rutulians." Ascanius said no more. The
Trojans follow his words with a shout, and cry aloud for joy, and raise
their spirits to the stars.

It chanced that then the god Apollo of the flowing hair from the
region of the sky was looking down upon the Italian lines and the
town, throned on a cloud; he with these words addresses victorious Iulus:
"Go on, my boy, in this your youthful valour. This is the way to heaven,
O son of gods, and future sire of gods. 'Tis meet and right that under
the race of Assaracus all wars destined to come in the future should
subside in peace; nor can Troy contain you." As thus he spake he drops
from the lofty sky, he parts the blowing breeze, and flies straight to
Ascanius. Then he transforms his appearance into that of old Butes.
He had first been armourbearer to Dardanian Anchises, and trusty
guard at his palace-gate; next did Ascanius' father give him as an
attendant to his son. Apollo seemed to come in all things like the old
man, in voice, and complexion, in gray hair, in arms that sounded fierce;
and thus he speaks to Iulus glowing with glory: "Content yourself with
this, son of Æneas, that by your arrow Numanus has fallen, and you
unhurt; the great Apollo grants you this as your first glory, and envies
you not a weapon like his own; for the rest, while yet a boy, abstain from
war." Apollo thus had begun his speech, and then cut short his words,
and left mortal eyes, and far away from human sight melted into thin
air. The Dardan chieftains knew the god, and his heavenly arrows,
and heard the quiver rattle as he fled. So, warned by the words and presence of Phœbus, they make Ascanius quit the walls, though eager for
the fight; they themselves return back to the conflict, and expose their
lives to the danger of the open battle. The shouts pass along the whole
walls by the line of the bulwarks; they bend their strong bows, and
whirl their slings. The whole ground is strewn with darts; the shields
and hollow helms re-echo with the blows; the fierce fight thickens; so
thick the rain coming from the west in the season of the showery
Kids lashes the ground; with such a storm of hail the clouds precipi-
tate themselves into the sea, when Jove all grim with winds whirls the
watery tempest, and bursts the hollow clouds in the sky.

672—690. *Pandarus and Bitias open a gate of the camp, and sallying
forth repulse the besiegers.*

Pandarus and Bitias the sons of Alcanor of Ida, whom Hiæra reared
amidst the forest in the grove of Jove, youths as tall as the firs and
hills of their country, unbar the gate trusted to them by the command of
their leader; for they rely on their arms, and dare to invite the foe within the walls. They themselves within on the right hand and on the left
stand in front of the towers, armed with iron, and their tall heads
adorned with waving plumes: like as when two lofty oaks by the clear
flowing streams, either on the bank of the Po, or by the side of the
pleasant Athesis, rise together, and raise their shaggy tops to the sky,
and nod with their towering crown. In burst the Rutulians, as soon as

they saw the entrance wide open. Straightway Quercens, and Equicolus in beautiful armour, and Tmarus rash of soul, and martial Hæmon, throughout the whole line were either routed and fled, or lost their lives just at the threshold of the gate. Then fiercer and fiercer waxes the rage in their embittered hearts; and soon the Trojans come in force to the same point, and venture to engage in close fight, and sally forth further.

691—716. *Turnus comes to the rescue and slays Bitias and other Trojans.*

To the leader Turnus, as he raged in the opposite quarter, throwing the ranks in confusion, news came that the enemy glowed with fresh slaughter, and held the gates open. He abandons his enterprise; roused by savage wrath he rushes to the Dardan gate against the haughty brothers. And first by the dart which he threw he laid Antiphates low, for Antiphates first came in his course; of Theban mother was the youth, the bastard son of noble Sarpedon; forth flies the Italian cornel through the yielding air, and fixed in his heart pierces deep into his breast; the gaping bloody wound sends forth a foaming stream, and the iron point is warmed in his transfixed lungs. Then Meropes and Erymas, then Aphidnus with his hand he lays low, then Bitias of glowing look and furious soul; but not with a common dart; he would not have fallen by a common dart; but whizzing loudly came the swung falaric, whirled like the thunderbolt; it neither two ox-hides nor the trusty coat of mail with its double golden scales could withstand; suddenly down fell his monstrous limbs; the earth gives a groan, and the huge shield thunders over him. So on the Euboic shore of Baiæ may fall a pile of stone, which men lay in the sea, built of mighty masses prepared before; so does it come down and draw its ruin with it, and dashed deep into the sea there it lies; the main is filled with tumult, and the black sand dashed up. Then with the sound trembles steep Prochyta, and Inaryme placed by Jove's behest no soft coverlet on Typhœus.

717—777. *Pandarus shuts the gate and encloses Turnus within the camp, who slays Pandarus and many others.*

Hereupon Mars, god of war, put new spirit and strength into the Latins, and roused keen courage within their souls; but on the Trojans he sent flight and black fear. From every side the assailants flock, for now was given means of fight in abundance, and the warrior god lighted on each soul. Pandarus sees his brother lying with outstretched body; he knows the present state of their fortune, how the turn of war now swayed events. He swings the gate with great strength, turning it on its hinges with an effort of his broad shoulders, and leaves many of his friends shut outside the walls in the stern fight; whilst others he shuts in with himself, and receives them as in they rush; fool! for he saw not the Rutulian prince in the midst of the troop bursting in; and by his own act he shut him in the town, like a savage tiger amongst the spiritless sheep. Forthwith a strange light gleamed from the warrior's eyes, and his arms rattled dreadfully; his blood-red crests quiver upon his head, and from his shield he shoots forth glittering flashes. The men of Æneas, suddenly affrighted, knew well the hated face and giant limbs. But mighty Pandarus springs forward, and burning with rage at his brother's death, speaks thus: "This is not the bridal palace of Amata, nor is this the centre of Ardea which within the walls of your country encloses you: the camp of your foes you see; there is no power of exit hence." To him with a smile spake Turnus with untroubled soul: "Begin, if in your heart be any courage, and close with me in fight; you shall go and tell Priam how here too you have found an Achilles." So spake he. The other strove with all his strength, and hurled his spear all unfashioned with its knots and rough bark. The air received the blow; Saturnian Juno turned aside the wound it should have made, as on it flew; in the gate is fixed the spear. "But not so my weapon shall you escape, which my right hand wields with strength; unlike to you is he who owns this sword, and deals this wound." He spoke, and rose, as high he lifts his sword, and with the steel cleaves the centre of the forehead between the temples, cutting the giant face with hideous gash. A crash is heard; the earth is shaken with the monstrous weight. The dying man stretches upon the ground his fallen limbs, and armour spattered with the bloody brain; in equal parts his head is shared and hangs from either shoulder. The Trojans turn, and scattered fly in hurried panic; and had the conqueror forthwith thought but this, that with his hand the barriers he should burst, and let his comrades in through the gates, that day had been the last to the war and the nation alike. But rage, and frenzied thirst of blood, drove him burning onwards right against the foe. First Phalaris he overtook; then Gyges hamstrung from behind; their spears he snatches up, and hurls them at the backs of the flying herd; Juno supplies strength and vigour to the chief. To these he adds Halys as companion in death, and Phegeus with his shield transfixed; then ignorant on the walls, and stirring fight, Alcander he slays and Halius, Noëmon and Prytanis. Lynceus went to meet him, and called his comrades, whom Turnus from the right with brandished sword and effort from the rampart anticipates; at once his head, struck down in conflict close by single blow, lay at a distance with his helmet. Next did he slay Amycus, who cleared the woods of game, unrivalled in his happy skill of anointing his arrows and arming their points with poison; and Clytus he slew, the son of Æolus, and Cretheus the Muses' friend, Cretheus the Muses' mate, to whose heart dear were songs ever, and harps, and harmonies attuned upon the strings; ever of steeds, and arms, of men and battles, did he sing.

778—818. *At length Mnestheus and the Trojans drive Turnus to the walls, from which he springs, like Cocles, into the river, and swims back safe to his companions.*

At length the Trojan captains, for they heard of the slaughter of their men, join together, even Mnestheus and Sergestus keen in fight, and see their comrades straggling in flight, and the enemy within the walls. And Mnestheus said: "Whither next, or whither do you mean to fly? Have you any other walls, any other battlements, besides these? Shall one single man, and he, my countrymen, hemmed in on every side by your ramparts, shall he make such havoc through your town, and feel no vengeance? Shall he send so many of the best of our youths to the shades of death? For your unhappy country, and your ancient gods, for the great Æneas have you no pity, feel ye no shame, ye cowards?" By such reproaches are they fired with wrath, and rally, and in close battalion halt.

Turnus little by little withdraws from the fight, making for the river, and the quarter girt by its waters. Thereupon the Trojans with greater spirit press on him; they shout aloud, they mass their bands; as when a crowd of men press hard upon a savage lion with weapons pointed at him, the beast terrified, yet grim, glaring fiercely, steps backwards; and neither does rage and courage suffer him to turn in flight, nor can he, though he desire it ever so much, press forward through darts and hunters. Just so did Turnus hesitate and retire, yet with steps deliberate, whilst his soul boils with rage. Nay even then twice did he pierce to the heart of the foe, twice did he drive their troops in rout and flight along their walls. But the whole band quickly from the camp unite, nor does Saturnian Juno dare to supply him with strength to fight against them; for Jove had sent Iris down through the sky from heaven, and she bore no gentle orders to his sister, should Turnus refuse to withdraw from the lofty walls of the Trojans. So then the warrior could not stand up against them with shield or sword; with such a shower of darts cast upon him on every side is he o'erwhelmed. With ceaseless rattling rings around his hollow temples his helmet, and with stones is riven its solid brass; the plume is struck away from his casque; nor can the bossy shield bear up against the blows; with spears the attack is redoubled by Trojans and by Mnestheus the captain, thundering in arms. Then throughout his whole body the sweat pours, and courses down in clammy stream; to recover his breath he has no power; a painful panting shakes his wearied frame. So then at last with headlong spring he throws himself with all his armour into the river. The god with his yellow flood received him as he came, and bore him off on his gentle ripple, and at length sent him back to his comrades with the blood washed off.

BOOK X.

1—15. *The council of the gods. Jupiter wonders at the angry passions of the celestials.*

MEANWHILE the mansion of Olympus the abode of the Almighty is opened wide, and a council is summoned by the father of gods and king of men to his starry throne; whence as he sits aloft he gazes on all lands, on the Dardan camp, and Latin tribes. They take their seats in the halls with folding doors. The king himself thus begins:

"Ye mighty Powers of heaven, why, I pray, is your old resolve turned backward? why is there such strife in your contentious hearts? I forbade Italy and the Trojans to clash in arms. What is this discord in disobedience to my commands? What fear has persuaded either side to take up arms, and provoke the strife of the sword? The right hour of war will arrive; see that ye hurry it not on; when fierce Carthage in days to come shall hurl on the citadel of Rome a mighty destruction, and open a way through the barrier of the Alps. Then will it be lawful to contend in the strife of hate, then to speed the course of war. Now let matters be quiet, and consent to ratify the peace we have agreed upon."

16—61. *Venus at great length inveighs against Juno, as the cause of so many troubles to the Trojans.*

In few words spake Jove ; but few were not the words in which golden Venus replied :

"O Father, thou eternal potentate of heaven and earth, (what other Power can I now find from whom to implore aid ?) thou seest the insults of the Rutulians, and how Turnus rides conspicuous in his chariot through the midst of the host, and is borne along in victorious war, swollen with pride. Their closed walls protect the Trojans no longer. Nay, within their gates, and on the very ramparts of their walls, they now mingle in fight ; and the trenches are floating in a deluge of blood. Æneas knows this not ; he is far away. What? wilt thou never permit them to be delivered from blockade ? Lo! a second time the walls of Troy, as it is born again, a foe threatens : a second host appears, and a second time against the children of Teucer rises from Ætolian Arpi the son of Tydeus. So I suppose that fresh wounds are in store for me, and I, thy child, have to expect the attack of a mortal man. If indeed without thy leave, and against thy heavenly will, the Trojans made Italy their aim, then let them atone for their sins, and see thou aidest them not with thy help. But if they did but follow the guidance of many an oracle, which Powers above and Powers below did give, who now can turn back thy will? who can found a new-made destiny? why need I remind thee how on the shore of Eryx their fleet was burned? or repeat the tale of the king of storms, and the raging winds stirred from Æolia's isle? or how that Iris was driven with a message through the clouds ? Now too she stirs up hell (this portion of the universe had as yet not been tried), and Alecto suddenly let loose on the upper air has raged like a bacchant through the midst of the towns of Italy. Touching empire I am no longer moved with hope ; that hope I once had, whilst fortune favoured. Now let theirs be the victory, whom thou wouldest have victorious. If there be no country which thy cruel wife will allow to the Trojans, I implore thee, father, by the smoking ruins of destroyed Ilium, may I be allowed to send Ascanius safe far away from this war, at least may the grandson be spared. Let Æneas indeed be tossed over strange seas, and follow the paths through which fortune leads him : but this my grandson may I save, and steal him from the fell fight. Amathus is mine, and lofty Paphos, and high Cythera ; I have a home at Idalia : let him lay aside his arms ; there let him pass his days inglorious. Bid Carthage lord it over Italy with mighty sway ; nothing from him and his children will thwart the Tyrian towns. Ah! what good to escape from the bane of war, and to have fled through the midst of Grecian fires? what good to have passed through so many dangers by sea, and o'er the wide land, while the Teucri search for Latium, and a new-created Pergamus? 'Twere better to have settled amidst the last ashes of their country, on the soil where Troy was once, and is no more. I pray thee, give the wretched back their Xanthus and Simois ; and grant, O father, to the sons of Teucer again to pass through the mishaps of Troy."

62—95. *Juno in her answer retorts the charge on Venus as the real cause of all these calamities to the race she favours.*

Then royal Juno inflamed with mighty wrath did thus reply :

"Why dost thou force me to break my deep silence, and divulge by words my hidden indignation? What god or man compelled Æneas to court war, or thrust himself as an enemy on king Latinus? Thou sayest, he sailed to Italy under the authority of Fate; nay say rather, he was driven by the ravings of Cassandra. Did I advise him to leave his camp, and trust his life to the winds? the fortune of the war and his walls to a child? Did I bid him seek a Tyrrhenian alliance and disturb peaceful nations? What god or what cruel power of mine drove him into this mischief? Where is Juno here? where in all this is Iris sent down from the clouds? It is hard, I suppose, if Italians surround with flames Troy at its birth, if Turnus settles in his native land, a prince whose grandsire is Pilumnus, whose mother is the goddess Venilia: what then? is it not rather hard that Trojans should attack Latins with the dark firebrands of war? plough with yoked oxen lands that are another's? carry off thence booty? What? is it right that they should choose alliances of marriage, steal betrothed maidens from their parents' bosom, plead for peace with branches in their hand, but put up arms on their vessels? Thou canst withdraw Æneas from the hands of the Greeks, and for a man offer a mist and empty air; thou canst transform ships into as many Nymphs: but that I should give any help on the other hand to the Rutulians, is an abomination. Æneas is ignorant and away; well, let him be ignorant and away. Thou sayest, 'I have Paphos and Idalium, I have lofty Cythera.' Why then dost thou meddle with a city big with the throes of war? why tempt rough souls of men? Was it I, as thou sayest, who endeavoured utterly to overthrow the tottering empire of Phrygia? What, I? or rather one who threw the wretched Trojans in the way of the Greeks? What was the reason why Europe and Asia rose to arms, and broke the covenant of peace by an act of robbery? Was I the leader who shewed a Dardan adulterer how to force his way into Sparta? or did I furnish the weapons, or kindle war through lust? Those were the days when thou shouldest have feared for thy beloved: now when it is too late thou risest against me in an unjust quarrel, and in bootless bickering bandiest words."

96—117. Jupiter declares that the Fates must not be interfered with. He confirms his declaration by an oath and a nod.

Thus pleaded Juno; and at once all the denizens of heaven murmured assent to either side. As when rising blasts bluster confined within the woods, and roll along their indistinct sounds betokening to mariners coming gales. Then the almighty Father, whose is the supreme power over the world, begins his speech. As he spake the lofty home of the gods is silent; earth trembles from her foundation; hushed is the lofty firmament; then the zephyrs lull themselves to rest; the deep smoothes its surface into calm. "Listen then," says he, "and let these my words sink into your souls. Since it is not permitted that the Italians should unite in compact with the Trojans; since your strife admits no end: whate'er to each is his fortune to-day, whate'er hope he opens out for himself, be he Trojan, be he Rutulian, difference none will I put between them; whether it be through fate that the camp is now blockaded by the besieging Italians, or through Troy's hapless mistaking, and ill-omened oracles. Nor do I absolve the Rutulians. Each man's own attempt shall bring its toil and issue. Jupiter is a king that rules indifferently for all. The Fates will find their way." By the waters of his Stygian brother, by the banks of the river of pitchy torrent fire with dark rapids, the Father nods in confirmation, and with his nod makes all Olympus quake. Thus ended parley. Then from his throne of gold Jove rises. Him in their centre the denizens of heaven attend to his palace.

118—145. *Again the Rutulians attack the Trojan camp.*

Meanwhile the Rutulians press around at every gate, eager to slay and kill the warriors, and to gird the walls with flames. But the legion of Æneas' men is hemmed in within their rampart closely blockaded; there is no hope of escape. The wretched men stand on their tall towers helpless, and line the walls with a thin circle. Asius the son of Imbrasus, and Thymœtes son of Hicetaon, and the two Assaraci, and Thymbris now advanced in years, with Castor, these formed the front line. Whom follow the two twin sons of Sarpedon, Clarus and Hæmon, who came from the hills of Lycia. Acmon of Lyrnessus striving with all his strength bears a huge stone, it seemed no small fragment of a mountain; Acmon was as great as his father Clytius and his brother Mnestheus. Some with darts and some with stones, they are eager to defend the town, or they prepare fire, and fit the arrow to the string. In the very centre stood he, who with reason was Venus' dearest care, lo! he was there, the Dardan boy; bare is his comely head, he glitters like a jewel set in yellow gold, to grace the neck or head; or like as ivory shines, when enchased by skill of man's device in box or ebony of Oricus; his locks fall profuse upon his milk-white neck, where a circle of ductile gold fastens them beneath. You too, Ismarus, the spirited clans beheld, as you shot arrows that dealt wounds, and tipped their reeds with poison; of noble birth were you, from a Lydian home; where rich are the fields, for the husbandmen till them, and Pactolus irrigates them with its streams of gold. There too stood Mnestheus; he had repulsed Turnus from the rampart of the walls, and the glory of the deed raises him aloft in fame; Capys too was there; from him Capua derives its name.

146—162. *Meanwhile Æneas sails over the sea with Pallas and his Etrurian allies.*

Thus they with one another engaged in hard warfare; Æneas in midnight was sailing o'er the seas. For when from Evander's town he has entered the Tuscan camp, straight to the king he goes; he tells the king his name and race; what he wants, what he can offer in return; what arms Mezentius is uniting, how violent is Turnus' will; he warns him, how little faith can be put in the chances of life; he mingles prayers with warnings. Quickly resolves Tarcho, and unites his forces, and makes a covenant with him; then, for free by fate they were to embark, the race of Lydia's stock embark, as Heaven willed; and trust a foreign leader. So Æneas' ship leads the van; beneath the beak was seen a chariot yoked with Phrygian lions; above seemed Ida hanging, a welcome sight to the exiles of Troy. Here sits the great Æneas, in his heart he revolves the chances and changes of war; ever close by his left sits Pallas: sometimes he asks about the stars, and the course of shady night; anon of what the chief had borne by land and sea.

163—165. *The invocation of the Muses.*

Ye goddesses, now open Helicon for me, and wake your song, telling what bands meanwhile accompanied Æneas from the Tuscan shores, arming their ships, borne along the main.

166—214. *The Etruscan captains and their troops. Description of the towns. The sorrow of Cygnus for Phaëthon. The population of Mantua.*

Massicus in front cuts the seas in his brazen Tiger; he led a band of a thousand youths, who left the walls of Clusium, and the city Cosæ; their weapons arrows, on their shoulders are light quivers, and death-dealing bows. With them is Abas stern in mien; his whole troop glittered with glorious arms; and the stern of his ship shone with the gilded image of Apollo. Six hundred youths tried in war had his native Populonia given him; whilst Ilva sent three hundred, Ilva an island rich in unexhausted mines of the Chalybes. Third came Asylas, interpreter was he of Heaven's will to man, obedient to him were the fibres of the victims, and the stars of the firmament, and the cries of birds, and the presaging fires of the thunderbolt. A thousand warriors he hurries onward in thick array with bristling spears. These are bid to follow him from Pisæ, Pisæ a town Alphean in origin, but built on Tuscan soil. Next Astur follows, the fairest chief of all the host, Astur proud of his steed and many-coloured arms. Three hundred swell the ranks, one spirit to follow Astur was in all, they whose home is Cære, who dwell in the fields of Minio, and the men of old Pyrgi, and unhealthy Graviscæ.

Nor would I pass you by, leader of the Ligurians, right valiant in war, Cinyras; nor you, Cupavo, though attended by few, from whose helm rises the plumage of a swan: love was the crime of your house, your device was your father's changed form. For they tell how that Cygnus through grief for his beloved Phaëthon, whilst he sings amidst the leafy poplars and the shade of the trees once his sisters, and whilst he beguiles his sad love by song, gradually received the white locks of old age with soft plumage, and left the earth, and rose upwards to the skies, singing as he rose. His son follows in his fleet the bands of warriors his equals in age, and propels the huge Centaur with oars; the monstrous figure-head threatens the waters, and high above the waves menaces the sea with a vast rock, and cuts the deep main with its long keel.

Another too rouses a troop from his native land, Ocnus was his name, the son of the prophetess Manto, and of the Tuscan river, who gave to you, Mantua, walls and his mother's name; Mantua rich in ancestors; yet not all of one race; there were three races there; in each race four peoples; of all these was Mantua the head; her strength was drawn from Tuscan blood. Hence too did Mezentius arm five hundred warriors against himself, whom their ship carried to the attack; the figure-head was the river Mincius, child of Benacus; he, garlanded with gray sedge, led them o'er seas in ship of battle.

Then comes Aulestes in heavy vessel; with a hundred oars that rise the waves are lashed; the waters foam, as their surface is upturned. Him bears the monstrous Triton; it is as though with his shell he terrified the azure seas; the shaggy front that he shews, as he swims, is that of a man as far as the waist, the belly ends in a fish; the foaming billow gurgles beneath the monstrous breast. So many chosen chieftains sailed in thirty ships to aid the cause of Troy, and cleft the briny plains with keels of bronze.

215—257. *The Sea-Nymphs, into which the ships of Æneas have been transformed, appear to Æneas out at sea, tell him the state of affairs, encouraging him with the hope of a great victory.*

And now had day yielded its rule o'er the sky, and the kindly goddess of light was traversing the middle of Olympus in her nightly-wandering car: Æneas, for anxious thoughts denied his limbs repose, sitting directs with his own hands the helm, and attends to the sails. And there behold! in the middle of his course the band of those who were once as his comrades meets the chief, those Nymphs, whom the kindly goddess Cybele had commanded to be deities in the sea, once ships, now Nereids; in a line they were seen swimming to his ship, breasting the waves, as many Nymphs now, as once on the shore had stood brazen prows. They know their former king from afar, and surround the ship, as with the circles of a dance. One of all there was, who seemed the readiest speaker, Cymodocea by name; behind she follows, and with her right hand holds the stern; the goddess rises above the water with her back, with her left hand as with an oar she glides along the placid waves. Then thus she addresses the wondering prince: "Do you watch, Æneas, king of heavenly race? Yes, watch, and slacken the bands of the sails. We are the pines of Ida cut from its holy crown, now rather the Nymphs of the sea, once your fleet. As the faithless Rutulian pressed us hard with fire and sword, your moorings we broke, and yet we fain had stayed; now o'er the sea we seek you. The mother of the gods in pity gave us this new form, and granted that we should be as goddesses, spending our lives beneath the waves. But know, that the boy Ascanius is penned within wall and trench in the very midst of darts, and the Latins bristling with martial spears. By this time the Arcadian horse united with the brave Tuscans hold their appointed ground. To oppose his centre troop to them, lest they should join with those in the camp, is Turnus' fixed resolve. Haste then, and with the rising dawn be the first to bid your comrades be called to arms, and take your shield; that which the lord of fire himself gave you, your invincible shield, whose edge he surrounded with gold. To-morrow's light, if you will not count my words as idle, will behold mighty heaps of slaughtered Rutulians." She spake, and, as she left, with her right hand she pushed the tall ship; she knew the way. Through the waters flies the ship, swifter than dart or arrow that rivals winds in speed. Amazed at the mystery is the Trojan prince, the son of Anchises; yet he comforts his heart by the happy omen. Then briefly prays looking up to the vault of heaven: "Kindly mother of the gods, thou queen of Ida, to whom Dindyma is dear, who lovest towered cities, and lions yoked in pairs to thy bits; be thou now our champion for the fight, and duly verify this omen, and favour, lady, thy own Phrygians with propitious advent." This and no more he prayed; and then meanwhile day returned in its orb, and hastened onward with full light, and chased away the darkness.

258—286. The prince comes in sight of his own camp. The besieged raise a shout. Turnus is still undaunted. He hastens to oppose the enemy as they land.

He first proclaims to his comrades to follow their standards, and have their spirits ready for action, and prepare for battle. And now he sights the Trojans, and his own camp, as he stands on the tall poop; when at that instant he lifts his blazing shield with his left hand. The sons of Dardanus raise a shout from the walls to heaven. New hope inflames their rage. They hurl a shower of darts. As when beneath the dark clouds the cranes of Strymon utter forth a boding voice, and stem the air of heaven, screaming as they fly before the south winds with happy cries. But to the Rutulian king and the Italian captains strange did seem that shout; till looking round they see the sterns turned towards the shore, and the whole sea as though it were flowing forward with the fleet. The crest of the prince's helmet blazes, and a flame seems to pour forth from the plume at its top, and the golden boss vomits forth mighty fires: like as when sometimes on a clear night blood-red comets blush with baleful light, or as is the blaze of Sirius, who rises bringing drought and disease to suffering men, and saddens the sky with ill-omened gleam.

Yet for all that daring Turnus lost not heart, eager first to gain the shore, and drive back from the land the coming foe. He waited not, but raised their souls by his words, he is the first to upbraid his friends. "You have what you prayed and wished for, the power to break through the foe sword in hand. On yourselves, my men, depends the war. Now let each remember his wife and home; now let each recall the glorious acts of his sires, their deeds of worth. Let us not wait, but rush to meet them at the breakers, whilst yet confused, and just landing, they stagger in their first steps. Fortune favours the daring." So he says, turning in his mind whom he might lead to the charge against the enemy, to whom trust the siege of the blockaded walls.

287—307. The landing of the fleet. Tarcho's ship is broken.

Meanwhile Æneas lands his comrades on gangways from the tall sterns. Many wait for the retiring of the spent wave, and jumping forward commit their bodies to the shoals; others land by means of oars. Tarcho surveys the shore, looking where the water does not surge, and the breakers do not roar, but the sea without dashing glides inward with the rising billows; thither he suddenly turns his prow, and adjures his comrades: "Now, ye chosen band, ply your stalwart oars, lift along your ships, bear them on, cleave with your beaks this unfriendly land, let the keel for itself cut deep its own furrow. Nor do I grudge to break my ship at such an anchorage, if I do but once gain the land." As soon as Tarcho had said this, his comrades rose to their oars, driving their ships amidst the foam on the Latin shore; until their beaks are on dry land, and all the keels settle unhurt. Yet not your ship, Tarcho, for dashed upon the shoals and hanging on a fatal ridge, doubtfully it balanced there long, struggling with the waves; then broke, and cast its crew into the midst of the water; the shattered pieces of oars and floating planks get entangled with the crew, and the retreating wave at the same time draws back their feet.

308—361.   *The battle on the shore.   Æneas' success gives an omen of the result.   But the Italians resist bravely.*

No sluggish loitering detains Turnus ; vigorous he hurries his whole line to meet the Trojans, and marshals it against them along the shore. The trumpets sound the notes of battle. The first to charge the rustic troops was Æneas ; this gave the omen of the issue ; he routed the Latin band, and slew Thero, the tallest of their company, who rushing forward made for Æneas ; the prince with the sword gashes his exposed side, piercing through the breastplate of brass, and the tunic rough with gold. Next he strikes Lichas ripped from his dead mother's womb, and, so, sacred to thee, Phœbus, in gratitude for this, that he had escaped the danger of the steel, when yet an infant. Soon after this he levelled in death hardy Cisseus, and giant Gyas, who were laying low the ranks with their clubs ; nought booted them Herculean arms and stalwart hands, or their father Melampus, though he had been Alcides' friend, so long as the earth supplied to the hero toilsome labours. Pharus was shouting with idle boast ; behold ! the chieftain hurls his spear and fixes it in the throat of the brawling braggart. You too, unhappy Cydon, while you pursue Clytius, whose cheeks are downy with the earliest auburn hair, your latest delight, had well-nigh fallen piteously, laid low by the hand of the Dardan chief ; then had you forgot your many loves ; but the serried band of brothers the sons of Phorcus met the prince ; seven were they, seven lances they hurl ; whereof some bound back from his helm or shield idly, some his good mother turned aside, and they but grazed his body. He to his trusty Achates says : " Hand me the weapons, be sure my right hand will not hurl e'en one in vain ; these are the darts that once pierced the bodies of Greeks on the field of Troy." So said, and seized his mighty spear, and hurls it. It flies, and strikes through the brazen shield of Mæon, tearing open breastplate and breast. His brother Alcanor comes to his help, and supports his falling brother with his hand ; still onwards flies the lance that sped, it transfixes his arm, and stained with blood still keeps its forward course ; the right arm of the dying man hangs from his shoulder by the tendons. Then Numitor, snatching the lance from his brother's body, aimed it at Æneas ; to pierce him, where he stood against him, was not granted ; the spear grazes the body of great Achates. Here Clausus of Cures, reliant on his strength and bloom of youth, comes up, and from afar smites Dryopes with tough lance that heavily was thrust, just under the chin ; he would have spoken, but at that moment both voice and life are gone, as his throat is pierced right through ; he with forehead strikes the ground ; from his mouth spurts the clotted gore. Three Thracians too, whose line traced back to the god Boreas, and three whom their father Idas and their fatherland Ismara sent, the Sabine captain slays amid the changing fortunes of the fight. Up runs Halesus, and Aurunca's troop ; comes to the help Neptune's son, Messapus, he conspicuous with his car. They strive to push back their foes ; now struggle these, now those ; at Italy's very threshold rages the conflict. As when in the vast sky contending winds raise their strife, equal is their fury, equal their strength; they will not yield to each other; the clouds, the sea, sway not either way; doubtful is the contest long; the winds continue struggling; all nature is in opposition. Even so did the Trojan and Tuscan lines meet; close is foot to foot, and man to man.

362—438. *In another part of the battle Pallas distinguishes himself. Lausus also fights bravely. The Fates did not permit that these two should engage.*

But in another quarter of the field, where the torrent had driven stones rolling to a great distance and shrubs torn from the banks, Pallas saw his Arcadians, untrained to attack on foot, fly before the pursuing Latins; the rough ground had perchance persuaded them to let their horses go; their leader, it was his last resource in distress, with prayers, then with bitter reproaches, excites their courage: "Oh! whither do ye fly, my comrades? by your doughty deeds, by the name of your chief Evander, by the victories you have won, by my own hopes, which have now succeeded to emulate my father's fame, I adjure you, rely not on swiftness of foot. By the sword must you break your way through the foe. There, where the thickest mass of men presses you hard, thither our noble country expects you and Pallas to go. It is not the power of any gods that distresses us sore; a mortal foe attacks, and we are mortals; we have as many lives, as many hands as they. Lo! the deep shuts us in with a mighty barrier of sea; there is no more land left for flight: is it the sea we shall make for, or the camp of Troy?" So he speaks, and in the centre charges the thick array of enemy; first meets him Lagus; his ill-starred fate brought the man; as he plucks up a stone of huge weight, Pallas pierces him with his hurled weapon, just where down the centre of his back the spine divides the ribs; he receives the spear fixed deep in his bones. Hisbo coming upon Pallas is too late, though he had hoped to be beforehand, for as he rushes on raging, reckless through the cruel death of his comrade, Pallas waits his attack, and buries his sword in his swelling lungs. Next he attacks Sthenelus and Anchemolus of the ancient race Rhœtus, who dared to pollute his step-mother's chamber. You too, Larides and Thymber, twin sons of Daucus, fell in the Rutulian fields, children just like each other; their own parents could not distinguish them, very pleasant it was to mistake them; but now a cruel distinction Pallas made; for Evander's sword struck off your head, Thymber; your right hand, Larides, lopped off seems to seek you, its master, whilst the fingers quiver with the remains of life, and clutch at the sword. The Arcadians were inflamed by his exhortation; now they gaze at the glorious deeds of the hero: mingled feelings of anger and shame arm them against the foe. Then Pallas transfixes Rhœteus as he was flying by in his chariot. Just so much as this was it that stopped the death of Iulus; for it was at Iulus that Pallas aimed his stout spear from afar; but Rhœteus in the midst flying from you, good Teuthras and your brother Tyres, intercepts the blow, and rolling from his chariot he strikes the Rutulian fields with his heels in the agony of death. As when wished-for winds having suddenly risen in summer, a shepherd fires the forest with flames that soon spread; the heart of the wood suddenly catches, and then extends at once o'er the broad plain the flickering flaming sword of Vulcan ; the shepherd sits on high gazing down on the conflagration in triumph : like this, all the courage of his comrades unites together, and helps you, Pallas. But Halesus keen in war advances straight against them, and draws himself within cover of his arms. He slays Ladon, Pheres, and Demodocus ; with his glittering sword he lops off the hand of Strymonius raised to his neck ; with a rock he strikes the face of Thoas, and scatters his bones mingled with bloody brains. His father warning him of fate to come had hidden Halesus in the forest ; but when the old man's aged eyes were relaxed in death, then the Fates laid their hands on the youth, and doomed him to fall by the weapons of Evander. At whom Pallas aims his spear, having first thus prayed : " Grant now, father Tiber, to the lance that I poise and hurl, a successful passage through the breast of the warrior Halesus. Thy oak shall hold these arms, the spoils taken from the man." The god heard his prayer ; whilst Halesus protects Imaon, the unhappy man exposes his undefended side to the Arcadian dart. But Lausus, himself a great part of the strength of the war, suffers not the troops to be daunted by the dread death of the hero ; and first he slays Abas who was opposed to him, Abas who was the pith and stay of the fight. The Arcadian men of war are laid low ; low are the Tuscans laid ; and ye Trojans too, lives that had escaped from the Greeks. So the ranks meet in battle with strength and captains fairly matched. The rear close up the line ; so thick the throng, they will not let weapons or hands move. On one side Pallas presses eagerly forward ; on the other side Lausus ; well-nigh equals in age were they ; both passing fair in form ; but yet fortune denied them return home. The lord of high Olympus would not however allow them to engage each with the other ; their own fates await them, for either soon to fall beneath a greater foe.

439—509. *Turnus attacks Pallas, who prays to Hercules. The god looks on with unavailing sorrow, but is reminded by his father Jupiter of the common lot of mortality. Turnus kills Pallas, but restores his body to his companions.*

Meanwhile his kindly goddess-sister warns Turnus to come to Lausus' aid ; Turnus in his swift chariot cuts through the midst of the line. When he saw his comrades ; " It is time," quoth he, " for you to desist from fight ; alone do I go against Pallas ; to me alone is Pallas due ; would that his parent were here to behold the fight." So he speaks ; his comrades give place from the appointed ground. But as the Rutulians withdraw, the youth thereupon wondering at his proud commands stares amazed at Turnus, o'er that giant form he rolls his eyes, scanning all afar with stern countenance. And with these words he meets the words of the monarch : "Soon shall I be glorious for having won the noblest spoils, or for a glorious death. My father is prepared for either issue. A truce to threats." He spoke, and advances into the centre of the ground. The blood of the Arcadians is chilled and stiffens within their hearts. Down from his chariot sprang Turnus ; on foot he prepares to go to fight hand to hand. Even like a lion, when from a commanding height he sees a bull standing far off in the plain, essaying the fight, then he bounds forward; like his was the look of Turnus, as he came. When Pallas believed that he was within reach of a cast of his spear, he would try his chance first, if perchance fortune would aid his venture, though with strength ill-matched; and thus he speaks, looking up to the high heaven: " By the hospitality my father once shewed thee, by the table, where thou a stranger didst sit, I pray thee, Alcides, help my great attempt; let Turnus behold me rob him in the moment of death of his blood-stained arms, and let his glazing eyes endure me as conqueror." Alcides heard the voice of the youth; deep was the groan he stifled within his heart, and he poured forth unavailing tears. Then the Father of the gods addresses his son with loving words : "To each man comes his appointed day; short and irreparable is the span of the life of all; but to enlarge the bounds of fame by valiant feats, that is virtue's work. Beneath the tall towers of Troy how many of the sons of the gods fell! yea, there fell too Sarpedon, my own child. Even Turnus his own fates now summon, and he has reached the goal of his allotted life." So speaks the Father, and turns his eyes away from the Rutulian fields. But Pallas hurls his spear with mighty strength, and snatches his flashing sword from his hollow scabbard. The spear flying, where the top of the protecting armour rises on the shoulders, lights in its course, and forcing its way through the rim of the shield, at length too grazed the great body of Turnus. Then Turnus brandishes for a long time his oaken spear, tipped with sharp steel, and thus he speaks: "See, whether my weapon be not more piercing." So he spake; the spear's point with quivering blow strikes through the centre of the shield, through all the plates of iron and brass, though so many times the folds of hide were cast round; it pierces the barrier of the breastplate, it passes into his strong chest. He in vain snatches at the reeking dart to tear it from his wound; by one and the same passage both blood and life follow. He falls upon the wound; his armour clashes over him; dying he bites the hostile land with bloody teeth. Turnus stood o'er him, then says : "Arcadians, remember to carry back my words to Evander; such as he deserves, Pallas I restore. Whate'er is the honour of a tomb, whate'er the solace in a burial, that I freely give. Dear will cost him his hospitality to Æneas." And as he so spake, he bestrode with his left foot the lifeless corpse, spoiling him of the belt of heavy weight with tale of horrible crime thereon inlaid; in one wedding-night a band of youths foully murdered, and bridal chambers dabbled with blood; a scene that Clonus the son of Eurytus had emboss-ed with much gold: in which, as his booty, Turnus now exults, and is glad to have won it. The heart of man knows not its coming fate and fortune, nor how to keep the bounds of moderation, when tempted to pride by prosperity. The time will come to Turnus, when gladly would he purchase at a great price never to have touched Pallas, and when he shall hate these spoils and the day he won them. But with many groans and tears his comrades crowding round bear Pallas back laid on his shield. Alas! to your parent you are to return, a source of great grief, and great glory. This was your first day at the war, this your last and fatal one: and yet you leave on the field great heaps of Rutulians slain.

510—605. *Æneas hearing of the death of Pallas makes a great slaughter of the enemy. The besieged Trojans and Iulus at last burst from the camp.*

And now it is no longer the mere rumour of a great misfortune, but a surer messenger that hurries to Æneas; he tells him his friends are at the very edge of ruin: 'tis high time, he says, that he hasten to the aid of the routed Trojans. With his sword he reaps down all the nearest ranks, and through the troops makes with his steel a broad path in his fury. Pallas, Evander, the whole scene is present to his eyes; the hospitable board, the first to which he as a stranger came, and the right hand of friendship then proffered. Then he takes alive four sons of Sulmo, as many of Ufens, to offer them as victims to the shades of his friend Pallas, and to pour over the flames of the funeral pile the blood of these captives. Then at Magus from afar he hurled the spear that he aimed; Magus warily runs under it; the quivering lance flies o'er the coward, who clasping his knees speaks thus in supplication: "By thy father's manes, by the hopeful promise of Iulus rising to man's estate, I pray you, spare my life for son and sire alike. I have a high-built house, therein lie safely stored talents of embossed silver; I have massy ingots of gold wrought and unwrought: on such a poor life as this the victory of Troy does not depend; nor can one such life make so great a difference." He spoke; Æneas answers thus: "As to the many talents of silver and gold you tell me of, keep them for your children. Such trafficking in war as you would have, Turnus was the first to close, even then when he slew Pallas. So feels my father's spirit, so feels Iulus." He spoke, and with his left hand holds the helmet of the suppliant, then bends his neck backward, and to the hilt drives in the sword. Not far from thence was Hæmon's son, priest of Phœbus and Trivia; the ribbons of the holy fillet adorned his temples; all his body glittered with his spangled robe and glorious armour: Æneas met this priest, and drove him before him; the Trojan bestrode the fallen man, and with the dreadful shades of death envelopes him; the arms spoiled from his body Sergestus carries back, a trophy to thee, great lord of war. Then Cæculus of Vulcan's race, and Umbro who came from the Marsian hills, reinforce the ranks. The Dardan chief rages against them. With his sword he smote off Anxur's hand, and the steel struck down the whole orb of his shield; Anxur had uttered some vaunting boast, believing that there was force in his words, and perchance lifted his proud soul to heaven, promising to himself gray hairs, and a length of years. Tarquitus springs forth to meet him in glittering arms, Tarquitus whom the Nymph Dryope bore to Faunus of the woods; he threw himself in the way of the raging chief. The prince drew back his spear, and with it pierces and holds his breastplate, and huge heavy shield; then as he pleaded in vain, and had many a prayer ready, he strikes his head to the ground; and, spurning the warm body, standing above, so speaks from his pitiless heart: "There now lie, you dreaded chief. No good mother shall bury you, nor cover your limbs in the sepulchre of your fathers; you shall be left to be the prey of wild birds; or the wave shall toss you sunk within its eddies, and hungry fish suck your wounds." Straightway he pursues Antæus and Lucas, warriors who fought in Turnus' van, and valiant Numa, and yellow-haired Camers, the son of noble-minded Volscens, the richest in land of all the Italians, once king in silent Amyclæ. Ægæon was such as this, of whom they tell that he had a hundred arms, and a hundred hands, fifty mouths and fifty chests, from which flames blazed, in the day when he fought against the thunderbolts of Jove with fifty clanging shields, and fifty drawn swords: even so Æneas raged victor o'er the whole plain, so soon as his sword's point tasted warm blood. Lo! next against Niphæus' four-horse chariot the hero goes, and met him face to face; the steeds, when from afar they saw the chief stalking along, raging dreadfully, turned in terror, and rushing back throw their driver out, and hurry the car off to the shore. Meanwhile Lucagus drives into the midst of the host in his chariot drawn by two white steeds; with him was his brother Liger; Liger wheels his steeds, turning them with the reins; Lucagus fiercely brandishes in circles his drawn sword. Æneas brooked not to see them rage with such fury; on he rushes, and shews himself in his great strength with his spear pointed at them. To whom Liger thus spake: "You see not here the steeds of Diomede, or the chariot of Achilles, nor the plains of Troy; here now in this land an end shall be put to the war, and to your life." Such words fly abroad uttered by Liger in his senseless vaunts; words in reply the hero of Troy is not careful to prepare; but hurls his lance against the enemy. Lucagus hangs forward as though in act to lash, and with his weapon's point urges his steeds; his left foot is stretched forward, he prepares for the fight; then a spear passes through the lowest rim of his shining shield, and pierces his left groin; knocked out of his chariot he rolls in the agony of death on the plain. Him the pious Æneas addresses with bitter words of scorn: "Lucagus, you cannot say the sloth of your steeds betrays your chariot, or that idle shadows makes them fly from the enemy; of your own choice you spring from your chariot and abandon your pair of steeds." So he spake, and seized the horses. The unhappy brother, falling from the same chariot, stretched forth his unarmed hands: "I intreat you, Trojan hero, by your own life, by your parents who bore you such a son, spare my life, and have mercy on my prayers." He would have added more; but the chieftain said: "Your tone is altered soon. So die. A brother should not from a brother part." Then with his sword he lays open his breast, where dwelt within his life. Such slaughter o'er the field the Dardan chieftain wrought, raging like the torrent of a stream, or a black tempest. At length burst forth, leaving their camp, the boy Ascanius, and the warriors in vain besieged.

606—632. *Juno obtains permission from Jupiter to rescue Turnus from death.*

Meanwhile Jupiter first addresses Juno: "O thou at once my sister, and my loving wife, 'tis forsooth as thou didst suppose, Venus alone (for surely thy judgment cannot err) sustains the hopes of Troy; these Trojans indeed have no hands vigorous in war, no martial courage forsooth, or endurance in dangers." To whom Juno submissively replies: "Why, fairest spouse, vex me sick at heart, dreading thy words severe? If my love had that power which it once had, and which it ought to have, thou wouldst not surely deny me this boon, almighty Jove, nor grudge my withdrawing Turnus from the fight, and keeping him safe for his father Daunus. Now then let him die, and lose his pious life for the Trojans' sake. And yet he has his name traced from the race of heaven, and Pilumnus is his ancestor in the fourth generation back; and oft with bounteous hand and many a gift he has enriched thy temples." To whom the king of ethereal Olympus briefly replies : " If what thou implorest for the youth doomed to early death is a respite from instant fate, and a span of life, and so thou interpretest my decree, rescue Turnus by flight, save him from imminent death. So far indulgence has a place. But if some deeper meaning is concealed beneath thy prayers for pity, if thou supposest the whole war can be altered or changed, idle are the hopes thou cherishest." Juno replied, bursting into tears : " And yet perhaps what thy words deny, thy purpose yet may grant ; perhaps life may remain ensured to Turnus. Not so; now a sad end awaits the youth, which he deserves not; or else I have no true forebodings. But rather, still, oh ! may I be the sport of idle fears ; and mayest thou, who hast the power, have the will to turn thy purpose to a better issue."

633—688. *The goddess deceives Turnus with the wraith of Æneas, which flying into a ship is followed by Turnus. He is carried out to sea, not without grievous complaints of the disgrace he involuntarily suffers, and is borne by the waves and winds to Ardea.*

She spoke, and forthwith from the lofty sky descended swift, girt with a tempestuous cloud, driving a storm before her through the air ; and flew straight for the Trojan lines and Laurentian camp. Then the goddess out of a hollow cloud fashions a thin phantom void of strength, a strange form of wondrous shape ; to make it like Æneas, she adorned it with the Dardan arms ; in it she imitates the shield and plumed helmet of the head of the hero chief ; gives it spectral words, a voice without thought, and shapes it with the gait of the prince as he walks in life : such are the flitting figures which they tell us appear of men after death, such are the dreams that delude our senses in deep sleep. But see ! the phantom joyously exults in the front of the line of battle, and with brandished weapons challenges the chief, and provokes him with taunts. Turnus rushes to the attack, and from afar hurls his whizzing lance ; the image turns its back and flies. But when the prince fancied that Æneas turned and yielded, excited with a bewilderment of joy he drank draughts of idle hope : "Whither do you fly, Æneas?" quoth he ; "forsake not, I pray, your betrothed bride. This hand will give you the land you sought with trouble o'er the waves." With shouts like these he follows, and brandishes his drawn sword ; he sees not that the winds bear his fancied joys. By chance a ship stood there, joined to a ledge of a lofty rock with planks stretching out, and a gangway ready laid ; in that ship was king Osinius borne from the shores of Clusium. Thither hurries the flying phantom of Æneas, and hastens to this hiding-place ; Turnus is as swift to pursue, and delays not an instant, and bounds o'er the high raised bridge. Hardly had he set foot on the prow, when Juno breaks the rope, and bears the ship quickly o'er the billows rolling back. Æneas meantime calls for the absent foe, daring him to fight ; and many of his troops he meets, and sends them down to the shades of death. Then the airy wraith no longer seeks a hiding-place, but flies aloft and fades into a dark cloud ; meanwhile the whirling tide bears Turnus far out to sea.

He looks back, he knows not what this means, he is ungrateful for a life saved, and raises his folded hands and lifts his voice to the sky: "Almighty Father, couldst thou think me worthy to be disgraced by such a crime, and could it be thy will that I should suffer such a dreadful punishment? Whither am I carried? Whence am I come? How shall I escape back? or with what character shall I return? Shall I ever again behold the Laurentian walls and camp? What will become of that valiant band of men, who followed me and my cause, and all of whom (oh, shameful crime!) I have left behind in the jaws of cruel death? E'en now I can see them struggling o'er the field, I hear the groans of the dying. What am I to do? What earth will yawn deep enough to swallow me? Nay rather do ye, O winds, pity me, on rocks, on crags (with all my heart I Turnus implore you,) dash the ship, or drive it into the cruel quicksands, where no Rutulians, no fame that I can feel, may ever follow me." So speaking, in his heart he fluctuates hither and thither; doubting, whether maddened by such a dire disgrace he should bury the sword's point and drive its keen edge through his ribs, or throw himself into the midst of the waves, and swimming make for the winding shore, and again return to fight the Trojans. Thrice either way he tried; thrice Juno's power restrained him, and pitied the youth's sorrow and checked his purpose. On glides the ship, cleaving the deep sea with waves and tide driving it on; and he is borne along to the ancient city of his father Daunus.

689—754. *Mezentius takes the place of Turnus. He slays many of the enemy.*

Meanwhile by Jove's warning fiery Mezentius reinforces the warriors, and attacks the Trojans in the hour of their triumph. Him meets the Tuscan line, with hatred all combined against one single man, on one their shower of darts they hurl. He stood firm, like a rock, which jutting into the vast deep, exposed to the fury of the winds, breasting the main, bears the collected force and threats of sky and sea, itself unmoved enduring; low on the ground he lays Hebrus the son of Dolichaon, and Latagus with him, and Palmus who was flying; Latagus he anticipates, striking his mouth and face in front with a stone, the huge fragment of a mountain; the craven Palmus hamstrung he leaves rolling on the ground; and gives the armour to Lausus to wear on his shoulders, the crested helmet to adorn his head. Next he slays Evanthes the Phrygian, and Mimas born at the same hour as Paris, afterwards his comrade; for on one and the same night Theano bore him to his father Amycus, and the queen the daughter of Cisseus pregnant with a torch bore Paris: Paris lies dead in his native land; the Laurentian soil holds Mimas unknown to fame. And like a wild boar driven from the high hills by biting hounds, whom pine-clad Vesulus has defended for many years, for many years his lair has been the Laurentian marsh; there has he fattened on the thick reeds; when he is among the toils, he stands at bay, and rages fiercely, and raises his bristles on his back; not a man has the courage to shew anger or approach nearer; but they attack with darts thrown from afar, and shouts in which there is no risk; whilst the undaunted beast turns deliberately on every side, gnashing with his teeth, and shaking the spears from his back. Just so, though righteous is their anger against Mezentius, yet there is not a man of them who dares to meet him close with drawn sword; with darts from afar, and noisy shouts they provoke him. From the land of old Cortona came Acron; he was a man of Greece; an exile he fled ere his marriage was finished; Mezentius saw him afar throwing into confusion the centre line, as he shone brightly with his crest, and the purple robe woven by his betrothed. Like a hungry lion often roams round the pen defended by high walls, for maddening famine tempts him, if perchance he perceives a rapid running roe, or a stag butting with tall horns, he rejoices gaping frightfully, and raises his mane, and remains stooping o'er his booty's entrails; foul gore bathes his greedy maw. So fiercely rushes spirited Mezentius against the thickest of the foe. Unhappy Acron is laid low, and strikes the dark ground with his heels as he dies, besmearing with gore the broken weapon. Orodes was flying; but he did not deign to slay a flying man, nor to inflict an unforeseen wound with the thrown spear: but meets him face to face, running up, and engages with him, man against man, stronger not by stealth, but in valiant arms. Then o'er the fallen warrior he trod with foot fixed and lance: "Orodes once so proud lies low," quoth he, "no contemptible portion of the war." His following comrades raise the shout of triumph. The dying man breathing out his spirit said: "Whoe'er you are, not long shall I be unavenged, nor shall you long exult in victory; you too like end awaits, and soon shall you lie on the same field." To him with smile, but smile of wrath, Mezentius replies: "Now die: about me the father of gods and king of men will surely see." He spoke, and from his body drew the point. Then iron sleep and rest not soft closed the eyes of the fallen man; their orbs are shut in everlasting night. Cædicus slays Alcathous, Sacrator kills Hydraspes; and Rapo ·Parthenius, and hardy stalwart Orses; Messapus slays Clonius and Ericetes son of Lycaon; the one as he lay on the ground, thrown by his ungovernable steed; the other on foot he on foot killed. Lycian Agis stepped forward; and yet Valerus, not without his part in his ancestor's valour, lays him low; then Salius conquers Thronius, himself to fall by Nealces, renowned for throwing the lance, and for shooting the arrow that surprises from afar.

755—790. *The fortunes of the battle are equal till Æneas wounds Mezentius.*

Now did cruel Mars divide equally the sorrows and mutual deaths on either side; by turns they slew, and by turns were slain, victors and vanquished alike in either host; for neither party knew what it was to fly. The gods in the palace of Jove pity the vain fury of both armies, and grieve there should be such woes to mortal men: Venus and Juno, Saturn's daughter, gaze, but with different hopes; the ghastly Fury rages in the midst of thousands. Then did Mezentius brandishing a huge spear stalk excited o'er the plain; as great as Orion, who, walking on foot through the deep waters of the very middle of the sea, making himself there a path, yet rises above the billows with his shoulders; or carrying down an ancient ash from the summit of the mountains, has his feet on the earth, his head shrouded by the clouds of heaven: such was the appearance of Mezentius, as he advanced with his giant arms. On the other side Æneas, having seen him from afar, prepares to go and

meet him. Undaunted remains Mezentius, awaiting his noble foe, standing massive in his might; then measuring with his eyes the space of his
spear's cast; "Now," said he, "may my own right hand, my true divinity,
and this my dart that I brandish propitious help me; I vow that you, my
Lausus, clad in the arms taken from the body of the pirate Æneas, shall
yourself be the trophy." He spake, and hurls from afar his whizzing
lance; it flies, then glances from the shield, and from afar pierces noble
Antores between his side and bowels; Antores was the comrade of Hercules; he came from Argos, then to Evander attached himself, and settled
in an Italian town: the unhappy man is laid low by a weapon meant for
another, and looks up to heaven, and as he dies remembers his beloved
Argos. Then pious Æneas hurls his spear; it passed through the hollow
round shield made of triple brass, through the linen folds, through the
woven workmanship of three bulls' hides; at last its point fixes in his
groin; further it carried not its force, now spent. Quickly from his thigh
Æneas, glad to see the blood of the Tuscan chief, draws his sword, and
eagerly presses on his confused foe.

791—832. *The valour of Lausus. He saves his father. He will not be
　　persuaded by Æneas to retire, and is slain by him. The Trojan pities
　　the youth, and spares his armour, and gives up his body.*

Lausus in his affection for his beloved father groaned deeply at the
sight; tears coursed down his cheeks. Here I, as far as in me lies, will
tell of the misfortune of your cruel fate, and of your noble deed, in hopes
that late posterity may not disbelieve so generous an exploit; nor will
I pass you by in silence, youth, who deserve to be made memorable. The
father, trailing his foot, helpless and hampered now withdrew, dragging
his enemy's lance fixed in his shield. The son burst forward, and
mingled in the fray; then as Æneas rose, lifting his hand to deal a
blow, he came under the sword's point, and sustaining the attack delayed the chief; his comrades follow shouting loud; whilst the father protected by the son's shield withdrew; and cast their darts, and with
missiles from afar keep off the foe. Æneas, chafing, covered by his shield,
stands at bay. Even as it happens if stormy clouds descend rattling
in a shower of hail, in every direction each ploughman and each husbandman flies at once from the fields; the traveller lies hid in safe screen, either
under the bank of a river, or the arching roof of a tall rock, whilst it rains
on the land; hoping that, when the sun is returned, they may employ
the day in industry: thus Æneas, on every side overwhelmed by darts,
sustains the whole storm of war, as it thunders on his head; meanwhile
upbraiding Lausus, menacing Lausus: "Whither do you rush to instant
death, and venture on attempts too great for your youthful strength?
Duty and love beguile you to forget." But none the less the youth
exults madly; and now higher rose the fierce wrath of the Dardan captain,
and the Fates spin the very last threads of the life of Lausus; for Æneas
drives his strong falchion through the body of the youth, burying it deep;
and the sword's point passed through the shield, the light armour of the
menacing youth, and through the coat which his mother had woven with
threads of ductile gold; the blood filled his bosom; then life sadly withdrew through the air to the shades below, and left his body. But when

Æneas saw the face and countenance of the dying prince, his face o'er-spread with strange paleness, he groaned deeply in pity, and stretched his hand forth, and the image of his own parental love touched his heart: What now to you, lamented boy, for this your honoured deed, what shall the pious Æneas give you worthy of such a noble soul? Keep your arms, in which you delighted; I restore you to the spirits and ashes of your fathers, if aught such rights avail. And yet this may comfort you in your sad death; you fall by the hand of the great Æneas. He is the first to chide his hesitating comrades, and raise the dead from the ground; the blood dabbled the locks that had been dressed with care.

833—908. Mezentius sees his dead son, and, though wounded severely, mounts his horse Rhœbus, and attacks the Trojan chief. The horse has sympathy for his master. Both horse and rider are slain by Æneas.

Meanwhile the father by the stream of the Tiber dried the wound with running water, and refreshed his body, reclining against the stem of a tree. At a little distance from the branch hangs his brazen helmet, and his heavy arms lie idle on the grass. Around stand his chosen warriors; he himself weak, short of breath, rests his drooping neck, with his long beard hanging down o'er his breast; many a question he asks about Lausus, many a messenger he sends back to recall his son, and bear the warnings of his sorrowing sire. But Lausus lifeless was borne on his shield by his weeping comrades; great warrior was he, conquered by a great wound. Far off a father's mind foreboding woe knew the meaning of their lamentations. He disfigures his grey hair with much dust, and stretches both his hands to the sky, and hangs o'er the corpse: "My son," said he, "could such a fond love of life detain me, that I should allow you, my child, in my place to sustain the attack of the enemy's hand? Am I your father saved by your wounds? do I live by your death? Alas, not till now did wretched I know the misery of exile; now is the wound driven deep. Yes, and I too, my son, dis-honoured your fair name by my crimes, banished as one hated from land and ancestral throne. I should have paid the penalty I owed to my country and the detestation of my subjects; to all forms of death I ought to have surrendered my guilty life. Now I live, and do not yet leave life and light; but leave them I will." As he speaks, he raises him-self on his weak thigh; and though the deep wound palsies his strength, yet with spirit unabated he bids his steed be led forth. This to him was glory and solace; on this his horse he had come forth victorious from every fight. He addresses the animal that seems to mourn, and thus begins: "Rhœbus, long (if aught be long in this our mortal life) you and I have lived. To-day you shall either bring back with me the bloody spoils, and head of Æneas, and avenge with me the sorrows of Lausus; or if no force can open out a way, with me you shall die. For you, my gallant steed, I believe, the commands of strangers and Trojan lords will not deign to obey." He spake, and was taken up on his back; there he placed his familiar limbs, and armed both his hands with sharp-pointed javelins; his brazen helmet glittered on his head, shaggy was its plume of horse's hair. So, swift he sped into the centre of the foe ; there surges in his heart great shame, and the madness of wrath, and sorrow mingled with it. Then he called on Æneas thrice with loud voice ; and Æneas knew the voice, and joyful prays : " So may the great Father of the gods, so may Apollo in heaven grant ; may you begin the fight." He spake no more, but met him face to face with attacking spear. To whom Mezentius : " Cruel foe, why do you try to frighten me, now you have robbed me of my son? That way alone could you destroy me. I fear not death; no god I hesitate to defy. Cease. See I am come, as one about to die. But first I bring you these gifts." He spake, and hurled his lance against the foe ; then in the shield fixes another, and then another dart, wheeling round in a great ring ; the golden boss sustains all the spears. Three times round Æneas, who stood firm, did he ride in circles to the left, throwing lances with his hand ; three times did the Trojan hero carry round with him a great wood of iron on his brazen buckler. At length, when weary of such long protracted delay, and of plucking from his shield so many darts, hard pressed in the engagement of an unequal fight, after many a thought he bursts forth, and hurls his spear between the hollow temples of the charger. The steed raises himself erect, and lashes the air with his heels, and encumbers his thrown rider, falling on him, and, tumbling headlong o'er his prostrate master, lies on his shoulder. Trojans and Latins alike make the welkin ring with fervent cries. Æneas flies forward, snatching his sword from its scabbard, and standing over him says : " Where is now the fiery Mezentius, and the fierce spirit of his soul?" In answer the Tuscan, as soon as looking up to the air he drew in the breezes of heaven, and recovered his senses, thus said : " Insulting foe, wherefore do you thus upbraid and threaten me with death? There is no guilt in slaying me ; this was not the condition on which I came to battle : these were not the terms of contest which my Lausus covenanted for me. I beg for one favour alone; if there is any mercy to be shown to a conquered foe, suffer my body to be covered in a grave. I know that bitter is the hatred of my countrymen that surrounds me ; I entreat you, protect my body from this wrath, and consign me to a grave which I may share with my son." He speaks, and offers his throat to the expected sword, and pours forth his soul in a deluge of blood that floods his arms.

BOOK XI.

*1—28. Æneas makes a trophy of the spoils of Mezentius. He gives
directions for the funeral of those slain in battle.*

MEANWHILE the Morn arose and left the ocean: Æneas, though his
sorrows urge him to give full time for the burial of his comrades, and his
soul is troubled by the death of his friend, yet, as conqueror, paid the
vows he owed the gods at the break of day.   He lopped the branches
from the stem of a great oak, and planted it on a mound, and clothed
it with glittering arms, the spoils taken from the captain Mezentius, a
trophy to thee, thou mighty lord of war.   Hereto he fastens the crests
that drip with blood, and the warrior's weapons broken short, and his
breastplate which the enemy's blows had pierced in twelve places; he
fastens the brazen shield to the left arm, and on the neck hangs the sword
with ivory hilt.   Then, as the whole company of captains throngs around
and closes him in, he thus begins to exhort his triumphing comrades:
The main work is done, my friends; away with all fear touching what
remains; see here are the spoils, here taken from the haughty king are
my first offerings; and what my hands have raised here, is all that is left
of Mezentius.   Now we must march to the king, and Latin walls.   In
your hearts be ready for arms, and let your hopes anticipate success in
war, that you be not ignorant, nor hindered by delay, as soon as the
gods show their will for us to pluck our standards from the ground, and
to lead our men forth from the camp; and that no thoughts, sluggish
through fear, slacken us.   Meanwhile let us consign to the earth the
unburied bodies of our comrades; this is the only respect we can pay to
those who are deep down by Acheron.   Go, says he, honour with the
last gifts those noble souls, who with their blood have purchased for us
this land for our country; and first of all let Pallas' body be sent to the
mourning city of Evander; he lacked not valour, when the dark day of
death carried him off, and sank him in an untimely end.

*29—58. The lamentations of the Trojans and Æneas over the dead
body of Pallas.*

Thus as he speaks he sheds tears, and walks back to the threshold,
where was laid out the lifeless body of Pallas, watched by Acetes now
advanced in years: in days of old he had been armourbearer to Arcadian Evander, but not so happy are the auspices with which he then
went as appointed guardian to his beloved foster-son.   Around were
standing all, the band of servants, and the Trojan throng, and the
daughters of Ilium with their sad hair dishevelled according to usage.
But when Æneas entered by the lofty doors, then loud are the lamentations they raise to the sky, as they beat their breasts, and the palace
resounds with their sorrowful mourning.   The prince himself as he beholds the head of Pallas propped up, and his countenance white like snow,
and the gaping wound made by Italian spear in his smooth breast, thus
speaks, as the tears gush forth: Lamented boy, ah! could fortune, coming
to me with smiles, yet envy me this, that you should not see my new realm,
nor ride victorious to your father's home?   Such were not the promises

that I gave your father touching you at my departure, as he embraced
me when I departed, and said he sent me to the hope of a mighty empire;
and yet in fear reminded me how warlike were the men, how that we
had to fight with a hardy race. And now he on his part, much beguiled
by idle hopes, perchance is making vows, and loading the altars with
gifts; we in sorrow attend with bootless rites a lifeless youth, who is no
longer in debt to any of the gods of heaven. Unhappy father, you will
see the bitter funeral of your son. Is this our return, is this our expected
triumph? Is this the way I keep my solemn promise? But yet, Evander,
you shall not look on your child smitten by shameful wounds, nor shall
you pray for a dreadful death after your son has survived his honour.
Alas me! how great a protection Italy loses, and you too, Iulus.

*59—99. The dead body of Pallas is sent with due honour and many
lamentations to his father Evander.*

He ended his tearful lamentation, and bids the piteous corpse be
raised, and sends a thousand men chosen from the whole troop, to assist at the last respect to the dead, and to be present at the father's tears;
a scanty comfort in a mighty sorrow, yet due to the wretched father.
With industry others weave wicker-work and a pliant bier made of the
twigs of arbutus, and pliant boughs of oak, and overshadow the raised
couch with a canopy of leaves. Here they lay the youth on the top of the
rustic litter: in beauty, like a flower cropt by a maiden's hand, either a
tender violet, or a bending hyacinth, from which as yet neither its bright
colours nor fair form is gone; but no more does its mother-earth cherish
it or supply it with vigour. Then Æneas brought forth two vests stiff
with gold and purple, which Sidonian Dido taking pleasure in her work
with her own hands had long ago wrought for him, and had separated
the threads with tissue of gold. With one of these the sorrowing prince
clothes the youth as with his last ornament; with the other as with a
wrapper he veils the hair that is to burn in the fire; many besides are
the prizes from the fight with the Laurentians which he heaps together,
ordering the spoil to be brought forth in long array. He gives beside the
steeds and arms whereof he had stripped the foe. He had pinioned too
the hands behind of those whom he meant to offer as victims to the ghost
of his friend, when he would sprinkle in the flame the blood of the slain;
and he bids the chieftains themselves bear the trunks clothed with the
arms of the enemy, and that they be marked with the names of the foe.
Unhappy Acetes is led along, worn by many a year; sometimes he wounds
his breast with his closed hand, then with his nails his face, then grovels
on the ground stretched at his full length. They lead too in procession
his chariot stained with Rutulian blood. Behind comes Æthon, his war-
horse stripped of his trappings; as he paces on, he weeps, and wets his
face with big drops. Others carry his spear and helmet, his other arms
the victor Turnus possesses. Then follow a sad phalanx, Trojans, and
all the Tyrrhenians together, and Arcadians with reversed arms. When
the whole line of attendants had passed in long procession, Æneas stopped, and with deep-drawn sigh added these words: "Us hence to fresh
tears the same horrid destiny of war summons. Hail to me for the last

time, mighty Pallas; for ever farewell." He said no more, but walked to
the lofty walls, and turned his steps to the camp.

100—138. Drances and others come from the Latin city to ask leave to
bury their slain. Æneas gives them a gracious reply. A truce of
twelve days. .

And now came ambassadors from the Latin town, they were veiled
with boughs of olive, they entreated his grace: would he deign to give
them back the bodies that lay stretched o'er the plains by the sword, and
allow them to rest beneath barrows of earth; there ought, said they, to be
no contest with men vanquished and bereaved of the air of heaven; he
should, said they, spare those whom he had once called hosts and kinsmen. Whom good Æneas honours with his grace, for they sued a boon
he could not grudge to give, and farther adds these words: "What fortune undeserved has involved you Latins in so sad a war, that you
should avoid our friendship? You ask of me peace for the lifeless, slain
by the chance of Mars: I would gladly grant it to the living too. I had
not hither come, unless the fates had granted me a home and abode;
nor do I wage war with the nation: your king abandoned my friendship,
and preferred to trust the arms of Turnus. It were fairer surely that
Turnus should face this death. If he is ready to finish the war with his
own hand, and to chase the Trojans hence, he should have engaged with
me with these weapons. Then let him live, to whom God or his own
right hand has given life." So spake Æneas. They stood as men amazed
in silence, and turning to each other, gazed and looked each on his
neighbour. Then Drances, old in years, whom youthful Turnus had
made his deadly foe by hate and accusation, thus in turn replies to what
the Trojan first had said: "O great in fame, but greater still in arms,
hero of Troy, by what praises shall I extol you to the skies? Shall I
admire you more for justice or for your exploits in war? We indeed will
gratefully bring this reply back to our native town, and will unite you to
king Latinus, if fortune shall show us any way thereto. Let Turnus seek
an alliance for himself. Nay, and it will be a pleasure to us to raise the
massive walls which the fates allow, and to carry on our shoulders the
stones for Trojan towers." He so spake, and all with one consent ap-
plauded in agreement. They covenanted for twelve days, and under the
protection of the truce Trojans and Latins mixed together wandered
through the forests on the hills without risk. The tall ash resounds to
the iron hatchet; they fell pines that towered to the sky; and continually
with wedges they cleave the heart of oak and the fragrant cedar, and
carry mountain-ashes on their creaking wagons.

139—181. The description of the grief of Evander. His sad speech o'er
his dead son.

And now winged Fame, the messenger that goes before great grief, fills
the ears of Evander, and the palace and city of Evander—that Fame,
which but lately bore the news of Pallas as victor in Latium. The Arcadians were seen to rush to the gates, and according to the old usage they
snatched up torches for the funeral; the road glitters with the long row of
flaming brands, and far and wide shows the fields distinct and clear. To
meet them come the crowd of Phrygians, and unite their lines, which

lament aloud. Now as soon as the matrons saw them enter the town, they fire the sorrowing city with their cries. But Evander no force can hold, he comes into the midst. When the bier was lowered, he threw himself on Pallas, there he clings weeping and groaning, and through excess of sorrow it was only hardly at last that a passage was freed for his voice : " Such were not the promises you gave, Pallas, to your parent, how that you would be more cautious in tempting cruel Mars. I knew full well the power of youthful glory in arms, and of honour only too sweet in the first field. O wretched essays of my boy, and cruel rudiments of a war too near at hand, and oh my vows and prayers heard by none of the gods, and you my stainless spouse, happy in your death, spared this sorrow. I on the other hand by living outlived my destiny, only to survive and be left a father when my son is gone. O that I had followed the arms of my allies the Trojans, and been o'erwhelmed by Rutulian darts! O that I myself had given up the ghost, and that this procession were bringing me, not Pallas, home! Yet would I not blame ye, Trojans, nor our treaties, or right hands united in hospitality; this lot is due to my old age. But if an untimely death did await my son, it will be a comfort to think he first slew thousands of Volscians, and fell leading the Trojans into Latium. Nay I myself would not wish to honour you with another funeral than that which pious Æneas, and the great Trojans, and the Etrurian captains and all the Etrurian host deign to give. Great are the trophies they bear taken from those whom we see your hand has slain. You too, Turnus, would now stand a mighty trunk clad in arms, had my son's age and strength of years been fairly matched with your's. But why does an unhappy father detain the Trojans from arms? Go then, and forget not my message to your lord. If I linger still in hated life, now that Pallas is gone, your right hand is to blame ; you see it owes Turnus to father and son alike. This is the only place open for your services and for fortune's gifts. The joys of life I reck not ; joy were a crime in me; but this I long for, to take my son the news down to the world below."

182—202. *The Trojans bury their dead.*

Meanwhile Aurora raised her kindly light for wretched men, bringing back their work and toil. Already father Æneas, already Tarcho had raised the pyres on the winding shore. Hither each man bore his kinsmen's bodies after the usage of their sires: they place beneath the funeral fires, and lofty heaven is hidden in darkness by the murky smoke. Thrice round the lighted piles they rode, clad in glittering arms; thrice on their horses they made the circuit of the sad funeral fires, and uttered loud laments. The earth is bedewed with tears, their arms are bedewed ; to the sky rises together the cry of men, and clang of trumpets. Next, others throw on the fire the spoils taken from slain Latins, helmets and ornamented swords, and bits, and wheels that glow with speed; others cast on the flames well-known emblems, their friends' own shields and unlucky weapons. Around, many huge oxen are sacrificed to Death ; and they cut the throats of bristly boars and cattle taken from all the fields around, and throw them into the fire. Then all along the shore they gaze at their comrades blazing in death, and keep the half burnt relics, nor can they tear themselves away, till dewy night turns round the vault of heaven now studded with the brilliant stars.

203—224. The Latins do the same. Turnus is condemned by some. By others he is still supported.

And no less too did the unhappy Latins raise in a different part of the plain innumerable pyres, many of the bodies of their countrymen they bury in the ground, many on the other hand they carry away and bear them to the neighbouring fields, and send them back to the city. The remainder, a vast heap of slaughtered men crowded together, they burn unhonoured and without a name; then on every side the dreary plains seem to vie with one another in gleaming with many a fire of death. The third morning had dispelled the damp shades from the heaven: sorrowing they raked together in heaps the ashes and confused mass of bones on the pyres, and covered them with a warm mound of earth. But further, within the houses, even in the city of wealthy Latinus, was heard especially the tumult of sorrow, and there was the greatest portion of the prolonged grief. Here it was that mothers and unhappy daughters, here that the loving hearts of sorrowing sisters, and orphan children execrate the accursed war and the nuptials of Turnus; they bid him in person with his own arms, his own sword, decide the contest, as he claimed for himself the realm of Italy and the first place of honour. Drances bitterly aggravates this, and solemnly declares that none but Turnus is invited, none but Turnus is challenged to decide the contest. At the same time many are the opinions, various the words in favour of Turnus, the great name of the queen shelters him; his own famous renown resting on well-earned trophies sustains the hero's claims.

225—242. The ambassadors that had been sent to Diomede return.

Amidst these passions of party, in the midst of the raging disturbance, lo, to increase their fears, sadly returning from the great city of Diomede, the ambassadors bring back their answers; they tell that fruitless was all their labour spent and great toil; bootless had been their gifts, their gold, their earnest prayers; either the Latins must find other help in arms, or must sue for peace from the Trojan prince. In the greatness of the sorrow King Latinus himself fails to give advice. That by the decree of the Fates, and by the manifest will of heaven, Æneas had been brought to Italy, they were warned by the wrath of the gods, and by the newly-raised tombs before their eyes. So then the king summons by imperial mandates within his lofty palace a great council, even the first men of his citizens. They meet together, and flock to the regal halls along the crowded streets. There sits in the centre he who was oldest in years and first in kingly power, but with no countenance of joy, Latinus. And here he bids the ambassadors, returned from the Ætolian city, tell the answers that they bring, and demands to hear all the replies, each in due order. Then were all tongues hushed, and Venulus in obedience to his word thus begins to speak.

243—295. They report the speech of Diomede in which he told of his own sufferings, of those of other Greeks, of the valour and piety of Æneas, and recommended them to make peace with the Trojans.

"We have seen with our eyes, O citizens, Diomede and the Argive camp, and having performed our journey, we passed safely through every risk, and we touched that hand by which fell the realm of Troy. He had been conqueror, and was founding in the fields of Iapygian Garganus the city Argyripa, named after his native people. When we are admitted, and liberty is granted to speak before him, we offer our gifts, we tell him our name and country, who had made war on us, what reason had drawn us to Arpi. Having heard us, he thus replies with calm words; 'O happy nations, realms of Saturn, ye ancient men of Ausonia, what fortune disturbs your rest, and persuades you to provoke such a war as you know not? As many of us as with the sword attacked the lands of sacred Ilium (I speak not of all the sufferings we endured while warring 'neath the lofty walls, nor of the heroes whom Simois of evil name overwhelmed,) have endured unutterable torments through all the world, and paid the full penalty of our guilt, a band whom even Priam might pity. This knows well the fatal storm Minerva sent, and the cliffs of Eubœa, and avenging Caphareus. From that warfare we have been driven to shores far apart; Menelaus, Atreus' son went an exile even to the columns of Proteus; Ulysses saw the Cyclops of Ætna. Need I mention the realm of Neoptolemus, and the ruined home of Idomeneus? or the Locri dwelling on the shores of Libya? The monarch of Mycenæ himself, the leader of the great Achæans, fell by the hand of his wicked wife; after Asia was conquered, there lay in ambush another combatant, the adulterer. Then to think that the gods could grudge my being restored to my country's altars and beholding my beloved wife and fair Calydon? Now too portents of horrible appearance pursue me, and my comrades lost to me have fled into the sky on wings, or wander along the streams transformed into birds, (alas! for the shocking punishments my companions suffer), and they fill the rocks with their wailing cries. Such punishments as these were to be looked for by me since the day that in my madness I attacked the persons of the gods, and with a wound outraged the hand of Venus. Do not indeed, do not urge me to such battles. I have no war with Trojans since the overthrow of Troy; nor do I remember with pleasure my old misfortunes. The gifts which you bring to me from your country, take to Æneas instead. We have stood and met each other's fierce darts, and have engaged in combat: believe one who knows from experience how great he rises to charge with his shield, with what swiftness as of a whirlwind he hurls his spear. Had the land of Ida borne two more such men, the Trojan unattacked had come against the cities of Inachus, and the fates had been changed, and Greece were in mourning. So far as there was delay at the walls of Troy that resisted so long, it was by Hector's and Æneas' hand that the victory of the Greeks was checked, and was protracted to the tenth year. Both were renowned for courage, both for excellence in arms; the latter was superior in piety. Let your right hands be united in treaty, as you may; but beware that arms do not clash with arms.' Thus, excellent prince, you have both heard at once the reply of the king, and what is his opinion touching the mighty war." Scarce had the ambassadors so said, when various was the murmur that ran along the confused assembly of the Ausonians; as when rocks delay rapid rivers, and a roaring rises from the imprisoned flood, the neighbouring

banks re-echo to the splashing waves. As soon as their feelings were
appeased, and the confused hum subsided, the king, having first invoked
the gods, begins from his lofty throne.

296—335. *King Latinus consults the assembly. He suggests that they
    should either offer the Trojans some land, or timber to build new
    ships.*

"I could have wished, Latins, and it had been better that you had determined before this the affairs of the state; and not at such a time to
collect a hurried assembly, when the enemy is sitting before the walls.
O citizens, we wage ill-omened war with the race of heaven, with men
unconquered, whom no battles exhaust, who e'en when conquered cannot
desist from the steel. As to any hope, if you had any in the alliance
of the arms of Ætolia, lay it aside. Each man must hope in himself
alone; how poor this hope is, you see. How great the ruin in which all
else lies smitten down and prostrate, is before your eyes, and in the
midst of you. Yet I blame no one. Our valour has been as great as it
could be; we have contended with the whole strength of our realm. So
then I will lay before you the judgment of my distracted mind, and briefly
will inform you; do you give me your attention. I have an ancient tract
of land lying along the Tuscan river, extending far towards the setting
sun, even beyond the borders of the Sicani; the Aurunci and Rutulians
sow there their grain, and with the share plough the stiff hills, or graze
their roughest ridges. Let all this district and the pine-clad region of the
lofty mountain be ceded to the Trojans to win their friendship; and let us
set forth equal terms in our truce, and invite them to share our realm;
let them settle down, if so great be their desire, and found their walls.
But if their mind be to obtain other territories, and go to another people,
and they can be content to depart from our soil, let us build them twice
ten ships of Italian heart of oak, or more if they can man them; all the
timber lies ready by the water; let them direct the number and size of
the ships; let us give brass, and hands to work, and docks. Further it is
my opinion that a hundred Latin orators of the noblest rank should go to
bear our offers, and ratify the treaty, bearing before them in their hands
olive-branches of peace, carrying as gifts talents of ivory and gold, and
the curule seat and state robe, emblems of our regal power. Consult
for the public weal, and come to the aid of our afflicted fortunes."

336—375. *The character of Drances. He speaks in favour of peace; he
    upbraids Turnus as the author of all their misfortunes.*

Then that same Drances, a bitter enemy of Turnus; for the glory of
the prince vexed him with envy half-concealed, and with malign feelings
goaded him; liberal with his wealth, and ready in tongue, but his hand
was slack in war; in counsel he passed for no vain adviser, powerful in
cabals; his mother's nobility gave him high descent, but doubtful was the
descent he derived from his father; this man rises, and inflames and
aggravates the general wrath with these words: "The subject is obscure
to none, it needs no words of mine, on which you consult us, excellent
king. All with one consent allow they know what the fortune of our
people demands; but they fear to speak openly. Let him give us liberty
of speech, and lower his blustering pride, on account of whose unlucky

auspices, and ill-omened obstinacy—I will speak, though he threatens me with arms and death—we see that so many glorious heroes have fallen, and that the whole city is sunk in sorrow, while he attacks the Trojan camp, and yet puts his trust in flight, and menaces heaven with arms. There is one gift still, which beside those you bid be sent and assigned to the Trojans, there is one, excellent king, which you should add; let no one's violence prevent you from giving your daughter to a noble son-in-law in no unworthy marriage, you who are her father, and ratify this peace for us by an eternal compact. But if so great terror possesses our minds and breasts, let us earnestly entreat him, and beg for his grace, that he would deign to yield and give up his own rights to the king and the country. Why do you so often expose your wretched citizens to evident perils, O you, who are the source and cause to Latium of our present troubles? There is no safety in war; peace we all beg of you, Turnus, we beg of you the only pledge of peace that cannot be violated. I first, I, whom you pretend am your enemy—and I can hardly deny I am—see I come as suppliant, pity your countrymen, lay aside your obstinacy, and as one beaten, give way. In our rout we have witnessed enough of death, and have seen the desolation of widely-extended lands. Or else, if your renown stirs you, if you can conceive such courage in your breast, if your heart is set on a kingdom for your dowry, venture, and boldly bear your breast to meet your foe. What forsooth, that to Turnus there may be a royal bride, are we, worthless souls, an unburied unlamented crowd, yes, are our bodies to be strewn o'er the plains? 'Tis time for you, if you have any vigour, if aught of your ancestral valour remain, to look him in the face, who challenges you to battle."

376—444. *Turnus in a fervid speech denies that he has been defeated, charges Drances with cowardice, appeals to their feelings of honour, professes his readiness to meet Æneas in single combat.*

At these words the fury of Turnus blazed forth; he groans, and bursts forth this answer from the depths of his heart: "You, Drances, I must allow, have a plenteous abundance of words, then when war demands hands; and when our senators are summoned, you are the first to come. But it is not the time to fill the council-house with words, which big and blustering fly from your mouth safely, so long as the rampart of our walls keeps our foe at bay, and the trenches do not yet swim with blood. Continue then to thunder with eloquence, after your usual fashion, and do you charge me with cowardice, yes, you, Drances, for your hand has strewn such heaps of slaughtered Trojans, and far and wide you adorn the fields with trophies. The power of vigorous valour you may easily try; and we have not truly far to go to look for foes; they are standing all round our walls. Let us rush to meet them! Why do you lag behind? Will your powers of fighting always be in your vain braggart tongue, and those feet of your's fleet to run away? Was I beaten? or who, you foul slanderer, could truly say I was beaten, who saw the Tiber swell and rise with Trojan blood, and all Evander's house fall with the hope of its stock, and the Arcadians stripped of arms? Not such did Bitias and huge Pandarus prove me, and the thousands whom I victorious sent to hell on the day when I was inclosed by the walls, and cooped in by

the enemy. No safety in war? Fool, go chant such words to the Dardan
man, and the side you have passed to. Then go on, and do not cease to
confound all with great terror, and thus to extol the power of a twice
conquered people; in the opposite scale to depress the arms of Latinus.
Now too the captains of the Myrmidons begin to tremble at the arms of
Phrygia, now too the son of Tydeus and Achilles of Larissa; and the
river Aufidus runs backward to his source from the waves of Adria. This
is as true as the wicked contriver pretending alarm at a quarrel with me,
and embittering the calumny by a feigned fear. Such a soul as your's
you shall never lose by my hand; cease to trouble yourself; let it dwell
with you, and remain in that breast of yours. Now I return to you,
father, and your great deliberations. If you place no further hope in our
arms, if we are so entirely forlorn, and because our troops have been once
defeated we are utterly fallen, and Fortune has no steps backward, let
us pray for peace, and hold out our helpless hands. And yet, in the
name of heaven, if there be any of our wonted valour, he seems to me
above others happy in his efforts and noble in soul, who, lest he should
see such a disgrace, has fallen in death, and once for all bitten the ground
with his teeth. But if we have still means, and a body of youth as yet
untouched by the sword, and there still remain to help us the cities and
nations of Italy; if to the Trojans too no bloodless glory has come—for
they too have their deaths, and the storm of war has passed alike o'er all,
—why, dishonoured, do our hearts fail us at the very threshold of war?
Why before the trumpet sounds does a quivering seize our limbs? Many
a thing has time and the changing sway of shifting ages altered for the
better; many men has Fortune in her alternations made sport of, and
then again placed on a solid footing. No help to us will be the Ætolian
and his Arpi; but Messapus will be, and fortunate Tolumnius, and all
the captains sent by many a tribe; nor small will be the glory that will
attend the picked men of Latium, and the Laurentian fields. There is
too Camilla of the noble nation of the Volsci, leading a troop of cavalry,
and bands arrayed in glossy brass. But should the Trojans summon me
alone to the combat, and that is settled, and I obstruct so much the common weal, Victory does not so hate or so avoid my hands, that I should
decline to venture aught for so glorious a hope. I will go and meet him
with spirit, though he should prove himself a second great Achilles, and
put on arms as good, wrought by Vulcan's hands. For you all and for
my father-in-law Latinus, I, Turnus, second to none of my forefathers in
valour, devote this soul. Æneas challenges me alone. I pray, he may
do so. And let not Drances rather than I, if here work the anger of the
gods, expiate it by death, or if it be a field of glory, bear off the palm."

445—531. *Meanwhile Æneas advances to the city. Then a tumult
arises. Preparations are made for fighting. A supplication of
matrons. Turnus full of spirit gives various orders. Camilla
offers with the cavalry to meet the enemy's horse. Turnus hastens to
occupy the passes of the hills.*

They thus in words contending discussed the crisis of their fortunes;
Æneas forwards moved his camp and line. So the news spreads through
the royal halls with a mighty tumult, and fills the city with great terror,

that the Trojans in full battle array and the Tuscan host were descending from the river Tiber over the whole plain. Straightway the minds of the people were confused, and their hearts disturbed, and their anger stirred with no gentle goads. In haste they call for arms for their hands; the youth shout for arms. The fathers sadly weep and mutter doubts. Hereupon on every side a mighty clamour with varied discordant cries rises to the skies. Just as when in a deep forest perchance there settle flocks of birds, or by the fishy river of Padusa the hoarse-throated swans scream along the noisy pools. "Nay," said Turnus, for he seized the occasion, "do ye, O citizens, summon a council, and sit and talk in praise of peace; let them in arms attack our realm." He spake no more, but hurried forth, and swiftly bore himself from the lofty hall. "Do you," said he, "Volusus, order the maniples of the Volsci under arms, and lead the Rutulians. Do you, Messapus, and Coras with your brother, bid the armed cavalry scour the whole plain. Let some strengthen the approaches to the city, and man the towers, let the remainder with me bear arms, whither I shall bid them." Immediately there is a rush to the walls from every quarter of the town. Latinus himself, his people's father, abandons the council and his weighty purposes, and confused by the sinister aspect of the times prorogues the meeting, often blaming himself for not having made advances to receive Dardan Æneas, and admit him as son-in-law in his city. Others dig trenches in front of the gates, or carry up stones and stakes. The hoarse-voiced trumpet brays the signal for war and blood. Then matrons and boys girded the walls with a varied ring; the last effort summons all. Further, to the temple-height of the citadel of Pallas the queen rides up the street attended by a great retinue of matrons; she bears gifts; near her attends the maiden Lavinia, the fair cause of all the evil, with beauteous downcast eyes. The matrons follow in procession, and fume the temple with incense, and pour forth their sorrowful prayers, standing at the threshold of the lofty building: "Lady of arms, queen of war, Tritonian maid, shiver the lance of the Phrygian pirate, and lay his body prone on the earth, and prostrate him before the lofty gates." Turnus himself with eager ardour arms himself for the battle. And anon he has donned his glittering coat of mail bristling with scales of brass, already are his legs enclosed with golden greaves, his temples are yet bare, his sword is girt to his side: he glitters in his golden harness, as he rushes down from the high citadel; he exults in his spirits, his hopes already reach his foe. As when a steed has broken his fastenings and escaped from his stall, at last he is free, he has won the open plain, so he runs either to the pastures and the herd of the mares, or, wont to bathe in the familiar running stream, he bounds forth, he neighs with head aloft, he prances in wanton liberty, whilst his mane plays o'er his neck and shoulders. Then comes forward to meet the chief, Camilla, attended by the Volscian line; close to the gate the queen sprang from her horse, the whole troop imitate her and in a moment vault to the ground from their steeds: she speaks thus: "Turnus, if the brave can justly on themselves rely, I dare and undertake to meet the cavalry of Æneas' men, and alone to go and engage the Tuscan squadron. Allow me with my hand to essay the foremost perils of the war ; do you on foot halt before the walls, and guard the battlements." Turnus replied to this, with his eyes fixed on the wondrous maid : "O glory of Italy, O maiden, what thanks shall I try to express, or how repay you? But now, since your soul is far above such returns, with me share the toil. Æneas, as report, and the scouts that we have sent bring back certain news, gives us no rest, but has sent forward the light-armed cavalry to shake the fields ; he himself, passing the height of the hill across the desert country o'er the ridge, is drawing near to the city : I prepare the stratagems of war in the hollow narrow path through the wood, that I may blockade the double pass with my armed troops. Do you await the attack of the Tuscan cavalry and engage with them in pitched battle ; with you shall be spirited Messapus, and the Latin troops, and the squadron of Tiburtus ; do you take on yourself the cares of a general." So he speaks, and with like words encourages Messapus and the allied captains to the fight, and goes straight against the foe. There is a valley with a winding gorge, formed for fraud, and the stratagems of war ; dark banks close it in on either side with steep descending woods ; hither leads a narrow path, and a strait pass, and a scanty approach bears the traveller on. Above this, on the cliffs and on the highest peak of the hill, there lies table-land little known, and a safe place of retreat, whether from the right or left you mean to rush to the fight, or to take your stand on the ridge, and roll down huge masses of rock. Hither the youthful warrior hastened along the familiar road, and seized the vantage-ground, and took up in the woods a post to thwart the foe.

532—596. *The story of the father of Camilla, Metabus, of the maiden's childhood, her education, her life in the woods, the dedication of herself to Diana. Diana predicts her death, and bids Opis avenge her and bring her body from the battle-field.*

Meanwhile Latona's daughter addressed swift Opis in the celestial abodes ; Opis was one of the virgins of her troop and heavenly band ; thus sadly did Diana speak : "Now to the cruel war Camilla goes, O virgin, in vain is she girt with my arms, though dear to me beyond all other daughters of the earth ; for this is no new fancy of Diana, nor is my heart touched with a sudden affection. Metabus was driven from his kingdom by his people's hatred and his own haughty violence, and as he departed from the ancient city of Privernum, he took with him, as he was flying through the very midst of the battle of war, his infant child, as the companion of his exile, and called her by her mother's name Casmilla, changing it a little into Camilla. He bore her in his bosom before him, and made for the distant ridges of the lonely woods. On every side cruel weapons pressed him hard, and around were hovering the Volsci with soldiers spread far and wide. So, to cut short his flight, Amasenus swollen foamed to the very top of its banks ; so great a storm of rain had burst from the clouds. ·He, preparing to swim, is delayed by his love for his infant child, and fears for the dear charge. As in his mind he turns over all thoughts, suddenly, though scarcely, he settles on this resolve : perchance in his hand the warrior bore a huge weapon, of solid knotty well-seasoned heart of oak ; to this he fastens his child bound with the bark of sylvan cork, and attaches her, a light burden, to the middle of the spear, which poising with his stalwart hand, he thus speaks looking up to the sky : 'Kindly goddess, thou that dwellest in the woods, virgin daughter of Latona, I myself her father vow this child here as a handmaiden to thee ; bearing through the air thy dart her earliest weapon, thy suppliant she flees from the foe.' Receive, I adjure thee, O goddess, thy servant, who is now trusted to the uncertain breezes." He spake, and drew his arm to his shoulder and hurls the lance ; the waters resounded ; over the swift river ill-fated Camilla flies attached to the whizzing spear. But Metabus—for the great troop now pressed him hard—trusts himself to the stream, and successful plucks from the grassy turf the spear with the child as a gift dedicated to Trivia. No towns received him beneath their roofs or within their walls ; nor would he in his wild life have complied with such an offer ; he spent a pastoral life upon the lonely hills. Here did he rear his child in the thickets and amidst the tangled lairs of the beasts, by the breast and with the milk not of a woman but of a mare of the herd, pressing the udder to feed her tender lips. And as soon as the child began to plant her steps on the soles of her infant feet, he armed her hands with a pointed lance, and hung bow and arrows from the shoulder of his little darling. Instead of gold on her hair, instead of the covering of the long robe, the skin of a tiger hangs from her head down her back. Even at that early age she hurled childish darts with her tender hand, and whirled round her head a sling with neatly fitted thong, and brought to the ground the Strymonian crane, or the white swan. Many were the matrons in the towns of the Tyrrhenians who in vain wished to have her for a daughter-in-law ; Diana contented her ; and, a maiden, she cherishes an unchanging love for her darts, and her virgin estate. And oh, that she had not been possessed with the desire of such a warfare, nor ventured to attack the Trojans ; she would now be my dear comrade, and one of my train. But come, since she is pressed hard by an untimely death, glide, Nymph, down from the sky, and visit the land of Latium, where the fatal fight is opened with inauspicious omens. Take these weapons, and draw from the quiver the avenging arrow ; whoever violates her holy form with a wound, be he Trojan, be he Italian, no matter which, by this arrow let him atone with his blood. Afterwards I in a hollow cloud will bear the body of the lamented maiden, and her arms not despoiled, to her tomb, and restore her to her country, there to rest." She spake ; and Opis lightly gliding through the air of heaven sounded in her flight, with her form surrounded by a dark storm-cloud.

597—647. The cavalry engagement. It remains doubtful at first. Many fall on either side.

Meanwhile the Trojan troop draws near the walls, and the Etrurian captains, and all the host of the cavalry, arranged according to their numbers into squadrons. Neighing over the whole plain prances the steed with trampling feet, and strives against the tightened reins, turning this way and that ; then far and wide the field bristles with spears, as though it were of iron, and the plains glitter with lifted arms. Then too Messapus to meet them, and the active Latins, and Coras with his brother, and the wing commanded by the maid Camilla, appear in the plain to face the foe, and point forward their spears, drawing their right hands far back, and brandish their darts ; and the riders draw near, and the neighing steeds glow with ardour. And now either side advance to within a spear's cast, then suddenly halt ; then raise a shout, and in a moment rush forward, and urge their maddened steeds ; at the same time on every side they pour forth darts as thick as snow, the sky is covered with shade. Forthwith Tyrrhenus and spirited Aconteus with effort charge each other with lances, and first of all fall with mighty crash, dashing together and shattering their steeds. breast against breast ; Aconteus was cast from his saddle, and like a thunderbolt, or heavy missile from an engine sent, is hurled to a distance, and scatters his life into the air. Straightway the lines are confused, and the Latins put to flight throw their shields behind their backs, and turn their horses to the walls. The Trojans drive them before them ; Asilas foremost leads the squadrons on. And now were they close to the gates, and again the Latins raise a shout, and turn their pliant necks ; then the others fly, and back are borne with reins quite slack. As when the sea rushes forward with alternating swell, at one moment it rolls to the land, and casts its wave o'er the rocks, and foams, and pours over the farthest sand with its covering surge ; then again rapid retires backward, and in its flow sucks the stones, and flies, leaving the shore with its retiring waters. Twice did the Tuscans drive the Rutulians turned towards the walls, twice, forced to yield, they look often behind them, protecting their backs with their shields. But when they met in their third charge, they mingled together all their ranks, and man singled man : and then were heard the groans of the dying, and in pools of blood are arms and bodies together, and mixed with the slaughtered men roll the horses between life and death ; a fierce fight arises. Orsilochus hurled his lance at the horse of Remulus, for he dreaded to approach the rider him-self, and left the iron point beneath its ear. The wound makes the prancing steed rage and rear, and impatient of the blow throw on high his feet, and lift its breast upright. His master rolls on the ground flung from his horse. Catillus lays Iolas low, and Hermitius, a man of mighty soul, of mighty frame and arms ; his head was bare, his auburn locks were seen, bare were his shoulders ; wounds have no terror for him ; huge he is, exposed to weapons. The spear quivers as it passes through his shoulder, and driven through him doubles the warrior with agony. On every side black blood pours forth ; as they strive with the sword they deal death, and aim at glorious ends the meed of wounds.

648—724. *The glorious exploits of the maiden warrior. She slays many. Her skill in riding. Her swiftness on foot, when she outstrips the horse of the lying Ligurian.*

But in the midst of the slaughter exults the Amazon, with one side bared to the fight, Camilla girt with a quiver ; and at one time she throws in quick succession the tough spears with her hand, then unwearied she seizes in her right hand a strong axe. Golden is the bow that rattles on her shoulder, she wears the arms of Diana. She too, if ever driven back she retires, shoots arrows in her flight, turning her bow to the foe. But around are her chosen comrades, both the maiden Larina, and Tulla, and Tarpeia, shaking her brazen hatchet, daughters of Italy, whom divine Camilla chose for herself, to be her glory, good handmaids both in peace and in war. As when in squadrons the Amazons of Thrace trample Thermodon's frozen stream, and war in painted arms, either around Hippolyte, or when martial Penthesilea returns in her chariot; amidst the cries of the mighty throng the female bands exult with their crescent shields. Whom first, whom last, fierce maiden, do you lay low with your dart? or how many bodies of dying men do you stretch on the ground? Eunæus first, his father was Clytius; whose open breast, as he faces her, she pierces with the long spear of fir-wood. He falls, vomiting streams of blood, and bites the gory ground, and in the act of death writhes with his wounds. Then she slays Liris and Pagasus; one of whom tumbles from his stabbed horse, and tries to collect his reins, the other comes to the help, and reaches forward his unarmed hand to support his falling friend; headlong they both fall alike. To these she adds Amaster, son of Hippotas; and pursues, pressing upon them with her lance hurled from afar, both Tereus and Harpalycus and Demophoon and Chromis: and as many darts as the virgin warrior threw with her hand, so many were the Trojan men that fell. At a distance the huntsman Ornytus clad in strange armour rides on an Apulian steed; the warrior's broad shoulders were covered by a hide taken from an ox; his helmet was the yawning mouth and jaws of a wolf with its white teeth; a rustic pike arms his hand; he himself turns everywhere in the midst of the troop, o'ertopping all by his whole head. Camilla transfixes him surprised; it was easy, when she had routed the whole troop; and then speaks thus with bitter soul: "You must have thought, Etruscan, you were hunting quarry in the woods; the day is come to refute your boasts by the arms of a woman. And yet you shall bear no light glory to the ghosts of your fathers, telling how you fell by Camilla's dart. Next straightway she attacked Orsilochus and Butes, two giants of the Trojans; Butes was turned away from her, she pierced him with her spear's point between his coat of mail and helmet, where, as he sat in his saddle, his neck was seen, and the shield was hanging from his left arm; then pretending to fly, and chased through an ample circle, she eludes Orsilochus, and gets within the ring, and pursues the pursuer; then she rises high in her saddle, and with redoubled blow drives her strong battle-axe through the armour and bones of the man; he entreated and prayed for mercy oft; the wound drenches his face with the hot bloody brain. The warrior son of Aunus who dwelled in the Apennines comes across her path, and at the sudden sight stood still as one alarmed; he was not least among the Ligurians, so long as fate allowed him to deceive; and he, when he plainly sees that by no fleetness he can escape the fight, or turn aside the queen who pressed him hard, began to contrive his fraud with policy and craft, and thus he says: "What so wonderful, a woman trusting in her gallant steed? Give up your flying horse, and venture to fight me hand to hand on fair

ground, and gird yourself for a battle on foot: soon will you know, to
whom shifting fortune will bring a mischief." He spake, and she, maddened and stung with the indignation of courage, hands her horse to her
attendant, and stands her ground in arms fairly matched, on foot with
drawn sword, undaunted with her unemblazoned shield. The young
man thought he had prevailed by craft, and off he flies, he lags not, he
is borne away in flight with his reins turned aside, and urges his swift
steed with his iron spur. "Foolish Ligurian, in vain elated by your
haughty soul, to no purpose have you tried the slippery tricks of your
country, nor shall your fraud carry you off safe to cheating Aunus." So
speaks the maid, and swift as fire upon her rapid feet she passes the
horse in speed, then meets him face to face, then seizes the reins, and
takes a punishment from the blood of her enemy: as easily as a hawk,
a sacred bird, flying from a high crag, overtakes on her wings a dove
high up in a cloud, and seizes it, and holds it, and tears it open with its
talons ; then blood and feathers rent from the dove fall from the sky.

725—835. *Tarcho upbraids his men for yielding to a woman. He restores
the fight. Then as Camilla pursues Chloreus, Arruns, having first
prayed to Apollo, wounds her. Arruns escapes by flight, Camilla dies,
with her last breath sending a message to Turnus.*

But with no careless eyes the Father of gods and men watches the fight,
as he sits aloft on the summit of Olympus. The Father stirs up Tarcho
the Etruscan to the fierce battle, and with no gentle spur inspires his
wrath. So midst the slaughtered men and yielding lines Tarcho is borne
on his steed, and encourages the squadrons with varied words, calling on
each by name, and cheers the beaten back to fight: "What fear, O Etruscans, ye who can ne'er be stung by shame, ever sluggish, what utter
cowardice possesses your souls? A woman scatters and drives you
before her, and turns these lines to flight. To what purpose wear ye iron,
or carry idle weapons in your hands? But no laggards are ye for love
and wars by night, or when the bent flute calls to the Bacchic dance, ye
are not slow to be ready for the feast, and for the cups on the loaded
table—such is your taste, such your passion—when the augur announces
the sacrifice propitious, and the well-fed victim invites you to the deep
groves." He spake, and spurs his steed into the throng, himself too prepared to die, and furiously charges full on Venulus; he pulls him from his
steed, and with his right hand grasps him round; and, carrying him before
him, bears him away at full speed with mighty strength. A shout is raised
heavenward, and all the Latins at once turn their eyes one way. O'er the
plain flies Tarcho, swift as fire, bearing with him the armed chieftain ;
then from the end of his own spear he breaks off the iron point, and feels
for an open place where to direct a deadly wound ; he on the other hand
resists and keeps from his throat the hand, and baffles strength by
strength. As when a tawny eagle flying on high bears off a serpent
it has seized, and fastens its feet to the prey, and clings to it with his
talons : but the wounded snake writhes its coiling folds, and bristles with
scales erect, and hisses with its tongue, raising itself on high ; the bird no
less plies it as it struggles with taloned beak, and at the same time lashes
the air with its wings : even so Tarcho in triumph bears his prey from the

Tiburtian line. Following the example and success of their chief, the Etrurians charge. Then Arruns doomed to death first circles swift Camilla with dart in hand, and with deep craft, and tries where fortune would come easiest. Wheresoever the impetuous maiden bears herself, through the midst of the line, there Arruns·stealthily follows, and silently tracks her course ; where she returns victorious, bringing back booty from the foe, there the young man cunningly turns his rapid reins. He essays first this approach, then that, and traverses every circuit, and persevering shakes his fatal spear. Perchance Chloreus, sacred to Cybele, once her priest, was glittering conspicuous from afar in Phrygian arms, urging his foaming horse, which a skin fastened with gold and feathery scales of brass defended. The rider, bright in foreign purple and Tyrian dye, shot his Cretan arrows from a Lycian bow ; golden was the bow that rattled from his shoulder, and golden was the helmet of the seer ; his saffron cloak and rustling linen folds he had bound in a knot of yellow gold ; embroidered with the needle was his tunic, and his barbaric greaves. The huntress maiden, either that she might hang the Trojan arms on the gate of the temple, or show herself decked in golden spoil, was blindly following him alone in all the contest of the battle, and heedlessly through the whole line she was inflamed with a woman's love of booty and plunder. Then at length Arruns seized his time, and from his ambush brandishes his dart, and thus addresses the heavenly Powers in prayer : "Highest of the gods to me, Apollo, guardian of holy Soracte, whom first we honour, for whom is fed the blaze of pines piled up, whose votaries we, passing through the fire in the strength of our piety, press the soles of our feet on many a burning coal, grant, almighty father, that by my arms may be abolished our dishonour. I beg not for any spoils nor trophy of the vanquished maid ; other exploits will give me glory. If this dread pest does but fall by the wound I inflict, I will return inglorious to my native town." Phœbus heard, and in his purpose gave success to half the vow, the other half he whistled down the wind ; he granted to his prayer to lay Camilla low, smitten by a sudden death ; he suffered not his mountain-home to see the chief return ; and the storms bore his words to the south winds. So, when the spear hurled from his hand whizzed through the air, all the Volscians at once turned their keen minds and eyes towards the queen. She heeded neither the rustling air nor whizzing lance, nor the weapon coming from the sky, until the spear, onwards borne, was fixed beneath her bare breast, and driven in, drank deeply of the maiden's blood. Her confused attendants rush together, and catch their falling queen. Before the rest flies off terrified Arruns with fear and mingled joy ; nor does he dare further to trust his spear, nor meet the maiden's weapons. As when oft a wolf having slain a shepherd or a great steer, conscious of his daring deed, straightway by a pathless journey betakes himself to the lofty mountains, before the hostile darts pursue, and lowering his tail he places it quivering beneath his belly, and makes for the woods ; thus Arruns in terror bore himself out of sight, and content to escape, mingled in the midst of the armed troop. She with dying hand draws the weapon forth ; but within her bones the iron point remains fixed to her side with a deep wound. Fainting she sinks ; her eyes sink in the coldness of death ;

her colour, once so bright, left her face. Then, as she breathes her last, she thus addresses Acca, one of her companions of equal age; Camilla trusted her alone out of all the rest to share with her her troubles, and thus she speaks: "Acca, my sister, so long has power been given me; now the cruel wound despatches me, and all around grows black with mist. Escape, and bear these my last words to Turnus; I bid him take my place in the fight, and keep the Trojans from the city. And now farewell." As she spake these words, she slowly forsook her reins, sinking to the ground unwillingly. Then, all cold, she freed herself little by little from her whole body, and bent her drooping neck and head oppressed by death, abandoning her arms: her soul with a groan flies disdainful beneath the shades. Then indeed mighty is the shout that rising strikes the golden stars; when Camilla falls the battle waxes fiercer still; thickly they charge in arms all the host of the Trojans together, and the Etrurian captains, and the Arcadian squadrons of Evander.

836—867. Opis, according to the injunctions of Diana, avenges the death of Camilla, and shoots Arruns with an arrow.

But Diana's watch, Opis, from the beginning was sitting on high upon the summit of the hills, and viewed the battle without fear. And when from afar in the midst of the shouts of the youths raging in the conflict, she saw Camilla visited by a sad death, she groaned, and uttered these words deep from her breast: "Alas, O maiden, too cruel is the punishment you have paid for essaying to attack the Trojans in war. Nor has it availed you that you honoured Diana in the woods, or that you wore on your shoulder our quiver. Yet your queen will not leave you dishonoured in the very hour of doom, nor shall this death be without fame throughout the nations, nor shall you have to bear the name of one who died unavenged. For whoever has violated your form with a wound, shall atone his guilt by a deserved death." There was a great tomb made of a mound of earth, of King Dercennus of old, the Laurentian, beneath a high mountain; it was shaded by an umbrageous oak; here first the beauteous goddess from her swift flight stays her course, and views Arruns from the summit of the barrow. As she saw him exulting in soul, and swelling with vain pride, "Why," says she, "do you go away from hence? Hither direct your course; hither come to certain fate; that you may receive a reward due for Camilla's death. What, shall such as you die by the arrow of Diana?" She spake, and like a Thracian huntress took from her quiver a swift arrow, and drew her bow with the soul of vengeance, and stretched it far, until the bent ends met, and now level are her hands, with her left hand she touches the point of the iron arrow, with her right her breast. In an instant Arruns heard at once the whizzing arrow, and the whistling air, and the iron point was fixed in his body. Him as he gasped and sobbed his last groan his forgetful comrades leave in the unknown dust of the plain; Opis on her wings is borne to Olympus and the sky.

868—895. The Latin horsemen are routed, and are driven to the walls of the town, for which even the matrons fight.

First flies, their queen lost, Camilla's light squadron, the Rutulians fly in confusion; even Atinas, keen in fight, flies; and the scattered captains and the thinned troops make for safe ground, and with steeds turned in flight speed to the walls. Nor could any one sustain with weapons the charge of the Trojans dealing death, nor stand against them; but they carry behind them their slack bows on their sluggish shoulders, while the hoof of the steeds shakes in their speed the crumbling plain. To the walls rolls the dust in turbid clouds of murky darkness, and from the watch-towers the matrons, smiting their breast, raise the cries of women to the stars of the sky. Those who in their course first burst into the open gates, are hard pressed by a hostile throng in confused line; nor do they escape a miserable death; but just at the threshold, at the battlements of their own homes, they are pierced, and expire. Some haste to shut the gates, they dare not open a way for their friends, or receive them within the walls, as they pray; and a most piteous slaughter follows of those who with arms defended the entrance and those who rushed on arms. Shut out were they before the eyes and gaze of their weeping parents, and part roll into the steep trench, as ruin presses on them, while part blind with terror, and urging their steeds with loosened reins, batter against the gates and the posts with hard bars. The very matrons on the walls in the extremity of the contest—true patriotism points the way, they had seen Camilla—in eager haste hurl darts with their hands, and with tough oaken clubs, with stems and stakes hardened in the fire they rival steel, and are the foremost in zeal for death in front of their walls.

896—915. *Turnus on hearing the news of the defeat of the cavalry leaves the defile. Both he and Æneas pitch their camps.*

Meanwhile Turnus' ears are filled in the forest by cruel news, and to the youthful prince Acca is the bearer of a mighty trouble, that the Volscian troops are cut to pieces, Camilla slain, the enemy rushing on in full force, and carrying all before them in successful war; that the terror now reaches the very walls. He as one frenzied, for so the cruel will of Jove demands, abandons the hills he had occupied, and leaves the woody ground, a position difficult to attack. Scarce had he got out of view, and reached the plain, when father Æneas enters the undefended defile, passes the ridge, gets clear of the dark wood. So both swiftly march to the walls with their whole force, not far distant the one from the other. And at the same time Æneas beheld from afar the plains thick with rising dust, and saw the Laurentian lines; and Turnus recognized warlike Æneas under arms, and heard the tramp of advancing infantry, and the snorting steeds. And straightway had they begun the fight, and tried the chance of war, but rosy-coloured Phœbus was just bathing his weary horses in the Iberian sea, and bringing back night, as daylight melts away. They pitch their camp before the town, and raise their ramparts round.

BOOK XII.

1—80. *The anger of Turnus is increased by the defeats of the Latins. Notwithstanding the intreaties of Latinus and Amata, he resolves to challenge Æneas to single combat.*

TURNUS, when he sees that the Latins are shattered and disheartened by unsuccessful war, that the fulfilment of his own promises is called for, that men's eyes make him their mark, burns all the more with rage implacable, and higher lifts his pride. As in Carthaginian plains, the mighty lion, his breast grievously wounded by the hunters, then at last wakes his weapons, and exultingly makes his shaggy muscles start from his neck, and dauntlessly shivers the deep-fixed javelin of his assailant, and roars with bloody mouth; even so in Turnus, once inflamed, the fury swells up more and more. Then he thus addresses the king, and stormily begins his speech: "No delay is caused by Turnus; no pretext have the spiritless people of Æneas for striving to recall their words, and revoking the compact they have made: I go to meet my enemy. Bring the sacrifice, my father, and formally declare a truce. Either with this right-hand of mine I will send down to Tartarus the Dardan, that runaway from Asia (let the Latins sit still and see the sight); and will refute with my single sword the charge that is laid against us all; or let him be master of the vanquished, let Lavinia be yielded him to be his bride." To him with mind composed Latinus replied: "Youth of matchless spirit, the more you surpass in fierce valour, the more thoughtfully is it meet that I should deliberate, and anxiously balance every chance. You have the realm of Daunus your father, you have many towns, captured by your might; Latinus too has gold and goodwill for you. There are other maidens in Latium and the fields of Laurentum, they too of no ignoble birth. Suffer me, with all disguise removed, to unfold these thoughts, unpleasing to utter though they be. Withal do you receive this into your heart: I was forbidden to unite my daughter with any one of her former suitors; and such was the warning of all gods and men alike. Overcome by love for you, overcome by our kindred blood, and by the tears of my sorrowing queen, I burst through all the ties that bound me; I robbed my son-in-law of his betrothed; I took up unhallowed arms against him. You, Turnus, see what calamities, what wars have pursued me ever since that time, what grievous toils you above the rest endure. Twice conquered in a great battle, we scarce maintain within our city the hopes of Italy; the streams of Tiber still run warm with our blood, and vast plains are white with our bones. Wherefore do I so oft retrace my plans? What madness changes my resolve? If I am prepared to attach them to me as my allies in case Turnus is destroyed, why do I not rather dissolve the strife when he is unharmed? What will the Rutulians, my kinsmen, what will the rest of Italy say, if—fortune refute my words!—it come to pass that I have betrayed you to death, while you seek to win my daughter, and by marriage to unite yourself with me? Consider the changes and chances of war; pity your aged father, whom now in sadness his native Ardea holds, separated far from you." The rage of Turnus is not a wit tamed by these words; it mounts still higher, and is made worse by the attempt to cure it. As soon as he gained the power of utterance, he thus began to speak: "The trouble you take for my sake, I pray you, my excellent sire, for my sake lay aside, and suffer me to purchase honour with death. We too, my father, scatter darts, and no weak weapon with our hand, and blood flows from a wound dealt by us. Far from him will his goddess-mother be, to wrap her fugitive in a cloud, a woman's craft, and hide herself in unavailing gloom." But the queen, filled with terror at the strange conditions of the combat, ever wept, and, resolved to die, clung to her fiery son-in-law: "O Turnus, by these tears I shed I entreat you, by your respect for me (if any respect for Amata touches your soul)—you are now the sole hope, you the sole comfort of my joyless age; the honour and throne of Latinus reside in you; on you reposes all our sinking house—one thing I beseech; cease to engage in fight against the Trojans. Whatsoever fortunes await you in this contest, await me also, Turnus; with you I will leave this hateful light, and not see Æneas my son-in-law, myself his captive." Lavinia heard her mother's words, with burning cheeks bathed in tears; for a deep blush shot fire into her veins, and overran her glowing face. As when with crimson dye one stains the ivory of India, or mixed with many a rose white lilies blush; such hues the maiden showed upon her countenance. He is distracted with love, and fastens his looks upon the maiden; he is still more frantic for the fight, and thus in few words addresses Amata: "Do not, I intreat, do not attend me, when marching to the strife of savage Mars, with tears, nor with an omen so fatal, O my mother: for indeed to delay his doom is not within the power of Turnus. Idmon, be my herald to bear to the Phrygian prince these words of mine, that will not please his ear; so soon as to-morrow's dawn, borne upon crimson wheels shall blush in heaven, let him not lead the Teucri against the Rutulians; let the arms of the Teucri be still, and the Rutulians; with our own blood let us decide the issue of the war: on that plain let Lavinia be sought in marriage."

81—106. *Turnus arms himself for the combat with Æneas.*

When he had spoken these words, and with haste gone back into the house, he calls for his steeds, and rejoices to view them prancing before his eyes, the coursers which Orithyia herself gave to grace Pilumnus, whose whiteness passed the snows, whose speed the gales. The ready grooms stand round, and with the hollow of the hand pat the sounding breasts of the horses, and comb their flowing manes. Next he himself puts around his shoulders his corslet rough with gold and white orichalcum; withal, he fits on for ready use his sword and shield, and the horns of his ruddy crest; the sword, which the lord of fire had himself made for Daunus his father, and dipped it white with heat in the Stygian flood. Straightway he strongly grasps a mighty spear, which stood beside him, rested against a great pillar in the heart of the mansion, the spoil he took from Actor the Auruncan, and shakes it till it quivers; crying aloud: "Now, O my spear, that never failed my call, now the hour is come, it was valiant Actor that wielded you once, it is the hand of Turnus that wields you now: grant that I may strike down the body, and with strong hand tear and rend away the corslet of the Phrygian eunuch, and soil in the dust his curls, tricked with the heated iron, and wet with myrrh." Such is the frenzy that drives him on, and flashes start from all his glowing face ; a fire sparkles in his fierce eyes.   As when a bull raises fearful bellowings, the prelude of the fray, and trains himself to throw into his horns his wrath, pushing at the trunk of a tree, and with his blows defies the winds, and spurns the sand in practice for the fight.

107—133.   *The field is prepared for the conflict between Æneas and Turnus.*

And no less Æneas, meanwhile, dauntless in the armour given by his mother, whets his warlike spirit, and stirs himself with wrath, glad that the war is settled by the compact offered him.   Then he cheers his comrades and the fear of his sorrowing Iulus, expounding the fates, and bids the envoys carry back to king Latinus his resolved reply, and propose the terms of the peace.   The following daybreak had scarce begun to sow the mountain-tops with light, when the horses of the Sun are just arising from the depths of the flood, and from uplifted nostrils breathe the day.   Rutulians and Trojans marked out and made ready the field for the contest, beneath the walls of the great city ; and in the midst hearths and grassy altars to their common gods ; others brought the spring water and the fire, with linen veils, and brows with vervain bound. Forth comes the host of the Ausonidæ, and troops armed with the pilum pour out from the crowded gates : hence, in various arms, rushes all the Trojan and Etruscan army, as completely arrayed in steel, as if the rude battle of Mars were calling them on.   Moreover, in the centre of their thousands, the captains themselves are fluttering, in the pride of gold and purple ; both Mnestheus the child of Assaracus, and stout Asilas, and Messapus the tamer of horses, the progeny of Neptune.   And so soon as at a signal given each man retires to his own position, they fix in earth their spears, and lean their shields on the ground.   Then, eagerly streaming forth, mothers and the unarmed rabble, and nerveless old men, thickly crowd the towers and house-tops ; others stand by the high-built gates.

134—160.   *Juno, to save the life of Turnus, urges Juturna to break the truce.*

But Juno, as she looked out from the summit of the slope that is now called the Alban hill (then the mount had neither name nor honour or renown), surveyed the plain and both the lines, the array of the Laurentes and of the Trojans, and the town of Latinus.   Straightway she thus spoke to the sister of Turnus (a goddess addressing a goddess, who is mistress of the meres and murmuring streams ; this place of honour Jove, high king of heaven, dedicated to her, the recompense for her ravished maidenhood): " Nymph, beauty of the rivers, right dear to my heart, thou knowest that thou art the one whom I have favoured above all the maids of Latium, that have ascended haughty Jove's unduteous couch, and cheerfully have established thee in a share of heaven ; learn, to prevent thee from accusing me, the cause of thy trouble.   So far as fortune seemed to permit, and the Parcæ allowed the course of Latium's state to be prosperous, I protected Turnus, and the walls of thy city.   Now I see that the youth is hastening to meet destinies he cannot withstand; and the day appointed by the Fates draws nigh, and their power that is against him. I cannot view with my eyes this conflict, this treaty. Do thou, if thou darest to give thy brother any more effectual aid, proceed, it is thy proper part: perchance a better fortune will yet reach the unhappy." Scarce had she spoken, when Juturna shed from her eyes a stream of tears, and again and again smote with her hand her beauteous breast: "This is not the time for tears," says Juno, Saturn's child; "make speed, and if any means there be, rescue thy brother from death; or do thou awake the war, and shatter the compacted truce. It is I who prompt thee to be bold." With these exhortations she left her there wavering in purpose, and distracted by the grievous wound of the mind.

161—216. *The chiefs enter the field. The vows of Æneas and Latinus.*

Meanwhile the monarchs advance; Latinus, surrounded by a mass of state, is carried in a chariot drawn by four steeds; twelve golden beams circle his dazzling brows, the ensign of the Sun, his grandsire; drawn by two white horses Turnus comes along, waving in his hand two shafts with broad heads of steel. After him father Æneas, the author of the Roman line, blazing with starry shield and arms of heaven; and beside him Ascanius, the second hope of mighty Rome, come forth from the camp, and the priest in spotless robe presented the offspring of a bristly sow, and ewe never shorn, and brought the victims to the flaming altars. They, with eyes turned towards the rising sun, offer in their hands the salted meal, and with the steel mark the victims on the top of the brows, and pour a libation from the bowls upon the altars. Then pious Æneas draws his sword, and thus makes his prayer: "Now, O Sun, be thou my witness, and this land attest my prayer, for whose sake I have been able to endure toils so hard; and thou Almighty father, and Juno, child of Saturn; now, now, O queen, more kind, I pray; and thou renowned Mavors, that art the sire who dost govern all wars beneath thy sway; and Springs and Streams I call; and all that is worshipped in high heaven, and all the Powers in the dark blue sea; if perchance Victory side with Ausonian Turnus, it is covenanted that the vanquished withdraw to Evander's town: Ascanius shall quit these fields, and the people of Æneas shall not hereafter renew the war, and make a fresh incursion, or harass this kingdom with the sword. But if it prove that Victory makes the battle our own (as I rather believe, and so may Heaven's will rather sanction!) I will neither bid the Italians obey the Teucri, nor do I claim for myself the sovereignty; let both nations, unsubdued, enter under equal conditions upon an everlasting compact. I will ordain rights and divinities; let my father-in-law Latinus hold the rule in war, let him possess the fixed command; for me the Teucri shall set up my walls, and Lavinia shall give the town her name." So spoke Æneas first; after him Latinus follows thus, gazing up to heaven, and uplifts his right-hand towards the stars: "These same Powers I call to witness, O Æneas, Earth, Sea, Stars, and the twin offspring of Latona, and Janus of double front, and the might of the gods below, and the sanctuary of unpitying Dis; these vows let the Father hear, who ratifies treaties with his thunderbolt. I touch the altars, and adjure the fires that burn between us, and the deities: no term of time shall break this peace, this compact of the men of Italy, whatever be the issue of events; and no force shall make me willingly swerve; not if it spill the land into the main, confounding both in a deluge, and dissolve into Tartarus the sky; as this sceptre,"— for in his right-hand he chanced to bear a sceptre,—"will never shoot forth twigs nor foliage of tender leaf, since once and for ever hewn away in the woods from the bottom of its stem, it has lost its parent, and has shed beneath the steel its leaves and sprays; once a tree; now the craftsman's hand has cased it in adorning brass, and given it to the fathers of Latium to bear." With such words they mutually confirmed the compact, in the midst of the gazing lords. Then over the flame they slaughter the victims duly hallowed, and from the living bodies snatch forth the vitals, and with laden chargers pile the altars high.

217—276. *Juturna, in the form of Camers, incites the Rutulians to break the treaty. Tolumnius, encouraged by an omen, hurls his spear into the ranks of the Arcadians, and kills Gylippus.*

But in the eyes of the Rutulians the combat had now long appeared unequal, and their minds were distracted with manifold anxiety; still more so at this moment, when by nearer view they perceive that the champions are ill-matched in strength. Turnus deepens the feeling, as he advances with silent step, and with downcast eye humbly pays his homage to the altar; and so do his bloodless cheeks, and the paleness in his youthful frame. So soon as his sister Juturna saw that this rumour was gaining ground, and that the hearts of the crowd were wavering and unsettled, into the midst of the array, in form made like to Camers (whose ancestral descent was glorious, and his father's name renowned for bravery, and himself right valiant in arms), into the midst of the array she plunges, knowing well the course of events, and flings abroad various reports, and thus she speaks: "Are you not ashamed, Rutulians, to risk a single life for all these men so brave? Is it in numbers or in force that we do not match the foe? Lo, these are all the Trojans and Arcadians, and the host of destiny, Etruria the enemy of Turnus. Should we close in fight, scarce has every second man of us an antagonist. He indeed will mount in fame to the gods above, to whose shrines he devotes himself, and undying will be wafted through the mouths of men: we, our country lost, shall be forced to obey proud masters, we who now have sat down idly on the field." With such words the resolution of the warriors is fired ever more and more, and the murmuring steals on through the lines; even the Laurentes, and even the Latins are swayed. The men that just now hoped for rest from battle and safety for their fortunes, now wish for arms, and pray that the compact be made void, and pity the hard lot of Turnus. To these words Juturna adds another greater sign, and gives an omen in the height of heaven, one that more forcibly than any other excited the minds of the Italians, and beguiled them by its prodigy. For flying in the reddened air the tawny bird of Jove was seen to chase the fowls of the shore, and the noisy throng of the winged train: when suddenly swooping towards the flood he greedily bears away the choicest swan in his crooked talons. Aroused were the spirits of the Italians, and all the

birds clamorously turn from flight—a wondrous sight to view—and
darken with their wings the sky, and, formed into a cloud, press close
upon their enemy through the air; until the eagle, vanquished by their
force and the very weight of his victim, gave way, and dropped the prey
from his talons into the stream, and fled far away into the clouds. Then
do the Rutulians hail with shouts the omen, and make ready their troops
for the fight; and foremost the augur Tolumnius speaks: "This, this
it was that I oft besought with prayers. I accept the sign, and acknowledge the will of the gods: led by me, by me, grasp the sword, ye
wretched men, ye whom a greedy adventurer scares in war, like feeble
birds, and savagely wastes your shores. He will take to flight, and
spread his sails far away across the deep. With one mind marshal your
troops in close array, and in war defend your ravished prince." He
spoke, and running forward hurled his lance against the foes that faced
him: the whizzing shaft gives forth a noise, and truly cleaves the air.
In a moment it is done: in a moment there is a mighty cry, and all
the battalions are disordered, and their hearts are heated with the
tumult. The flying spear, as the beauteous forms of nine brethren
chanced to be stationed opposite, each one of which number a faithful
Tuscan wife had borne to Arcadian Gylippus, pierces through the ribs
one of these, a youth of noble form and flashing arms, in the middle
of the body, where the woven sword-belt presses tight upon the belly,
and the buckle bites the clasped edges of the belt, and tumbles him on
the yellow sand.

277—323. *The fray becomes general, and many are killed on both*
sides. Æneas, while he attempts to check the conflict, is wounded
by an unknown hand.

But his brethren, a gallant band, and fired with grief, partly draw
forth their swords, partly snatch up the missile steel, and blindly rush
on. Against them speed forth the troops of Laurentum. Hereupon in
a returning tide flock on Trojans and men of Agylla, and Arcadians
with arms inwrought. So all are possessed with the same passion to
decide the issue with the steel.

Instantly they strip the altars: through all the sky flies thick the
hurtling storm of darts, and heavy falls the iron rain: wine-bowls and
brasiers they bring to battle. Latinus himself flees away, carrying back
the gods spurned by the disannulling of the treaty. Others harness
horses to their cars, or with a spring fling themselves upon their steeds,
and with drawn swords join the fray. Messapus, eager to dissolve the
truce, affrights by riding at him the Tuscan Aulestes, a king, and
wearing the kingly escutcheon; he falls backward in retreat, and is
miserably thrown against the altars that stand in his way behind, upon
the head and shoulders; then Messapus hotly flies upon him with his
spear, and from the height of his horse grievously smites him with his
beamy shaft, in the midst of his entreaties, and thus he speaks: "This
blow has reached him; this, a goodlier victim, is offered to the great
gods." The Italians crowd to the place, and strip his limbs yet warm.
Chorinæus, standing in the way, snatches from the altar a half-burnt
brand, and full in the face of Ebusus, as he comes on, and intends a

wound, dashes the flame : out blazed all his beard, and the scorched hair gave forth a stench : his antagonist, following up the blow, seizes with his left-hand the long locks of his bewildered foe, and, pressing his knee upon him with all his might, fastens the man against the ground : so, he smites him with the point of his sword. Podalirius following with naked blade the shepherd Alsus, as in the front of the host he hastens through the shower of darts, threatens him from above ; the other with the sweep of his axe meets his foe, and cleaves him through the midst of his brow and chin, and bedews his armour all over with the scattered brain. Stern quiet loads his eyes, and iron sleep ; his eyelids close to everlasting night. But pious Æneas, with head exposed, stretched forth his unarmed hand, and with a shout called upon his men : " Whither are ye rushing? or what means this sudden rising quarrel ? Restrain your rage, I pray you : the truce is now concluded, and all conditions settled ; I alone am permitted to engage in combat : leave me to myself, and drive away your doubts ; I with my own hand will form a binding league : these sacred rites make Turnus now my due." While he uttered these cries, and these words were on his lips, lo, an arrow with whizzing wings lighted on the hero : by what hand discharged, by what blast impelled, who it was, whether chance or god, that bestowed so great renown on the Rutulians, is unknown ; lost is the glory of the illustrious deed ; nor did any one make his boast in the wound of Æneas.

324—382. *Turnus is encouraged by the retreat of Æneas from the field. His deeds of valour.*

Turnus, when he sees Æneas retiring from the host, and his captains dismayed, glows and burns with sudden hope ; he demands his steeds and arms withal, and with a proud leap bounds upon his car, and with his own hands plies the reins. Many a valiant frame does he give to death in his winged course ; many does he roll on earth half-slain, or trample down ranks with his chariot, or snatch up lances and shower them on the fugitives. Even as when bloody Mavors, stirred to battle beside the streams of cold Hebrus, clashes his shield, and, as he wakes the war, gives rein to his maddened steeds ; they across the open plain fly forth before the south winds and Zephyrus ; the utmost bound of Thrace resounds beneath the tramp of feet, and all around him speed along faces of gloomy Dread and Anger and Ambush, the followers of the god ; like him Turnus amid the thickest of the fight with vigour urges his steeds that smoke with sweat, trampling on his foes miserably slain ; the rushing hoof dashes up sprays of blood, and mixed with gore the sand is trodden down. And in an instant he consigned to slaughter Sthenelus and Thamyris and Pholus, the first two in close conflict, the other from afar ; from afar he slew both the sons of Imbrasus, Glaucus and Lades, whom Imbrasus had himself reared in Lycia, and adorned them both with equal arms, either to join in close combat, or on the courser to outstrip the winds. In another part Eumedes rushes into the midst of the fray, the child renowned in war of ancient Dolon, in name the likeness of his grandfather, in soul and strength of his sire ; who, in days of yore, dared to claim for his own the car of Pelides as his price, to go a spy into the camp of the Danai ;

to him Tydides rendered another price for such a deed of daring ; and he does not aspire to the horses of Achilles. Him when Turnus descried from afar on the open plain, having first pursued him o'er the wide space with his fleet dart, he stays the course of his car, and leaps down from the chariot, and comes upon him half-dead and prostrate, and, with foot planted on his neck, wrenches the sword from his hand, and dyes the glittering blade deep in his throat, and speaks this taunt besides : " See, Trojan, you measure as you lie the fields and the Italy you thought to win in war ; this is the prize they bear away who dare to provoke me with the steel ; thus they found their walls." With the cast of his spear he sends to bear him company Asbutes ; and Chloreus, and Sybaris and Dares and Thersilochus, and Thymœtes, tumbled from the neck of his horse that threw its rider. Even as when the blast of Thracian Boreas roars across the Ægæan deep, and chases the billows to the shore ; where the winds chance to swoop, the clouds flee along the sky ; so before Turnus, wherever he cleaves a path, the ranks give way, and the lines turn in hurried flight ; the warrior is borne onwards by his own force, and the breeze ruffles the plume that streams against the course of the chariot. Phegeus brooked him not as he pressed along with exulting heart ; he threw himself in the way of the car, and with his right-hand plucked aside in full career the mouths of the horses that foamed upon the bit. As he is dragged along, and hangs from the yoke, the broad lance overtakes him while exposed, and fixing deep tears through the corslet of double mail, and scarce wounds slightly the surface of his body. Yet he, guarding himself with his shield, turned round and was advancing against his enemy, and drew his sword to succour him, when the wheel and axle with the force of its onward career struck him down headlong, and tumbled him on the ground ; and Turnus pursuing him lopped away with the sword his head between the extremity of the helmet and the uppermost rim of the breastplate, and left him headless on the sand.

383—440. *The wound of Æneas is miraculously healed by the aid of Venus. His farewell to Ascanius.*

And while victorious Turnus works these deaths upon the plain, mean-while Mnestheus, and trusty Achates, and Ascanius by his side set Æneas in the camp stained with gore, supporting with his long lance each successive step. He is frantic with rage, and strains to pluck out the head of the broken shaft, and cries for the quickest means of remedy ; bids them cut the wound with the blade of the sword, and cleave open to the bottom the hidden seat of the shaft, and let him go back into the war. And now came to the spot Iapis son of Iasus, beyond all other men beloved by Phœbus, he upon whom in former time Apollo, inspired with passionate love, cheerfully offered to bestow with his own hand his peculiar arts, his own attributes, the gift of augury and the harp and flying arrows. He, that he might delay the doom of his sire sick to death, chose rather to know the virtues of herbs and the practice of healing, and exercise unfamed the silent arts. Æneas was standing in the bitterness of rage, leaning on his mighty spear, amid a vast throng of warriors and his sorrowing Iulus, himself untouched with tears.

The skilled old man, his robe rolled back and girt high in the fashion of his tribe, with healing hand and the sovereign herbs of Phœbus makes many a hurried attempt, in vain solicits with his hand the dart, and oft with biting pincers tugs the steel. No fortune guides his path, no means of succour does Apollo create ; and ever more and more dread alarm deepens o'er the plains, and disaster draws nearer and nearer. Already they see the sky become a column of dust ; and horsemen ride close up, and darts fall thickly into the heart of the camp. To heaven goes the dismal cry of men that fight and men that fall beneath un-pitying Mars. Hereupon his mother Venus, distracted by her son's un-merited agony, plucks from Cretan Ida a stalk of dittany with downy leaves and feathery purple bloom ; well-known is the plant to the wild goats, when winged arrows chance to fix deep in their body. It was this that Venus brought, her form enveloped in a cloud of gloom ; this she steeps in streams poured into shining vessels, and secretly medicates the cup ; and sprinkles health-giving juices of ambrosia, and fragrant panacea. With this water, though he knew it not, aged Iapis bathed the wound ; and in a moment all pain readily fled from the body, all the blood was stanched from the bottom of the wound ; and now the shaft without an effort followed the hand and dropped to the ground, and his strength renewed returned to its former vigour. "Hasten with speed to bring the hero's arms! Why stand ye still?" Iapis cries aloud ; and foremost fires their souls against the foe. "It is not by human aid, not by the methods of art, that this is brought to pass, nor is it my hand that saves you, Æneas : one greater than I, a god, is at work, and sends you back to greater deeds." The prince with eagerness had cased his ankles all around in gold for the battle, and loathes delays, and brandishes his lance. When the shield is fitted to his side, and the corslet to his back, he clasps Ascanius, and throws his armed frame around him ; and printing a light kiss through his helmet, speaks to him thus : "From me, my boy, learn valour and true toil ; from others fortune. My right-hand now will guard you safe in war, and lead you where high prizes are to be won. Be sure that you remember, when in its course your youth has grown to ripeness ; and as in your mind you look for patterns among your kinsmen, let Æneas your sire, and Hector your uncle stir your soul."

441—487. *Juturna foils the efforts of Æneas to encounter Turnus.*

When he had uttered these words, he strode in mighty stature through the gates, brandishing his ponderous spear ; withal in crowded array Antheus and Mnestheus haste along, and all the host forsake the camp and stream forth. Then the plain is troubled with a dark cloud of dust, and the ground stirs and shakes beneath the tramp of feet. Turnus saw them as they came on from the opposite rampart ; the Ausonians saw them ; and an icy shudder thrilled even through their bones. First Juturna, before all the Latins, heard and recognised the noise, and quailed and fled away. The hero wings his way, and speeds his dark troop o'er the open plain. As when a tempest, bursting forth from heaven to earth, passes o'er the midst of the main, alas, the hearts of the wretched husbandmen, boding from afar, begin to quake ; it will bring wreck to the trees, and havoc to the crops, and lay waste all things far and wide ; the winds fly on before, and waft the din to the beach ; like it the Rhœteian captain urges on his host to meet the foe ; in close array they all throng to the marshalled battalions. With the sword Thymbræus smites the huge Osiris, Mnestheus Archetius ; Achates cuts down Epulo, and Gyas Ufens ; the augur Tolumnius himself falls, who had been the first to hurl his lance against the foe. A shout is raised to heaven, and the Rutulians in turn give way, and haste in dusty flight across the 'fields. He himself neither deigns to strike down to death those that turn their backs, nor moves to meet those who face him with fairly-matched steps, nor those who fling the shaft ; Turnus alone he tracks and searches in the thick darkness, him alone he calls to the combat. Distraught in soul with fear of this, the warrior-maid Juturna tumbles down amid the reins Metiscus, the charioteer of Turnus, and leaves him fallen far from the pole of the car ; she mounts herself, and with her hands directs the flowing reins, wearing all the marks of Metiscus, both voice and form and arms. As when through the great mansion of a wealthy lord a black swallow flits, and traverses the lofty halls, gathering its little store of food, and morsels for its twittering nestlings, and noisily flies, now along spacious colonnades, now round watery pools ; like it Juturna is borne by the coursers through the midst of the foes, and in her rushing car manœuvres to every point her flight ; and now here, now there, she shews her brother in his triumph, and suffers him not to close in fight ; far out of the way she flies. No less Æneas threads mazy circles to meet him, and tracks the warrior, and with loud voice cries to him through the shattered ranks. As often as he cast his looks upon his foe, and challenged on foot the flight of the winged steeds, so often Juturna turned back and drove away the chariot. Alas, what is he to do? In vain he is swayed by a changeful tide, and discordant thoughts summon his mind to contrary points.

488—554. *Æneas, provoked by the javelin of Messapus, gives up the chase of Turnus, and attacks the Rutulians.*

Against him Messapus, light of foot, as he chanced in his left-hand to carry two pliant javelins tipped with steel, hurled one of these, aiming with unerring force. Æneas halted, and drew himself within cover of his arms, sinking down upon his knee ; yet the forceful spear bore away the point of his helmet's peak, and struck away from his head-piece the top of the crest. Then it is that his wrath arises, and overcome by the treacherous ambush, when he perceives that the steeds and car are driven far away, having oft taken Jove to witness, and the altars of the violated truce, he now at last plunges into the midst, and, backed by Mars, terribly awakes a dreadful carnage without distinction, and flings loose all the flowing reins of wrath. What god can now describe for me so many dreadful deeds, who in song can tell of the carnage on either side, and the fall of the captains, whom now Turnus, now the hero of Troy rout over all the plain in turn? Was it thy will, O Jove, that nations destined to live in endless peace should close in combat with rage so fierce? Æneas encountered Sucro the Rutulian (this conflict first stayed in fixed position the Teucri in their onset), and without long delay smote him on the side, and, at the point where death is quickest, drove through the ribs and frame-work of the breast the cruel sword. Turnus fighting on foot met Amycus and hurled him from his horse, and slew also his brother Diores, smiting the one with his long spear, as he came on, the other with the edge of the sword ; and the severed heads of the two he hung from his car, and bore them on, dripping with dews of blood. The former sends to their doom Talos and Tanais and the brave Cethegus, meeting the three at once, and ill-starred Onytes, by name Echion's son, Peridia was the mother who bore him. The latter slays the brethren sent forth from Lycia and Apollo's fields, and a youth who in vain detested battles, Arcadian Menœtes, whose craft and poor abode had been about the streams of Lerna, haunt of fish ; unknown to him was the business of the great, and rented was the land his father sowed. Even like flames from different points thrown in upon a dry forest, and thickets of crack-ling laurel ; or as when in rushing career down from mountain heights foaming torrents roar aloud, and gallop to the main, making each his own lane of devastation ; with no less might the twain, Æneas and Turnus, speed through the fray ; now, now, surges up the wrath within ; mangled are breasts that know not how to yield ; now with all force they press to meet the wound. The former strikes down headlong Murranus, who loudly boasted the ancient names of generation on gene-ration of ancestors, and all his line derived through Latin kings, with a crag and ponderous whirling rock, and tumbles him on the ground ; him the wheels roll prostrate down beneath the reins and yoke ; upon him with many a blow trample the hoofs of his coursers in full career, and regardless of their lord. The latter speeds to meet Hyllus as he rushes on with boundless rage at heart, and hurls the javelin at his gold-clad brows ; right through his helm the spear fixed fast within the brain. Nor did your right-hand, O Cretheus, bravest of Greeks, rescue you from Turnus ; nor did the gods he served protect Cupencus at the approach of Æneas ; he presented his breast to meet the steel, nor did the resistance of his brazen shield avail the hapless man. You too, Æolus, the Laurentian plains saw meet your fate, and on your back o'erspread a length of earth. You fall, you whom the Argive phalanxes could not lay low, nor Achilles, the destroyer of the realm of Priam. Here was your goal of doom ; a lofty mansion was yours beneath Ida, a lofty mansion at Lyrnessus ; on the soil of Laurentum is your grave. The whole of the armies are utterly intermingled, all the Latins, all the men of Troy ; Mnestheus and stout Serestus, and Messapus, tamer of horses, and brave Asylas, and the Tuscan phalanx, and the squadrons of Arcadian Evander ; each man, on his own account, struggles with the utmost strain of his powers. No pause, no respite ; a fearful strife they wage.

555—613. *Æneas, moved by Venus, attacks and sets fire to the city. The suicide of Amata, and the despair of Lavinia and Latinus.*

It was here that his beauteous mother inspired Æneas with the resolve to march towards the walls, and turn his host against the city with all speed, and rout the Latins with unlooked-for carnage. He, while tracking Turnus through the several hosts, hither and thither shot his glance around; he views the town exempt from share in so fierce a conflict, and quiet and unharmed. Straightway he is fired with the vision of a greater fight. He summons his captains Mnestheus and Sergestus and the brave Serestus, and occupies a mound, whither all the rest of the Trojan legion quickly muster, and in close array lay not aside their spears or shafts. He, standing in the midst on the lofty rampart, addresses them thus : "Let no man delay to perform my words ; on this side Jove takes his stand ; and let no man be slower to obey me because my enterprise is sudden. This day I will utterly raze the city, the cause of the war, the very heart of the realm of Latinus, unless they consent to receive the curb, and as conquered men submit to me, and will lay level with the ground his smouldering roofs. Am I to stay forsooth, till it be the pleasure of Turnus to await our onslaught, and till the conquered warrior choose again to meet us? This, my citizens, is the life, this the heart of the unholy war. Quickly bring brands, and with flames claim back the broken truce." So he spoke ; and they all, their hearts inspired with equal zeal, form a wedge, and in a dense mass make their onset against the walls. Suddenly scaling-ladders are seen, and the unexpected flash of fire. Some hurry to the gates, and kill the first they meet ; others hurl the steel, and shadow the sky with darts. Æneas himself among the foremost stretches his hand towards the walls, and with loud voice accuses Latinus ; and takes Heaven to witness that he is forced to resort to arms again ; that the Italians are now twice his foes, that this is the second compact they have broken. Dissension springs up among the affrighted citizens ; some urge that the town be opened, and the gates laid wide to the Dardans, and drag to the battlements the king himself ; others bring arms, and set themselves to defend the walls. As when in the crevices of a pumice-rock a shepherd tracks out the bees that lurk within, and fills the nest with bitter smoke ; they within, alarmed for their safety, hurry to and fro throughout their waxen camp, and with loud buzzings whet their rage. The black and noisome vapour rolls through the mansion ; then with stifled hum the crags resound within ; the smoke goes upward to the empty air. This catastrophe besides befel the dis-heartened Latins, which shook the whole city to its foundations with sorrow. The queen, when from her dwelling she beholds the foe advance, the walls beset, and fire-brands flying to the roofs, no Rutulian host anywhere to meet the enemy, no troops of Turnus, unhappily believes that the warrior has perished in the strife of battle ; and, troubled in spirit by the sudden pang of grief, cries out that herself is the cause and guilty source and spring of woes ; and when she has spoken many distracted words through the frenzy of sorrow, resolved to die she violently tears her purple robes, and twines from a lofty beam the noose of an abhorred death. So soon as the wretched women of Latium heard of this fatal disaster, first Lavinia, her daughter, her yellow hair and rosy cheeks disfigured with her own hand, after her, all the throng rave with grief around ; with mourning loud the palace resounds throughout. From hence the news is spread abroad through the whole city. Men's spirits droop; with garments rent Latinus goes along, stunned by his consort's doom, and city's wreck, shamefully besmearing his grey hairs with unclean dust ; and oft he blames himself, that he has not before received Æneas of Troy, and made him his son-in-law besides.

614—696. *Turnus hears the tumult from the city. His address to Juturna. Finally he rushes back to the city, and calls upon the armies to cease from the battle.*

Meanwhile upon the distant plain the warrior Turnus chases the few stragglers, now more slow, and now less and less pleased with his coursers' victorious pace. To him the breeze wafted a cry mingled with vague alarms ; and the noise of the bewildered town, and its woeful murmur, struck upon his listening ears. "Ah me ! why are the walls troubled with grief so loud ? or what means this cry so sad, which flies from the distant city?" So he speaks, and in distraction pauses, drawing in the reins. And him his sister, since transformed into the shape of Metiscus, she was governing car, and steeds, and reins, challenges with these words : "By this path, Turnus, let us follow the men of Troy, this path by which victory opens out the readiest way. Others there are who can stoutly defend their homes : Æneas lowers over the Italians, and stirs the tumult of battle ; let us too, with our might, inflict upon the Trojans bitter deaths. You will leave the field, unequal neither in number of the slain, nor in the honour of war." Turnus in reply : "My sister, from the first I knew you, when you were foremost by craft to break the truce, and devoted yourself to this warfare ; and now it is in vain that your divinity would be concealed. But by whose will are you sent down from Olympus to endure toils so hard ? Was it to view your hapless brother's piteous fall ? For what avail the deeds I do ? or what good fortune now assures me safety ? Myself before my eyes I have beheld Murranus while he cried aloud upon me, than whom no dearer one to me survives, meet his doom, a mighty man, and vanquished by a mighty blow. The hapless Ufens fell, that he might not look on my disgrace ; the Teucri have his body and his arms. Shall I even suffer our dwellings to be razed to the ground? this only wanted to complete my shame ; and shall I not with my hand refute the words of Drances? Shall I turn my back in flight ? and shall this land see Turnus a fugitive ? Is it so passing hard to die ? Ye Powers of the dead, be ye gracious to me, since the goodwill of the gods above is turned from me. A holy spirit I will descend to you, and one that knows not that disgrace, a man never unworthy of his mighty forefathers." Scarce had he said these words, lo, through the midst of the enemy, Saces is borne along upon his foaming steed, wounded with an arrow in the front of his countenance ; and on he speeds, by name beseeching Turnus : "Turnus, in you is our last relief ; pity your friends ! Æneas thunders in arms, and threatens to hurl down the topmost heights of the Italian towers, and give them to destruction ; and now the fire-brands are flying to the roofs ; on you the Latins cast their looks, on you their eyes ; king Latinus himself in muttered words doubts what sons-in-law to invite, or to what alliance to incline. Moreover, the queen, your surest friend, has perished by her own hand, and in wild dismay has fled the light. Alone before the gates Messapus and brave Atinas strive to rally the host ; around them on each side stand crowded battalions, and an iron harvest bristles with pointed blades ; you o'er an empty field drive round your car." Bewildered at the changeful show of events, Turnus stood aghast, and paused in speechless gaze ; in the bottom of his heart surges boundless shame, and frenzy mixed with grief, and love goaded by fury, and the consciousness of valour. So soon as the mists were swept away, and light came back to his mind, full of trouble he turned the glowing glance of his eyes towards the walls, and from his chariot looked back upon the mighty city. But lo, curling between the floors, a flaming torrent rolled its waves to heaven, and encompassed the tower, the tower which he had himself reared up with jointed beams, and placed upon wheels, and spanned with lofty bridges. "Now, now, my sister, fate prevails ; cease your efforts to keep me back ; where God, and where cruel Fortune calls us, let us follow. It is my purpose to face in fight Æneas ; my purpose to endure all the bitterness of death ; nor, my own sister, shall you longer see me tainted with dishonour ; let me first, I implore you, indulge this fit of frenzy." He spoke, and from his car with speed leapt down upon the plain ; and through foes, through darts he rushes on, and leaves behind his sorrowing sister, and in fleet career bursts through the centre of the host. Even as when, torn away by the wind, or washed down by a torrent of rain, a crag shoots headlong from a mountain-top, or is undermined and loosened by the course of years, the crashing rock with mighty force comes rushing down, and bounds along the ground, sweeping with it forests, herds, and men ; so through the shivered ranks Turnus hurries on to the walls of the town, where the earth is deepest drenched with flowing blood, and the air is loud with the whiz of spears : and beckons with his hand, and withal begins in loud tone : "Refrain now, ye Rutulians, and you, ye Latins, check your darts ; whatever fortune there is, is mine ; it is righteous rather for me alone in your behalf to expiate the broken truce, and with the sword decide the fight." All that stood between gave way, and left a space.

697—765. *Æneas and Turnus meet in combat. The sword of Turnus is shattered against the Vulcanian armour, and he is forced to flee before Æneas.*

But father Æneas, when he heard the name of Turnus, leaves the walls, and leaves the height of the battlements ; and turns to headlong haste all delay, cuts short all designs, exultant with delight, and in his arms like dreadful thunder sounds. Great as Athos, or great as Eryx, or as he himself, father Apenninus, when, towering to the sky, he resounds with his quivering oaks, and rejoices in his snowy top. Now it was that with all eagerness, both Rutulians and Trojans, and all the Italians turned their gaze, and they who occupied the height of the fortress, and they who were battering with the ram the foundations of the walls ; and from their shoulders they took off their arms. Latinus himself is amazed, that mighty men, born in distant quarters of the world, have met together in conflict, and are contending with the sword. So they, as soon as the plains lie open with empty tract, when in rushing onset they have hurled their lances from afar, speed to close combat with shields of clashing brass. Earth yields a groan; then with the sword they redouble blow on blow; fortune and valour are blended into one. Even as when on mighty Sila or the peak of Taburnus two bulls with levelled horns charge on to deadly fight; trembling the keepers flee; dumb with dread stands all the herd, and the heifers doubt who is to be lord of the forest, whom the whole herd is to follow. They in turn with ponderous force give wound for wound, and pushing hard drive deep their horns, and bathe their necks and shoulders in a stream of blood; with their bellowing all the forest echoes: like them, Trojan Æneas and the Daunian hero close with meeting shields; a mighty clashing o'erflows he sky. Jove himself holds forth two scales with balance poised, and in them puts the opposite fortunes of the two, which of them the sinking scale is to doom, with the weight of which death is to incline. At this moment Turnus springs forth, thinking to do it safely, and with all the force of his body rises to swing his sword upraised aloft, and strikes. Aloud exclaim Trojans and anxious Latins, and the armies of both are thrilled with suspense. But the faithless sword snaps short, and in the very stroke forsakes the fiery chief, now lost, unless flight remain to succour him. Swifter than the East wind he flies, the instant he beholds a hilt he knows not, and his hand disarmed. Fame tells that he, while in headlong haste he was mounting his chariot equipped to begin the fray, in his hurry caught up the weapon of his charioteer Metiscus. It long endured, whilst the Teucri turned their backs in scattered flight: so soon as it met the god-wrought armour of Vulcan, the mortal blade, like fragile ice, snapped asunder at the blow; the fragment flashes on the tawny sand. So Turnus in confusion speeds his flight o'er the distant plain; and now this way, now that, he wheels in aimless rounds; for all about the Teucri hemmed him in with crowded circle; and on this side a spreading marsh, on that the lofty walls surround him. And no less Æneas, though his limbs, made slower by the wound of the arrow, sometimes thwart him and refuse their speed, pursues him close, and hotly presses with his stride on the stride of his frighted foe; as when perchance the hunter hound has surprised a stag shut in by a river, or hedged round by the terror of the crimson feather, and, running and barking, plies him hard; the other, on his part, panic-struck by the snare and the steep bank, doubles in various flight a thousand ways; but the nimble hound of Umbria with open mouth ne'er leaves him, and now, now seizes him, and as in the act of seizing, snaps his jaws, and is baffled by the empty bite. Then a loud cry is raised; and river-banks and pools repeat the echo round; and all the sky tumultuously resounds. He flies, and as he flies upbraids all the Rutulians, calling on each man by name, and earnestly demands his trusty sword. Æneas, on the other hand, threatens death and instant doom, if any man approach, and scares the trembling foes, oft menacing destruction to the town, and though wounded presses on. Five full circles they cover in their race, and thread through as many more, this way and that. And of a truth not slight nor sportive is the prize they play; but the life and blood of Turnus is their stake.

766—842. *Faunus and Juturna aid Turnus in the fight. Juno's appeal to Jupiter. She yields to the ordinance of fate, and is appeased by the promises of Jupiter.*

It chanced that here had stood a wild olive with its bitter leaves, sacred to Faunus, a tree by sailors once revered, where, when rescued from the waves, they used to fix up their offerings to the god of Laurentum, and hang their votive garments; but the Trojans had without respect cut down the hallowed stock, that they might make their charge upon an open plain. Here stuck the spear of Æneas; hither its force had borne it, and kept it fixed in the tough root. The Dardan stooped to grasp it, and strove by force to wrench away the steel, and follow with the javelin him he could not catch by speed of foot. Then it was that Turnus, dazed with fear, said: "Pity me, Faunus, I beseech thee; and thou, most gracious Earth, keep fast the lance, if I have alway maintained thy honours, which contrariwise the men of Æneas have profaned in war." He spoke, and invoked the help of the god to hear no fruitless vows; for Æneas, though he struggled long, and persevered at the tough stock, could not by any efforts unlock the hard wood's bite. While fiercely he tugs and strains, the Daunian goddess, changed back into the form of the charioteer Metiscus, runs forward, and restores to her brother his sword. Then Venus, indignant that such power was granted to the daring Nymph, drew near, and plucked away the weapon from the heart of the root. They, at full height, in arms and soul repaired; the one relying on his sword, the other dauntless and towering with his lance, stand face to face, panting in the strife of war. Meanwhile the monarch of almighty Olympus addresses Juno, as from a saffron cloud she views the fight: "What then shall be the end, my queen? what at last remains? Thou thyself knowest, and dost confess thou knowest, that Æneas, as a national divinity, is owed to heaven, and by destiny wafted to the stars. What is thy purpose? or with what hope lingerest thou in the cold clouds? Was it fit that a god should be profaned by a mortal's wound? or that the sword (for what power could Juturna have without thee?) when plucked from Turnus should be restored to him, and the might of the vanquished be increased? Now at length cease, and be swayed by my intreaties; and be not in silence wasted by grief so deep, and from thy sweet lips let thy mournful cares often flow forth to me. The final hour has come. On land or on the deep thou hadst power to persecute the Trojans, to kindle a fearful war, to taint a house with disgrace, and poison with woe a marriage-feast. To venture farther I forbid thee." So spoke Jove first: thus with humble look the goddess, child of Saturn, replied: "Because indeed this will of thine was known to me, great Jove, I reluctantly forsook Turnus and his land. Nor wouldst thou otherwise now behold me, all alone in my aërial seat, suffer good and bad alike; but girt with flames I would stand even within the battle-array, and draw on the Teucri to a deadly fight. I confess I inspired Juturna to succour her hapless brother, and for the sake of his life sanctioned her still greater deeds of daring; but yet not that she should hurl the lance, not that she should bend the bow; I swear by the inexorable source of the Stygian fount, the only name of awe imposed upon the gods of heaven. And now I indeed give

way, and with loathing leave the fight. This favour, which is withheld
by no ordinance of fate, I intreat of thee for the sake of Latium, for the
majesty of thy own people; when presently they shall with an auspicious
marriage (so let it be!) confirm the peace; when they shall form a union of
laws and covenants; bid not the Latins, the children of the soil, to change
their ancient name, nor to become Trojans, and be called Teucri; nor
command the men to alter their speech, or change the fashion of their
dress. Let there be Latium, let there be Alban kings, through every age;
let there be a Roman line strong in Italian valour; Troy has perished;
let her name have perished too." To her with a smile replied the author
of men and things: "Thou art Jove's sister, and the child of Saturn
second in power; dost thou roll within thy breast such mighty waves of
wrath? But come, and lower the rage thou hast in vain begun;. I give
thee thy wish; and vanquished and willing yield myself to thee. The
men of Ausonia shall keep their ancestral tongue and customs; and as it
now is, their name shall be; mixed in blood alone the Teucri shall settle
in the land; I will add besides a ceremonial, and forms of sacred rites,
and make them all Latins of one speech. Sprung from them thou shalt
behold a people, which shall arise partly of Ausonian descent, surpass
both men and gods in piety, and no nation so faithfully as this shall celebrate thy honours." To these words Juno gave compliance, and with joy
reversed her design. Meanwhile she withdrew from heaven, and left the
cloud.

842—886. *Jupiter prepares to withdraw Juturna from her brother.*
Description of the Diræ. One of these is sent to give the sign of the
death of Turnus. Juturna acknowledges the sign, and sadly departs.

When this is ended, the Father resolves in his heart another purpose,
and prepares to withdraw Juturna from her brother's side. Diræ by
name are called two sister fiends, who, with Tartarean Megæra, at one
and the selfsame birth were born to dismal Night; she wreathed them
each alike with snaky coils, and gave them wings of wind. These by the
throne of Jove, and portal of the angry king are seen, and deepen the
fears of suffering men; whenever the monarch of the gods wields dreadful
death and plagues, and terrifies with battle guilty towns. One of these
from the height of heaven Jove sends swiftly down, and bade her as an
omen meet Juturna. She flies along, and down to earth is borne with
rapid swoop: even as an arrow, driven from the string through a cloud,
which, armed with the venom of cruel poison, a Parthian or Cydonian has
shot, a shaft of point incurable, whizzing, and untraced, cleaves the fleeting shades. So moved the child of Night, and sought the earth. When
she descries the host of Ilium and the troops of Turnus, in a moment
contracted to the shape of a little bird, which sometime perching by night
on tombs or desolate roofs, unwelcome sings her late song through the
gloom; changed into this form, the fiend flies noisily backwards and forwards close before the face of Turnus, and lashes with her wings his
shield. A strange lethargy unnerved his limbs with dread, and his locks
stood up with horror, and his speech was choked in his throat. Then his
sister Juturna, so soon as she recognizes the scream and flapping wings
of· the fiend, rends in grief her loosened hair, disfiguring with her nails

her face, and with her hands her breast: "How can your sister help you
now, my Turnus? or what course now is left to my cruel self? By what
art can I keep you in the light of life? Can I confront so dread a monster? Now I leave the field. Affright me not in my fear, ill-omened
birds; I know well the lashing of your wings, and your funereal scream;
and am well aware of the proud commands of sovereign Jove. Is this
the reward he renders me for my ravished maidenhood? Wherefore gave
he me an everlasting life? Why is the ordinance of death reft from me?
else now certainly I could put an end to woes so deep, and pass through
the shades, by the side of my hapless brother. I immortal! nay, will anything I possess be sweet to me without you, my brother? O that some
abyss of earth deep enough would yawn to receive me, and send me,
goddess though I be, deep down to the world of the dead!" So much
the goddess spoke, and with many a groan wrapped her head in her azure
mantle, and plunged into the depths of the river.

887—952. *The last effort of Turnus. He feels his powers benumbed by
the presence of the fiend. The narrative of his death.*

Æneas presses on against the foe, and brandishes the tree, his spear's
mighty staff, and thus he speaks with fierceness of soul: "What now is
your next means of delay? or why, Turnus, do you still shrink from me?
It is not in speed of foot, but in close fight, with biting arms, we must
contend. Change yourself into all shapes, and compass aught you can
in valour or craft; wish on pinions to search out the starry heights, or to
hide yourself enclosed within the hollow earth." The other, shaking his
head: "Your savage words, fierce foe, affright me not; the foes that me
affright are Heaven and Jove." No more he speaks; and glancing round
beholds a mighty stone, a mighty stone it was and old, which chanced
to lie on the plain, set for a landmark of the field, to keep away conten-
tion from the lands. Scarcely could twelve picked men upheave it on
their shoulders, such human frames as earth produces now. He caught
it up with hurrying hand, and flung it at his foe, he, a hero, rising to his
height, and running hard. But neither in running, nor in his movement,
does he feel his proper self, or as he uplifts in his hand, and hurls the
ponderous stone: his knees totter; his blood is chill and curdled with
cold. Besides, that very crag he cast, as it whirled through the empty
void, passed not over all the space, and failed to reach its mark. Even
as in sleep, when in the night-time languid rest weighs down the eyes,
we seem in vain to wish to run with eagerness a distant course, and in
our very efforts feebly sink down; the tongue is powerless, our usual force
of body serves us not, and neither words nor voice attend our will: so
from Turnus, by whatever brave attempt he strives to win, the fell goddess withholds success. Then various feelings work within his breast.
He stares at the Rutulians and the town; and hesitates in dread, and
shudderingly fears that the lance is upon him; and sees not whither he
can escape, nor by what means of assault he can advance against his
enemy, nor his car anywhere, and the charioteer, his sister. Against him
as he hesitates, Æneas waves his fatal shaft, choosing with his eye the
opportunity, and with all his might he flings it from afar. Never do
crags resound so loud, hurled forth by the battering engine, nor do claps

so great crash forth from the thunderbolt. On like a gloomy whirlwind flies the lance, bearing dread doom; and unseams the hem of the corslet, and the outermost circles of the sevenfold shield; griding it passes through the midst of his thigh. Beneath the blow, with doubled knee, down falls the mighty Turnus to the ground. With a groan the Rutulians rise, and all the mountain echoes around, and far and wide the lofty groves repeat the cry. He, a humble suppliant, lifting the eyes, and stretching forth the hand of prayer: "I have in truth myself deserved, nor deprecate my doom: use the advantage fortune gives you: if you can be touched with any feeling for a hapless parent, I beseech you (you too had such a father in Anchises), pity the age of Daunus, and give me back alive to my friends, or, if you please, my body reft of life. You have conquered, and the Ausonians have seen me stretch forth my hands, a conquered man. Lavinia is your bride. Press not to further deeds of hate." Æneas, fierce in arms, stood still, rolling his eyes, and checked his hand. And ever more and more the words began to melt him as he paused; when o'er the shoulder was unhappily seen the sword-belt, and the cincture of young Pallas glittered with its well-known studs; Pallas, whom Turnus with a wound had vanquished and slain, and now wore on his shoulders the ensign of his foe. The Trojan, when he had gazed his fill upon those spoils, the memorials of bitter grief, fired with fury, and terrible with wrath: "Shall you, clad in the spoils of my friends, be snatched from me? Pallas, Pallas, with this blow makes you a sacrifice, and draws his vengeance from your guilty blood." With these words, full in his breast he plunges deep the steel, in the heat of wrath; but coldly droop the other's limbs, and with a sigh the affronted soul flies forth beneath the shades.

INDEX.

[The references are to the pages.]

A.

Acestes (Trojan prince in Sicily), generous, 86; hospitably receives the Trojans, 143; chides Entellus, 150; his arrow gives an omen, 152; one who sympathizes, 156; city named from, 156

Achates (friend of Æneas), may represent Agrippa, 79; attends Æneas, 88, 162, 268

Achilles, restored Hector's body, 92, 108; combat with Æneas, 158; kings of Macedonia descended from, 176

Æneas, his character great fault of Æneid, 80; his lamentation in the storm, 84; encourages his friends, 86; meets his mother, 88; comes to Carthage, 91; his grateful speech, 94; begins the tale of his adventures, 97; sees vision of Hector, 103; his useless efforts, 105; checked by his mother, 109; rescues his father, 112; loses his wife, 112; goes to Delos, 115; to Crete, 116; to the Strophades, 118; to Buthrotum, 119; coasts along Italy to Sicily, 124; coasts along Sicily, 127; Dido's love for, 128; pleads the command of Jove, 134; leaves Carthage, 139; received by Acestes, 143; celebrates games, 143; prays to Jove for rain, 155; sees his father in a dream, 156; lands at Cumæ, 159; consults the Sibyl, 160; finds golden bough, 163; descends to the lower regions, 164; reaches Elysium, 172; hears from his father the doctrines of philosophy, 174; sees in a mystic valley the future heroes of Rome, 175; enters the mouth of the Tiber, 178; fortifies his camp, 181; sends gift to Latinus, 181; sees vision of the river-god, 195; visits Evander, 197; receives celestial arms, 206; sails over the sea with Etruscan troops, 227; sea-nymphs appear to, 229; slays many men, 231; grief at death of Pallas, 235; slays Lausus, 240; Mezentius, 242; gracious reply to Latins, 245; praised by Diomede, 248; advances to the city, 251; pitches his camp, 260; field prepared for his combat with Turnus, 263; his prayer, 264; is wounded, 267; is miraculously healed, 269; his deeds of valour, 271; threatens to burn the city, 272; his combat with Turnus, 275; his victory, 279.

Æneid, the imperial poem, 78; truly Roman poem, 78; hence faults and merits, 79; in what sense a religious poem, 79; speaks to the heart, 81; compared with Iliad, 80; has many faults, 81; chiefly the character of Æneas, 80; compared with Georgics, 81

Æolus (god of winds), his cavern, 83; Juno (goddess of air) begs help of, 83; Neptune bids him bluster at home, 85; storm of, 158; island (Lipare) named from, 202

Agrigentum (Girgenti), its giant walls, 127

Agrippa, perhaps represented by Achates, 79; his figure on the shield, 207

Alba Longa, fathers of, 82; founded by Iulus, 87; kings of, 87, 175; origin of name (white), 121

Alecto (fury), summoned by Juno, 184; fills the queen with frenzy, 185; enrages Turnus, 187; rustics, 188; returns to lower world, 189

Alphesibœus sings of charms, 25, 26

Alternate couplets, 16, 17, 23, 24

Amata, her frenzy, 185; her love for Turnus, 262; her suicide, 272

Anchises, struck by lightning, 110; encouraged by sign, 111; is carried by his son, 112; mistakes oracle, 116; is better advised, 117; his prayer, 119; dies at Drepanum, 127; his troubled phantom, 135; a seer, 143; his familiar spirit, 144; appears in vision, 156; meets his son in Elysium, 173; Evander remembers him, 197; his memory recalled, 279

Ancus, king of Rome, somewhat boastful, 176

Andromache, her affectionate sorrows, 120; sad parting, 121

Anna, encourages Dido's love, 128; her entreaties, 137; is deceived by her sister, 138; her misery, 141

Antenor, founder of Padua, 87

Antony, perhaps represented by Turnus, 79; his figure on the shield, 207

Apollo (Phœbus), warns the poet, 21; visits Gallus, 28; of Thymbra, 72, 115; archer god, 115; bids Trojans seek their ancient mother, 116; sailor's dread, 119; of Claros, 121; pitied Troy, 160; shrine and holydays of, 161; keeps promise to the ear, 166; Actian, 208; snow-white portal of, 208; praises Iulus, 221; of Sóracte, 258; his various gifts, 268

Arethusa (fountain and nymph), glides under the sea, 28, 127

Aristæus, story of, 72

Ascanius, see Iulus.

Atlas (sage and mountain), his lore, 97; description of mountain, 133; bearer of the sky, 175

Augury, happy omen from, 90; interpretation of, 266; Apollo, giver of, 268

Augustus, his insipid character, 80; had not a court like a modern one, 80; character a misfortune to Æneid, 80; about to rise to heaven, 33; his fame, 55; his happy age, 88; celebrated Actian games, 78, and game of Troy, 79; his glory at Actium, 207; triumph at Actium, 79, 208; exaggerated praises of, 175

Aurora (morning), pale, 41; blushing, 124; early, 125; bright, 143; unclouded, 144; rosy, 170; saffron, 178; brings-back toil, 246; borne upon crimson wheels, 262

Avernus (lake), channels of, 46; its woods, 122: noisome, 163; according to Virgil derived from Greek ἄορνος (birdless), 164

B.

Bacchus, wild dances of, 20; his buskins, 43; goat sacrificed to, 50; his hymns and masks, 50; cause of offence, 52; his orgies, 76, 134, 186; dances and cups, 257; of Naxos, 116; his travels, 175; of Nysa, 175

Bees, emblem of toil, 31; easily offended, 66; active in spring, 66; their swarming, 66; their battles, 67; their flower-garden, 67, 68; their republic, 68, 69; compared to Cyclops, 69; shortness of individual life, eternity of race, 69, 70; loyal creatures, 70; their natural enemies, 70; sickness and remedies, 71; method of renewal of their race, 71; simile of, 91; another simile of, 173

Bough, golden, 162, 163; Charon recognizes it, 167; is deposited at Pluto's palace, 172

Britons, separate from the world, 8, 13; woven in tapestry, 54

Brutus, stern patriot, 176

Bulls, fierce are the battles of, 59; rivers represented as, 73, 166

Byrsa, Carthage citadel of, 89; wrong derivation of name, 89

C.

Cacus (robber), story of, 198, 199

Cæculus found on the hearth, 176

Cæsar, Julius, represented by Daphnis, 10, 19; his murder, 42; his descent from the Alps, 176

Camilla, warrior maiden, 194; her generous offer, 252; the story of her childhood, 253, 254; her exploits, 256; her death, 258, 259; is avenged by Opis, 259

Camillus bringing back the standards, 176

Capitol, passage of triumph up to, 176; supposed abode of Jove, 201; immoveable, 217

Carinæ, street in Rome, sumptuous, 201

Carthage, dear to Juno, 82; newly founded, 88, 89; building of, 90; its harbour, temple, theatre, 91; character of people, 91, 95; future foe of Rome, 140; simile of its destruction, 141; war with Rome, 224; ironical mention of, 225

Cassandra, warns in vain, 102; loved by Corœbus, 104; dragged from temple, 105; not listened to, 117; phantom of, 154; ravings of, 226

Catiline, his punishment, 207

Cato, censor, 176; of Utica, 207

Cattle should be chosen carefully for breeding, 55; gently to be cared for, 57

Cerberus charmed by the song of Orpheus, 75; by honey cake, 168

Ceres sustains life, 32; yellow, 34; teacher of men, 35; poppy dear to, 37; golden, 38; to be adored by husbandmen, 39; lawgiver, 129

Charon, grotesque description of, 165; awed by golden bough, 167

Charybdis, description of, 122; dreaded, 124; instrument of Juno, 184

Circe, power of, 26; her groves and lights and magical powers, 178

Cleopatra perhaps represented by Dido, 79; her figure on the shield, 207, 208

Client, fraud against, punished hereafter, 171

Cocles, in Ennius' annals, 79; defends bridge, 207; Turnus represents him, 224

Corinth, triumph over, 176

Corydon, his desperate love, 13, 14; matched with Thyrsis, 23; victorious, 24

Crete, Jove's isle, 116; Trojans settle in it, 116; pestilence there, 116; Labyrinth in it, 153; represented in sculpture, 160

Creusa lost to her husband, 112; her phantom, 113

Cybele, mother of the gods, her mysteries, 116; her crown and family, 175; her promise from Jove, 210: her awful appearance, 210; her showy priest Chloreus, 258

Cyclades, voyage through, 116

Cyclops, bees compared to, 69; a hundred monstrous, 126; forges of, 202

Cyrene (nymph), sorrow for, and aid to her son, 72, 73, 74

D.

Damœtas, his quarrel and singing match with Menalcas, 15, 16, 17

Damon, his complaint, 25

Dante, his relation to Virgil, 6

Daphnis represents Julius Cæsar, 10; ideal shepherd, 19; his apotheosis, 20; patron of rural life, 20

Dardanus, sprang from Italy, 117, 182; common origin to people of Epirus and Italy, 123; founder of Troy, 172; descended from Atlas, 197

Dares, a braggart, 149; beaten by Entellus, 151

Death, inexorable, 55; sickness drawing on to, 64; no room for, 70; in many a shape, 105; to be found with one's own hand, 110; interest of, 136; prayed for, 137; approach of, 141; undeserved, 162; even after it, woes remain hereafter, 168; image of, 170; lingering, 204; Cleopatra pallid at approach of, 208; tranquil, 217; father living by a son's, 241; happy in, 246; expiates anger of Heaven, 231; description of, 259; not so passing hard, 273; bitterness of, 274

Decii, glory of Italy, 46, 176

Defile, description of, 189

Deiphobus, cruel murder of, 169, 170

Delos, Latona's isle, 54; once floating, 115: temple there, 115; Trojans visit it, 115; the dances of Apollo in, 131

Destiny, see Fate.

Diana, simile of, 92; of triple countenance, 138; her care of Hippolytus, 193; tells the tale of Camilla's childhood, and dedication of herself, 253, 254; predicts her death and bids Opis avenge her, 253, 254

Didactic poets, Virgil prince of, 30; modern rather follow Horace, 31

Dido may represent Cleopatra, 79; her sorrow at Tyre, 89; founds Carthage, 89; her retinue and fair form, 92; her modest speech, 93; her passion, 96, 128; her hunting-party, 130, 131; her reproaches, 135; her despair, 137; her funeral pile, 138; her death, 141, 142; flames of funeral pile, 142; her phantom in the mourning fields, 168

Diomede, Æneas' combat with, 84; his testimony to Æneas, 248

Dogs useful to husbandmen, 62

Donatus (so called), his life of Virgil, 1; appears to be true in the main, 2

Drances may represent Cicero, 79; embassy to Æneas, 245; his character, 249; his speech against Turnus, 250; his taunts shame Turnus, 273

Dreams of Dido about her husband, 89; of Æneas about Hector, 103; of Dido about her loneliness, 137; of Æneas about his father, 156; true and false, 177; of wondrous phantoms, 179; of Æneas about the river-god Tiber, 195; simile of, 278

Dryden, quoted, 1, 4, 7, 8, 80; mentions the Sortes Virgilianæ, 4

E.

East wind (Eurus), its fury, 45; Riphæan, 61; horses of, 106; swifter than, 199, 275

Eclogues of Virgil, artificial, 9; contrast with the Idylls of Theocritus, 9; disregard of consistency in, 9; comparison of the 4th with Isaiah, 10; beauty of the 5th, 10; their faults and merits, 11; imitation of them by later poets, 11; superiority of them to most modern pastoral poetry, 11

Elissa, Phœnician name of Dido, 135

Elysian fields, description of, 172

Ennius, his Annals, a national poem, 79

Epicurus, his tenets, 1; his account of the creation of the world adopted, 10, 22; his philosophy, 40, 52; life of ease, 52, 53

Etruria, brave, 53; righteous wrath of, 204; their camp, 206; their captains and troops, 228; their cavalry, 254; taunts against their luxury, 257

Euryalus, his merit and beauty, 148, 149; his race, 149; episode of, 212; his death, 217; lamentation of his mother, 218

Eurydice all but recovered, 75

Evander, Æneas visits him, 197; his worship of Hercules, 200; his honourable poverty, 201; makes Etruscans allies of Trojans, 203; his sad farewell to his son, 205; his lamentation for his slain son, 246

F.

Fabius restores state by delay, 176

Fabricius, rich in scanty store, 176

Fate, its steadfast will, 18; Æneid, epic of, 79, 80; things grow worse by its rule, 36; Jupiter unrolls its hidden book, 91; will find its way, 121; Juno inferior to, 184; nought can change, 184: may however be delayed,

184, 237; willing follower of, 197; its will, 204; smiled upon by, 204; fates counter to fates, 184, 211; Jupiter may perhaps control, 237; free by, 227; summon men, 236; give a home and kingdom, 245; walls allowed by, 245; permit men to deceive, 256; expounded to the timorous, 263; intend present war, future peace, 270; prevail, 274

Fauns, invoked, 32; aboriginal, 200

Faunus, son of Picus, his oracle, 179; glorious race of, 182; aids Turnus in the fight, 276

Feast on African shore, 86; at Carthage, 96, 97; in an isle of the Strophades, 118; in palace of Helenus, 121; on coast of Italy, 180; Etruscan, 257

Feelings, kindly inspired by Mercury, 88; change of, to joy, 158

Forest, hardy and useful trees of, various in kind, 51, 52; fire in, 49; Æneas meets his mother in, 88; description of, 163; mystic bough in, 163; fiend lurks in, 188; on banks of Tiber, 196; of wide extent, 216; trees cut down in, 245

Forum, Roman (campo Vaccino), cattle lowing in, 201

Funeral, description of, 163, 164, 246, 247; anniversary of, 143

Furies, Envy dreads, 54; charmed by Orpheus, 75; of a guilty race, 120; seen by Pentheus and Orestes, 137; iron chambers of, 165; grim stream of, 167; the eldest of, 171; dreadful appearance of one, 187; glance of, 207; fell, 208; under name of Diræ, 277; Tisiphone, 65; Alecto, 184; Megæra, 277

G.

Gallus, friend of Virgil, 1; joined with the nine Muses, 1; praises of him by Virgil lost, 1; his death, 1; love for Lycoris, 28; comforted by men and gods, 28; his passionate complaint, 29

Games, (1) boat-race, 145; (2) foot-race, 148; (3) boxing-match, 149; (4) archery, 152; (5) game of Troy, 153

Garden, useful to bees, 68; description of one near Tarentum, 68

Georgics, unlike Hesiod's Works and Days, 30; not much indebted to Aratus and Nicander, 30; contrast of them with Lucretius' poem, 30; not much imitated by modern poets, 31; begun, B. C. 37, 31; not a practical work, 31; melancholy tone in them, 31; the most finished of Virgil's writings, 32; unreality in them, 32; sympathy with nature in them, 32; contrasted with Æneid, 81

Ghost of Creusa, 113; restless, appeased, 115

Glory, sudden revelations of, 90, 94, 109, 111, 117, 155, 221

Goats, enemies of Bacchus, 50; a hardy and valuable flock, 60

Gods, of the country invoked, 32, 33; of our land, 42; those of the Æneid compared with the Iliad, 80; the constraint of, 82; regard the benevolent, 94; rulers stand fast by, 104; arbitrary will of, 106; watch evil deeds, 108; fighting against Troy, 110; invited to a share of spoil, 118; lords of sea, 124; guardians of a dying queen, 140; invoked in boat-race, 147; possess realm of spirits, 164; fear to perjure themselves by the Styx, 166; vengeance belongs to, 170; bless men's purpose, 183; his own strong passion to each man as one, 212; pity man's vain fury, 239; altars too common, 263

Golden age, description of, 18; encouraged idleness, 35; to be established by Augustus, 175

Gossrau, his commentary on the Æneid, 7

H.

Hannibal, great enemy of Rome, 140; passage of the Alps by, 224

Harbour, land-locked, 85; another, 124; Tiber gives one to the Trojans, 178

Hatred, unrelenting, 81

Hector, picture of, 92; vision of, 103; his mother's thought of, 108; his grave, 149; kept Greeks at bay, 211; compared to Æneas, 248

Heinsius, his noble edition of Virgil, 7

Helenus, king in Epirus, 120; entertains Æneas, 121; reveals the fates, 121, 122; his gifts, 123

Hercules, poplar sacred to, 24; boxing-match with Eryx, 150; dress of, 191; punishes Cacus, 199; worship and praises of, 200; intercedes in vain for the life of Pallas, 234

Hesiod, practical writer, not imaginative, 30

Heyne gives an account of editions of Virgil, 7

Hive, where it should stand, and with what plants near it, 65, 66; construction of, 66; how bees to be re-called to, 67

Honey, how and when to be taken, 70

Horace, friend of Virgil, 1; mentions Virgil nine times, 2; Lord Lytton's remark on, 8; usual model of modern didactic poetry, 31

Horses, shape, colour, age, to be observed, 55; famous ones, 55; to be well fattened, 56; gadfly to be kept from, 57; should be treated kindly, 57; swift as the wind, 58; at times full of fury, 59; sad death of one in the plague, 64; omen from, of war, and yet of peace, 124; in the game of Troy, 153; of heavenly breed, 183; one that had sympathy for his master, 241; simile of, 252

Hunt, description of, 131; in the Italian wood, 188

Husbandman, has many enemies, 35; taught by Ceres, 35; should be grateful to her, 33; needs many implements, 35; must watch the heavenly bodies, 36; can trust nature, 37; should not neglect religion, 39, nor the signs of change of weather, 40, nor the warnings of sun and moon, 41; finds in the fields sad records of war, 42; happiness of his life, 52

I.

Iarbas (African prince), slighted by Dido, 129; his jealous prayer to Jove, 132

Ida, leafy, 147; lofty, 151; pine forest on, 210; choir of, 210; hunter's hill, 212; representation of, 227; the queen of (Cybele), 229;

dittany from Cretan, 269; Lyrnessus beneath, 271

Ilioneus, spokesman of Trojan, 93, 182

Ilium (see also Troy), home of gods, 102; its glory gone, 104; sinks in flames, 110; stood against divine pleasure, 160

Infants, their piteous woe in Hades, 168

Iris, her various hues, 142; severs the lock of life, 142; in human form addresses Trojan matrons, 154; sent to Turnus, 208; glory of the sky, 209; forbids help to Turnus, 224; sent from the clouds, 226

Irony, instances of, 108, 135, 140, 187, 221, 236, 250, 278

Italy, praises of, 45; Virgil describes scenery of, 81; whence named, 93; called Hesperia mighty and rich, 93, 117; destined to Trojans, 117, 135, 216; nearer part occupied by Greeks, 122; low coast of, saluted, 124; Trojans coast along, 124; big with empire, 132; descendants of line of, 174; is excited, 190; its ancient tribes, 191; hardihood of its race, 220; daughters of, 256; not bidden to obey Trojans, 264; valour of, strength of Rome, 277

Iulus (Ascanius), once Ilus, 87; gives name to Julian house, 89; Cupid takes his form, 96; follows his father, 112; reminds Andromache of Astyanax, 123; a keen sportsman, 131, 188; a captain in the game of Troy, 153; upbraids Trojan matrons, 155; his playful remark, 180; shoots Sylvia's deer, 188; has a soul beyond his years, 214; slays a vain boaster, 221; is praised by Apollo, 221; second hope of Rome, 264; stimulated by the example of his father and uncle, 269

Ivory, gate of, 177; India produces, 33; weeps, 42; in art, 94, 172, 243, 262

J.

Janus, prophecy of his gates being closed, 88; with double forehead, 181; guardian, 190; gates opened by Juno, 190; citadel of, 201

Jesuits, their schools, 8; learned French, 7

Juno, her contest with fate, 80; causes of her anger, 82; stirs up a mighty tempest, 83; will one day favour Rome, 88; occupies Scæan gates, 110; to be conquered by vows, 122; guardian of marriage ties, 129; conversation with Venus, 130; pities Dido, 142; stirs up Trojan matrons, 154; her rage against Æneas, 184; calls up Alecto, 184; opens gates of war, 190; sends Iris to Turnus, 208; does not dare to help Turnus, 224; inveighs against Venus, 226; is taunted by Jove, 236; but rescues Turnus, 237; impels Juturna to break the truce, 263, 264; her appeal to Jove, 276; yields at last to fate, 277

Jupiter, appoints toil to be the lot of man, 35; his thunderbolt, 39; to be feared by grapes, 51; fed by bees, 68; unrolls the fates, 87; stirs up gods against Troy, 110; Anchises prays to him, 111; Iarbas prays to him, 132; warrant of his word, 142; his armour-bearer, 147; sends a great rain, 156; thunders in a cloudless sky, 180; shakes his ægis, 201;

Evander prays to, 205; convokes council of gods, 224; declares fates inviolable, 226; his nod, 227; declares limits of life and virtue, 234; his conversation with Juno, 236, 237; bids Juno yield, 276; predicts the piety of the Romans, 277; sends a fiend down, 277; the enemy of Turnus, 278

Juturna, nymph-sister of Turnus, in the form of Camers urges the breaking of the truce, 265; prevents Æneas from engaging with Turnus, 269, 270; in the form of Metiscus encourages Turnus, 273; still aids Turnus, 276; is at last forced to leave him, 277; her sad complaint, 278

K.

Keightley, 1, 7
Kings, two rival, in one hive, 67; reverence for, among bees, Parthians, and other people, 70; shall reign for 300 years in Alba, 87; a just, pious, brave king, 93; Anius king and priest at once, 115; succession of kings of Rome, 175, 176

L.

Labour, its praises in the Georgics, 31; bees the emblem of, 31; Jove's rule ordained it, 35; is victorious in difficulties, 35; needed in little things, 36; summer the special time for, 38; yet no season unsuitable, 38; needed in dressing the vine, 50
Labyrinth, puzzling bower, 153; famous bewilderment, 160
Lakes of Italy, Larius (Como), Benacus rising with boisterous turmoil (Garda), Lucrine with barrier, 46; living, 52; Avernus, 46, 163, 164; sacred to Trivia, 188; Ciminus, 192; Anguitia, Fucinus with glassy pool, 193; Stygian, 20
Laocoon, his wise advice, 98; his dreadful death, 101
Laomedon, faithless, 42; true children of, 119; treachery of race of, 139
Latinus, his descent, respect for religion, 179; kindly speech and gifts to the strangers, 183; passive resistance, 189; convokes council, 247; advises moderation, 249; his fruitless intreaties to Turnus, 261; his solemn vows and prayer, 264, 265; rends his garments, 273, his amazement, 274
Latium, race of, 82; hardy youth of, 181; why so called, 201; defeat of cavalry of, 259; Jove intreated for the sake of, 277; is not to be merged in the Trojans, 277
Lausus, contrast to his father, 191; fates forbid his engaging with Pallas, 233; episode of, 240; saves his father by his own death, 240
Lavinia, only child of Latinus, 179; promised to the stranger, 183; her mother's anger thereat, 185; becomes a bacchant, 186; is a suppliant at the temple of Minerva, 252; her modest beauty, 262; bewails her mother's death, 272
Lethe, poppies steeped in, 34, 159; description of, 173, 174

Love, hopeless, 13; frenzied, 29; conquers all the world, 29; drives all nature to fury, 58; god of, scorns the thunderbolt, 95; takes form of Iulus, 96; deep draughts of, 97; cannot be cured by sacrifices, 129; pride surrenders to, 136; restless, 138; its wasting power, 168
Lucretius, earnest writer, 30; followed by Virgil, 10, 22, 31, 64, 278
Lycidas, wonders at what Mœris tells him, 27; begs Mœris to sing, 27, 28

M.

Mæcenas, dedications to him, 32, 43, 54, 65
Mœris, tells how poetry is powerless, 27; repeats verses of Menalcas, 27; his memory fails him, 28
Manlius, guard of Tarpeian rock, 207
Mantua, Virgil's property near, 1; sacred tree at, 5; scenery of, 9; too near to Cremona, 27; hapless, 46; whence named, 228; the races of, 228
Marcellus, praises of the two, a lament for the younger's early death, 176, 177
Mars of civil strife, 42; chariot of, 55; father of Romulus, 87; walls of, 87; Thrace sacred to, 114; Gradivus, 114; the dread of, 190; car and wheels made for, by the Cyclops, 203; wolf of, 219; lord of war, 222; governs all wars, 264; his river, shield, steeds, dreadful retinue, 267
Melancholy tone of Georgics, 31, 36, 55
Melibœus, forced to leave his farm, 12; congratulates Tityrus, 13; adjudges prize to Corydon, 24
Menalcas put for Virgil, 10; has lost his farm, 10, 27; his contest with Damœtas, 15, 16, 17; praised by Mopsus, 21; songs by him, 27; his return looked for, 28
Mercury, fiery planet, 39; inspires kindly feelings, 88; his flight to earth, 133; bids Æneas quit Carthage, 133; warns him in a dream, 139; son of Maia, forefather of Evander, 197
Messapus bears a charmed life, his troops, 192; foremost chief, 194; captain of cavalry, 252; attacks Æneas, 270; with Atinas rallies the host, 274
Mezentius, despiser of gods, 191; his monstrous cruelty, 204; his exploits, 238, 239; his own hand his god, 240; saved by his good son, 240; lamentation over his son, 241; his death, 242; spoils of, 243
Mincius river with waving rushes, 23; its winding course, 54; child of lake Benacus, 228
Minerva (Pallas), loves citadels, 17; inventress of olive, 32; hurls Jove's lightning, 83; her skill built wooden horse, 97; her fateful Palladium, 100; her statue animated for temporary life, 101; cruel Tritonis, 102; gleams with Gorgon, 110; clashes arms, 124; work of the loom her art, 148; her armour, 203; theft of her Palladium, 211; the storm which she sent, 248; procession to her temple, 252
Minos, Roman prætor, 79; his realm (Crete), 159; shakes the judicial urn, 168
Mnestheus, house of, Memmius derived from,

144; his address to his crew, 176; repulses Turnus, 224

Mopsus praised by Menalcas, 20

Mourning Fields, abode of those crossed in love, 163

Muse, invocation of, 18, 82, 178, 191, 228; set forth Jove as the beginning, 16; brought back by Virgil, 54; Cretheus, mate of, 223

Mythological subjects trite, 54

N.

Nautes, his sage counsel, 156

Neptune, produced the first horse, 32; his monstrous herds, 73; his serene majesty, 84; calms storm, 85; destroys the walls of Troy, 109; god of Ægean, 115; bull sacrificed to, 116; promises safety to Trojan fleet, 158; his horses, car and retinue, 158; fills sails with favouring winds, 178; on the side of Augustus at Actium, 208; Troy built by, 158, 211

Niebuhr, accounts Virgil useful to the antiquarian, 4; unfavourable judge of Æneid, 3, 78

Night, fatal to Troy, 102; calm, 124; gloomy, 125; silent, 138; bright, 178; goddess invoked, 180; deception of, 216; ends mourning, 247; her dire progeny, 277

Nile, whose stream flows proudly, 54; overflowing, 71; sevenfold in terror, 175; calling vanquished to his dark-blue lap, 208; ebbing with fertilizing waters, 209

Nisus, his love for Euryalus, 148; through him his friend wins the race, 149; episode of him and Euryalus, 212; his generous conduct, 212, 213; his exploits, 215; avenges his friend and dies, 217

North wind (Aquilo, Boreas), cold of, little recked of, 24; penetrating, 34; grim, 40; steady, 58; mares run towards, 59; sent to aid of mariners, 127; Alpine, 137; Thracians descended from, 231; roaring across the Ægean deep, 268

Numa, his peaceful reign, 175

Nymphs, easy-tempered, 15; wept for Daphnis, 19; Dictæan, 22; beloved by shepherds, 23; throng of, 29; sister-nymphs, 52; names and occupation of, 72; sisterhood of, 73; revere Proteus, 73; grotto home of, 85; one of the race of, 89; worshipped, 114; cry aloud on mountain-top, 131; retinue of Neptune, 158; prayed to, 180; Egeria one of them, 193; from whom rivers take birth, 196; Carmentis one of them, 201; ships transformed into, 211; appear to Æneas out at sea, 229

O.

Olives, invented by Minerva, 32; what soil fruitful in, 47; easily reared, 51; dear to peace, 51, 197

Omens, from blasted oaks, 12; from the crow on the left-hand, 27; from fire, 111; from Dido's funeral pile, 142; from Acestes' arrow, 152; from playful word, 180; religious soul stirred by, 183; comfort from, 229; from first success, 231; though deceitful hailed with shouts, 266

Oracles, oaks revered, as by Greece, 43; terrible response of that of Apollo, 99; that at Delos ambiguous, 115; that of Faunus beneath Albunea, 179; holy ones of heaven, 197

Orion, stormy, 93; his belt and sword, 124; watery, 129; fierce setting of, 192; in the seas and on the hills, 239

Orpheus, his descent and sad death, 75, 76; holy bard in Elysium, 172

P.

Padus (Eridanus, Po), monarch of rivers, 42; with horns gilded, 73

Palæmon, a judge who cannot decide, 16, 17

Palinurus (pilot), loses his course, 118; waits for clear sky, 124; yields to foul weather, 142; beguiled by the god Sleep, 159; his death, 159; his sorrows in Hades, 166; his partial consolation, 167

Pallas, see Minerva.

Pallas (son of Evander), meets Æneas, 196; Evander's farewell to, 205; compared to morning star, 206; sits by Æneas in the ship, 227; his courage, 232; Hercules intercedes for, 234; his death, 234; honour to his dead body, 244; his father's lamentation for, 246

Pan, his art and office, 14; would allow himself vanquished, 19; Arcadia's god, 28; would not suffer reeds to rest idle, 25; Lord of Tegea, 32; gift to the Moon, 62; Lupercal called from Lycæum, 201

Parthians, famed for bow, 29; whose trust is in flight, 54; their reverence for their kings, 70; begin with arrows the prelude of the fray, 72; restore Roman standards, 190; shoot arrows armed with poison, 277

Penates (household gods), hapless, 53; carried by Æneas over the sea, 90; Hector commends them to him, 103; embraced by bay tree, 108; must not be touched by bloody hands, 112; appear in a nightly vision, 117; sprinkled with blood, 128; invited to a feast, 143; in vain rescued, 154; faithful bid to hail, 180; vanquished, 194; objects of adjuration, 213

Personification, of Envy, 54; of Honour, 88; of unnatural Fury, 88; of Fame, 131; of Grief, Fear, Hunger, Death, Toil, Sleep, bad Delights, War, 165; of Discord, 208; of Dread, Anger, Ambush, 267

Philomela (nightingale), her feasts, gifts, flight, 22; simile of her sorrows, 76

Philosophy, doubtful to what school Virgil belongs, 1; hardly suited for, 31; expounds doctrines of Epicurus, 22, 52; materialistic preferred, 40; Æneid, how like Stoic dissertation, 80; doctrine of the soul of the universe, 70, 174

Phlegethon, joined with Chaos, 164; waves of torrent fire, 170

Pictures of Trojan war, 91

Plague, cause of destruction, pollution, misery, 63, 64, 65; wastes the Trojans in Crete, 116

Plough, difficult description of, 36; has not its meed of honour, 42; marks city's walls, 157; rich Galæsus had a hundred, 188

Ploughing, to begin early, 33; cross ploughing recommended, 34

Pluto (Dis), Tænarus deep portal of, 75, 207; lock holy to, 142; nether home of, 156; unsubstantial realms of, 164; bridal chamber of, 167; battlements of, 170; Alecto hateful to. 184; Amsanctus vent of, 189; sanctuary of unpitying, 264

Pollio, a poet, 17; in his consulship a happier age is to begin, 18

Pompey, Priam's death may represent his, 79; has with him all the East in battle array, 176

Porsena, in act of menace on the shield, 207

Portents, at death of Cæsar, 42; no uncertain ones given by Minerva, 101; at Polydorus' grave, 114; before Dido's death, 137; intimate Heaven's wrath, 156; of coming strangers, 179; Turnus undaunted by, 211; of horrible appearance pursue Diomede, 248

Priam, his sorrows represented in a picture, 91; his kindness to the captive, 100; his palace, 106; his death, 108; his noble race, 148, 214; Greek sorrows that even he might pity, 248

Procne (swallow), her breast marked with her bloody hands, 66

Proteus, old man of the sea, 73; his wonderful transformations and knowledge, 74; column of, 248

Pyrrhus (Neoptolemus) descends from wooden horse, 102; his exploits, 107; slays Priam, 108; marries Andromache, 120; slain by jealous Orestes, 120

Q.

Quirinus (Romulus), victorious, 54; united with his brother Remus, 88; captured arms hung up to, 176; his crooked wand, 181; state robe of, 190

R.

Ramsay, Allan, natural pastoral poet, 11

Religious rites, attention to, 39; duly observed, 76, 77; observance of, part of Roman character, 80; gods jealous of their observance, 83; power of, 122; unavailing against love's frenzy, 129; polluted by prodigies, 137; part of feasts, 73, 96, 144, 180, 198, 200; at the Sibyl's shrine, 160; at the mouth of hell, 164; in honour of Hercules, 200; attention to, unavailing against fate, 237; observance of, before a peace, 264

Richter, his judgment of the Æneid, 78

Rome, highly exalted above all other towns, 12; the Sun showed pity for, 42; beauty of the world, 53; walls of lofty, 82; boundless empire of, 87; Hector's prophecy of, 103; kings and heroes of, 176; panegyric of, 176; its business to rule the nations, 176; mighty wealth of Rome, 196; site of, 201; forum of, 201; triumph of, 208; Alban and Latin, and Italian, rather than Trojan, 277; distinguished for piety, 277

Romulus, prayer to him to preserve Augustus, 42; son of Ilia and Mars, 87; marked with glory as a tenant of the sky, 175; made a grove a refuge, 201; birth of, 206; the thatch of his palace freshly covered, 207

S.

Sacrifices, see Religious rites.

Sarpedon slain, 84; Jove did not save him, though his own son, 234

Saturn, cold planet of, 39; his crooked knife, 51; the life he passed on earth, 53; once king in Latium, 175; old god, 181; righteous character of children of, 182; land and citadel of, 201

Scenery contrasted with sorrow and death, 81, 138, 188, 193, 195, 216, 217, 220, 240, 241, 244, 254, 269, 270, 271, 275

Scipios, stout in war, 46; bane of Libya, 176

Sculpture on doors of Apollo's temple, 159, 160

Scylla, her barking monsters, 22; pays the penalty of her sin, 40; her cliffs and caverns, 86; description of, 122

Servius, character of his commentary, 4; useful to antiquarian, 80

Sheep, a lowly subject, but original, 59, 60; care required for, 60; diseases of, 63

Shield of Turnus, 194; of Æneas, compartments of, 206, 207; circle of sea, 207; centre, battle of Actium, 207, 208; flight of Cleopatra, 208; triumph of Augustus, 208

Ships, one sunk in the sea, 84; twenty in number at first, 90; twelve swans sign of the twelve missing, 90; Ilioneus begs they may be repaired, 93; built at the foot of Ida, 114; tempest-tossed, 118; sail in haste from Carthage, 139; set on fire by the Trojan matrons, 155; all saved, but four, 156; enter the Tiber, 178; threatened by Turnus, 210; transformed by Cybele into sea-nymphs, 211

Sibyl, books of, 10; Cumæan hymn of, 18; cavern, leaves and prophecies of, 122, 123; her inspiration, 160; her instructions, 162; guide into hell, 164; mistress of the groves of Avernus, 171

Silenus, his song, 22

Similes, in Georgics of chariot race, 42; battle array, 48; north wind, 58; wave, 58; Cyclops, 69; nightingale, 76; in Æneid of good man, 85; busy bees, 91; Diana, 92; bellowing bull, 102; fire and stream, 103; wolves, 104; snake, 105, 107; winds, 106; river, 107; doves, 108; ash, 110; oaks and cypresses, 127; doe, 129; Apollo, 131; sea-bird, 133; bacchanalian, 134; ants, 136; oak, 137; destruction of Carthage, 141; rainbow, 144; charioteers, 145; dove, 146; snake surprised, 147; city or fort beleaguered, 151; labyrinth, 153; dolphins at play, 154; misletoe, 163; walk by moonlight, 164; leaves and birds in autumn, 165; moon rising, 168; bees, 173; Berecynthian mother, 175; top, 185; seething caldron, 187; wave, 188; rock, 189; centaurs, 191; swans, 192; watery ray, 195; earthquake, 199; rent of fire, 202; industrious matron, 202; morning-star, 206; Ganges and Nile, 209; wolf, 209; famished lion, 215; poppies, 217; wild beast, 219; eagle, 219; storm of hail, 221;

lofty oaks, 221; pile of stone at Baiæ, 222; lion at bay, 224; rising blasts, 226; a jewel and ivory, 227; cranes of Strymon, 230; contending winds, 232; forest on fire, 232; lion and bull, 233; Ægean, 236; phantoms and dreams, 237; rock, 238; wild boar, 238; hungry lion, 239; Orion, 239; traveller hid in safe screen, 240; hyacinth, 244; rivers on rocky beds, 248; flocks of birds, 252; horse, 252; advancing and retiring waves, 255; hawk and dove, 257; eagle and serpent, 257; wolf, 258; lion and hunters, 261; crimson dye, 262; bull preparing for battle, 263; Mars stirred to battle, 267; Boreas across Ægean, 268; approaching storm, 269; swallow's flight, 270; flames and streams, 271; bees in nest, 272; descending crag, 274; Athos, Eryx, Apennines, 274; two bulls fighting, 275; hound in pursuit of stag, 275; poisonous arrow, 277; dreams, 278; stones from engine, and thunderclaps, 279

Soil of different kinds, 33; even when idle not unthankful, 34; produces various trees, 45; some best for grazing, some for corn, 46; how to discover its powers, 47

Soul of universe, bees inspired by, 70; its doctrine expounded, 174

South Wind (Auster, Notus), let in on flowers, 15; whistling of, 21; devising ill, 41; tendrils of vine fear, 49; dusky and lowering, 59; chilling, 71; whirls ships towards reefs, 84; cloudy, 156; overwhelmed mariners, 166; cranes fly before, 230; wishes borne to, 258; steeds of Mars flee before, 267

Styx, dark, 37; has nine circles of stream, 75, 168; harpies rise from, 118; gods fear to perjure themselves by, 165; bark of, 167; Æneas and Sibyl cross it, 167; Jove ratifies his word by, 110, 237; name of awe imposed upon the gods, 276

Suicide, Virgil's opinion of, 168

Sun, its path in zodiac, 37; a true monitor to the farmer, 41; warns of revolutions, 41; eclipsed at Cæsar's death, 42

Sylvia, her sorrow for her pet deer, 188

T.

Tacitus, imitates Virgil, 3; peculiarities of, 3

Tarquin kings, 176; banished, 207

Tartarus, description of, 171

Tempest, descriptions of, 39, 83, 84, 118, 156; calming of, 85; threatening of, 142

Theocritus, genuine writer, 9; prince of pastoral poets, 11; his muse (of Sicily) referred to, 18

Thomson, his Seasons not very like Virgil, 31; praised by Johnson, 32

Threshing-floor to be solid and level, 36

Thyrsis matched with Corydon, 23; defeated, 24

Tiber, Tuscan, 42, 203; Lydian, with gentle current, 113; whate'er it may be, 144; description of its mouth, 178; river-god appears to Æneas, 195; calms his swelling flood, 196; receives Turnus in his yellow flood, 224; Mezentius rests on its bank, 241; swelled with Trojan blood, 161, 250

Timavus, rocks of great, 24; of Iapia, 63; its roaring stream, 87

Tityrus, his ease and safety, 12; represents Virgil, 9; grateful to Octavianus, 13

Trees, various modes of rearing, 43; grafting and budding of, 44; each sort of, has its varieties, 44; different on different soils, 45

Triumph, description of Roman, 208

Trophy, description of, 243

Troy, city of Laomedon, 42; story of fall of, 97; Cæsar descended from, 88; a mimic, 121; game of, 154; walls built by Neptune, 158; persecuted gods of, 161; a second, 184; not yet vanquished, 203; trials of, 212; gods do not mean to destroy the race of, 215; mishaps of, 225; at its birth, 226; tall towers of, 234; delay at its walls, 248; let its name perish, 277

Tullus, will break his country's repose, 176; dragged the traitor's body, 207

Turnus, suitor for Lavinia, 179; visited by the Fury, 186, 187; demands war, 189; his form, arms and troops, 193, 194; stirred up by Iris, 208; would burn the fleet, 209; cares not for portents, 211; his exploits, 222; like Cocles, 79, 223, 224; undaunted, 230; slays Pallas, 234; deceived by the wraith of Æneas, 237; counts life a loss, 238; his fervid speech, 250; occupies the passes of the hills, 253; leaves the defile, 260; resolves to fight Æneas in single combat, 261; arms himself for the fight, 262; his deeds of valour, 267; hears the tumult from the city, 273; engages with Æneas, 275; flees before him, 275; his last efforts, 278; his powers benumbed, 278; his death, 279

U.

Ulysses, his crew transformed, 26; for what known, 98; crafty malice of, 99; accursed, 102; guards the booty, 113; his country, 119; prince of Ithaca avenged his comrades, 126; instigator of crimes, 170; wily in words, 220; saw the Cyclops of Ætna, 248

Unburied, their hard lot in Hades, 166

V.

Varius, united by Horace with Virgil, 2

Varus, Virgil excuses himself from celebrating, 21; yet has sung of him, 27

Venus, myrtle dear to, 24; complains to Jove of her son's lot, 87; appears to him disguised as a huntress, 88; her glory revealed, 90; substitutes Cupid for Iulus, 95; bids her son save his family, 109; her conversation with Juno, 130; begs of Neptune a safe voyage for the fleet, 157, 158; obtains arms for her son from Vulcan, 202; brings them to her son, 206; inveighs against Juno, 225; wounded by Diomede, 248; brings dittany to heal her son's wound, 269; plucks her son's weapon from the stock of the tree, 276

Vines, many kinds of, 44; part of the glory of Italy, 45; soil best suited for, 46; how to be prepared for them, 48; their proper order on plains and slopes, 48; trenches for, 48; to be planted in spring, 49; luxuriance of, to be pruned, 50; goats the especial enemy of, 50; storms dreaded by, 51

Virgil, friend of Gallus, 1, 10; his fondness for Naples, 2; his amiable character, 2; his friendship with Horace, 2; opinion of him among later Romans, 3; Sortes Virgilianæ, 4; opinions of him by the Christian fathers, 4; notions of him in the middle ages, 5; why Dante chose him as guide, 6; criticism supplants legends, 6; editions of Virgil, 7; influence of Virgil on modern poets, 7; on education, 8; recovers his land, 9; how an unreal poet, 11; yet without rival, 11; not a philosopher, 31; only mention of himself by name, 77

Volcano, description of, 125

Vulcan, his fire, 38; left his infant on the hearth, 191; father of the monster Cacus, 198; made arms for Achilles and Memnon, 97, 202; his forge in Vulcania, 202; lord of fire, 208; Turnus professes not to need his arms, 211; makes arms for Æneas, 203, 251.

W.

Weather, signs of bad, 39, 40; signs of fine, 40; how the moon and sun predict changes in, 41

Wraith, description of, 237

Wordsworth, his opinion of Virgil, 81

Y.

Yews of Corsica to be shunned by bees, 27; not to be near a hive, 66

Youth, brilliant complexion of, 94; shining in, 107; beauty of, 139; flower of, 148; recommends virtue, 149; relying in, 150; early dawn of, 212

Z.

Zephyrs, ever shifting, 19; unbind earth, 38; home of, 40; warm breezes of, 49; their call, 60; lingering, 68; summoned by Neptune, 84; favouring, 116; to be summoned by Mercury, 132; favourable, 143; lulled to rest, 226

Zones, description of the five, 237

CAMBRIDGE: PRINTED BY C. J. CLAY, M.A. AT THE UNIVERSITY PRESS.

www.ingramcontent.com/pod-product-compliance
Lightning Source LLC
Chambersburg PA
CBHW020507270326
41926CB00008B/775